Managing THE Shopping Center

$

CONTRIBUTING AUTHORS
Alan A. Alexander, CPM®
A. Alexander Bul, CPM®
Harold J. Carlson, CPM®
Thomas Dobyns
Colette A. Frederick, CPM®
Joe J. Lancaster Jr., CPM®
Robert J. Lofton, CPM®
Cyrena S. Movitz, CPM®
Marshall W. Reavis
Gary R. Sligar, CPM®
E. Wayne Tomlinson, CPM®

EDITORIAL CONSULTANTS
Leo Koltz, CPM®
Robert J. Lofton, CPM®
Richard F. Muhlebach, CPM®

Keith F. Levine,
Publishing Manager

Jeannie L. Glickson,
Project Editor

Managing THE Shopping Center

Institute of Real Estate Management
of the NATIONAL ASSOCIATION OF REALTORS®

430 North Michigan Avenue, Chicago, Illinois 60611

ACKNOWLEDGMENTS

Dollars and Cents of Shopping Centers. Copyright © 1981. *Standard Manual of Accounting for Shopping Center Operations.* Copyright © 1971. Reprinted by permission of the Urban Land Institute, Washington, D.C.

Management I Institute Course Material. Copyright © 1979. *Shopping Center Report.* Copyright © 1975. Reprinted by permission of the International Council of Shopping Centers, New York, N.Y.

International Standard Book Number:
0-912104-60-0

Library of Congress Catalog Card Number:
82-84485

Printed in the United States of America
Third Printing, 1985

Foreword

The Institute of Real Estate Management (IREM) of the NATIONAL ASSOCIATION OF REALTORS® is an organization of professional property managers that certifies property managers who have distinguished themselves in the areas of education, experience, and ethical conduct. IREM offers property managers and the public an expansive program of courses, seminars, books, periodicals, audiovisual kits, and other educational activities and materials. *Managing the Shopping Center* has been prepared as part of this professional program.

The objective of this text is to present the processes and procedures involved in effectively managing shopping centers. To achieve this objective, it was necessary to solicit the participation of a number of real estate professionals. The following people served as contributing authors and/or editorial consultants:

Alan A. Alexander, CPM®, CSM, president of Alexander Consultants, a Burlingame, California, firm that specializes in the management, leasing, consulting, and development of income-producing properties throughout the West Coast of the United States. Alexander has been a frequent guest speaker at IREM's national meetings, has written articles on shopping center management for IREM's *Journal of Property Management*, and is a member of IREM's national faculty. He has also taught several courses for the University of Shopping Centers of the International Council of Shopping Centers (ICSC).

A. Alexander Bul, CPM®, CSM, president of Henry S. Miller Management Corporation and executive vice president of

Henry S. Miller Companies, Dallas, Texas, and director of the School of Real Estate and Urban Development at the University of Texas—Arlington. Previously, Bul was city manager of Midland, Texas, and, before that, zoning administrator for the city of Dallas. He is active on IREM's national faculty. He is a past president of the Greater Dallas Board of REALTORS®, the Dallas-Fort Worth Chapter of IREM, and the Dallas Apartment Association.

Harold J. Carlson, CPM®, CSM, MAI, CRE, president and chief executive of Harold J. Carlson Associates, Inc., a Mount Prospect, Illinois, firm that specializes in shopping center management, marketing, and consulting. Before forming his own company, Carlson was vice president and general manager of Randhurst Corporation, which manages—among other centers— Randhurst Center, a shopping mall with retail space in excess of one million square feet. Carlson has contributed numerous articles to such publications as the *Journal of Property Management, Shopping Center World,* and *National Mall Monitor.* He also publishes a monthly newsletter on shopping center management, *The Carlsonreport.*

Thomas Dobyns, JD, an attorney who owns his own law firm in Orange, California, and specializes in real estate law. Dobyns has handled investment property leases for Tishman West Management Corporation in Orange County, as well as for other clients. He is an instructor of real estate law at the University of California—Irvine. He has also taught seminars through California's Department of Real Estate. He has served as a volunteer attorney for IREM's Orange County Chapter, and he has frequently spoken to this group on a variety of legal topics. Dobyns is also a licensed real estate broker.

Colette A. Frederick, CPM®, asset manager with Joe Foster Management Company, Dallas, Texas. Ms. Frederick was previously investment manager, real estate operations, for the Prudential Insurance Company of America, Chicago, where she managed a portfolio in excess of $125 million and 3 million square feet, and served as the midwestern coordinator of a space remeasurement program. Before that time, Ms. Frederick was a broker for the shopping center division of Baird & Warner, Inc., Chicago.

Leo Koltz, CPM®, vice president of Baird & Warner, Inc., Chicago, and general manager of the firm's shopping center division. Koltz is responsible for the development, management, and leasing of Baird & Warner's shopping center properties. He is a member of ICSC and has lectured frequently at ICSC seminars. He has written numerous articles on the rehabilitation and remodeling of shopping centers; some of these articles have appeared in the *Journal of Property Management.*

Joe J. Lancaster Jr., CPM®, CSM, president of Arcus Development Corporation, a commercial real estate development firm in Dallas, Texas. Lancaster teaches numerous courses in shopping center development for ICSC and for the National Association of Homebuilders, and has taught undergraduate courses in real estate development at Southern Methodist University in Dallas. He is a contributing author of the book *The Real Estate Handbook,* published by Dow Jones-Irwin in 1980. Lancaster is a member of the Urban Land Institute.

Robert J. Lofton, CPM®, president of Boyle Management Company and vice president of Boyle Investment Company, Memphis, Tennessee. Boyle is engaged in all areas of real estate management, including commercial, industrial, and residential properties. Lofton is a past president of IREM's Memphis Chapter. He serves on IREM's national faculty, and also teaches real estate management at Memphis State University.

Cyrena S. Movitz, CPM®, regional real estate manager of VMS Realty, Inc., Chicago. At VMS, Ms. Movitz is asset manager of a $150 million portfolio of shopping centers and office buildings. Previously, she was vice president of management at the Greenfield Company in Philadelphia, and, before that, a property manager and leasing representative for the Rouse Company in Columbia, Maryland. She has presented several national seminars for IREM on shopping center leasing, and she is a member of IREM's national faculty. Ms. Movitz has also served as treasurer of IREM's Philadelphia Chapter.

Richard F. Muhlebach, CPM®, CSM, president of TRF Management Corporation, Bellevue, Washington. TRF specializes in the development of shopping centers and office buildings throughout the Pacific Northwest and in Alaska. Muhlebach acts as a consultant for neighborhood, community, and regional shopping centers, as well as for mixed-use developments. He is a member of IREM's national faculty, is an instructor for ICSC's University of Shopping Centers, and has taught real estate at the college level.

Marshall W. Reavis, PhD, Associate in Risk Management, CPCU, associate professor of finance at DePaul University, Chicago. Reavis is a frequent speaker on insurance and risk management. He has a number of publications to his credit, and he contributes an insurance column to the *Journal of Property*

Management. Reavis serves as a consultant to several insurance organizations and insurance companies, and was formerly executive director and dean of the Insurance School of Chicago. He is publisher and chairman of the board of Insurance Education Specialists, Ltd., which provides training materials to the insurance industry nationwide.

Gary R. Sligar, CPM®, vice president of Lincorp, Inc., and partner with Lincoln Property Company Associates, Dallas, Texas. Among Sligar's responsibilities for the Lincoln company is the management of Lincoln Centre, a 2 million square foot multiuse high-rise office complex. Sligar previously worked for Balcor Property Management, Inc., where he was regional director of the southwest region's shopping center division. He has guest lectured on real estate topics at several colleges and universities, including the University of Tulsa in Oklahoma.

E. Wayne Tomlinson, CPM®, vice president of Storey, Tomlinson, and Company, a Nashville, Tennessee, leasing management firm that specializes in commercial and income-producing properties in 6 southeastern states. Tomlinson's firm is currently involved in the leasing and management of 30 shopping centers with a total retail area in excess of 3 million square feet. Tomlinson has taught several IREM courses, and has served on the Education Committee of IREM's Middle Tennessee Chapter. He is a past director of the Nashville Chapter of the Building Owners and Managers Association.

Contents

ix

Preface

Real estate is a rapidly changing field, and the management of real estate property of any kind has become a complex discipline. The management of shopping centers, in particular, demands a very high level of professionalism. *Managing the Shopping Center* has been written to assist managers of shopping centers in improving their professional skills and to guide them through the entire shopping center management process.

From the conception of the project, the authors' goal was to create a textbook that was authoritative, comprehensive, practical, and concise. Although intended primarily for the beginning student of shopping center management, the book is also suitable for the experienced shopping center manager who wishes to review a particular topic, or as a self-study guide for anyone who seeks a more thorough understanding of shopping center management.

There are three basic manners in which a real estate manager may be employed to oversee the operations of a shopping center. First, and perhaps most common, the manager may be employed by a property management firm and assigned the responsibility of managing a center property. In this situation, the manager is involved in fee management in an agency relationship with the client. Second, the manager may be employed and paid by an owner of a particular shopping center to act as the owner's direct representative in dealing with tenants and overseeing all other daily activities. Third, the manager may be employed by an institution, such as a bank, an insurance company, or a pension fund, to manage its portfolio of properties.

Rather than focus on the differences between these three approaches to shopping center management, this book stresses the similarities. Regardless of whether they are on-site administrators of sprawling superregional shopping centers, with over 200 tenants, or acting as managers of small neighborhood strip centers, all property managers can gain from this book the basic knowledge needed to manage any type of shopping center property.

Beginning with the manager's initial assignment to a center, problems will undoubtedly develop—in the creation of a management plan, in the development of an effective tenant mix, in the preparation of effective promotional plans, in the maintenance of the property. Shopping center managers, however, can learn to view the problems they face as opportunities—opportunities to refine their administrative talents, opportunities to create more efficient and cost-effective operations, opportunities to achieve the owner's objectives, opportunities to demonstrate professionalism in property management.

In a natural, logical, and detailed manner, this book analyzes each of the opportunities that await property managers in specific areas of shopping center management. *Managing the Shopping Center* supplies practical knowledge to anyone who is—or wishes to be—professionally engaged in the management of shopping centers.

The authors wish to thank several people for their significant contributions to the publication of *Managing the Shopping Center*. The editorial consultants, Leo Koltz, CPM®, Robert J. Lofton, CPM® (who was also one of the contributing authors), and Richard F. Muhlebach, CPM®, reviewed the entire manuscript prior to publication and offered criticisms and suggestions that helped make the book comprehensive and authoritative. A. Alexander Bul, CPM®, one of the contributing authors, also served as project coordinator, and helped in the book's overall development. David C. Nilges, CPM®, vice president, The T. W. Grogan Company, Cleveland, Ohio, and chairman of IREM's Publishing Committee for 1981 and 1982, provided important assistance and input.

Nancye J. Kirk, former publishing manager and current executive assistant to the executive vice president of IREM, played a central role in the conception and early development of the project. Keith F. Levine, publishing manager, took over the management and coordination of the project, and shepherded the book into reality. Jeannie L. Glickson, project editor, wove our individual contributions into a cohesive, lucid text. Norman Baugher, The Chestnut House Group, Inc., Chicago, provided effective, attractive designs for both the inside and the outside of the book. Joel D. Meisles, executive director of retail development, U.S. Shoe Corporation, Chicago, provided valuable input for the retailing chapter. Dr. William T. Beadles, CLU, national insurance education adviser, State Farm Insurance Companies, Bloomington, Illinois, provided a thoughtful review of the insurance section. To all of these people, to any others who helped but whom we may have inadvertently neglected to mention, and of course, to our families, we are grateful.

Introduction to
the Shopping Center Industry

Woodfield Mall, an enclosed shopping center located in a northwestern Chicago suburb, contains approximately 2,267,000 square feet of gross leasable area. To convey the immensity of this mall, it can be noted that the Empire State Building, one of the largest office buildings in the world, standing 102 stories, contains 1,790,433 square feet of gross leasable office space. The size of Woodfield Mall, by this comparison, is staggering. Woodfield's more than 200 tenants cater to the shopping, entertainment, and service needs and demands of thousands of people every day of the week. Woodfield Mall is one of the largest superregional shopping centers that has been built in this country, and it is representative of the extent to which this massive shopping center industry has grown.

Off Center is an enclosed shopping mall that stands in the inner city of Chicago. Off Center contains 11 tenants and approximately 55,000 square feet of tenant space. Off Center, as its name implies, stands in an area slightly removed from the main downtown Chicago district. This shopping center, however, has an appeal of its own. Off Center tenants sell high-quality, designer merchandise at discount prices, and thus provide an attraction that appeals to a wide public.

In yet another part of the city of Chicago, specifically in the far west side of the city, stands Brickyard Shopping Center, another enclosed mall. Brickyard, which contains just under one million square feet of tenant space and 121 tenants, is an unusual regional center because it is located in the inner city rather than in the suburbs. Industry practitioners refer to a zone such as this, that peripheral area between the city and suburbs, as the *twilight zone*. The twilight zone will be discussed in more detail later in this chapter, but suffice it now to say that the twilight zones in many cities stand ripe for shopping center development.

Water Tower Place is a specialty center that stands in Chicago's upper-income Gold Coast area, on North Michigan Avenue's "magnificent mile." Tourists visit Water Tower every day of the year, and local residents use the center for their daily shopping needs. Water Tower's 130 tenants and approximately 2.9 million square feet of tenant space provide a strikingly beautiful setting for shopping, entertainment, and a simple enjoyment of attractive architecture. Besides its elegantly designed atrium, which appears to be surrounded by a forest of tropical plants, Water Tower contains seven stories of specialty stores, two large department stores, and numerous restaurants. The small tenants at Water Tower range from an old-fashioned cookie maker to a clock shop, movie theatre, toy shop, and several fashion boutiques.

All of the properties just described are shopping centers, although very different types of shopping centers and in very different types of locations. The reader is thereby introduced to probably the most noteworthy characteristic of the shopping center industry today: There is great diversity in the types, designs, and locations of shopping centers that are being built and purchased. There are now specialty centers, built on the basis of an imaginative theme. There are shopping centers being built in previously untouched areas, such as the central city. These and others will be discussed in this introductory chapter. Investors in the industry are rediscovering old properties and recognizing the fact that instead of bigger shopping centers, great possibilities lie in the development of existing properties and in the tapping of previously untouched markets.

To appreciate the changes that have occurred in the industry, it is useful to look back upon the history of the shopping center. Shopping centers are unusual phenomena on the basis of their rapid growth rate alone. This amazing growth is plainly demonstrated in the fact that nearly 18,000 shopping centers have been built in this country since the end of World War II.

The shopping center industry, therefore, has a relatively short but nonetheless fascinating history. The industry has evolved tremendously since the early 1920s, when what is recognized as the first shopping center, Country Club Plaza, in Kansas City, Missouri, was built on a 40-acre lot five miles south of the heart of the city. Less than fifty years later, in 1981, the entire shopping center industry in this country generated a total of some *$400 billion* in sales. This is a *400 percent* increase in sales from 1964. The shopping center industry has essentially revolutionized the world of retailing.

This introductory chapter will offer readers a brief history of this rapid evolution and provide an overview of the major types and designs of shopping centers that are being developed today. In the latter part of this chapter, the reader will come to realize that whatever the type, size, or location of the shopping center, it is the property manager who plays a vital role in determining the success of the investment. Therefore, property managers must recognize the new demands that will be placed on them and be able to change with the industry.

History of the Shopping Center

The American shopping center industry did not begin with the first shopping center built in this country. The tradition that a center be used to cater to a public's shopping needs has existed for centuries and actually originated in ancient town markets. In colonial America, the seaports—among them, Boston, New York, and Philadelphia—served as major trading centers, primarily because these cities stood in the most convenient locations for shipping and receiving goods from other countries. As towns began to develop in other, inland areas of this country, it was primarily the town's access to the waterways that determined whether it would become a major trading center. Cleveland, Ohio; Detroit, Michigan; Chicago, Illinois—all of these cities, which were to become major industrial areas—stood on major waterways, to and from which goods could be easily shipped.

During the early 1700s, towns in the Midwest and West, undeveloped yet in many respects, had public square areas, where people could buy and sell merchandise. From this public square, the city's downtown district gradually developed into what it is known to be today.

Therefore, two general points about shopping areas can be established. First, major trading centers tend to be concentrated in cities that are most accessible to people and transportation. This factor of location, as readers will find in several chapters of this book, is one of the most important determinants of a shopping center's success. Second, the idea of a center that provides all of the buyer's shopping needs emerged very early in this country, notably in the public squares of colonial America.

Major changes occurred in this country throughout the 19th and 20th centuries. During the latter 1800s, the Industrial Revolution first took hold of this nation, and in time, brought permanent changes to the working life and economic means of most of the American public. New, more efficient means of production emerged, and the country began its ascent to becoming eventually the greatest industrial power in the world.

One of the most significant advances to modern life occurred in the early 1900s. This was when the automobile was first produced. This development allowed people to drive long distances quickly, and in time, the automobile provided the primary means of transportation to shopping centers. A distinguishing feature of most shopping centers, as a result, is the parking lot that is available for free, convenient customer parking.

During the first part of the 20th century, the country also endured a world war, soon followed by the Great Depression. The economy eventually recovered from the depression, but soon afterward, the United States entered World War II. Following this war, a population boom exploded, which dramatically increased the size of the total population. The needs and demands of that population encouraged the expansion of retailing centers.

After World War II, for the first time, the "American Dream" became possible for many Americans. That dream—the dream of owning a home—had before that time been unrealistic for most people. Many programs were enacted to aid home buyers and to make suburban living more convenient. For war veterans, there were mortgage loans backed by Veteran Administration guarantees. The Federal Housing Administration (FHA) was created. President Eisenhower initiated the interstate highway program, which led to the development of an elaborate highway system—which made it easier for suburbanites to commute to and from the city. There were also federal programs to aid educational programs and waste disposal services in suburban areas. Along with a simple desire of many people to leave the problems and congestion of the big city, these factors combined to encourage a massive exodus to the suburbs.

Shopping center developers followed the population to the

suburbs. They began by building small, neighborhood centers that contained from 10 to 12 tenants. Grocery stores were among the first tenants to move from downtown areas into suburban shopping centers. These grocery stores, therefore, first established themselves as the anchor—that is, the major—tenants of many neighborhood centers. Many of these anchor grocery stores stand in the same positions today. Neighborhood centers catered to the public's immediate buying needs—food, drugs, and services—and so these were the original functions of the American shopping center.

Before 1950, department stores' activities in the suburbs were slight. By the mid-1960s, however, over half of all department store sales were in suburban shopping centers. Once again, then, the amazing growth of this industry is demonstrated.

Gradually, shopping center developments became larger. The first enclosed shopping mall opened in the mid-1950s, but it was during the 1960s that the enclosed mall gradually became an American institution. The mall became a social gathering place; the mall has now attained its position as a solid representation of modern, suburban America. The shopping center mall offers the public one-stop, temperature-controlled shopping with convenient, free parking.

The shopping center mall turned out to be the real estate investor's dream. During its early years, the mall ranged in sizes from 500,000 to 800,000 square feet. Today, as mentioned earlier, it has grown to sizes of more than 2,000,000 square feet. The mall was ideal for small retail stores because these small stores could share in the customer traffic generated by the anchor tenants. The mall, therefore, provided a major divergence from the downtown retailing area.

The 1970s were generally profitable years for shopping center developers. Developers continued to expand during this time, building superregional centers in many metropolitan areas of the country. With the 1980s, however, several significant events occurred that generally altered developers' plans. As prices of nearly all items increased, consumers' disposable incomes declined. The costs for housing, food, clothing, medicine, and transportation all increased, and the public grew far more discerning in what it bought and how much it spent. Interest rates increased to record highs. Furthermore, many shopping center developers had depended on the baby boom generation to demand and consume an abundance of all goods. When the baby boom generation matured, however, in general it wanted smaller families. The population that was to support the grand-scale, suburban shopping developments, in sum, never came to be. All of these factors had major consequences for the shopping center industry.

As a result, new trends in shopping center development emerged during the time, and developers began to view the entire industry with different eyes. The 1980s will be remembered as a time that, in most metropolitan areas of the country, first saw the saturation of regional shopping centers. It will be remembered as a period when retail tenants at shopping centers began to demand smaller spaces. The 1980s will be remembered as a time when these large centers first lost their one-time status as the "darlings" of investment real estate. The 1980s will probably continue to be characterized as a period when shopping center developments will not be restricted by form, size, or location. Today, there are many possibilities for shopping center development. By broadening their view—mainly out of necessity—developers have begun to realize new investment opportunities in the shopping center industry.

The 1980s and Beyond

What do the 1980s and beyond hold for shopping center investors and developers? We have looked briefly at the ways this massive industry has evolved. Let us turn now to new alternatives that have emerged as realistic and profitable shopping center investments.

First, it should be understood that in some parts of the country, notably the South and the West, investments in regional shopping centers continue profitably. Florida is an example of a state where growth of the shopping center industry has not been seriously curtailed. The main trend of the industry, however, has been a slowdown, particularly in the development of large shopping center malls. In nearly all other, major metropolitan areas, there is a saturation of regional and superregional centers, and although many of the types of existing centers continue to prosper, the demand for new, similar types of centers virtually does not exist.

Beyond the traditional suburban shopping mall, however, developers have renewed their interest in the central city. Many neighborhood and small convenience centers—which will be described in detail later in this chapter—are being built in cities rather than in suburban areas. Some urban analysts see the beginnings of a population movement back to the city. They see tendencies among the middle class to shun their suburban, split-level homes and move back to the central city. Smaller families, changed lifestyles, energy shortages—all of these are considered factors that explain a movement back to the cities. This movement is encouraging shopping center developers to look again at central city locations. There, many developers are building and succeeding with smaller shopping centers.

Next, many developers have given a second look to many of the *middle markets* of the country. Middle markets are areas that are so thinly populated or appear to be so limited in growth potential that developers by-passed them during the initial surge of development. Indeed, developers are recognizing the demand for such centers in these primarily nonmetropolitan regions of the country. The potential for success is there.

There is also the so-called twilight zone of development, which was mentioned earlier. The twilight zone refers to the peripheral zone that lies between the city and the suburbs. In this twilight zone, some developers are discovering a region that has not yet been saturated by large regional centers. Brickyard Shopping Center, noted earlier, is a prime example of a twilight zone development. Brickyard is a superregional center located in an area that developers had previously overlooked. Developers realize now that these twilight zones provide another large, untouched area for shopping center investments.

Next, the industry is almost certain to witness an increase in the number of recycled, rehabilitated, and converted shopping centers. The reasons are clear: Marketing in the United States has never been a static discipline. Rather, it changes constantly with the times and the competition. It is very difficult, if not impossible, to market an aging center. Therefore, existing centers, to maintain their positions in the market, must somehow be changed to keep pace with the newer centers. The public undoubtedly will choose the newer, more modern environment. Repackaging existing centers, therefore, is likely to become common in protecting and preserving existing centers.

Finally, the ingenuity of shopping center developers is clearly demonstrated in the rise in the number of specialty center developments. Water Tower Place, mentioned at the beginning of this chapter, is such a specialty center. Its attraction is its unique architectural theme, the unique offerings of its tenants, and the draw of its many restaurants. These attractions are the major distinguishing features of a specialty center.

Shopping center developers, therefore, today have an assortment of possibilities available to them. No longer is there a single formula that will determine success in the shopping center industry. Different types, sizes, and locations of shopping centers are being successfully developed today.

Types of Shopping Centers

The shopping center industry has traditionally been characterized by four basic types of centers, based primarily on size and on the types and number of anchor tenants. These four types of centers are neighborhood; community; regional, including superregional; and specialty centers. There are both *anchor* tenants and *satellite* tenants in most shopping centers—with the exceptions of most specialty centers and some neighborhood centers. An anchor tenant is a key tenant that will attract other businesses as well as consumers to the center. Anchor tenants provide the major attraction to a shopping center. A satellite tenant is a smaller tenant that stands in a secondary, ancillary position to the anchor. The following is a brief look at each type of shopping center. Following that is a discussion of another type of shopping center that has received considerable notice in recent years—the convenience center.

Neighborhood Center

For many years, especially during the 1960s, neighborhood centers were the forgotten stepchildren of the industry. Today, many developers are realizing that, in some ways, the industry has come full circle: The industry is witnessing a reawakening to the neighborhood center.

Neighborhood shopping center owners have known for many years that small can indeed be beautiful and quite profitable. The prosperity of the neighborhood shopping center continues. During the early 1980s, these smaller neighborhood centers, in general, had a greater increase in their net operating income than did the larger center ("Neighborhood Shopping Centers Bloom," *Wall Street Journal,* October 28, 1981). Neighborhood centers have become more appealing, largely because they are easier in time, effort, and money to establish and to operate.

By definition, a neighborhood center contains one anchor tenant, usually a supermarket. In recent years, many neighborhood centers have undergone major facelifts. The most noticeable change in these neighborhood centers is in the size of the grocery store anchor. Traditionally, this store was about 20,000 square feet in size. Today, many of these stores are being replaced with 30,000 to 60,000 square feet supermarkets that sell everything from groceries and hardware to cosmetics and clothing.

In general, experts of the industry believe that the neighborhood center in a highly dense area will continue to hold a steady market and maintain a healthy profit. The typical drawing radius of a neighborhood center in a very dense area is one mile and a half. In a rural area, the drawing area can extend to several miles. Neighborhood centers range in size from 50,000 to 200,000 square feet of gross leasable area. They cover from 4 to 10 acres of land.

Community Center

A community center is larger than a neighborhood center, and to qualify as a community center, its anchor must be a junior department store, a variety store, a discount center, or a major hardware store. Most community centers also contain a selection of wearing apparel stores, home furnishing stores, and service tenants, such as an optometrist or insurance agent.

Many of these community centers were built during the latter 1950s and throughout the 1960s, before the grand-sized superregional centers were built. As a result, the designs of many community centers are outmoded. What seemed new and interesting for shoppers in earlier decades, today, in many cases, cannot compete with the variety offered at the regional centers or with the simple conveniences of the neighborhood centers. Therefore, one of the greatest hopes for community centers rests with professional management. The community center must develop its own identity—perhaps through conversion, a change in the tenant mix, or remodeling. The community center, as any shopping center, must be able to attract a steady flow of consumers, through whatever special offerings can be provided and advertised.

The trading area for a community center in a highly dense region is up to a radius of three miles, or about a five-minute drive time. In a rural area, the trade area may extend much farther. The community center draws from several neighborhoods. Community centers range in size from 100,000 to 300,000 square feet of gross leasable area, and most of the sites cover an area from 10 to 30 acres.

Regional Center

Regional and superregional shopping centers are the giants of the industry, and yet, in comparative terms, they are only a small segment of the market. They represent less than *five percent* of all shopping centers in this country. Nevertheless, the regional centers have changed the industry so significantly that despite their relatively small numbers, they have had an enormous impact on all types of shopping centers. It was in regional centers that numerous shoppers first discovered the conveniences and enjoyment of shopping centers, and it was in regional centers that shopping centers first provided stiff competition to many downtown districts.

Most regional centers have two or more full-line department stores, and today, most also have an enclosed mall. A superregional center, by definition, contains 1,000,000 square feet or more of gross leaseable space. A superregional center generally has three or more full-line department stores and covers over 50 acres of land.

Most regional and superregional centers do not have a supermarket within their malls. In general, the grocery shopping trip is not served by a shopping trip to the regional center. There is, however, in many cases, a large grocery store located close to the shopping center property. During the 1960s, the regional mall was heavily advertised as a total entertainment package with special events, such as antique shows or musical events often taking place in the mall. In more recent years, however, the emphasis has turned more to promoting the shopping center as a fashion environment, as the center sponsors fashion shows and special displays of stylish clothing.

Specialty Center

The specialty center is unlike the other types of centers that have been discussed so far. The specialty center generally contains no department store anchor or supermarket anchor tenant. A specialty center is based on a unique feature or on the creative use of an existing building. Water Tower Place, an example of a specialty center, as noted earlier, does contain two department store anchors. Yet, it is Water Tower's impressive architecture, its interesting mix of tenants, and its many restaurants that qualify it as a specialty center.

Most specialty centers stand in high-tourist trade areas. Most successful specialty centers have tenants that appeal both to local residents and to tourists. Most specialty centers can draw on a regular basis from only a limited area. The owner's best defense, therefore, is to keep the project relatively small. In general, the specialty center should cover between 50,000 to 70,000 square feet.

One factor that appears to be important in determining the success of a specialty center is the center's proximity to middle-to-upper-income residential neighborhoods (Christopher Carneghi, "Specialty Shopping Centers: Factors of Success and Failure," *Appraisal Journal* [October 1981], p. 563).

Many shops at specialty centers carry high-priced, luxury items, as opposed to necessity items, which are generally purchased at department or discount stores.

Specialty centers can be open-pedestrian malls or climate-controlled, enclosed malls; single-level buildings or multistory buildings. Because they appeal to a more narrow segment of the overall market, specialty centers are more sensitive to economic fluctuations than are the other, more traditional types of centers.

Convenience Center

A more recent development in the shopping center industry has been the increased interest in convenience shopping centers. These are small grocery stores that stand with a dry cleaner, fast food restaurant, or drugstore. A convenience center is readily identifiable by its prime tenant, a convenience food operation, such as a 7-Eleven or a White Hen Pantry.

Convenience centers are relatively modest, yet profitable properties that have given investors, who otherwise would be unable to get involved with shopping center investments, the opportunity to invest in this market. Given the fast lifestyle to which many Americans have grown accustomed, the continued popularity and profitability of these convenience centers can be expected.

There are yet other types of shopping centers that are becoming popular, but those that have been discussed here are the most common. Some of the other types of centers will be discussed in later chapters of this book.

Shopping Center Design

In addition to knowing the classifications of shopping centers by their size and basic function, the property manager may also be asked to help determine the basic shape and design of the center. The layout of the center has an impact on the placement of tenants within the center and on the general aesthetic nature of the property. Just as there is great diversity today in the types of centers being developed, so is there diversity in the designs of these centers. The developer and manager of a new center have control over many factors, determining many factors that they would not be able to control in other types of retail settings. The design of the shopping center is one of these factors. There are many traditional shopping center designs, which will be discussed. Also discussed will be some of the new designs being tried, particularly in the development of specialty centers.

Strip Center. A strip center is a linear group of stores, which may or may not have an anchor tenant. Most strip centers are located along major thoroughfares. Many such centers have a canopy that extends over the pedestrian walkway in front of the line of stores. The parking lot lies between the public street and the stores.

The strip, which should be no longer than a convenient walking distance, is a common design for neighborhood centers. A grocery store, which assumes the anchor role in many of these centers, lies either in the middle of the strip or at one end. A typical strip center layout appears in Exhibit 1.1.

L-Shaped Center. The L-shaped center is the most typical, physical layout for a shopping center. Ideally, it will be located at the intersection of two major thoroughfares, and the shops in the L will face toward the street. Easy-access parking is located between the stores and the streets. Generally, service and deliveries are in the rear of the stores, where there may also be parking for tenants. Many developers have tried to deviate from this basic design but have changed their plans when the

EXHIBIT 1.1. *Typical Strip Center Layout*

—————————————— Highway ·—————————————

Parking lot

Alternate anchor tenant	Satellite spaces	Anchor tenant	Satellite spaces

Delivery/service area

EXHIBIT 1.2. *Typical L-Shaped Center Layout*

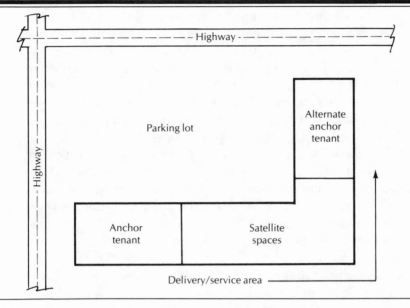

visibility or access to stores in the center were reduced. Some of these centers have two anchors, often one at each end of the L shape.

The L-shaped center is especially suitable for large neighborhood and small community centers. A sample layout for an L-shaped center appears in Exhibit 1.2.

Cluster Center. Many older regional centers still do not have enclosed malls. Rather, the major tenants are scattered on the property with the support stores located between them. These layouts are called *cluster centers*. In most of these centers, parking is available near each major tenant. In recent years, some cluster centers have been enclosed by malls. A sample cluster center layout appears in Exhibit 1.3.

T Center. The T-center layout places tenants in the shape of a T, with three anchor tenants located at each end of the T shape. A problem with this layout is that one anchor tenant is not visible from the front entrances of the other two anchors, although some practitioners consider this an advantage for the smaller tenants. The layout encourages shoppers to stop at the smaller stores rather than move directly to the anchors. A typical T-center layout appears in Exhibit 1.4.

Dumbbell Shape. The dumbbell layout places two anchor tenants on either end of a rectangular-shaped center, with the smaller tenants placed between them, thus encouraging shoppers to notice the smaller stores on their route between anchors. A double dumbbell is a layout in which four anchor tenants lie on either side of a center court in the formation of a square, and the smaller tenants lie between the majors and the center court. A sample dumbbell center layout appears in Exhibit 1.5.

Other Patterns. Triangles, U shapes, and pentagons are other shapes that have become common for regional and super-regional center layouts. The advantages of these patterns lie in the location of the anchors and secondary anchors, which are always at extreme points in the design. Notice this basic advantage in the sample layouts of a U center and a triangle center, as presented, respectively, in Exhibits 1.6 and 1.7. Consumers walking between the anchors in such layouts become prospective shoppers for the satellite merchants located between the extreme points.

Specialty centers are also being built in a variety of shapes and designs. An old movie theatre; a renovated warehouse; a mixed-use, high-rise condominium building; and a small shopping center—these are only some of the many variations in shopping center patterns that have been tried in recent years.

EXHIBIT 1.3. *Typical Cluster Center Layout*

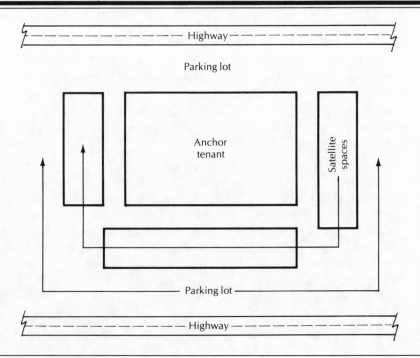

EXHIBIT 1.4. *Typical T-Center Layout*

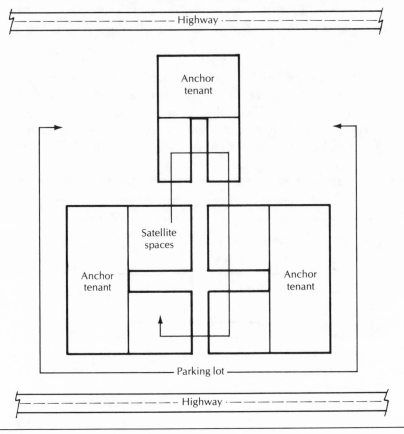

Net Operating Income

Whatever the type or design of a shopping center, it will probably be management that will determine the investment's success. This book is for the property manager, who can affect the earnings of the property—whether the center is a neighborhood, specialty, or superregional center. Readers will see throughout this text that whatever the type of center, the basic functions that property managers serve will generally determine whether the investment as a whole can succeed. The bottom line—the *net operating income (NOI)*—will be the property manager's and the property owner's primary and ongoing concern. The NOI equals the gross earnings from the investment, minus any operating expenses before debt service has been subtracted. Throughout this book, readers will learn how the property manager can effectively increase the property's NOI.

To begin, the relationship between the owner and the manager will determine how well the manager can understand and ultimately achieve the owner's investment goals. During the development of a new center, it will be the property manager's involvement and expertise that may very well determine whether the investment can achieve a high NOI. An organized plan for managing the property—the management plan—will be necessary for the successful operation of the center. The plan should take into account all the necessary operations for the successful management and functioning of an existing property.

The manager will often be involved with the shopping center

EXHIBIT 1.5. *Typical Dumbbell Center Layout*

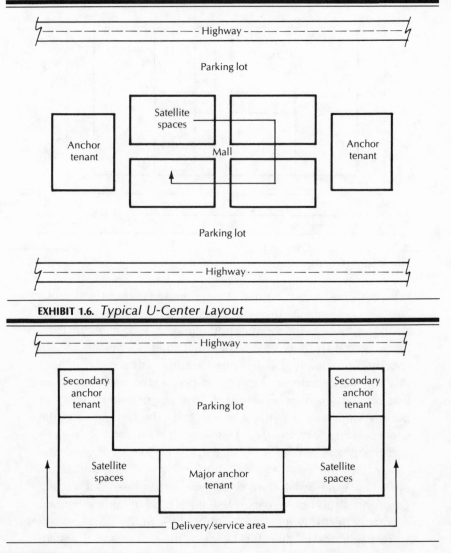

EXHIBIT 1.6. *Typical U-Center Layout*

EXHIBIT 1.7. *Typical Triangle Center Layout*

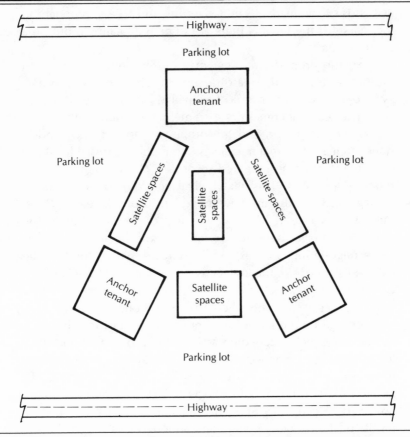

project from its conception. A development idea must be backed by market evidence showing that there is a demand for such a shopping center. The property manager, therefore, will probably be required to conduct market analyses to test whether a strong market demand exists for the center. Market analyses will then be required on a periodic basis throughout the property's life.

The manager's immediate concern upon taking over an existing center will be the handling of building operations, including maintenance, life safety, security, and energy conservation at the property. These are concerns that indeed will both directly and indirectly affect the NOI. The manager will quickly learn that the owner's income, for example, depends on tenants' income, and if an excellent maintenance plan is not instituted at the center, both the owner's and the tenant's income are likely to suffer.

The manager may be asked to assist the owner in selecting

an appropriate mix of tenants for the center, given the specific demands of the market. The tenant mix must be appropriate to the market if the tenants there are to earn a healthy profit on a continual basis.

Next, the property manager may be required to assist with the preparation of the lease document, although an attorney, as readers will learn, should be involved throughout this process. The lease document is extremely important to the property owner, however, and the property manager must understand at least the major clauses. As much as possible, these documents must be prepared to protect the property owner's financial interests. The next logical concern to the property manager will be the effective negotiation of the leases. Here, the owner stands to lose a great deal of income, should the property manager bend to too many of the tenants' demands. Lease negotiating is an extremely delicate matter but must be handled expertly if the owner is to find both strong tenants and beneficial leases.

A major concern that will confront the property manager very early on will be the advertising and promotion of the shopping center. An effective, ongoing advertising, promotion, and publicity campaign is needed to ensure a steady flow of consumers to the property. The property manager must also become familiar with the two important subjects of insurance and real estate taxes. These programs often have major consequences on the profits of the property owner, and although it is suggested that experts be called on to handle both of these programs, the manager would be well-advised to acquire at least a working knowledge of both.

Next, the accounting and reporting procedures of the shopping center will be important to the extent that the records of any investment contain essential information. Clear, concise, and thorough accounting records are necessary if the property is to be run in an organized, orderly manner. Finally, the property manager who acquires at least a basic understanding of the world of retailing stands in an advantageous position. The manager may be able to help retailers improve their sales, which, in turn, will ultimately affect the property owner's earnings. The manager can learn the retailers' concerns and be able to communicate with the entity around which the shopping center exists.

All of these topics are discussed in detail throughout the chapters of this book. Each is vitally important to the job of the property manager. Each is vitally linked to the success of the investment. How each concern is handled will ultimately affect the property owner's bottom line: the net operating income.

To manage the property effectively, the property manager must acquire a working knowledge of all of the topics discussed throughout this book. Although each type of shopping center property will pose unique problems and unique circumstances, the goal of this book is to present basic concepts and practical knowledge that can be used for the management of any type of shopping center.

An important distinguishing feature of any type of shopping center is the interrelationship that exists among the tenants, the property manager, and the property owner. In no other type of real property investment does each party have such a major impact on the others' financial success. The effective performance of each party is critical to the success of the other parties and of the investment. Likewise, each individual tenant will affect the other tenants. This critical interrelationship is unique to shopping centers, and this important concept will be evident throughout the book.

Conclusion

Shopping centers have taken on a distinct role in the retail structure. The emphasis in shopping center development, however, appears to be changing from a philosophy of "bigger is better" to one of "less is more." Investors have higher costs, less available funds, and a consuming public that grows increasingly more aware of budgetary constraints. The best choice, then, for investors is to change with their markets—which is what they have always had to do. This is where professional shopping center managers can assume their responsibilities. The industry is depending on them.

There are many different types and forms of shopping centers, and shopping center investors are just beginning to realize their opportunities in markets that were once bypassed. Practitioners divide shopping centers into four main classes: neighborhood, community, regional, and specialty. The small convenience center has also gained considerable attention in recent years. For any type or size of center, however, the property manager stands in a prime position to affect the investment's net operating income.

Property managers should always be looking for new

approaches to attract the buying public to their centers, sponsoring, for example, cultural activities or special events. The future of the shopping center industry depends on the active participation and expertise of property managers.

Review Questions

1. Discuss shopping center development during the 1970s—the surges and the trends, the negative aspects.
2. Discuss four potential new areas of shopping center development that hold great promise for the 1980s.
3. What are the four major types of shopping centers?
4. Why have neighborhood centers become more appealing to shopping center developers?
5. What factors will determine a specialty center's success or failure?
6. Discuss the advantages of an L-shaped center.
7. What is NOI, and why is it so critical to the shopping center owner?
8. How can the property manager affect the investment's NOI?

2

Management's Relationship with the Owner

Although a successful shopping center is the product of many forces, real estate practitioners have tried to identify the single most important factor that will determine whether a shopping center will prosper as a real estate investment. One theory that is backed by considerable evidence is that the success of a shopping center depends primarily on the relationship that exists between the owner and the manager. If the owner of a center is unwilling to spend an adequate amount of money to maintain the center, both the physical property and the financial investment will suffer. There will be little that the property manager can do to overcome that basic lack of support. If, on the other hand, the owner is willing to make a full commitment to the center, as both a financial investment and a functional property, the project is more likely to succeed.

Management plays a direct role in determining whether the property investment will achieve a satisfactory net operating income (NOI). Before the critical relationship between the manager and the owner can be clear, it is necessary to understand what property management—specifically, shopping center management—involves. Shopping center management entails the traditional, day-to-day obligations of managing any real property:

Collecting rents.
Paying bills.
Seeing that repairs are completed.

Maintaining the full occupancy at market rents.

Submitting regular reports on income and expenditures.

Scheduling contacts with current tenants at the center and prospecting for new tenants.

Conducting managerial functions in relation to the center's merchants' association.

The full responsibility of the property manager, however, goes beyond these daily duties and often takes on long-term investment goals. Property management's objectives, therefore, can be expanded to include the following:

Maintaining the highest possible net operating income (NOI)—income before debt service payment—without damaging the property's future productivity.

Enhancing the property's appreciation and thereby increasing its market value.

Analyzing the real estate tax obligations for the property and prorating taxes.

Implicit in all of these objectives of property management is management's basic obligation to the property investor, which is to fulfill the investor's financial objectives. The manager's ability to achieve the owner's goals underlies the relationship between the two parties. A professional property manager can increase a property's income and enhance its value—two of the chief objectives of ownership—in different ways:

The manager can maintain or improve the property as a physical asset, rather than allowing the property to deteriorate.

The manager can establish an image or character of the shopping center that attracts customers to the stores and appeals to current and prospective tenants.

The manager can institute programs and policies that will directly increase the income of the property as an investment.

The relationship between the owner and the property manager, therefore, is critical to the success of a shopping center. This chapter will explore the association between the two parties. Beginning with an exploration of the various types of shopping center ownership, this chapter will then discuss the objectives of owners, the impact of risk on investors' attitudes, and the ability of a shopping center investment to meet the owner's objectives. Following this, the chapter will describe the management agreement, which formalizes the relationship between the

MANAGING THE SHOPPING CENTER

property manager and the owner. Finally, the chapter will discuss various methods that are used to compensate the manager for providing professional services.

Typical Investors in Shopping Centers

Shopping centers have general characteristics that distinguish them from other investments and, in some cases, from any other type of income property. Although it is difficult to define the "typical" shopping center investor, it is possible to describe the most common types of shopping center ownership. First, however, before the most common types of owners can be understood, it is necessary to recognize the similarities shared by nearly all types of shopping centers:

1. A center is a merchandising complex with a relatively large investment in long-term, illiquid assets—a major portion of which are *wasting assets*. A wasting asset is one that deteriorates with time.
2. Most shopping centers' fixed assets are encumbered with heavy mortgages that are generally higher than those of other types of real estate investments.
3. As much as 75 percent of the land is unproductive, yet even in the unproductive area, there will be concerns about maintenance, security, and traffic.
4. As with other property investments, the market value of a shopping center is based on a capitalization of its net operating income stream.

Although these are the shared qualities of shopping centers, there is also great diversity in the types of owners and centers. The following is a discussion of the major forms of ownership.

Sole Proprietorship

The sole proprietorship is the most basic form of real estate and shopping center ownership. A sole owner maintains complete ownership and control of the property. The sole proprietorship is generally easy to form: Usually it can be arranged if the property manager has a state real estate broker's license and obtains a business license from the city in which the shopping center will be located. The sole proprietorship is also advantageous from the point of view of income taxes. The federal government considers any income from the investment as a part of the sole proprietor's income, which must be reported only once—on the individual investor's income tax return.

Rarely do large-scale operations choose the sole proprietorship, for two main reasons. First, with this type of ownership, the owner has unlimited liability. With unlimited liability, the investor has little protection against financial losses and essentially must assume all of the financial risks of the investment. An individual owner also has a limited amount of capital, and raising more capital, which is usually a requirement for large property investments, is difficult.

On the other hand, the sole proprietor does maintain absolute control of management. This control includes the right to decide how to spend cash flow generated by the property or even the choice to sell the shopping center. The investor can make decisions quickly and efficiently, and the property manager need not become embroiled in conflicts between partners.

The developers of many smaller centers—strip centers, in particular—are individual entrepreneurs who build and retain ownership on their own accounts. Many of these individuals started as homebuilders and developed neighborhood centers as a means of enhancing the value of nearby properties. Other individual owners are general contractors, builders, or other small investors. In the case of a builder or contractor, the construction of an income-producing property, such as a shopping center, is often only one facet of their business.

Partnership

The Internal Revenue Code defines a partnership as "a syndicate, group, pool, joint venture, or other organization, through or by means of which any business, financial operation or venture is carried on, and which is not a corporation, a trust or estate." Together, general and limited partnerships represent a large portion of all real estate ownership.

A partnership characterized by two or more owners, called the "partners," often represents a pooling of both capital resources and administrative skills. For example, a partnership may be formed to join individuals who have capital to invest with individuals who have the skills to develop, lease, build, finance, or manage a shopping center. In some partnerships, only a few of the partners assume an active role, and the other partners assume a passive role in the administration of the investment. An owner of land might pledge the land as a contribution to the partnership but leave all responsibility for the creation and operation of the center to the other partners. At least one of the partners must be willing to accept unlimited liability for the actions and obligations of the partnership.

In a general partnership, all partners agree to accept unlimited liability. Typically, these general partners enjoy all of the benefits of ownership and, to some extent, are active in managing the partnership. In a limited partnership, in addition to one or more of the general partners, there are limited partners who accept only limited liability and only limited responsibility. Many limited partners are individuals who are involved in only one facet of the partnership's operations. A lawyer, an accountant, or any individual who merely puts up capital might be a limited partner.

A partnership offers real estate investors many tax advantages, and, for this reason, it is a popular form of ownership. In general, it offers the same tax advantages as a sole proprietorship. A partnership is not a taxable entity. Instead, the partnership reports items of gross income and deductions as a single entity, and the partners, in turn, include these items on their individual income tax returns. The government measures the partnership's profits and losses in proportion to the investment of each partner. The specific arrangements are spelled out clearly in the partnership agreement.

Corporation

By legal definition, a corporation is "an artificial being, invisible, intangible, and existing only in contemplation of law" (Dartmouth College vs. Woodward, 17 U.S. 518, 1819). A corporation is a legal entity, but it possesses many of the same rights and obligations as individuals.

The stockholders of a corporation are the owners of the firm; each shareholder's ownership consists of a portion of the total shares of stock owned by all shareholders. In an open corporation, many individuals own the stock, and it is possible to buy shares from current stockholders. A closed corporation is owned by only a few individuals.

Corporations that are involved in real estate investments face a double-tax bind. First, the net income earned from the property is subject to income taxes. When the remaining income is distributed to the stockholders, either as dividends or as a result of liquidation, it again is subject to an income tax. Investors generally view this double tax as the main disadvantage to the corporate form of ownership. Another problem is that a corporation—unlike a partnership—cannot offer its shareholders the benefits gained from losses for tax purposes.

On the other hand, the corporate form of ownership provides a number of distinct advantages; one of the major benefits is that shareholders have a voice in managing the corporation. The shareholders elect a board of directors to run the corporation for them. The board then has the responsibility of choosing officers and managing the activities of the company. In this way, the corporation operates through centralized management. In addition, the corporate form provides for the firm's preservation since the corporation is a legal entity. Also, owners can buy and sell their shares freely.

Finally, with the corporate form, the individual shareholder is not liable for financial debts that result from damage claims. Many investors consider this characteristic—*limited liability*—the corporation's most valuable attribute.

A *Subchapter S corporation* is an offshoot of the corporation. Classification as a Subchapter S corporation allows shareholders to choose partnership-type taxation, which most investors prefer to the corporation's double tax. The obstacle, however, is that when the Subchapter S corporation requires financing, as most do, lenders generally want the stockholders to be personally liable for their debts. Also, qualifying for a Subchapter S corporation is difficult. Only 25 or fewer shareholders can belong to the entity, and the corporation can earn no more than 20 percent of its income from passive investment income. Another problem is that although tax losses can be passed on to stockholders, each person's share of the loss may not exceed the cost basis of individual stock holdings, just as with a partnership. This restricts investors from using depreciation and amortization to reduce their taxable income.

Many large institutional owners opt for the corporate form of ownership. Life insurance companies, commercial banks, savings and loan associations, and, to a lesser extent, pension funds, are all entities that use the corporate form for real estate ownership.

Syndications and Joint Ventures

Investment in real estate offers opportunities for several investors to pool their resources through a syndication or a joint_ venture.

A *syndication* is an association of individuals bound together by a business enterprise in which the members have a mutual interest. The syndication represents an ongoing, legal relationship. A joint venture, which differs only slightly has been defined as a "special combination of two or more persons who jointly seek a profit in a specific venture without any actual partnership or corporate designation." Thus, unlike a syndication, investors set up a joint venture for a single, specific business purpose. After the purpose has been served, the joint venture is dissolved. "Joint venture" in Japanese translates to English as "same bed ... different dreams," which is an appropriate reminder of what is involved with such a venture. The investors in a joint venture are united by a single purpose, but their ultimate aims in real estate may be very different.

Syndicating came into general practice as a method whereby several individuals could combine their funds to invest in a large real estate property, a property investment larger than any one individual could purchase alone. Even those who have large sums to invest may prefer owning portions of many properties rather than owning all of one or two. In addition to pooling capital, another advantage of syndications and joint ventures is that many of them have skilled real estate professionals advising them on the acquisition and operation of the properties.

Beyond representations of ownership forms, to a large extent, syndications and joint ventures are simply ways of "putting together deals." The form of ownership—the way title is held—can be arranged in a number of ways, depending on the investment objectives of the parties. Tax considerations become particularly important. The following are the methods that are most frequently used:

Tenancy in common.
Corporation.
Simple trust.
Complex trust.
Partnership.

The members of a syndication own all shares of stock. This arrangement limits the liability of members of the syndication and offers the benefits inherent in the corporate structure. Still, the double tax implications work as an argument against the corporate form of syndication. The corporate form is most common in syndications where the title-holders take an active role in the investment, and the exchange requires long-range activity. Another general prerequisite for the corporate form is that the income tax plus the tax on liquidation do not greatly exceed the tax that the shareholders would pay as sole proprietors.

For some situations, other forms of organizations will be better than the corporate form, as, for example in the following: if the main objective is short-range appreciation in properties that produce relatively small income; if the business activity required is not substantial or risky; or, if the investor's purpose is to reduce taxable income from other sources. Partnerships, trusts, and tenancy in common structures are especially well suited for tax shelter investments that involve more than one investor. Following is a short discussion of some of these alternatives:

A *tenancy in common* occurs with the acquisition of property under different titles, although the co-owners retain the right to hold and occupy the property, in conjunction with the other co-owners. In day-to-day operations, a tenancy in common works much like a common stock corporation. Each participant in the syndication owns an undivided, fractional interest in the property. Despite the simplicity and favorable tax treatment, however, a tenancy in common has a number of disadvantages. The main problems relate to high personal liability and the cumbersome elements involved in decision making and property transfers.

Simple trusts are common in states where land trust ownership is acceptable. A bank or similar body of trustees holds the title to the property, and members of the syndication hold beneficial interest in the trust. The trustee must respond to directions, as stipulated in the trust agreement. For income tax purposes, a title held in trust is treated as a tenancy in common.

A *complex trust* offers all the advantages of a corporation, short of incorporation. In this trust arrangement, title is taken and held by a trustee; the same trustee also holds considerable control over management. The extent of this control requires careful documentation in the trust agreement.

The final possibility for setting up a syndication is the partnership. The limited partnership, in particular, is the most common form of ownership among syndications. The limited partnership offers the basic legal advantage of limited liability to the investors and favorable tax treatment. Each investor is a limited partner.

The characteristics of the individual forms of ownership vary considerably in the advantages and disadvantages that they offer a property owner. Therefore, the specific objectives of the owner will affect the form of ownership chosen. A list of basic objectives for investing in real estate has been proposed:

Regular return.
Capital gain.
Tax shelter.
Use.
Entrepreneurial return (Professor Richard U. Ratcliff, *Valuation for Real Estate Decisions* [Santa Cruz, CA: Democrat Press, 1972], p. 174).

With the addition of pride of ownership, this list summarizes all of the goals that any real estate investor might have. Because these objectives are central to the ownership of real estate, it is worthwhile to discuss each of them.

Regular Return. Implied in the goal for a regular return is the requirement of a dependable cash flow. Typically, when a regular return is the primary goal, the investor will try to find a commercial property with strong credit tenants. The investor has a better chance of attaining financial security if the major tenant, such as a supermarket chain, a theatre, or a discount store, has a credit rating of AAA, the highest rating that can be received; and if that tenant's base rent is net or nearly so. A full *net lease* requires the tenant to pay a pro rata share of the shopping center's common area maintenance costs, real estate costs, the cost of insurance, special tax assessments, and maintenance costs for the building. Maintenance expenses will include the costs for the replacement or repair of electrical, plumbing, and roof parts, and the replacement or repair of the heating, ventilation, and air conditioning system (HVAC).

Capital Gain. Other investors are less concerned about current cash flow and instead direct their attention to reselling the property for a profit at a future date. Such investors are seeking a lump-sum profit at the time of sale and anticipate receiving the favorable capital gain tax treatment on the appreciated amount.

A capital gain offers an attractive objective, enough so that some investors direct more concern to the capital gain than to the property's cash flow. Still, it is important that the cash flow be high enough to meet fixed charges so that the investor need not contribute additional capital.

Investment for Tax Shelter. Equipped with a basic understanding of tax regulations and rulings, the property manager can work toward maximizing the investor's after-tax financial position. Taxes are extremely important in real estate transactions, as will be discussed in detail in chapter 11, "Insurance, Risk Management, and Taxes." Many syndicators and investors from high tax brackets consider real estate's tax shelters the primary reason for investing in property. Investors earn an income from the property, most of which is sheltered for income tax purposes. In addition to sheltering current cash distributions from the property, real estate can also create excess tax losses, which can be used to offset income from other sources.

It is not the purpose of this chapter to examine the field of taxation in depth (this is reserved for chapter 11). Still, to understand the relationship between owner and manager, it is necessary that the basic concepts of income taxes be considered. Taxes play a significant role in almost all real estate decisions.

Five important tax questions arise whenever real estate is purchased or sold:

1. When is a gain or loss recognized, and when can a gain be postponed?
2. How is the amount of gain or loss measured?
3. What is the basis for depreciation allowances and for determining future gain or loss?
4. What method of depreciation should be employed?
5. Is gain or loss ordinary or capital in nature? (Paul F. Wendt and Alan R. Cerf, *Real Estate Investment Analysis and Taxation* [New York: McGraw-Hill, 2nd ed., 1979], p. 70).

Federal tax laws, to a large extent, work in the favor of real estate investors. The law permits certain deductions in determining the investor's taxable income. The major deductions are depreciation, interest payments, property taxes, and operating expenses. Since depreciation allowances reduce taxable income and hence reduce the taxes payable, depreciation essentially increases cash flow. Depreciation is an expense on paper and does not constitute an actual cash outflow. It often does not reflect even a decline in the value of the property. Still, it is important for tax considerations, since, depending on the circumstances, there may be at the same time, a positive cash flow and no taxable income—that is, a tax shelter.

A discussion of the deductibility of interest and taxes as well as of depreciation warrants some mention of the concept of leverage. *Leverage* is the use of borrowed funds as a means of obtaining an asset-producing property. As such, leverage is an important concept in the field. Wendt and Cerf thus define leverage:

Leverage is a measure of the relationship of the amount of funds put in the venture by the owner as compared to the amount supplied by creditors. Leverage tends to magnify the percentage gain (or loss) on the owner's investment. Leverage permits higher depreciation deductions since these are based on the total amount of improvement rather than on the owner's equity *(Real Estate Investment Analysis and Taxation,* p. 72).

Leverage can be either positive or negative. Negative leverage can pose certain dangers for the property investor who overemphasizes tax benefits at the price of ignoring other important investment factors. Property managers should caution investors against this tendency. There have been cases where the inherent appeal of a tax shelter to high tax-bracket individuals has led to unsatisfactory, long-term returns on investments. Furthermore, a positive cash flow, regardless of the tax shelter, is an advantage for an investor, and its importance should not be diminished. On the other hand, the opportunity for leverage—that is, the opportunity to use someone else's money—is a primary distinguishing quality of investing in real estate.

Another tax consideration relates to an objective of ownership that was just mentioned—that is, capital gains and losses. Both capital gains and losses receive preferential tax treatment. Gains are taxed at a lower rate than ordinary income, and losses are subject to special treatment.

Accumulation. Many investors look to real estate as a way of building estates. Real estate investments offer ways of accumulating and storing wealth. The accumulated income, in turn, may be contributed to heirs or endowed to charity. As a contribution to charity, the investor obtains a deductible tax allowance.

One of the advantages of a real property investment is that it can offer collateral for borrowing purposes. This is yet another approach to the principle of accumulation.

Use. Real estate is acquired for use, often for the investor's own occupancy. Owning property has many advantages over the alternative of renting space. In some large shopping center developments, the major anchors—such as department stores or grocery stores—own their own buildings as well as a tract of land sufficient for their own parking needs. These tenants then agree on a working arrangement with the owner of the center. This concept was first used in the late 1950s. Many developers were unwilling to pay the high cost of building a department store, particularly in light of the relatively low rent that they would probably receive for the space. The developer, therefore, would sell to each department store a pad, or space, at a reasonable price, and the two parties would enter into a reciprocal agreement. This agreement, specifically the *Reciprocal Easement Agreement (REA)*, describes the necessary cross easements and all other pertinent details.

Entrepreneurial Return. Some investors are driven by their enterprising desires to invest in real estate. The builder who develops primarily to secure a profit is an example. When the development has been completed, this investor must decide whether to retain ownership or to change the investment vehicle. The landowner who seeks a joint venture with a developer as a way of holding land with improvements is also demonstrating the entrepreneurial urge. The landowner's profits should increase because of the enhanced land value.

The Element of Risk. Inherent in all these investment objectives is a common denominator, and that is risk. To the equity investor, risk fuses the chance of loss with the chance of gain. Investors differ in their willingness to take financial risks. In general, however, if all other aspects of the investments are similar, investors tend to pay more or accept a lower rate of return for a safe investment than for a risky one.

On the other hand, some investors have "gamblers' instinct." They agree to accept the higher risks of loss in return for the chance of a substantial gain. Such investors are willing to pay the price for speculative property unlike conservative investors, who tend to think of any risk as too expensive.

Given the reality that every investment involves some element of risk, an investor must evaluate probabilities. Basic questions that arise are these:

What is the certainty of projected income flow and reversion?
What is the stability of the forecasted income stream?
What is the likelihood of achieving the projected income in regard to quantity and quality?

One basic certainty is change, however slight the changes may appear to be in the short term. All long-term predictions carry with them an element of risk and the expectation of change. Investors can identify conditions and assess them with relative ease in the present. When they project into the future, however, investors must anticipate variations. The probability that these variations will occur increases in direct proportion to the time span over which the projections are made. No real estate investment comes with guarantees of financial success, but investors have their own attitudes and their knowledge of the market to guide them.

Do Shopping Centers Achieve Usual Investor Objectives?

Given these broad objectives, how well do shopping centers fare as real estate investments? To answer this question, it is helpful to look at two of the basic principles of real property value: (1) the *principle of anticipation;* and (2) the *principle of substitution.*

According to the principle of anticipation, people buy real estate because they anticipate that ownership will lead to future benefits. Value, therefore, is created by the anticipation of future monetary benefits. This principle is related to the principle of substitution, which holds that price is generally determined by the buyer's notion of the gains that substitute investments would provide. This principle also affirms the idea that the value of a property is set by the acquisition cost of a similar property. The comparison property is equal to the subject property both in terms of value and desirability.

It is useful to consider the element of risk and its relationship to an investment. This relationship has always been important in evaluating real estate investments, as indicated by the following prospectus, which was written in 1973:

The business of investing in real estate is highly competitive and is subject to numerous risks, including changes in general or local economic conditions, neighborhood values, interest rates, availability of mortgage funds, real estate tax rates and other operating expenses, the possibility of competitive overbuilding and of the General Partner's inability to obtain full occupancy of the properties, governmental rules and fiscal policies, acts of God and other factors which are beyond the control of the General Partner (Balcor/American Express, Inc.).

All of the factors that should have been considered during the long decision-making process leading up to the development of a center are related to the specific investment objectives. These factors include population trends; consumer purchasing power; present and projected competition; the site selected; the sizes and types of stores; market characteristics; and present and future transportation facilities in the area.

Given the quantitative objectives, combined with assorted nonfinancial goals that are important to some investors, how do shopping centers rate as investments? In terms of profit earned, do shopping center owners generally receive more than they invest? Most investors and analysts would answer yes to these questions, ranking shopping centers quite high in overall investment appeal.

There are many explanations for this. One important factor is that shopping center investments work as a hedge against inflation. It is primarily the use of percentage leases in most shopping centers today that makes the center investment appealing as an inflation hedge. Inflation forces retailers to raise their prices, which, in turn, should increase their gross profits and their percentage rent obligations. This, however, presents the shopping center investment in ideal terms. As developers and retailers have seen during periods of high inflation, high sales, and subsequently high percentage rents, profits can disappear quickly. Nevertheless, as it will be explained in the tax section of this book, various tax clauses in tenants' leases offer the investor added protection against rising costs. Few forms of investment property offer these built-in safeguards against inflation. Experiences in the marketplace over the past five to ten years suggest that institutional investors are not alone in considering shopping centers sound investments. The profile of the typical investor changes with the scale of the investment and the condition of the economy. Yet, with most shopping center investments, the potential for fulfilling investors' objectives remains high.

If shopping centers are solid investments that do meet owners' objectives, what can managers do to guarantee that the investment will meet its stated goals? This question leads into a discussion of the various methods of management that can be used for shopping centers and the differences between these management styles.

The management of a shopping center can be handled in many different ways. The systems and arrangements that the owner of a regional center with complete, in-house capabilities might employ will not be the same as what will be used by the owner of a single strip center. Similarly, the methods used for convenience centers will be different from those used in an urban development or a fashion-oriented or discount center. Although these obvious differences exist, all centers share certain characteristics. The following guidelines for managers were first published in 1964, and yet they remain valuable to managers today:

1. The architect determines a building's beauty; the management determines its success.
2. Every building worth managing has a personality worth developing.
3. A well-managed building is distinguished by its individuality; a poorly managed one, only by its street number.
4. Management policies should be formulated with an eye toward community trends.
5. Experience points the middle course between giving too much and losing a profit, or giving too little and losing a tenant.
6. Efficient management smoothly coordinates the interests of both owner and tenant.
7. To attend to a complaint is to minimize it; to ignore it is to magnify it.
8. Mangement that disregards maintenance will eventually have nothing left to manage.
9. True efficiency in real estate management is the product of years of experience (Arthur Eckstein, *Kansas City Realty,* newsletter of July, 18, 1964).

There are five basic arrangements for handling the management of shopping centers, although many variations are possible. Each arrangement will be discussed.

Management by Owner-in-Absentia

It is questionable whether management by owner-in-absentia can rightfully be called management. Frequently used in strip and community centers, this type of management arrangement implies that the owner and the property manager give little, if any, attention to the property.

As competition within investment real estate continues to increase and shows no noticeable signs of declining, it is improbable that this form of administration can be effective, except in isolated cases or for very brief periods of time.

Management by Owner or Owner's Organization

In many small centers, the owners control management directly. The properties, therefore, receive the personal attention of the owner, although in many cases, the owner does not have an office at or nearby the center.

Most center owners hire their own staff or a contracted staff that handles maintenance, repair, security, public relations, and any other function related to the upkeep and promotion of the building. Some owners get directly involved with the merchants' association programs; some owners may want the center staff to work with the merchants' association; and others might hire an advertising agency or a freelance promotional writer. In many respects, it is the manager's skills at applying the talents that are available that will determine whether the center succeeds.

An essential part of the manager's job, then, is to know what tasks must be completed, to organize the jobs, to set priorities, and to be able to delegate responsibilities. In many regional and superregional centers, a three-tiered structure represents owner and management. The top tier is the main office, with its concentration of specialists, who handle the activities that should be centralized—for example, insurance, accounting, and personnel management. The middle plank represents the administration at the regional level. Finally, the on-site staff is the bottom tier. These employees are responsible for the property's daily upkeep, including the operation of plumbing, security, and heating.

A variation of this method involves a completely autonomous on-site staff that is responsible for all management activities. In some cases, an on-site manager can fill similar duties at two or more centers, if the two properties are located near each other, as in, for example, one metropolitan area.

Agency Management

Legally, an agent is a person or company who has the authority to act for another. Most property managers are fundamentally agents, and therefore, they operate in an agency relationship with the owner, who is the client. The property manager is entrusted with the care and operation of the property.

In lease negotiations, purchasing, rent collection, bill payment, and management reports, the property manager acts as an agent. Agency management is also called *fee management*. It is a contract arrangement, whereby the owner hires a professional manager or a management company. This method can have applications for all sizes and types of centers.

Asset Management

Although dependent on other fields, asset management differs enough from the three methods of management already mentioned to warrant special attention.

An asset manager understands not only the daily requirements of the property's operations, but is also aware of the broader financial aspects of the shopping center. It has been suggested that a competent manager should be both a property manager and an asset manager, and many managers do fill this dual role. Asset management is bringing to the field a new branch of awareness and responsibility.

An asset manager must understand the investment objectives of the owner and understand the differences inherent in the legal forms of ownership. The manager must also know and be able to apply the principles of real estate management. The asset manager should develop a long-range plan, based on the owner's objectives, and re-evaluate and update the plan at least annually. The asset manager must also develop a management plan, which will identify various financial opportunities for the property owner. For an asset management program to be effective, the manager and property owner must agree on all general matters related to the property.

Consultative Management

Finally, there is a system of management that might be called consultative management. The objective in consultative management is to provide professional management at a price that the property owner can absorb. This is a difficult task since the property that requires the most intense management is generally the one whose owner can least afford such management.

In consultative management, the professional manager or management firm serves the owner in a role similar to an outside member of a board of directors. Among the duties the consultant might provide would be the following:

Schedule inspections—perhaps monthly or semimonthly.
Report on inspection.

Advise on leasing strategies, merchandise mix, and tenant selection
and placement.

Maintain the property and understand maintenance and repair
techniques.

Purchase insurance.

Any necessary work would become the job of the owner, subject to the consultant's periodic review.

Which Arrangement Is Best?

Each form of management offers the field worthwhile services;
likewise, each has clear drawbacks. The long-range plans that
the manager and owner agree on become the critical test of
whether management is doing its job properly. The plans serve
as a basis for comparison. Ultimately, management must be able
to maximize the potential for the center's long-term prosperity.
Good management, in general, can overcome mistakes that
were made during the planning and leasing stages of a shopping center's development.

Regardless of who manages the center or of how it is managed, some basic standards must stand in the forefront of the
manager's priorities:

1. Management must have a set of objectives—as clear, specific, and
   quantitative as possible.
2. A strategic philosophy must be developed. This type of strategy
   should not be confused with a financial forecast, which deals only
   with the investment's future in dollar terms.
3. Management must seek answers to such questions as: Where does
   the center stand in the marketplace? What purpose does the
   shopping center serve in the community? Who are the customers?
   In promotional terms, how can they be reached?
4. Management should think more in terms of profit improvements
   rather than in terms of cost cutting—the first is positive; the latter is
   negative.

The various methods of management cannot be classified
according to the size of the center. There is no clear formula
for determining whether a center should have an on-site manager. Typically, however, centers of fewer than 250,000 square
feet do not have on-site managers, whereas those of 300,000
square feet and more typically do. Centers that fall between
these two sizes have a less obvious need for on-site manage-

ment. Most neighborhood and community centers do not have a full-time resident manager. In specialty centers, however, where many tenants occupy relatively small units, there will probably be a need for on-site staffing, even though the square feet in many of these areas is 200,000 feet or less. There is a good reason for this. Generally, small independent tenants in all types of shopping centers cause most management activity: The more small independent tenants contained in the center, the greater the management activity. Therefore, specialty centers, which contain nearly all small, independent tenants, are management intensive, and most require an on-site manager. The particular demands of specialty centers create another reason for on-site management. Most of these centers contain exclusive shops that sell high-priced merchandise. The stores must be protected, and the situation often demands the presence of a property manager. Another reason is that many of the sites of these specialty centers pose safety and security problems. Many specialty centers are old, rehabilitated buildings, where any number of malfunctions can occur. In many cases, a property manager is needed on-site at all times, to alleviate potential problems.

In considering the relationship between size and management styles, it is worth noting that most centers rightly fall into the "small" category. Two-thirds of all shopping centers in the United States cover 100,000 feet or less. As noted in chapter 1 of this book, fewer than *five percent* of all shopping centers fit into the regional classification, and yet so much of the industry's concern is directed at this small percentage. Likewise, most of the industry's discussions on management styles concentrate on this small slice and virtually ignore the small- and medium-sized centers that dominate the market.

Most small- and medium-sized centers hire an outside contractor or a part-time evening worker to handle parking lot sweeping and landscaping. Many such centers, as a result, appear in ideal order only for the first few hours in the morning following the nightly cleaning.

In small centers, the property manager may visit only weekly or perhaps even less frequently, which can create numerous problems. The daily demands of any type of shopping center are great: Leases must be enforced. Delinquent tenants must be pursued. Vacancies must be filled. Events to attract consumers to the center must be planned. The building itself demands constant attention: Roofs leak. Parking lots accumulate dirt and trash. The parking lots begin to crack. The list goes on.

Who, then, is to manage the small- and medium-sized development, and how is it to be managed? Strip centers, in particular, are subject to a number of problems. Although the following list is not exclusive to small centers, it does reflect major problems that small centers share:

1. A poor public image.
2. Problems with access and parking.
3. Physical deficiencies.
4. Weak demand for space at the center.
5. Poor location.
6. Loss or lack of a major tenant (E. Wayne Tomlinson, CPM®, "Strip-Style Shopping Centers: Problems and Opportunities," *Journal of Property Management* [November/December, 1979], pp. 298-300).

These are all major problems, and certainly none of them should be discounted. Yet, a creative manager and a willing and interested owner can transform these ills into opportunities. The manager, for example, can campaign locally for improved public transportation that may result in greater traffic at the center, or perhaps a change in the tenant mix can be effected. Whatever the case, the recognition of a problem must come before any possible solutions can be considered. Therefore, a good manager will look for problems and potential problems and on finding them, search for realistic solutions.

In addition to the size of the center, the choice of a management method will also correspond to the type of owner. Some large corporations may find it expedient to employ the manager directly. Other, equally large institutions may choose to hire a locally based manager or management firm to oversee the centers it owns in a specific geographic area; this manager then would report to the corporation's central staff. Many partnerships grant to one of the partners the role of property manager. Joint ventures that hold wide interests are more likely to hire a local management firm to handle all management responsibilities.

In all cases, the scope of the manager's activities is subject to the property owner's preferences. Some management teams, including possibly both the manager and the employees, may function in almost purely custodial capacities. The other responsibilities and authority may be vested in a home office or centralized staff. Still, other management staffs will be given full responsibility to manage the property. Although the manager might react to the latter guidelines as a comforting display of confidence from the owner, the manager would actually have few practical guidelines on which to operate.

Regardless of the ownership entity, the property owner, with the suggestions and contributions of the property manager, will set the goals and objectives of the shopping center. The owner's priorities will continually affect all decisions made by management. The three most common ownership goals are periodic income, capital appreciation, and pride of ownership. In addition to these, many other forces are at work, and each requires consideration. One of the most critical factors is the owner's personal income tax obligations.

Ideally, the owner's goals and objectives will be stated clearly; in practice, however, few owners actually do this, even though a clear understanding of these objectives is essential to a good relationship between the manager and the owner. If the owner has not established objectives, the management team should suggest that this be done, beginning with a simple listing of the manager's operational responsibilities. Reference here is to professional management, which means either an employer of the owner or a fee manager. Responsibilities for both types of managers are similar and are appropriate for all sizes of centers:

Physical property management.
Financial (rental collections, disbursements, etc.).
Budgets and budget monitoring.
Leasing and public relations.
Projections and cost/benefit studies.
Promotion, publicity, and marketing.
Maximization of income and minimization of expenses.

When both the manager and owner agree on the extent of the manager's responsibilities, the two parties together can develop a property analysis and management plan. Chapter 4 will discuss the management plan in detail. The goal is that the property be managed successfully, which ultimately will mean income to the manager and a healthy cash flow and profit to the owner.

After an owner and a manager have decided to establish a business relationship, they must develop a management contract. A sample management contract appears in Exhibit 2.1. Most authorities agree that an acceptable management agreement contract should include at least the following six items:

1. An adequate description of the property to be managed.
2. Precise name and address of the owner and manager.
3. Management fees.
4. A clear statement of the responsibility and authority of the manager and any limitations placed upon operation of the property.
5. Provisions for adequate protection to both parties from risks of agency.
6. Length of term of the agreement and termination provisions.

The owner and the manager rely on each other. The owner who hires a manager depends on the manager to assure a steady profit from the investment. The manager depends on the property owner, who has assumed the risks of a real estate investment. The relationship between the owner of the property and its manager can be complex, and in many ways, it reflects a mutually dependent partnership. To avoid problems and potential disputes, therefore, the agreement must be explicit in stating the relationship and the rights and obligations of both parties.

Just as a well-drawn lease for a tenant in a center should resolve many problems before they occur, so will a clearly thought-out management agreement answer questions before they occur. The relationship between the owner of the center can be one of the following:

Principal and agent.
Owner and independent contractor.
Employer and employee.

The extent of management services to be provided under each of these relationships varies little from one form to another; however, the specific obligations can vary significantly.

One difference might involve the costs of payroll and employee benefits. If the association is that of employer and employee, the owner must pay all wages and benefits related to

EXHIBIT 2.1. *Sample Management Contract*

MANAGEMENT CONTRACT

AGREEMENT made this _____ day of _____19 ____,
between an Illinois corporation (herein called "Agent," and _____
_____ (herein called "Owner"):

Witnesseth

IN CONSIDERATION of the mutual promises and covenants herein contained, Owner and Agent agree as follows:

1. Owner hereby appoints and employs Agent as the sole and exclusive managing and renting agent of Owner's premises, commonly known as _____
_____ , for the period from _____
19 ____ to _____, 19 ____. Thereafter this Agreement shall continue in effect from year to year unless and until terminated as hereinafter provided. Either party may terminate this Agreement by giving notice in writing of intention to terminate at least thirty (30) days prior to said _____, 19 ____, or by giving notice in writing of intention to terminate at least thirty (30) days prior to the end of any extended yearly term.

2. Agent hereby accepts such appointment and employment for and in consideration of the compensation hereinafter provided, and agrees to use its best efforts in managing and keeping said premises rented to desirable tenants.

3. Owner hereby authorizes Agent to perform the following in the name of, for the account of, and at the expense of Owner:

    A. Execute all leases, renewals or extensions or agreements for the rental, occupancy, or operation of said premises, or any part thereof.

    B. Institute all legal actions or proceedings for the collection of rent or other amounts from said premises, or the ousting or dispossessing of tenants or other persons therefrom, and engage attorneys for any such matters.

    C. Hire, promote, discharge and supervise employees as Agent may determine advisable to be employed in the care, management or operation of said premises. It is understood and agreed that all such employees are in the employ of owner solely, and that Agent is in no way liable to such employees for their wages or other compensation, nor to Owner or others for any action of omission on the part of such employees.

    D. Make or cause to be made all repairs, replacements, alterations, additions, improvements and decorations in and to said premises as Agent may determine advisable. The expense incurred for any one item of same shall not exceed the sum of _____
    _____
    Dollars ($_____) unless authorized by Owner, except under such circumstances as Agent shall deem to be an emergency.

    E. Purchase all supplies and materials as Agent may determine advisable.

    F. Make all contracts for electricity, gas, fuel, steam, water, telephone, window cleaning, rubbish removal, laundry service, exterminating, equipment maintenance, and other services, or such of them as Agent shall deem advisable.

(continued)

EXHIBIT 2.1. *(Continued)*

G. Subject to Owner's approval, advertise said premises or portions thereof, prepare and secure signs, plans, circular matter and other forms of advertising.

4. Agent shall render to Owner a monthly statement of receipts and disbursements.

5. A. All monies furnished by Owner as working funds and all monies received by Agent for or on behalf of Owner shall be deposited by Agent in a bank mutually approved by Owner and Agent in account(s) maintained by Agent and not mingled with the funds of Agent, and shall be disbursed by Agent in such amounts and at such times as the same are required to pay for obligations, liabilities, costs, expenses and fees (including, without limitation, the compensation of Agent as hereinafter provided) arising on account of or in connection with this Agreement.

B. Owner shall pay all obligations, liabilities, costs, expenses and fees arising on account of or in connection with this Agreement.

C. Owner shall reimburse Agent promptly for any monies which Agent may elect to advance for the account of Owner. Nothing herein contained, however, shall be construed to obligate Agent to make any such advances.

D. Agent shall not pay from such account(s) interest or amortization on mortgages, taxes or assessments unless Owner, in writing, directs Agent to do so.

6. Agent is clothed with such other general authority and powers as may be necessary or advisable to carry out the intent of this Agreement.

7. Owner agrees to comply with all statutes, ordinances, laws, rules and orders of any federal, state or local government or department or officer thereof having jurisdiction in said premises respecting the use, operation or construction thereof, as well as with all orders and requirements of the local Board of Fire Underwriters or any other body exercising similar functions.

8. A. Owner agrees to indemnify and hold and save Agent free and harmless from any and all damages or injuries to person or property, or claims, actions, obligations, liabilities, costs, expenses and fees by reason of any cause whatsoever when Agent is carrying out the provisions of this Agreement or acting upon the directions of Owner. It is expressly agreed that the foregoing provision of this sub-paragraph shall survive the termination of this Agreement, but this shall not be construed to mean that Owner's liability does not survive as to other provisions of this Agreement.

B. Agent shall not be liable to Owner for any error in judgment, nor for any good faith act or omission in the execution of this Agreement.

C. Owner agrees to procure and maintain during the term of this Agreement comprehensive general public liability insurance, including property damage insurance, elevator liability insurance, steam boiler insurance, workmen's compensation insurance, and such other insurance as may be advisable for the protection of Owner and Agent. In each such policy of insurance, Owner agrees, upon request of Agent, to designate Agent and its officers, employees and agents as assureds. The insurance carrier and the amount of coverage in each such policy shall be mutually agreed upon by Owner and Agent. A certificate of each such policy issued by the carrier shall be delivered to Agent, and shall provide that Agent shall receive at least ten (10) days prior written

(continued)

EXHIBIT 2.1. *(Continued)*

notice from the carrier in the event of cancellation or any material change therein.

D. To the extent permitted by its insurance policies, Owner does hereby waive and release any and all claims which it may have against Agent for damages to said premises or contents therein to the extent that such damage is covered by Owner's insurance policies.

9. Owner agrees to provide, equip and maintain a suitable office in said premises for the use of Agent in the discharge of Agent's duties under this Agreement, and Owner agrees to assume the expenses incurred in connection therewith.

10. Owner hereby grants Agent the privilege of displaying Agent's signs in and upon said premises announcing that said premises is under Agent's management.

11. A. Owner agrees to pay Agent--

a. For management: _____ percent (_____%) of all amounts collected for rent, electric current, and from all other sources whatsoever;

b. For renting: On any new lease, a full commission, and on any renewal or extension of lease, or continuation of tenancy upon a statutory or month-to-month basis, a half commission.

B. All inquiries for any leases, renewals, extensions, continuations of tenancy, or agreements for the rental, occupancy or operation of said premises, or any part thereof, shall be referred to Agent, and all negotiations connected therewith shall be conducted solely by or under direction of Agent.

C. If Agent is called upon to perform any services not customarily a part of the usual services performed by a managing agent, it is agreed that Agent shall receive additional compensation therefore in an amount agreed upon between the parties.

12. During the term of this Agreement, Owner hereby appoints and employs Agent as the sole and exclusive agent of Owner in and for the sale of said premises, or any part thereof. If during the term hereof said premises, or any part thereof, shall be sold or exchanged, Owner agrees to pay Agent a full commission.

13. Upon and after the termination of this Agreement by lapse of time or otherwise, Owner shall recognize Agent as broker in pending negotiation with respect to any lease, renewal, extension or continuation of tenancy, or any sale of said premises and, additionally, shall recognize Agent as broker with respect to any persons to whom Agent shall have submitted or shown said premises during the term hereof with respect to any lease, renewal, extension, continuation of tenancy or sale, and in the event of consummation thereof, regardless of by whom such consummation is effected, Owner shall pay to Agent a commission.

14. All notices to be given hereunder shall be in writing and shall be sent by United States registered mail, return receipt requested, postage prepaid, addressed to Owner at _____

or to such other addresses as may from time to time be given as provided in this Paragraph 14. Any notice mailed as herein provided shall be deemed and treated to have been received on the date of mailing.

15. Agent is not and never shall be liable to any creditor of Owner or to any claimant against the property of Owner. Nothing contained in this Agree-

(continued)

EXHIBIT 2.1. *(Continued)*

ment shall constitute or be construed to be or create a partnership or joint venture between Owner and Agent. This Agreement shall be binding upon the parties hereto, their heirs, legal representatives, successors and assigns, and may not be changed orally but only by a writing signed by the party to be changed thereby.

IN WITNESS WHEREOF the parties hereto have executed this Agreement the day and year first above written.

By _____

_____

_____

_____

_____

employees, including unemployment compensation costs, withholding tax, and statutory insurance. Almost always, under this arrangement, the employer must also adhere to specific hiring regulations. If the relationship between the owner and manager is one of principal and agent, the owner principal may have to assume similar employer responsibilities, unless specifically stated otherwise in the agreement. Where the relationship is one of owner and independent contractor, the owner generally does not have to pay state or federal taxes, social security withholdings, or workers' compensation. In this case, the owner is also not liable for actions caused by "willful or gross negligence" of the independent contractor. There is only a fine distinction between a relationship of principal/agent and one of owner/independent contractor. Fee management or agency management generally refers to a relationship between principal and agent. The agent, in turn, may hire independent contractors (e.g., roofers, pavers, painters) to perform specific tasks.

A management agreement must contain specific clauses and follow a certain format. These clauses will be discussed next.

Identification of Parties

The two parties to the agreement—the property owner and the property manager—should be carefully identified. The legal description of the entity that is employing the manager should be stated.

If the property owner is a corporation, the agreement should specify the state of incorporation and the corporate address. If the owner is a limited partnership, the general partner will probably submit the agreement. If it is a general partnership, the contract should be entered into either by all the partners or by one who is vested with the authority to contract for management. Most sole proprietors become directly involved as the owners in signing the agreement form. Special care must be taken to state the accurate name, address, and legal entity of the manager or management firm.

Property Description

The property manager must assure that both parties clearly understand what property is to be managed. If all buildings and other improvements belong to the property owner and the land is clearly identifiable, the name of the shopping center and its address or bounding streets may suffice. Still, it would be better to include a satisfactory legal description and a site or plot plan as an exhibit in the contract.

If the major tenants own their own buildings, the land nearby, and the parking areas, the owner's specific obligations to these tenants must be defined. Likewise, the responsibilities of the property manager must be specified. Most agreements between the store and the center owner state the specific duties of both parties. The REA (Reciprocal Easement Agreement), discussed earlier, or the *RCOE (Reciprocal Construction, Operating, and Easement Agreement)* are the most common of this type of agreement. The documents describe the developer's buildings, the store tracts, and the shopping center site, and define and describe the common area. Typically, they also include agreements related to repair, maintenance, operations, alterations, parking requirements, and restoration. With an REA, the property owner or property manager usually maintains the major tenant's parking lot and other common areas.

The contract will spell out the standards of operation, especially in regard to maintenance and repairs. All common areas may be maintained and operated by a common contractor, mutually acceptable to all owners; all parties then would share the costs for this contractor. In many cases, the common contractors are the property managers who accept and perform the work, either with their own staffs, the center's staff, or with outside contractors.

One of the parties, often one of the anchor tenant stores, may want to assume responsibilities for maintenance and repair of the proportionate common areas that it owns. The frequent result, however, is that the party becomes virtually independent of the rest of the center. This arrangement can only lead to problems for the property manager. One store might choose to turn its parking lot lights off at a different hour than the rest of the center. Another store might use a careless lot-sweeping contractor that creates problems for the rest of the property. Similar complications can occur with respect to trash removal services, landscape contractors, and snow removal operators. Consistency and uniformity are important goals in the operation of a shopping center.

If one of the store owners elects to assume this maintenance responsibility, the manager may regard this as a warning of the tenant's displeasure with the quality or costs of the common contractor's work. The property manager should make every effort to satisfy all parties in the agreement, to avoid the inherent danger of divided responsibilities.

Terms of Agreement

The agreement between the owner and the manager must answer many questions concerning the relationship between the two parties. The agreement must specify when the contract begins and ends. It must state the policy that regulates extension of the agreement or specific provisions for renewal. Cancellation requirements should be stated. The contract should stipulate the proper method that either party must use to give notice to end the agreement. The method for calculating fees during an extension or because of an early termination also should be included in the agreement. These concerns are important, and although they might not all be addressed in the clause that deals with the contract term, they warrant attention somewhere in the agreement.

Responsibilities, Authority, and Duties of Management

It is critical that the owner and manager clearly define the services that management will provide and its specific duties and responsibilities. The agreement should also set the boundaries of the manager's authority.

From the owner's standpoint, the list of duties and responsibilities will serve as the basis for selecting an individual or firm to manage the center. The advantages to managers are even more obvious: They can budget and plan far more efficiently if the contract details what services will be expected.

The duties and responsibilities most commonly turned over to a property manager include the following:

Management. Many contracts require the agent to accept the employment to manage (or to rent and manage) the property. This wording may further provide for the agent to be diligent in exercising these powers and duties. It may also provide for the agent to furnish the services of its organization for such purposes.

Monthly Statements. Most contracts contain provisions requiring the manager to furnish the owner with detailed monthly operating statements or receipts, expenses, and charges for the preceding accounting period. The manager also may have to turn in receipts of expenses and charges. Chapter 12 discusses these reports in detail. During some periods, the property may be operating under a deficit, as disbursements and charges are higher than income. The management contract should provide for such occurrences. The clause should state that the owner must maintain a minimum balance in an operating account, and that the manager will not be required to advance funds.

Most contracts make reference to an agreed-upon chart of accounts and to the types of financial reports that the owner will require from the manager. This might involve vouchers that cover all expenses and disbursements paid during the month. Most owners request an itemized list of all rents in arrears; some want an aging schedule that details the receivables and states how long the debts have been outstanding, e.g., 30, 60, or 90 days. Some owners may require a payroll list that shows the occupations and wages of employees hired by the agent.

Normally, the managing agent will be required to keep detailed records that describe the management of the center, and the owner will have access to these records at all times. Every agreement should also contain a provision that grants authority to the owners' accountants to audit the books and records when appropriate.

Separate Bank Account. Owners are rightfully concerned about the hazards of their properties' funds being commingled with the managing agent's funds. Most owners, therefore, insist on a clause in the agency agreement obligating the agent to deposit all funds collected from the operation of the center into a trust account. This account should be in a bank approved by the owner and separate from the agent's personal accounts. To simplify matters, the agent should be allowed to endorse checks that are made out to the owner, for deposit in this trust account.

Fidelity Bond. Most owners prefer that the managing agent obtain a company fidelity bond in an agreed-upon amount and that it be made conditional upon the faithful performance by the agent of management duties, including an accounting for all funds. The two parties can reach a settlement on the exact amount of the bond. That amount should be at least equal to, if not greater than, the largest sum the agent is likely to deal with at any time during the course of the operating year.

Employees. The agreement should specify the staff that the agent will furnish and who the agent will carry on its own payroll. The contract should also specify the job titles of personnel who will be involved in the operation of the center and will not be direct employees of the agent. Normally, the agent will pay these employees from the property owner's funds, but they will be considered employees of the managing agent. Generally, the property manager is responsible for hiring, training, supervising, and, if necessary, firing employees.

Operating Budget. Some management agreements contain a provision requiring the agent to develop an annual operating budget and an income and expense projection for the center. Most such projections will include common area expenses, and, if appropriate, enclosed mall expenses. The contract should specify the date that the agent must furnish budget figures for the property owner's approval.

Tenant Contact. Although some property managers and owners might simply assume it, stating in the contract the manager's obligation to handle routine contacts with tenants may be appropriate. This would include meetings with store owners, managers, or representatives from retailing operations that own their own buildings but still are part of the center.

Service Contracts. Most management contracts give the agent the authority to negotiate various service contracts at the owner's expense. Most of these contracts will require the owner's approval. There may be separate contracts, for example, for fuel, supplies, exterminating services, trash removal, mechanical equipment, or housecleaning.

Merchants' Association. The contract should request that the manager cooperate with the center's merchants' association and its staff and serve as the owner's representative on the association's executive committee or board of directors. It is common, especially in large, enclosed malls, for the agent to hire a marketing director, who then works with the merchants' association or administers the center's promotional funds.

Utilities and Real Estate Taxes. Most contracts request that the managing agent maintain contact and negotiate all necessary agreements with appropriate government agencies. This might involve real estate taxes, special assessments, or utility bills. The contract might contain a provision stating the costs that the agent would pay "on behalf of the owner in accordance with approved budgetary allowances."

Rental Collections. Rental collection is one of the owner's major concerns. Rental payments represent the owner's cash flow. The management agreement should discuss rent collection, percentage rents, and record maintenance for gross sales reports in computing percentage rents. Most contracts go further, stating the agent's authority to terminate tenancies upon consent of the owner, and to sign and serve notices that the agent considers necessary. In most agreements, this section also allows the manager to take various actions at the expense of the owner, provided that the agent has the owner's written consent. Tenant eviction and recovery of possession of the occupied premises may be the final outcome. Most contracts also give the agent permission to settle, compromise, and release such actions or suits to reinstate tenancies, but again only with the owner's approval.

HVAC Equipment. In most enclosed malls and in some open malls, the managing agent must take responsibility for the mechanical equipment that furnishes heating, ventilating, and air conditioning to the mall. The managing agent also might supervise the operation and maintenance of this equipment, either with an outside contractor or its own staff.

Repairs. This clause grants the agent the responsibility of handling repairs on the property. It may state only that the manager handle major repairs at the center and its common areas. It may go further, taking into account minor repairs, the installation of tenants' alterations, or the purchase of necessary supplies.

Most agreements require that the property manager report any unusual conditions to the owner immediately. The agreement should specify what constitutes an "unusual condition." For example, most agreements have a provision requiring the agent to secure the owner's approval on all expenditures in excess of some agreed-upon amount. Monthly and recurring operating charges and emergency repairs in excess of the maximum should be excluded from this requirement of advance approval.

The owner would probably prefer that the manager agree to charge all expenses at net cost. The owner, thus, would receive credit for any rebates, commissions, discounts, and allowances.

Outside Services. Many management contracts provide that the agent may procure any necessary outside services, subject to the owner's written approval and at the owner's expense. These services may include the fees of attorneys, real estate appraisers or consultants, architects, engineers, or advertising agencies.

Indemnity. Within the contract, an indemnification clause is necessary to hold the manager harmless for liability arising from the property's operation. The owner seeks indemnification from the agent, and the agent seeks indemnification from the owner. The intent is to seek protection from the danger of claims, losses, and liabilities arising out of damage from accidents or casualty at the center. In some cases, the agent may not be covered if clear negligence can be established.

Insurance. Every shopping center should be insured, and the management contract may assign responsibility for maintaining coverage to the agent. Typically, the management agreement provides that the agent will, on the owner's behalf and at the owner's expense, maintain the insurance that will cover the owner and the agent against a variety of perils. This coverage will include workers' compensation policies, liability insurance, and property damage liability. It may provide that the agent obtain additional coverage, including coverage for fire, steam boiler failure, and rent loss. As a rule, this insurance is not subject to cancellation or change, except after a 10-day, prior written notice to the agent or owner. Chapter 11 will discuss insurance coverage and risk management in detail.

Office. Many management agreements require that the owner furnish the agent with a rent-free office in the shopping center. In most cases, this office is designated as both the office of the manager and the office of the center.

Compensation. In this clause, the owner agrees to pay the agent a specific sum for all management services. This can be a specific amount per month or a stipulated percent of the monthly gross receipts from the operation of the premises. If the latter approach is taken, gross receipts should be defined to clarify whether tenants' payments toward common area operations, real estate taxes, and insurance claims are included along with rent and percentage rent payments. A more detailed discussion of management fees appears later in this chapter. Most management agreements provide separately for leasing commissions. Different levels of commission may be charged for replacement tenants versus new tenants, as well as those cases where options are exercised. There may be other services for which the owner will agree to compensate the agent. This could involve rehabilitation and construction management responsibilities or other casualty restoration work. Or, the contract might not be so specific but rather set down guidelines more generally, as the following contract clause does: "If an agent is called upon to perform any services not customarily a part of the usual services performed by a managing agent, it is agreed the agent shall receive additional compensation in an amount agreed upon by owner and agent."

Exclusive Rights to Sell or Lease the Property. It is reasonable for the managing agent who is also handling leasing to have the exclusive right and authority to enter into new, replacement, or renewal leases. At the same time, the owner may reserve the right to withdraw a portion of the center's gross leasable area from the market at any time and for any reason. On the other hand, most managing agents do not have exclusive rights regarding the sale of the property. A manager who is qualified to sell the property may seek to obtain the exclusive listing for the property.

The Management Fee and How It Is Computed

Many standardized management agreement forms that are readily available provide that the management fee will be a specific number of dollars per month, or an agreed-upon percentage of the monthly gross receipts from the operation of the premises, whichever is greater. Nevertheless, these are not the only two ways that management fees are determined.

The fee should reimburse the management firm for all its costs and still provide a margin for profit. Thus, five methods of computing management fees become possible.

Method one is a minimum fee that includes operating costs, plus a pro rata share of start-up costs, and a profit—or a percentage of the gross income, whichever is greater.

Method two is a minimum fee (similar to method one) or a percentage of net operating income, whichever is greater.

Method three is a flat retainer fee, often used in the case of distressed properties. This retainer may include certain lease renewal fees, or leasing commissions may be in addition to the flat charge.

Method four is a cost-plus approach, whereby the management firm accounts for the jobs and factors in a profit and overhead loading.

Method five involves a variation of any of the foregoing methods, plus an incentive related to an agreed-upon measurement.

Each method has specific advantages and disadvantages. Different factors about each property will govern which method of fee structuring would be most appropriate. The following discussion explores each of these methods.

Method One: Minimum Fee

Many shopping center owners today are paying a minimum fee for management instead of the alternative, a percentage of gross income. A percentage of gross income, determined by the market, is easy to calculate. The method is criticized, however, because it fails to consider the fact that the owner benefits not from gross income but from net income. When the fee is based solely on gross income, the management firm also has little incentive—beyond professional pride—to keep down expenses. There is, however, an incentive to keep prices down, to the extent that the manager wishes to be rehired and wishes to maintain a strong reputation within the property management field.

Yet, tying the fee to a market-determined percentage of gross income gives management some incentive to increase rents or to take other actions that might increase sales volume. When percentage rents go up, gross income will also increase.

This approach to setting a management fee is based on the assumption that the objectives of the owner and the manager are the same. This, however, may not be an accurate assumption. To the manager, the value of an account is tied to the effective gross income—the top line. The fee moves up or down with the gross. To the owner, however, value is a function of either the net operating income—the bottom line—or, more likely, the after-tax cash flow.

Assume that there are three shopping centers; each is growing at a different rate. One shopping center is growing in effective gross income and in operating expenses at equal rates. Another has a gross income that is growing at a higher rate than are expenses. Finally, income growth in the third center is lower than the increase in expenses. If the effective gross income and operating expenses grow equally, both ownership and management increase their "wealth," expressed in percentages. If the effective gross income increases at a slower rate than the rate at which expenses increases, however, for the owner, the value of the property increases, and the value of the account to the manager remains the same. When the rate of increase of effective gross income is less than the increase in expenses, then for the manager, the value of the account does not change; for the owner, value declines. This situation actually occurs quite often. The objectives of the manager and the owner, therefore, in many cases are quite different.

The manager would be indifferent to any of the growth cases. The owner, on the other hand, would be deeply concerned. A basic ownership goal is to maximize net operating income (income minus expenses) and its rate of growth.

In sum, as long as fees are based on gross income, the manager has little incentive to achieve maximum profit on the property. The best solution may be another form of fee structure. Nevertheless, readers should be aware that, despite its shortcomings, this method is widely used and accepted in the industry.

Method Two: Percentage of Net Operating Income

There is much to be said in support of a fee that is based on a percentage of the net operating income. When the management fee is tied to the top line, the effective gross income, the manager will not be so concerned with controlling operating expenses. If it is tied to the bottom line, the net operating income, however, the objectives of ownership and of management become the same. Both parties are concerned with both income items and expense items.

A case could be made for the property manager who increases the net operating income without changing the gross income. The manager is not being adequately compensated for the extra, cost-saving efforts that such efforts would entail. The solution? Introduce a form of incentive into the approach—for example, method five—which might better serve both the owner and the manager.

Method Three: Flat Retainer

A flat retainer fee is ideal for situations of distressed property. In this case, the investment is still too risky, and much work needs to be done before the search for tenants can even begin. A fee structure, related either to gross income or to net income, would be inappropriate. Few skilled practitioners of property management would be willing to extend the required efforts without first establishing a clear basis for compensation.

The development of the fee should reflect the amount of time necessary to analyze the situation. It might involve a scanning of the combined talents of many—both in-house and outside experts—who represent a variety of specialties. Conceivably, the manager's job could involve the following:

Analyses of traffic patterns and site characteristics.
Appraising.
Cash flow and tax analyses.
Competitive reviews.
Consumer profiles.
Definition and analysis of trade area.
Engineering evaluations of the property.
Feasibility studies.
Financing and refinancing projections.
Marketing and advertising programs.
Income and expense analyses.
Leasing and tenant mix analyses.
Real estate tax counseling.
Sales forecasting.

The list could continue. Most likely, each step would be priced and contracted separately. The more routine elements of property management—rent collection, maintenance, repair—could be priced in the same manner from one property to another.

Assuming that the center stands on sound financial grounds, it would be reasonable for the owner and manager to renegotiate, at a later date, the basis for the fee.

Method Four: Cost Plus

Basically, the owner of the cost-plus method views the fee of property management as another—although essential—remuneration and an additional cost of owning property. With the cost-plus method, the owner and manager must come to an agreement about the basic cost of management and the basic services that management will provide. This job should come as a welcome burden. Not only does it give both the owner and manager an idea of the cost of managing the property, it also details staff time and related expenses that will be involved in that task. Equipped with this knowledge, together the manager and owner can arrive at an equitable fee.

A worksheet, such as that in Exhibit 2.2, will help determine the fees for managing a shopping center of almost any size. Note that leasing is considered a separate service, and it has a distinct fee.

Also, as illustrated in Exhibit 2.2, a percentage is used for overhead and for profit. These percentages are subject to negotiation and market conditions. Travel and similar out-of-pocket expenses would be added to this fee, but at direct cost with no markup.

With this method, the management fee generally is subject to a review every year. How does this method rate? An owner could argue reasonably that the fee structure is invalid because it does not relate to either the top line or the bottom line. But, in its defense, it can also be said that the cost-plus method represents a professional approach to a professional skill. It attempts to achieve two reasonable results:

1. Establish a true cost of managing the property.
2. Produce a profit for the management company.

Management almost always operates under the constraints of a budget of income and expenses. Thus, the property owner not only is aware of these anticipated items but also can equate the stated fee to the project's income.

Method Five: Incentive Arrangements

Method five involves variations of the other four methods, but it also includes a form of incentive that is tied to performance. Management companies experience two economies that are common to most businesses; they are (1) *economies of scale* and (2) *economies of greater utilization*. With respect to economies of scale, the larger organizations generate sufficient volume to employ specialized talents. This talent, in turn, should lead to more efficient operations. Other economies of scale could relate to systems, controls, and computer programs—all of which tend to lower the unit cost of operation. The business volume that is handled correctly will utilize both human personnel and various service equipment, which is referred to as the economy of greater utilization.

EXHIBIT 2.2. *Management Pricing Worksheet*

MANAGEMENT PRICING

PROPERTY _____

NO. OF UNITS _____ RESIDENTS _____ OFFICES _____ STORES _____ BOAT SLIPS _____

AGE AND PRESENT CONDITION OF PROPERTY AND IMPROVEMENTS _____

MILES FROM OFFICE _____ NUMBER OF EMPLOYEES _____

GROSS COMMON AREA CHARGE _____

MANAGEMENT/LEASING _____ LEASING _____

	No. Per Month	Hours Each	Total Hours	Cost
I. Property Manager's Services				
A. Inspections	___	___	___	___
B. Site visits	___	___	___	___
C. Capital improvement supervision	___	___	___	___
D. Owner/investor/association meetings	___	___	___	___
E. Travel time: $ . . . per hr. X . . . hrs.	___	___	___	___
F. Office hours per month			___	___
G. Travel expense . . . mi. X . . . per mi.				___
TOTAL COST				___
II. Executive Services				
A. Owner/investor/association meetings	___	___	___	___
B. Site visits	___	___	___	___
C. Surveys/consultations	___	___	___	___
D. Inspections	___	___	___	___
E. Statement review	___	___	___	___
F. Budget preparation	___	___	___	___
G. Travel time: $ . . . per hr. X . . . hrs.	___	___	___	___
H. Travel expense . . . mi. X . . . per mi.				___
TOTAL COST				___
III. Accounting and Clerical Services				
A. Receipts accounted for—days per mo.	___	___	___	___
B. Disbursement: invoices, payments	___	___	___	___
C. Monthly billing	___	___	___	___
D. Payroll: checks issued	___	___	___	___
E. Owner/association statement preparation	___	___	___	___
F. Resident statement and preparation	___	___	___	___
G. Statement photocopying	___	___	___	___
H. Owner consultation	___	___	___	___
TOTAL COST				___
IV. Subtotal before Overhead and Profit				___

	Percent of Total			
V. Overhead and Profit				
A. General overhead (telephone, rent-ins, utilities, etc.)	___	___	___	___
B. Marketing	___	___	___	___
C. Profit and contingencies	___	Total Fee		___
VI. Total Monthly				___

The Institute of Real Estate Management has developed a classification of incentive plans. There are four main categories:

1. Rewards for exceeding performance standards;
2. Incentive fees based on net operating income;
3. Graduated fees; and,
4. Incentive fees based on occupancy rates.

Applied to shopping center management, each incentive plan must be explored separately.

First, if management is rewarded for exceeding performance standards, the question might be: What will the performance standards be? Standards might involve any of the following:

Filling vacancies in a timely fashion.

Exceeding a specified rental rate on any new or renewal lease negotiation.

Keeping operating expenses below a negotiated dollar figure per square foot of gross leasable area or leased area.

Completing a renovation or remodeling program within a stipulated time frame or financial budget.

Producing centerwide tenant sales volume in excess of a negotiated level.

Reducing delinquencies or improving the timeliness of rental collections.

The property owner and manager can negotiate a variety of performance standards. The two parties also can negotiate the incentive fee. The second type of incentive fee—based on net operating income—offers the manager a special incentive for increasing the net operating income by reducing expenses, reducing vacancies, or increasing rent.

The management agreement might provide for a center management fee based on a percentage of the gross income. If NOI exceeded an agreed-upon level, there would be a separate fee for the excess income payable to the management firm.

As an alternative, the incentive could be tied to the rents or the NOI established in an approved budget. Or, it could relate to increases in NOI over a three-year period.

Graduated fees—the third type of incentive plan—can be interpreted as a variation of the flat retainer method and might best be used in the management of troubled properties. A center with many vacancies requires more attention than one that is 95 percent occupied. A distressed property offers innumerable problems; therefore, there must be special incentives to encourage the management company to elevate the property investment to a stable financial position.

Graduated fees can be designed to go up or down. At first, the fees might be substantial, as all-out efforts are taken, for example, to lease, remodel, or repair the property. As the workload decreases, the fee might then be adjusted downward.

Readily adaptable to apartment management, incentive fees based on occupancy rates also might be applicable to shopping centers. This plan suggests that the primary goal is to maximize occupancy rates rather than to maximize the net operating income. The problem with this, however, is that the NOI could be greater with some vacancies than it might be with full occupancy. Therefore, the manager and owner must put great care into developing this method, such that it benefits both the owner and the manager.

Shopping center management is an extremely competitive business. The various fee structures provide an agent with an incentive for doing a superior management job. However, because of the competitive nature of the business, it is possible that managing agents will have a difficult time using the incentive fees of the cost-plus type or the fee based upon the cash flow improvement.

Conclusion

The relationship between the shopping center owner and the property manager is integral to the long-term success of the real estate investment. This holds true whether the owner is a sole proprietor, a partnership, or a corporation, and whether the manager is an employee of the owner, a fee manager, or a consultant. In all cases, the objectives of the owner—for a regular return, for capital gain, for a tax shelter, for accumulation of wealth, for use, for entrepreneurial return, or for pride of ownership—guide the manager in decisions that affect the shopping center.

A management agreement, preferably a written contract, formalizes the relationship between the owner and the manager. Carefully thought-out and thorough, this agreement eliminates the problems and misunderstandings that so easily could occur between the two parties. The agreement identifies the parties, states the commencement and termination dates, and the property, and prescribes the duties and responsibilities of both the owner and the manager. It also states how the management fee is determined. The fee might be based on a percentage of gross income or net operating income, it may be a flat retainer, it may be computed on the cost-plus method, or it may be based on an incentive program. Although the percentage-of-gross method is most common, a fee that is tied to the manager's performance appears most likely to create a successful relationship between the owner and the managing agent.

Review Questions

1. Given two of center management's primary objectives:
   (a) Maintaining the highest possible net operating income without damaging the property's future productivity; and
   (b) Enhancing the appreciation of the property and thereby its market value;

   compose two lists—one, of the forces that inhibit these objectives, and another, of the forces that encourage them. List at least five positives and five negatives.

   Decide which of the forces are the strongest and rank them accordingly. Next, develop a strategy for dealing with each critical force—increase the driving forces and decrease resisting forces.

   Identify the steps most likely to be successful. Concentrate on aspects that have the greatest chance of being corrected.

2. If you were in a position to develop a 100,000 square foot strip center, using some form of institutional financing, which form of ownership vehicle would you choose? Defend your decision by comparing it to other alternatives.

3. Select three types of owners of regional centers. Rank the following possible investment objectives from most important to least important to each owner:

   Capital gain
   Regular return
   Tax shelter
   Accumulation
   Use
   Entrepreneurial return

4. Leverage from financing can be positive or negative. Give examples of both. What can be done to enhance positive leverage or decrease negative leverage?

5. What qualities of shopping centers make them attractive investments? What negative qualities reduce their investment attractiveness?

6. For an asset management system to be effective, the manager

and the owner must agree on all general matters related to the property.

List five items that you believe would be most important from the owner's viewpoint.

List five items you think would be most important from the manager's point of view.

How can the differences, if any, be reconciled?

3

Developing the New Center

Plans for a new shopping center development have become more precise. A site has been selected, and the developer has decided on the size and type of the center. The developer has considered the market, studied consumers' buying habits, analyzed the region, and weighed the impact of local and national economic conditions. The ultimate question emerges: Should plans proceed for developing the new shopping center?

Shopping centers are costly real estate investments, and most shopping center developers are sophisticated practitioners who have been in the field for several years. Today, few of these developers would begin a new project without first obtaining solid evidence that it would succeed. Many smaller investors delve into neighborhood centers, and most of these smaller investors also have market evidence that supports their ventures. Whoever the investor, that person or group of people must weigh all factors carefully and follow certain "rules of the trade," which are guidelines that experts of the field have followed for many years.

The shopping center industry is still very new, so relatively few generally agreed-upon principles have emerged. In some ways, practitioners today have a firmer grasp of what *not* to do than of what they should do. Therefore, part of the value of this chapter will come from ideas of what property managers and developers should not do. These "do nots" are discussed in some detail in the latter part of this chapter.

What is the property manager's role in the development of a

new shopping center? That role varies, depending primarily on the demands of the developer. Some developers prevent the property manager from getting too involved in the process. Others give the property manager only the responsibility of handling the daily functions of the property. Still other developers depend almost entirely on the professional property manager's expertise. These differences in owners' preferences are discussed in more detail later in this chapter.

Property managers are skilled practitioners who know the steps that are needed for efficient programs of accounting, insurance, property maintenance, and promotion. Skilled property managers know their market, and they know how to select an appropriate tenant mix for that market. Property managers, however, must remember the limitations of their roles. They may or may not be allowed to participate in major decisions. They may or may not be allowed an open voice during the planning stage. They may or may not be expected simply to "operate the property" and be given few responsibilities beyond that. The choice, again, belongs to the developer, who is the property manager's employer.

Basically, during development, the property manager is in the best position to address the following questions:

1. Access in and out of the shopping center property.
2. Traffic flow within the parking lot.
3. Parking requirements.
4. Maintenance responsibilities and problems.
5. Building layout. The property manager should know, for example, if certain layouts will result in difficult tenant leasing.
6. Tenant mix selection.
7. Promotional activities.

The bias of this book is that property managers should be active participants during all stages of development—since the professional manager can offer an invaluable contribution to the investment.

For the purposes of this chapter, a condensed definition of a shopping center will bring sufficient meaning to the subject of development. The Community Buildings Council of the Urban Land Institute (ULI) defines a shopping center as the following:

A group of architecturally united commercial establishments built on a site which is planned, developed, owned, and managed as an operating unit related in its location, size, and type of shops to the trade area that the unit serves (J. Ross McKeever, Nathaniel M. Griffin, and Frank H. Spink Jr., *Shopping Center Development Handbook* [Washington, D.C.: Urban Land Institute, 1977], p. 1).

It is significant that this definition of a shopping center emphasizes three major functions: (1) planning; (2) management; and (3) the center's relationship to its trade area. This chapter will discuss all aspects of the center's development, with emphasis on these three topics. These three elements are generally the priorities of successful shopping center developers.

This chapter does not intend to turn the novice into a seasoned professional property manager with an expertise in development—although how nice it would be to read a book and then know it all. In truth, only attentive study and experience with the development process will produce professionalism. This chapter will present enough information to guide the reader in the proper direction.

Another point needs to be clarified at the beginning of this chapter, and that is that development does not refer exclusively to the creation or construction of a center. The term also suggests expansion, conversion, generation, or growth. Development can refer to a center that is undergoing changes, such as a major renovation program of modernization, conversion, or rehabilitation. Readers should keep that idea in mind throughout this chapter. Although this chapter deals specifically with the development of new centers, many of the same principles could also apply to the redevelopment of older properties. This point is important in today's market, since so much emphasis has been geared to the rehabilitation of existing buildings, rather than on the construction of new properties.

Development Objectives

Before aspiring shopping center developers embark on a new project, first they should define their own specific goals and objectives for the project. Commonly, developers will say that their goal is to earn a "nice profit," but they fail to mention all the factors that allow the center investment to achieve economic success. Profit is the main incentive for developing a new project—and it should be. Profitability, however, is too general a goal, and earning a healthy profit from the center depends on many factors. Listed below, in no special order, are four main objectives for a successful shopping center:

1. An aesthetically pleasing property.
2. Functional, serving a basic need.
3. Easily and inexpensively maintained.
4. Profitable—both initially and as a long-term investment.

Whether the proposed development is a small neighborhood center, a larger community project, or a superregional center with more than 1,000,000 square feet of gross leasable area, the developer should be concerned with the appearance of the improvements to be constructed on the land, which is a finite resource. (The term *gross leasable area [GLA]* has been adopted as a measurement of the total floor area designed for each tenant's occupancy and exclusive use.) The concern with appearance is not entirely altruistic. The developer does not ponder how attractive the property will be for the sole purpose of creating an object of beauty; rather, attention to aesthetics helps ensure leasing success and the approval of potential customers and tenants. An attractive, pleasing appearance is actually a prerequisite for the investment's prosperity.

The project should be functional and free of any unnecessary design features that detract from its intended purpose, which is to generate the maximum level of retail sales. In neighborhood and community shopping centers, the site plan is the single most important design element that will determine the functional capacity of the center. The site plan shows the placement of buildings, the location of tenants, and the design of the parking lot, driveways, and sidewalks. Site design is important for regional shopping centers, but it is not as critical. A regional shopping center draws from a much larger trade area and offers a much greater variety of merchandise. These characteristics create a situation where typical customers at regional centers plan to spend several hours shopping and are willing to tolerate more inconveniences than when they shop at the smaller centers in their local areas. One of the primary reasons for convenience and neighborhood shopping centers is that they offer a convenient place to shop for basic products and services. This convenience factor is a major element in their design.

Other design elements that can affect a center's functionalism—either positively or negatively—include the exposure and appearance of tenants' signs, placement and the number of parking spaces, size of the center and of individual stores in relation to the trade area being served, and the availability of store space to meet retail tenants' requirements.

The cost of operating and maintaining a shopping center is a key element in determining its economic success, a principle that holds true for all income properties. Maintenance is discussed in more detail later in this chapter and in extensive detail in chapter 6 of this book. It is worth mentioning here that some developers are moving in a dangerous direction in regard to maintenance: They are attempting so diligently to reduce costs during the design and development phases that they use and purchase inferior-quality products and equipment, resulting later in unreasonably high maintenance costs. Such short-sighted frugality does not pay off in the long term—and eventually will cause a multitude of problems. Here are a few examples:

Installing a poor-base asphalt parking lot rather than a lot with a high-quality base.

Encasing exterior canopy columns with stucco, which requires a high maintenance cost, rather than more expensive brick veneer, which requires virtually no maintenance at all.

Installing an inferior and inexpensive roof system, rather than a built-up roof designed to last 20 years or more without major repair or replacement.

In the typical neighborhood shopping center, the roof and parking lot represent the major items of physical maintenance expense. Developers and managers, therefore, should take special care during the design and construction phases of a new center to reduce the future costs of maintaining these two items. As demonstrated, such precautions may mean a higher initial cost, but the lower cost of maintenance will probably result in high cost savings for the owner in future years. Indeed, the anticipated future costs of all maintenance, repair, and replacement should be considered and ultimately influence the design criteria.

Development Team

Experienced practitioners have seen that the team approach generally works best for handling the development of a new shopping center. Each person on the team should be involved as early as possible in the project, and preferably during the conceptual phase. The only aspect in creating a new center that does not require the involvement of all team members is during site selection, when the developer selects a site. Even in this case, however, more than one team member gets involved.

A full development team consists of the following professionals:

Developer or project manager.
Architect.
General contractor.
Consulting engineers, designers, and architects (soil, civil, structural, mechanical, graphic, and landscaping).
Property manager.
Leasing agent.

Developers who refuse to involve other professionals at early stages and instead attempt to handle complicated and critical functions themselves are actually harming their own investments. They will almost certainly not save money in the long term, and they are flirting with economic disaster. The following discussion will describe the different roles and responsibilities that each team member should assume.

Developer. Developers are the "risk takers," the entrepreneurs who conceive projects and put all of the pieces together. Because developers bear the economic risks, they are also the ones who reap the rewards of success—or who suffer the liabilities of failure.

During the early stages in the development of a shopping center, the developer functions as a project manager. In that role, the developer's responsibility is to assimilate all the activities and recommendations of other team members. The developer has final decision-making authority, but a true professional will listen to the opinions of all members and consider their advice.

A developer, in sum, has the knowledge, experience, contacts, and money—or the ability to generate the money—to complete the project. Few people have this unique combination of talent and resources. There is evidence to suggest that some retailers will refuse to deal with a shopping center developer who does not have a proven record of past success.

Architect. The architect prepares a site plan design and supervises construction of the property. For a neighborhood or community shopping center, market conditions and the requirements of the major tenants generally dictate the site plan. The developer then must define the specifications for construction of the project. Smaller shopping centers generally offer the architect opportunities for creative design when the job enters the design stage of the structure's exterior. Architects should be careful before they suggest "creative" modifications to the site plan design unless they have an idea of how retailers and consumers will react to these changes. Modern architecture may be appealing to "avant garde" architects, but to shoppers and retailers the look may be "distasteful" or "ugly." Developers should also be hesitant before they agree to effect such changes. An architect could be recommending a plan based on little understanding of retailing, leasing, and market conditions.

General Contractor. Traditionally, the general contractor's main function has been to construct the project according to the plans and specifications that the architect has prepared and the developer has approved. This function remains the principal role of the contractor, but to make use of the contractor's expertise on construction, many developers prefer to know the opinions of the general contractor about other aspects of the property's construction during the design stage. In an economy of rising construction costs, the general contractor's knowledge of how to keep costs down without sacrificing quality may prove to be a valuable asset for the investor. The developer should arrange a series of meetings between the architect and the general contractor during the initial design and drawing stages to guarantee that the project is economically feasible.

Other Technical Experts. Consultations with many different types of technical experts will generally lessen the risks involved in planning a new shopping center. The developer should seek advice from soil, civil, structural, and mechanical engineers, and landscape architects. The prudent developer, for example, will commit to a purchase agreement for a particular site only when it is certain that the soil on the property is in good condition, and that utilities on and near the property are adequate and convenient. The costs of consultations with a soil engineer, to determine the condition of the soil, and a civil engineer, to determine the availability of utilities, are small compared to the costs that poor soil conditions or inadequate sanitary sewer facilities will create.

Property Manager. The property manager sits in the "hot seat"—and assumes general responsibility for everyone on the team. The property manager is the overseer, the delegator, the "foreman" of the industry. An experienced professional manager should be in charge from the very start of the development. This will help to ensure leasing success and to reduce operating expenses. Especially in an economy of high interest rates, the long-term success of an income-producing property depends largely on the abilities of the property management services, which is a theme that will run throughout this book. The property manager is an extremely valuable member of the development team.

Leasing Agent. If an adequate percentage of space at the new shopping center does not lease up within a reasonable period of time after opening, or if the rental rates achieved are too low to yield the necessary return on investment, the new project may be short-lived. A professional leasing agent offers some assurance against this possibility. A specialist in retail leasing will be able to assimilate information about market demand for additional retail space in the primary trade area and then realistically assess the rental rates that the property can achieve. In sum, a knowledgeable leasing agent—preferably one who specializes in shopping centers—can serve as a valuable consultant in the development of the center.

Stages in the Development Process

Unless the situation involves special circumstances—for example, a major tenant brings a site to a developer, or the market demand for additional retail space is significant—the development of a new shopping center should follow seven steps:

1. Site selection and acquisition.
2. Preliminary planning and design.
3. Major-tenant leasing.
4. Financing.
5. Final design and construction.
6. Small-tenant leasing.
7. Operational management.

Site Selection and Acquisition

There is an old joke in the real estate field. What, it asks, are the three most important factors in any real estate decision? The reply: (1) location, (2) location, and (3) location. This bit of humor carries with it a wealth of wisdom, and it has special meaning to the shopping center developer. Location plays a more important role for a shopping center than it does for nearly any other type of real estate project. Indeed, the location is the single most important factor to be considered in planning a proposed shopping center development. Its importance extends all the way from the general to the specifics of the location. The region of the country that is selected, the specific section of the city, the choice of the corner of an intersection—any of these can spell the center's success or failure. A poorly designed center with a weak tenant mix that stands in a prime location will probably fare better than an otherwise well-conceived project in a secondary location.

A shopping center with one or more major chain stores as tenants also has an inherent checks and balances system in the site analysis. Most large national stores use sophisticated site-selection procedures, including projections of a trade area's future demographic characteristics, retail sales potential, and anticipated competition. In some cases, developers can rely on these chain store retailers' market projections to assist them as they make site-selection decisions. This site-selection assistance, which is unique to the shopping center industry, is likely to be clouded, however, by the particular needs and demands of the major tenant. The characteristics of the trade area indeed may support the development of major-tenant stores, yet they may provide almost no substantiation for the development of small-tenant stores, which are necessary for the investment's success.

It may surprise some readers that an investor generally will not profit with a center development that contains only major tenants. It would seem that the most profitable centers would contain the largest, most prosperous retailers. This, however, is not necessarily true. Developers depend on the smaller tenants for a healthy NOI and strong cash flow. It is often the major tenants who have been granted rental and other concessions because of their credit, which is necessary for financing, and for the buying public and other tenants that the presence of these major tenants draws to the center.

The return on investment of $25 per square foot for a small-tenant's store, which rents for $10 per square foot per year, is greater than the return from a major tenant, whose rent is $6 per square foot per year and whose space will cost the developer the same amount per square foot to build. A shopping center developer, to earn a profit, must have a certain amount of "small-tenant, speculative lease space." The following example should illustrate the point.

Exhibit 3.1 presents a possible blueprint—Development A—for a neighborhood center. The two major tenants, an anchor

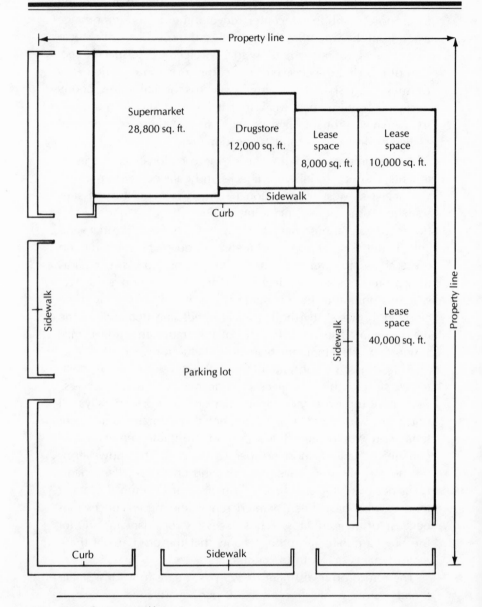

Square feet occupied by major tenants:

Supermarket	28,800 square feet
Drugstore	12,000 square feet

Square feet occuped by satellite tenants:

Lease space	8,000 square feet
Lease space	10,000 square feet
Lease space	40,000 square feet
Total gross leasable area (GLA)	98,800 square feet

EXHIBIT 3.2. *Possible Neighborhood Center Blueprint:*
Developer's Choice

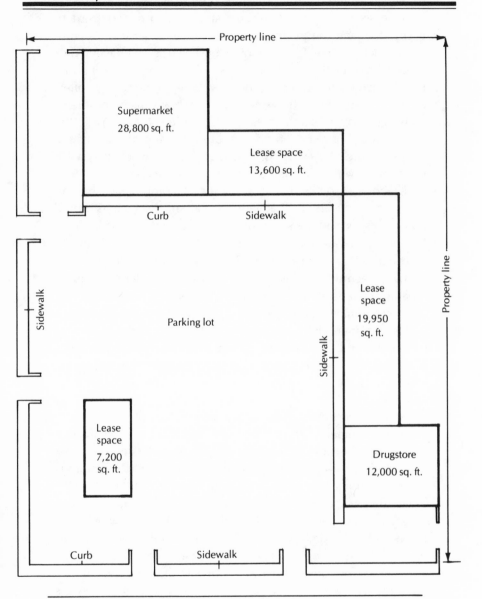

Square feet occupied by major tenants:

Supermarket	28,800 square feet
Drugstore	12,000 square feet

Square feet occupied by satellite tenants:

Lease space	13,600 square feet
Lease space	19,950 square feet
Lease space	7,200 square feet
Total gross leasable area (GLA)	81,550 square feet

supermarket and a large drugstore prefer this site plan for two main reasons. First, the two large stores stand directly next to each other, and the major tenants would consider this a significant drawing force for their own businesses. This layout provides a great deal of parking space, which is an added benefit for the large stores. From the developer's and the smaller-tenants' standpoints, however, there are two major problems with this layout. First, the great depth of the leased space in the center would prevent room for future expansion for any of the tenants—which poses the danger that tenants, when they wish to expand, will leave the center when their leases expire. Second, about 17 percent of the center's leasable space has no storefront exposure, a disadvantage that smaller tenants would object to strenuously, and a problem that would eventually harm the owner's financial interests as well.

The developer, instead, would probably urge a blueprint such as that presented in Exhibit 3.2, Development B. Here, the major tenants are separated with leased space between them, providing a consuming public between the major tenants. The space in Development B has less depth, which provides room for expansion and also generates a higher unit per square foot because there are more square feet of storefront leasable space. Finally, this layout provides adequate exposure for both large and small tenants.

Exhibit 3.3 presents an economic comparison of the two possible developments. If the total development cost per square foot is $45 for both plans, then the projected rates of return indicate that Development B would be financially advantageous from the property owner's viewpoint. The lower total of small-tenant leased square feet will result in lower maintenance, insurance, tax, and other administrative expenses, which will make up for the slightly lower effective gross income in Development B. Since from a retailing standpoint, the smaller tenants stand in a more advantageous position in Development B, the investment as a whole is more likely to prosper. Ultimately, as indicated by the economic comparison, Development B should yield a more profitable investment for the property owner.

Preliminary Planning and Design

The preliminary planning and design of a new shopping center constitutes an essential step toward the economic success of the project. In the initial site plan design, the developer must

EXHIBIT 3.3. *Economic Comparison*

Income	Development A (98,800 sq. ft.)	Development B (81,550 sq. ft.)
Supermarket (28,800 sq. ft. @ $7/ sq. ft.)	$201,604	$201,604
Drugstore (12,000 sq. ft. @ $6/ sq. ft.)	72,000	72,000
Lease space		
(8,000 sq. ft. @ $7/sq. ft.)	56,000	——
(10,000 sq. ft. @ $3/sq. ft.)	30,000	——
(40,000 sq. ft. @ $7/sq. ft.)	280,000	——
(13,600 sq. ft. @ $8/sq. ft.)	——	108,800
(19,950 sq. ft. @ $9/sq. ft.)	——	179,550
(7,200 sq. ft. @ $11/sq. ft.)	——	79,200
Common area maintenance @ $.30/sq. ft.	29,640	24,465
Less vacancy factor		
(5% of lease space rent and common area maintenance)	(19,170)	(18,989)
Effective Gross Income (EGI)	$650,074	$646,630
Operating Expenses		
Real estate taxes @ $.50/sq. ft.	$ 49,400	$ 40,775
Insurance @ .07/sq. ft.	6,916	5,709
Building maintenance	9,880	8,155
Common area maintenance	29,640	24,465
Management fee @ 5% of EGI	32,504	32,331
Legal, accounting, and miscellaneous	5,000	5,000
Annual Operating Expenses	$133,340	$116,435
NET OPERATING INCOME (NOI)	$516,734	$530,195

decide on several basic elements of the property, including the shape of the structure, its location, and the adequacy of its parking facilities. Alternative preliminary designs should be prepared before the developer offers a full commitment to purchase the site, which will offer assurance that, indeed, the project can be developed on the site. If possible, major tenants should be committed to lease agreements before the acquisition of the site. Most chain store retailers will agree to a lease on the basis of a mutually acceptable site plan and with an agreement that the developer will complete the improvements in accordance with plans and specifications that both the landlord and tenant have approved. The major tenant must be satisfied with the layout of the center and with its own location at the center. In many situations, the major tenant will demand a change in the building or parking lot layout in order to satisfy its needs.

In addition to the initial site plan design, the developer should consider the following items during the preliminary planning stage:

Zoning clarification. The manager must check city codes to ensure that such a commercial site is permitted, and that the developer will be able to obtain a building permit. Many "great" ideas have been spoiled when the developers have learned that a city code prohibits their plans.

Off-site costs. The developer will want to know how expensive the location is; that is, how accessible and costly supplies will be in that location.

On-site costs. The manager should determine whether the foundation, utility installation, and parking lot costs will fall within budgetary limits.

Local code requirements. The property owner or the property manager must check for local requirements regarding landscaping, building setbacks, building height, and parking-to-building ratios.

The preliminary planning and design phase should culminate in a workable site plan design, answering all questions about the availability of utilities, excess construction costs due to soil conditions, local code requirements, major-tenants' acceptance of the preferred site plan design, and store placements. During this phase, the property owner must involve all members of the development team, since each member stands in a position to offer valuable information. The developer who decides that the participation of all members would be too costly is likely to pay a much higher price later on when the property lacks the total professional appraisal that it demands.

Major-Tenant Leasing

Every neighborhood and community shopping center demands effective major-tenant leasing. As noted earlier, major tenants, by their desire to locate on a particular site, essentially, are the reason that a center is built. The anchor tenant draws most of the customers to the site. Other tenants will rent in the center because of the anchor or anchors. Obtainable rents from small tenants relate directly to the number and type of anchors.

Note, however, the important word "effective," which differentiates the leasing efforts of an astute developer from a novice, who is willing to accept most of the lease terms proposed by the major tenant. Those terms might include location requirements and tenant mix guidelines. Effective leasing is a time-consuming and extremely demanding process. Knowledgeable practitioners, who understand what lease terms are necessary for the success of the project, should assume responsibility for this job.

Knowledgeable developers also must realize, however, that they will often be forced to accept a very low financial return from the anchor tenant, if perhaps only to break even on the particular space. Since usually the developer must have an anchor tenant or the center cannot be built, the developer must look for the return that can be expected from the entire project. The developer, in this case, will have several other factors about the major tenant to consider:

1. How much common area contribution will the tenant agree to pay?
2. How much for tax contributions will the tenant agree to pay?
3. How large an insurance contribution will the tenant agree to pay?
4. How much maintenance responsibility will the tenant assume?
5. Does the tenant agree to become a dues-paying member of the merchants' association?
7. What percentage rent will the tenant agree to pay?
8. How much financing will result from this tenant's lease? Lenders will often not grant financing until the major anchors have been leased.

Negotiations with major tenants, therefore, can become a very delicate matter. Later chapters in this book will discuss the subjects of lease negotiations and tenant placement within a center. Presented here are four principles that managers and leasing agents should remember in negotiating with major tenants.

First, if the center will contain more than one anchor, these major tenants should stand separately, with ample space allotted between them for placing small tenants. With this arrangement, the property manager will stand in a better position for leasing to smaller tenants. The arrangement should also improve the trading volume of these smaller tenants, since they stand in a better physical location to benefit from the customer traffic generated by the majors.

Second, the rent that the major tenants will pay must be high enough such that the developer can earn a sufficient profit from the investment. This is one of the most difficult rules to adhere to in leasing space to major tenants. The tendency is to yield to all the demands of the large tenants. The developer should enter into lease negotiations with the attitude that if the tenant refuses to pay a rent high enough to ensure a desired profit, then negotiations with that tenant will cease. If this happens, the developer or the property manager should seek negotiations with another, similar type of tenant, who is more amenable to the developer's terms. However, as noted earlier, a very desirable tenant may be able to receive a rent that allows the property owner only enough income to break even on the space. In this case, it is the consequences of the tenant's presence that the owner believes will offset the large concession.

In lease negotiations that occur before the site plans have been developed, many major tenants will strive to obtain a good deal of control over the site design. The tenants want the maximum amount of exposure and adequate and accessible parking. These are necessary for the retailer's success; and the retailer has a legitimate right to demand them. On the other hand, some major tenants make unreasonable demands, and this is where developers must use their negotiating power. The third principle in leasing to major tenants, therefore, is that the developer maintain absolute control over "key items." What constitutes a "key item?" Specifically, the developer must have final approval of freestanding buildings; ensure the separation of major tenants; guarantee that the general design will promote leasing of small-tenant space and the eventual success of the project; and provide for sufficient landscaping, exterior lighting, and signs.

Finally, the developer and the major tenant must reach an agreement and understanding in regard to improvements that the developer will construct for the tenant. The developer should not accept an oral promise of some estimated amount of how much the tenant's building will cost to construct, nor should the developer agree to accept the tenant's plans and specifications for the building at a later date. During lease negotiations, the developer should request that the tenant furnish detailed construction plans. The manager can pass on these plans to development team members, who can determine the construction cost of the building and other improvements. The members can assess tenants' rents, based on cost estimates. The developer should exclude from the project any tenant that is unwilling to furnish preliminary store plans or demands an approval of rent before construction costs have been set. The executed lease agreement represents a binding contract between the landlord and tenant. All matters in lease negotiations are "two-way streets"—and both parties deserve fair treatment.

Financing

At the time of this book's writing, the whole concept of real estate financing had changed. High interest rates had made the traditional long-term, first-mortgage loan unrealistic for most developers. Although permanent financing was still available, many lenders interjected stiff, new requirements into loans that they issued. What did practitioners hope for the future? Some experts believed that traditional, permanent financing at lower rates would eventually become available again, when long-term economic stability set in. Others maintained that high interest rates had destroyed the fixed-rate loan forever. Still others expected interest rates to level off eventually, but to remain at higher levels than at any other period in history.

Most permanent financing available at the time of this book's writing included either of these two options: (1) ownership participation by the lender; or (2) participation by the lender in cash flow, above a predetermined level, for the life of the loan. Because interest rates had reached an unprecedented high, many lenders used high capitalization rates and debt-coverage ratios.

The *loan-to-value ratio* and the *debt-coverage ratio* are mechanisms that lenders have traditionally used to assess the safety of loans. The loan-to-value ratio is the amount of the loan compared to the value of the shopping center investment. During a period of high interest rates, however, the loan-to-value ratio becomes more academic than realistic. In a tight money market, investors cannot support debt services for 70 to 80 percent loans because high interest rates make money prohibitively expensive.

The debt-coverage ratio represents the relationship of a property's annual net operating income to its annual debt service. For example, if a shopping center's net operating income is $1,200,000 per year, and its annual debt service is $1,000,000, the debt-coverage ratio is $1,200,000:1,000,000, or 1.2:1; the property owner, therefore, has $1.20 available to service each dollar of debt. The ratio becomes critical as it becomes smaller, since this provides an indication that the property owner may have difficulty in servicing the loan.

At this writing, therefore, it had become virtually impossible for a developer to borrow 100 percent of the cost of a new shopping center development. Except when developers decided to contribute their own cash in the initial stage of their projects, most new shopping centers loans involved financial or equity partners who joined the developers as co-owners.

The developer generally should arrange for permanent financing before construction begins and preferably before the land is acquired. If the new development will not support the debt service, the developer should either abandon the project or postpone it until more favorable financing is available. Especially for a smaller developer, it is extremely risky to proceed with a project without a commitment for permanent financing, or with a commitment for financing that the property investment will not be able to support.

Most shopping center developers turn to commercial banks for *construction loans,* which are loans that provide money for needed labor and materials involved with the building of investment property. The interest rate on these short-term loans corresponds to the bank's prime rate, or to some other objective index. The interest cost of the interim, construction loan has become a major factor in the cost of developing a new center today. If a project begins when the prime rate is at a low point, there is a strong possibility that interim interest costs will exceed the amount that the developer originally estimated. The developer can try to prevent this by structuring rents paid by the major tenants such that these rents are a function of the interest costs of the property. Similarly, the amount of the permanent loan can increase or decrease, depending on rents that tenants will agree to pay, which may not be known until it is time to fund the permanent loan.

The developer may want to negotiate with the permanent lender for a loan commitment with little or no lease-up requirement. The permanent lender will generally be required to fund the loan after completion of construction, and after all major tenants have moved in and accepted the premises. Most lenders will not require additional lease-up of small tenant space for funding of the loan. Such an arrangement may sound ideal for developers, but unfortunately, this type of loan is quite difficult to obtain. Lenders need some assurance that the debt service will be paid; they need the assurance that the owner will have a steady income stream. For the developer, obtaining a loan without such a lease-up clause can mean the difference between the project's success and failure, or the simple feasibility of the entire project. The developer may be unable to lease space to the small tenants as quickly as projected in the original development plan. Many shopping center lenders will cooperate with

the developer, allowing certain concessions for funding requirements. If the lender does balk, the developer might suggest a
trade-off; for example, the lender may accept a loan commitment at a slightly higher interest rate, with no lease-up
requirement.

Final Design and Construction

If all members of the development team have performed their
jobs adequately, the actual construction of the project should
be the smoothest phase of the development process. It is
beyond the scope of this book to elaborate on proper construction techniques and individual building systems; however, some
general suggestions will be offered here.

First, the property manager, the architect, and the consulting
engineers should inspect the project at various intervals during
construction. Virtually no general contractor exerts complete
control over all of the subcontractors. The best insurance for the
developer that the finished product will meet the tenants', the
lenders', and ultimately, the consumers' requirements is periodic inspections during construction by different members of
the development team. The technicians, therefore, can identify
and solve most problems before they become irreversible.

A second recommendation is that the developer obtain an
agreement from the general contractor that states the maximum
amount needed to construct the project. The contractor will
base this amount on written plans that the architect and consulting engineers have provided, and that both the developer
and contractor have accepted in writing. Many construction
firms insist on a cost-plus or construction-management arrangement, where the general contractor assumes little or no fiscal
responsibility. Developers, however, strenuously resist this
arrangement. For developers, there is too much risk involved in
proceeding with a project without a guarantee of a maximum
construction cost.

Obviously, these suggestions do not apply to developers who
act as their own general contractors, which some developers
attempt to do. Property managers should take heed of the following warning, however, and so advise any of their clients who
decide to act as their own contractors: A skilled, professional
contractor should be hired for the project, unless the developer
can accurately and honestly be called an "expert" on
construction.

A third suggestion applies to the design stage of the project although implementation occurs during the construction stage. This suggestion is that each tenant space be provided with room for expansion. The profits of many existing shopping centers would be enhanced if the developers could expand the size of the stores when tenants' needs and market conditions so dictated. It is quite easy to allow for this extra space. To illustrate, if the major-tenant stores, which in general are the most expensive to construct, lie at either end of a long strip of stores, the developer can plan space for their future expansion by allocating more parking space near them. This preplanning could prove to be the key factor in a major-tenant's future decision to stay at the center.

Many neighborhood and community shopping centers have lost tenants because of the developer's reluctance or inability to expand the size of certain tenants' buildings when market conditions or retailing needs called for it. In this situation, the most likely move for this tenant is to relocate to a larger facility. The loss of key tenants can reduce the profitability of the project significantly.

The developer can best accommodate expansion of smaller retail stores by providing extra space in the rear of the buildings. Consider this: The typical supermarket today is approximately 180 feet in depth, but the average depth of speculative lease space in a neighborhood or community center is 80 feet or less. If the storefronts of the supermarket and the speculative lease spaces are aligned, then the smaller tenants will have the space in the rear of the building for future expansion. From the standpoint of growth, this would be preferable to aligning the rear walls of the stores. Nevertheless, few developers take this plan to action: Most developers do not even consider such expansion plans. Still, the idea has merit and is worth considering.

Small-Tenant Leasing

The sixth step in the development of a new shopping center involves leasing space to small tenants. This generally begins while the project is under construction, but most developers do not finish this step until sometime after construction has been completed. As mentioned earlier, and as it will come up in several parts of this book, small-tenant leasing is perhaps the most difficult—and one of the most essential—stages in the development of a new shopping center. Unfortunately, all too often it receives the least amount of attention, especially from the novice developer. The best person to handle these smaller retail spaces is a professional leasing agent, who specializes in the leasing of retail space and can determine the market demand for small-tenant space in a proposed new shopping center development. This leasing agent should be involved during the planning and design phases of the project. The property manager, whose role is discussed in the next section of this chapter, serves a valuable function in regard to the types, placement, and size of small retail tenants. As discussed earlier, small tenants produce cash flow for a shopping center development, which makes their presence at the center even more essential. On the other hand, too much small-tenant space at a center can be a detriment. The developer would be well advised to build conservatively; in general, constructing less space than the market can absorb.

Developers who are operating in areas unknown to them should conduct a detailed market analysis. Market analysis is discussed in detail under the chapter of the same name. The analysis should determine whether a demand for additional small-tenant space exists in the trade area of the new project. It is possible that a major tenant will be relatively easy to find for the new shopping center, but the analysis may also reveal that demand for small-tenant space does not exist. The developer who confronts this dilemma generally has little to do but abandon or restructure the project. If the analysis determines that consumers and retailers in the area would support the new development, the small-tenant leasing program should begin during the project's planning stage. Nevertheless, as mentioned, the developer will probably be unable to finalize the majority of small-tenant leases until the project is completed.

As much as the process has been analyzed and defined, no certified method will guarantee signed leases from every small-tenant prospect. Each leasing situation presents unique circumstances; likewise, each tenant's needs are different. Leasing is often a frustrating process for all parties: property managers, developers, and leasing agents alike. They would all like to have concrete steps that would work in all lease negotiations, but such guidelines do not exist. What option do practitioners have? They might want to wait for prospective tenants who will agree to the developer's terms, to come to them. That way, however, they probably will not find any tenants at all. On the other hand, they can take active steps to find strong tenants for the development. Ultimately, this can be their only choice.

Approaches to Locating Tenants. The measures outlined below by no means represent the only techniques that will be effective, or the only techniques that property managers and leasing agents should use. Nevertheless, these steps are basic to any leasing effort. The methods used for finding small tenants differ from those used for finding anchor tenants. Following are five principal ways of finding small prospective tenants:

1. Cold call visits. Leasing agents who visit retailers, study their needs, and pursue their interest stand in an excellent position for finding rent-paying tenants. These leasing agents have an advantage over leasing agents who wait for prospective tenants to call on them. However, cold call visits do have their drawbacks. The leasing agent must be certain that the prospective tenant desires a meeting, and that the leasing agent is not imposing on the prospective tenant's time. Some prospects may be disturbed by an unsolicited leasing agent who has no appointment. The leasing agent, therefore, should either be prepared to confront an occasional disgruntled tenant, or call or write for an appointment before any such contacts are made.

2. Prospecting in competitive projects. The successful leasing agent will see possibilities for finding prospective tenants almost everywhere. The older center in another section of the city may appear to be filled with satisfied tenants, but leasing agents should recognize that, on close inspection, many tenants may be found to be dissatisfied with the center or with the management of the center. Perhaps one tenant seeks additional space that is unavailable at the current location, or perhaps another tenant has been complaining for several months about the poor maintenance of the property. All of these problems spell opportunity for the aggressive leasing agent.

3. Approaching manufacturers, suppliers, and wholesalers. Manufacturers, suppliers, and wholesalers can provide information about companies that are entering an area for the first time or about companies that have expressed an interest in an alternative or second location. These sources probably can offer more aid to developers of new shopping centers that are being built in major metropolitan locations, since large companies tend to locate in urban areas. Nevertheless, the leasing agent should follow through on all available leads. Any source might eventually produce a signed lease. Trade associations, chambers of commerce, and local financial institutions also offer good sources for tenant prospects.

4. Written submittals to prospective tenants. The property manager can write to various types of tenants that use small-store spaces: national tenants, regional tenants, and local, multistory tenants.
5. Advertising. A project sign, direct mailings, print advertisements in professional magazines—any of these can be effective means of locating prospects. Property managers must remember, however, that these methods will be effective only when the leasing agent follows them up with personal contact. When a prospective tenant responds to an advertisement, the meeting between leasing agent and the prospect must follow promptly. If a prospect expresses interest—enough interest to respond to an ad—this is usually an indication that the prospect has already considered a relocation.

There are also several obvious sources that many leasing agents overlook in their attempts to find tenants. The Yellow Pages of the phone book is a good example. The telephone book contains a complete listing of all businesses in the area. The leasing agent can look down the list, call up businesses, and pursue a meeting with a decision maker of the organization. The telephone book can function as one of the leasing agent's most useful tools. At any rate, it provides a potential means for getting a "foot in the door."

When a prospective tenant has expressed an interest in the shopping center, immediacy is of primary importance. The leasing agent must act on the request at the first opportunity, since the prospect could quickly become a tenant in another project. Chapter 10 of this book will discuss promotional and advertising techniques in detail, and although the suggestions there apply mainly to a shopping center already in operation, the manager and leasing agent can apply the same principles to advertising during the development stage.

The final step in small-tenant leasing involves "closing the deal." If the location and the physical characteristics of the space meet the retailer's needs, the only factor that might block a successful lease closing relates to the property owner's or the tenant's budgetary constraints. Chapter 7, "Lease Negotiations," will discuss this process in more detail and will describe the terms in a lease that will have economic consequences for both the landlord and the tenant. As it will be noted in that chapter, the leasing agent must be skilled at negotiating the economic terms of a lease.

Never should the leasing agent assume that a deal cannot be made when problems that may seem insurmountable arise. For example, the landlord may have set a limit for the cost of improvements to the space. Perhaps that limit is considerably lower than what the tenant requires, and the tenant is unwilling to spend the amount of capital that would be necessary to improve the space. One solution to this problem may be to grant the tenant two or three months of free rent in exchange for the funds required to complete the leasehold improvements. If the free rent is in effect for only a short period, this arrangement may be beneficial to both parties. The tenant receives free rent, and the developer has certain capital expenses paid. Furthermore, for the property owner, vacant space represents an additional loss, so such a concession may produce even greater benefits. The leasing agent should identify all obstacles that stand in the way of negotiating a lease that is agreeable to both the landlord and the tenant. The property manager then must be creative in eliminating these obstacles.

The marketing effort for shopping center leases—for leases signed by desirable, rent-paying tenants—requires specialized knowledge and a great deal of persistence. The individual responsible for leasing new shopping center space should contact prospective tenants personally and at that, contact as many prospective tenants as possible. The agent should look on every business situation as a potential opportunity to find new tenants. The business section of the newspaper may indicate companies that are expanding or considering relocations. These leads represent potential prospects for the leasing agent.

The agent must allow sufficient time for the prospect to collect information, present it for in-house approval, review the market, study the location, and finally, arrive at a decision. For some leases, this entire process takes only a few days; for others, it may take many months. Many "hot leads" produce no results. Yet, once a prospect indicates an interest in leasing a space, the leasing agent must follow up immediately—not only to surpass the competition but also to show the prospect that reliable, dedicated individuals work for this reputable shopping center.

Operational Management

Ultimately, the purpose of this book is to define, explore, and establish the role of the manager in the modern shopping center. That is what is involved with the final step in the development of a shopping center. It will be referred to here as *operational management,* and it is nothing more than management in operation. Operational management refers to the day-to-day, ongoing management of the property, in accordance with specific procedures and a planned system.

Many shopping center developers treat property management as a kind of necessary evil; they, in turn, fail to create an atmosphere where the property manager becomes an active and effective member of the development team. In many cases, the manager who eventually will administrate the operations of a new, multimillion dollar shopping center is excluded from meetings during the development stage and is prevented from contributing ideas or comments. The manager in this case also fails to acquire a basic knowledge about the development plans and specific workings of the center.

Generally, however, the developer of a shopping center who solicits the recommendations of a knowledgeable property manager during the design phase of the project has much to gain: (1) The property will probably be less costly to maintain and thereby will generate additional cash flow; (2) the center will probably produce increased retail sales and higher percentage rents; (3) the value of the center will probably be enhanced. Basically, the income from an investment property—the net operating income—can increase through either higher revenues or reduced operating expenses, or both. Throughout the development process—from the selection of the site until the last space is filled—the experienced shopping center manager can offer advice that will enable the developer to meet these criteria for enhanced value.

Some Common Pitfalls

Earlier, this chapter noted that the "what *not* to dos" in developing a new shopping center were perhaps the most important knowledge of all. Although efforts in shopping center development have cooled somewhat in today's sluggish economy, developers are still constructing many different types of shopping centers. The developments range from superregional centers of 1,000,000 square feet to the convenience strip centers of only 20,000 square feet. Despite the differences in the size of the developments, the criteria for success remain much the same for all shopping centers. Similarly, the pitfalls encountered by shopping center developers share certain characteristics. The text will discuss six of the most common pitfalls.

Pitfall Number One. Acquiring raw land without conducting sufficient research is still a common error among all types of real estate developers. A site large enough to develop into a shopping center constitutes a substantial investment—for example, a 10-acre site at a cost of $2 per square foot results in a land cost of $871,200. Yet some developers would decide to proceed with this type of investment without first determining that a shopping center could be constructed on the site; that the project would be feasible; that financing could be obtained; or that a sufficient demand for small-tenant space existed at the projected rental levels.

Pitfall Number Two. The developer enters into a contract with an architect, which holds that the fee for the services is a function of the project's construction cost. This type of arrangement has no justification, however. One of the architect's main responsibilities is to reduce the costs for construction. When the architect's fee goes up because of increases in the construction cost of the new center, a conflict of interest would develop.

Pitfall Number Three. The developer agrees to a cost-plus or construction-management contract with a general contractor or construction firm. A cost-plus agreement in this case is where the developer pays the contractor for the cost of the project, plus a negotiated fee. The greater the cost, the higher the fee. This unnecessarily creates a great deal of risk for the developer. If the general contractor or construction firm refuses to assume any fiscal responsibility for the project, the developer probably should find another firm.

Rarely, however, can a developer find a general contractor or construction firm that will assume a fiscal responsibility for the entire project and guarantee the total construction price. The developer must assume that a project of this scope will undergo innumerable changes, including changes in cost. Developers who align themselves with the best architects available will have a budget cost on which they can generally depend. Each developer should also have a representative (usually a construction engineer on staff, or perhaps the developer) who will oversee the activities of the architect, the contractor, and the subcontractors. It can be this representative's responsibility, then, to analyze and recommend changes in the original plans and to address construction problems that arise during the construction process.

Pitfall Number Four. The developer allows the major tenants to dictate the site plan design, the placement of their stores, and the size or location of other buildings. The shopping center lease should represent a partnership between the landlord and both large and small tenants. The arrangement should achieve beneficial results for all parties. The developer should not and cannot allow the major tenants to dictate operations, and ultimately, perhaps, the success or failure of the project.

Pitfall Number Five. The developer overestimates the amount of small-tenant space that a new project should contain, given the market demand in the trade area. Similarly, the developer may design small-tenant space in the wrong location within the center or with the wrong spatial dimensions. Such drawbacks harm both the leasing of this space as well as the level of rent that can be obtained. A new shopping center development may work correctly on paper, but in brick and mortar, it may not work at all. The most common error in regard to small-tenant space is that the developer projects unrealistic rental rates. A developer may need to lease small-tenant space at $12 per square foot per year for the investment to be profitable. If the actual rents that tenants will agree to pay, however, is only $8 per square foot per year, and 40,000 square feet of speculative space has been constructed, then the actual annual gross income will be $160,000 less than originally projected.

Pitfall Number Six. The developer estimates construction costs unrealistically during the planning stage and then establishes rental rates with the major tenants that are below what is needed to earn a healthy return from the investment or to obtain a permanent loan. Developers can avoid this problem by studying, during the initial stages, the costs of construction and the rental rates in the area. Should a major tenant convince the developer to agree to a lower rent, the developer may well be tempted to lower the quality of the project so that construction costs will remain reasonable. Once again, however, the developer should be warned: An inferior parking lot, a reduced life for the roof system, or a low-quality floor—all of these curtailments will reduce construction costs, but their price will become evident later. The value of the property will probably decline, and the operating expenses will probably increase. Instead, the developer would do better to approach the major tenants and lender and try to renegotiate both the leases and the loans. Mistakes will happen, but there is no reason to compound one error with another.

Developing the New Center   93

Current market conditions present doubt and uncertainty to most shopping center practitioners, and yet it seems evident that during the 1980s, most convenience and neighborhood shopping centers will prosper. Interest rates for all types of financing, land costs, and construction costs have reached unprecedented highs. Recent fiscal and monetary steps taken by the federal government to counter the negative effects of a heated economy have interjected a multitude of involuntary restraints at a level never before experienced. Still, in spite of current political and economic conditions, the shopping center industry is generally doing well.

A well-located and well-planned convenience or neighborhood shopping center, professionally managed, and with a superior tenant mix, remains an ideal financial investment. This can be said, however, only with the assumption that about 50 percent of the total GLA is leased to credit tenants with long-term leases; that smaller tenants fill the remaining area at higher rentals with shorter-term leases; and that each lease requires the tenant to pay a percentage rent, all energy costs, and any escalations in other operational expenses. All of these factors help to make the shopping center investment an excellent hedge against inflation.

The shopping center thus combines the inherent attributes of reduced downside risk, guaranteed income over the short term, protection against increases in operational expenses, and the ability, with percentage rents, to increase income with inflation. What other multi-tenant income property can offer that kind of package? Virtually none. As described in chapter 2, one of the unique qualities of the shopping center is that the tenants, the manager, and the property owner develop what is similar to a partnership. Each member of the partnership involved in the operation of a shopping center depends on the skills and finances of the others.

A main reason for the increased interest in smaller centers is that the consuming public has developed a renewed interest in neighborhood facilities of all types. A gasoline shortage, coupled with an increase in transportation costs, has interested many consumers in shopping closer to home. Developers are realizing that bigger is not always better—an attitude that so predominated during the 1960s and 1970s, as superregional centers were built in several parts of the country. Today, property owners realize that they can also earn profits through a small but tightly run, well-maintained center.

The developer's ability to perceive changing consumer demands, to a large extent, will determine how well a new shopping center will fare. Today's consumer faces ever-rising costs and diminished purchasing power. The astute property manager and developer will recognize the limitations that these factors have put on a shopping center investment.

More shopping centers were built during the 1970s than during any other decade. Nevertheless, developers, tenants, managers, lenders, and equity partners must take a realistic look at changing market conditions. This is the only way that they can continue to earn high profits during the 1980s and beyond. Just as local, regional, national, and international socioeconomic environments are changing, the shopping center industry will also continue to change. Practitioners can hope they will not confront any unfortunate surprises, but the following changes can be expected:

Redevelopment of existing shopping center properties is likely to increase.

Energy almost certainly will continue to be a major factor to be considered in the design of new buildings, both for the developer's and the tenants' benefit.

Due to increased equity requirements for new developments, a greater percentage of new projects will probably have financial/equity partner arrangements joining the developer as a co-owner.

Minimum, guaranteed rents, as a percentage of tenants' total occupancy costs will probably decrease.

Chain store tenants, who previously leased space only in regional centers, are likely to locate new stores in selected neighborhood centers.

Because inflation is expected to continue, tenants are likely to accept leases with annual escalations in their minimum rents, along with percentage rents.

Supermarkets will probably no longer be considered essential as anchor tenants for neighborhood centers.

In certain locales, as petroleum-based products continue to escalate in cost, and the cost to maintain them increases, concrete will probably replace asphalt as the primary paving material.

The cost of land as a percentage of the total development cost will probably continue to decrease.

Conclusion

Developing a new shopping center demands the professional skills of all parties involved—from the property manager and developer to the leasing agent and contractor. The task is both an exciting and difficult one.

The seven basic steps involved in the development of any new center are the following: selecting a site; designing the project; leasing to major tenants; leasing to small tenants; arranging means of financing; supervising construction; and finally, overseeing all of these operations. To a large extent these steps overlap, since each is dependent on one or more of the others. Who controls the process? In some cases the developer does, and in other cases, it is the property manager. Yet, generally, the most successful projects have a management team, in which each member of the team controls a different step in the process, and all team members are allowed to contribute to the project.

The entire team—consisting of the developer, architect, contractor, consulting engineers, property manager, and leasing agent—can produce a truly prosperous development. Each person on the team, however, must be working toward the same goals. Throughout each phase of development, the team members should keep in mind the specific objectives of the developer.

Although it cannot control every intervening factor, a professional team is a strong force toward ensuring a profitable investment. The developer may spend more money by hiring a complete development team, but that cost will probably pay off many times over. It is generally not advised that developers attempt to carry out highly specialized tasks themselves. Many tasks in a shopping center development demand the assistance of an expert.

The development of new shopping centers has changed significantly in only the past few years. Investors are moving away from the superregional investments that so dominated the 1960s and 1970s. Now the focus is on smaller neighborhood, convenience, and specialty centers; and on renovations of existing properties. These economically strained times demand skilled managers who are aware of changing market conditions and changing consumer demands. The development process demands a solid team, whose members collectively understand everything about the shopping center industry and about the development of a shopping center.

Review Questions

1. What steps must be taken to ensure that the final commitment to purchase land required for the development of a new shopping center is not made until the developer is certain that the project can proceed?
2. Why should a developer be opposed to the traditional fee arrangement with an architect, where the architect's fee is based on the construction cost of the building(s)?
3. Is "cost plus" a reasonable method of compensation for the general contractor? Why or why not?
4. What is tenant mix? Why is it an important concept in the development of a new shopping center?
5. How should the major tenants be located within a shopping center?
6. List and explain five areas of revenue and five areas of operating expenses for a shopping center.
7. What are four common objectives of a shopping center developer?
8. List the various members of the development team, and discuss the role played by each member.
9. List and explain three common pitfalls in a shopping center development.
10. What effect might increased energy costs, which affect transportation costs, have on neighborhood shopping centers?
11. Explain what effect, if any, the installation of an asphalt rather than concrete parking lot will have on future operating expenses of a new shopping center. Why would an asphalt parking lot be chosen over a concrete parking lot, and under what conditions would this choice be reasonable?

4

Takeover of an
Existing Center: The Management Plan

Underlying the operation of a shopping center is the management plan. Every successful property needs a thorough management plan that states the objectives, short- and long-range recommendations, and the financial terms of the investment. The plan pulls together all of the analyses that have been conducted on the investment.

As a document, the management plan notes recommendations for the investment, including rental rates that tenants should pay, a maintenance schedule, staffing arrangements, and suggestions for financing. A skilled property manager, who understands investment property and knows the correct format for each of these documents, should prepare the plan.

As a process, the management plan represents flexibility. It synthesizes information that has been gathered about the property, and offers the owner and property manager an ongoing guide as they face decisions about the property's operation. Forces will change: market conditions, legal guidelines, financing alternatives, and interest rates, to name only some. Managers may learn of better ways of maintaining the property. They may notice new trends in the area; perhaps more families are moving in, or perhaps the area is becoming more commercial. The area may be suffering with a depressed economy, and consumers' buying power may be dwindling quite drastically. All of these considerations are part of the process. The management plan is ongoing, mainly because the property and the many forces that affect it change constantly.

This chapter will focus more on the management plan as a

process—as a changeable means of operation—than on the document. Managers must be aware of the proper format to follow, for example, in preparing a budget, but their most essential task is to keep the property functioning in a changing economy, with changing consumer demands and changing buying power.

Management Plan for an Existing Property.

The property manager assigned to an existing shopping center will confront a different situation than one who begins during the development stage. The takeover of an existing property offers both benefits and disadvantages for the property manager. The benefits are that the manager can look at the project from a more objective point of view, with little knowledge of the problems encountered during the development stage. The manager, therefore, has the opportunity to operate the property with few preconceived prejudices. Another advantage is that tenants have often already established a loyal clientele, which may reduce the manager's responsibility to attract new consumers to the center. On the other hand, there are certain drawbacks in being assigned to an existing shopping center. One is that although the manager knows relatively little about the property, major decisions will become necessary almost immediately. This means that the manager must learn as much about the property as quickly as possible while operating the center on a day-to-day basis. Tenants may try to take advantage of this temporary situation by promoting their own interests. The manager, therefore, should avoid hasty decisions during this period of transition, particularly decisions that favor tenants. Instead, the manager should use this time to grow more familiar with the property and the needs of the investment. This is the time to avoid premature solutions to complex problems.

The manager must gather many facts about the property. It is this collection, organization, assimilation, and evaluation of data about the property, the market, and the tenants that practitioners in the industry commonly refer to as the *management plan*.

A well-prepared management plan will become a "road map" for decisions about the property. If the manager bases the plan on inaccurate information, the decisions that result from it will ultimately reduce profits from the property investment. Once completed, the management plan should be used as a valuable resource. The manager should refer to it continually, and should update it in response to changes that occur in the local market and in the local and national economies.

The analogy of the management plan to a road map is actually quite an accurate one. Managing a shopping center without a plan—preferably an organized, written report—can be compared to driving from Los Angeles to New York without a map. The job may seem easy, but the driver will soon realize the great difficulty involved. Although the driver eventually may reach New York, many wrong turns and an enormous amount of frustration are virtually guaranteed. Likewise, it might seem easy to operate a property without a management plan, operating it in a trial-and-error fashion, taking "roads" that seem right, but may not be. Like the trial-and-error driver, however, the manager will face many problems, and the investment will probably deteriorate. At that point, it is likely that another manager in the market area will see the need for improvements and seize the opportunity with a well-organized program for the center.

In sum, managers should look on the management plan as a "given," as an essential tool for all properties that they manage. What does the plan contain? It begins with a full *market survey,* which notes all of the factors that affect the shopping center. This survey includes a study of the general region, of the direct market area, and of the competition. Then, the manager must take an objective look at the shopping center through a *property analysis.* The property analysis should include a thorough physical inspection (for example, the type of construction, the condition of the facility); an evaluation of the common areas, including the center's entrances and exits; and a review of how the property compares to the competition. These analyses provide the information necessary for a *rent analysis,* which is the third component of the management plan. In order to set optimal rents for the project, it is necessary to know what rents other shopping centers owners in the area are charging, and how the subject property ranks among its competitors.

Fourth, the management plan should contain an *analysis of alternatives,* which is a study of a property to determine its highest and best use. Such an analysis should include tests of economic feasibility for rehabilitation, modernization, or change of use. This chapter will present a systematic approach to deciding between the alternatives for operating a center. The chapter will then explain the logic behind any such decision. Finally, if the manager suggests changes for the property, the management plan should include a recommendation for financing. The financing market is extremely complex, and the manager should be able to provide valid reasons for selecting one form of financing over another. Therefore, it is another of the manager's many responsibilities to understand available financing and apply the form of financing that best suits the investment. However, because financing is indeed such a complex and important matter, it is also recommended that the investor obtain the advice of a mortgage banker.

Although the management plan is an analysis of the property, whoever prepares the plan must also consider the financial position, the motivations, and the long-term objectives of the owner. Equipped with the management report and a complete knowledge of the owner's investment needs, the manager stands in a position to recommend the best course of action for the property. The property owner should receive a complete copy of the management plan, which will include a list of necessary steps that the management team must take in order for the property to achieve the owner's stated goals.

Market Analysis

Chapter 5 will discuss market analysis for a shopping center investment. Because the market is central to the management plan, however, this chapter will offer an overview of the subject. As noted in chapter 1 of this book, a shopping center differs from other property investments primarily because the tenants' successes directly affect the owner's income. The owner and the tenants, therefore, share a concern with the market, a mutual concern that is unmatched in any other type of income property.

A market analysis for a shopping center is an assessment of the region, the neighborhood, and the competition. Readers who seek more in-depth information on the preparation of market studies can turn to the report *Market Analysis of the Shopping Center*, which was published in 1949 by the Urban Land Institute. This report, although published several years ago, contains timeless information on the proper development and administration of market studies. The report offers a clear and valuable guide to market research for shopping centers.

The market—the consuming public—ultimately determines whether the shopping center will prosper. It is therefore essential that the manager include a thorough analysis of the market in the management plan. This market analysis occurs at different levels.

At one level, the analysis should be simply a *demographic* breakdown. In a demographic analysis, the manager would be interested in learning the vital statistics of the region—the size, distribution, ages, and growth of the population. This data can be obtained from census reports, although the property manager should be aware that demographics can change quickly. There are still many other aspects of the region that could affect plans for the center. The climate, the available natural resources, industries, recreational facilities, schools, and competing businesses in the area will all affect the investment, and the manager should analyze each of these factors on an ongoing basis. The region's employment picture is also useful information. If one industry supports the region, an analysis of that employer would provide a strong statement about the region's stability.

A geographic obstruction, such as a major lake, river, or mountain range, will probably affect the area and the property. Any such natural barriers should be mentioned in the management plan, along with an expert's opinion of just what it means to the area and to the property. Likewise, if the property lies in a major tourist area or in an area heavily populated with office buildings, the manager should note this in the plan and project the impact it is likely to have on the investment.

Various federal agencies can provide data that will indicate economic trends in an area. Trade associations, the local library, local chambers of commerce, utility companies, and financial institutions are only a few of several organizations that will provide economic reports of the region. Essentially, the manager must read the events behind the figures. Another quality, therefore, befits the "ideal" property manager—and that is an astute perception of economic forces.

Finally, the property manager should note the economic prospects for the region. The future of the investment is the ultimate concern of all parties. After these projections are complete, the manager is ready to take a look at the neighborhood.

The management plan for a shopping center should contain an analysis of the neighborhood, or trade area, which represents the property's drawing power. *Trade areas,* which form the boundaries from which customers come to a shopping center, can be divided into three market zones: *primary, secondary,* and *tertiary.* Most center customers—from 70 to 75 percent—will come from the primary zone. These are the regular customers, who shop at the center at least once each week. The less frequent customers come from the secondary region, and they make up from 20 to 25 percent of the center's total sales. Finally, the center draws from a tertiary zone. This is the area from which infrequent customers come, those customers who visit the center once or twice in a year and amount to only about 5 percent of the center's total sales. These, then, are the three areas from which the center might attract customers. The main focus should be on the primary area, but the manager should analyze the demands and limitations of the shoppers from each of these zones.

Although important for each type of center, the primary market is most critical to the neighborhood center, since most such centers attract customers from an extremely small geographical radius. If shoppers in the primary region cannot support the center, the developer would be mistaken to think that the property could attract a sufficient number of consumers from secondary regions to support the investment.

Also, as part of the market analysis, the manager should conduct a physical inspection of the area. The general appearance of the neighborhood, as well as average prices at which homes are selling, the number of factories in the area, the number of businesses in the area, the condition of highways and expressways, the number of schoolhouses—all of these might offer the developer valuable clues about the area. The manager should also investigate the attitudes of the local government. A "no-growth" attitude—which is evidenced in a community with numerous zoning ordinances that restrict commercial development to varying degrees—would impose strict limitations on a shopping center owner's plans.

Property Analysis

After the market has been studied, the next area of concern is the property. Nearly all investors work with limited funds, and therefore, property managers must recognize what the demands of the property will mean in financial terms. That the property is clean and smooth-functioning will remain ongoing concerns. This is discussed in detail in chapter 6, "Building Operations: Maintenance, Life Safety and Security, and Energy Conservation." A well-maintained property will help foster good tenant/management relations, and it serves as one of the best promotions for attracting a continual flow of shoppers. The manager who fails in maintaining a well-kept, smoothly operating shopping center would lack credibility—let alone effectiveness—in requesting to tenants that they maintain their spaces.

A physical analysis of the property is always necessary. Ideally, this analysis will be conducted before the competitive survey, since the physical analysis will give the manager an idea of minimum standards to which the property should be compared. However, those standards are not an essential part of the property analysis, and the manager may want to set specific goals for each property. A sample form for use in a physical analysis of a shopping center appears in Exhibit 4.1.

Ultimately, the manager will use data gathered during this physical analysis to prepare the budget, predict future capital expenses, allocate funds for maintenance personnel, determine maintenance contracts, respond to tenants' complaints, and react promptly to emergencies. (A *budget* is a written prediction of the property's income and expenses over a specific time period.)

The managers themselves should conduct the physical inspection so that they will become familiar with the property. The property manager should carry a camera on the inspection, taking pictures of the center sign, directories, lamphoods, bicycle racks, trash containers, roof access ladders, fire controls, directional arrows in the parking areas, trash bins, roof equipment, and master meter areas. Any of these items may become important to the center's insurance policy. (A *master meter*, owned and operated by a utility company, measures the total amount of energy from one source that is required to operate an entire building.) To provide a reminder, the manager should also take pictures of items that demand repair, a condition that should become apparent during the inspection.

A thorough physical inspection might take several days, but it is well worth the manager's time. Through such an inspection, the manager obtains a broad view of the property and becomes familiar with the location of specific items, e.g.,ladders, turn-off valves, sprinkler clocks, timer switches, storage areas, meters, bike racks, trash receptacles, seating benches.

Operations Manual

The manager should also prepare an operations manual for the center. This is separate from the management plan, but it serves many of the same purposes as parts of the plan. The operations manual should contain information about the center for situations that demand quick decisions. The manual should include a site plan of the center and a list of tenants, the owner, and the manager, and their phone numbers, home addresses, and emer-

EXHIBIT 4.1. *Shopping Center Inspection Checklist*

Project: _____ Fund: _____
Address: _____
Inspected by: _____ Date: _____
Type of Inspection: Periodic _____ Pre-Acquisition _____ Other _____
Last Inspection: Date _____ By _____

I. Surrounding Area
   A. Character of Area: _____
   B. Access to Project: _____
   C. Street Conditions: _____
   D. Problem Areas/Comments: _____
   _____

II. Site
   A. Entrance Signs
     1. Number and location: _____
     2. General appearance: _____
     3. Visibility: _____
     4. Condition: _____

   B. Driveways and Parking Lots
     1. Driveways: Adequate width _____ Condition _____
     2. Traffic flow: Problem areas _____
     3. Parking stalls: Adequate no. _____ Adequate width _____
       Angled or 90° _____
     4. Directional signing: Condition _____ Adequate _____
       Painted on pavement _____
     5. Parking bumpers: Throughout lot _____ Partial _____
       Condition _____
     6. Paint striping: Condition _____ Years of life _____
     7. Drainage: _____
     8. Asphalt: Heavy-wear areas _____ Gravelling _____
       Alligator _____ Settlement areas _____ Other _____
     9. Concrete curbings _____

   C. Landscaping
     1. General appearance: _____
     2. Type of plants: _____
     3. Maturity of plants: _____
     4. Problem spots: Car damage _____ Pedestrian damage _____
       Erosion areas _____ Overwatering _____
       Bad soil conditions _____ Weeds _____
     5. Sprinklers: Adequate coverage _____ Bare spots _____
       Car damage _____ Exposed pipes _____

   D. Walls and Fences
     1. Retaining walls:
       Location _____
       Type _____
       Condition _____

(continued)

EXHIBIT 4.1. *(Continued)*

    2. Decorative walls:
        Location _____
        Type _____
        Condition _____
    3. Fences:
        Location _____
        Type _____
        Condition _____

E. Sidewalks and Ramps
    1. General condition: _____

F. Site Lighting
    1. Type and location: Mercury vapor poles ____ Wall-mounted ____
        Overhangs _____ Other _____
        Incandescent poles _____ Wall-mounted _____
        Overhangs _____ Other _____
    2. Adequacy _____
    3. Lights out _____ Lights broken _____ Lights shielded _____

G. Other Items
    1. Trelliswork, etc. (location and condition): _____

    2. Bike racks: Number _____ Condition _____
        Location _____
    3. Trash bins: Type of storage area _____
        Location _____
    4. Electrical cabinets: _____ Condition _____

H. Problem Areas/Comments: _____
_____
_____
_____

III. Building Exteriors
  A. Type of Construction and Finishes: _____
_____

  B. General Exterior Appearance: _____
_____

  C. Walls
    1. Masonry: Location _____
        Type: Concrete block _____ Slump stone _____
        Split face _____ Adobe _____ Brick _____
        Finish: Paint _____ Sealer _____ Condition _____
        Condition: Cracks _____ Mortar _____ Joints _____
        Other _____
    2. Stucco: Location _____
        Finish: Sand _____ Spray texture _____ Spanish _____
        Other _____ Integral color _____
        Condition: Cracking at windows _____ Other cracks _____
        _____ General workmanship _____

(continued)

EXHIBIT 4.1 *(Continued)*

3. Wood siding: Location _____
   Type: Plywood _____ Boards _____ Design_____
   Finish: Paint _____ Stain _____ Condition_____
   Condition: Cracks _____ Delamination _____ Nailing _____
4. Wood beams and trim: Location _____
   Type: Wood type _____ Paint stain _____
   Condition: Cracks _____ Shrinkage caps _____
   General appearance _____
5. Store front: Location _____
   Type: Wood mullions _____ Metal mullions _____
   Finish _____ Condition _____
   Glass: Clear _____ Bronze _____ Condition_____
   Spandrel/decorative panels: Type _____
   Color/finish _____ Condition _____
   Doors: Fully glazed _____ Partially glazed _____
   Other _____ Metal stiles _____ Wood stiles_____
   Excessive air gaps at frames _____
   Condition _____
6. Doors:
   Service doors: Roll-up _____ Sectional _____ Paint _____
   Condition _____
   Utility doors: Metal _____ Wood _____ Frames_____
   Dents _____ Paints _____ Condition_____
   Other doors: Location _____
   Condition _____

D. Soffits and Overhangs
   1. Location: _____
   2. Materials: _____
   3. Condition: Water damage _____ Cracks _____
      General condition _____

E. Roofs
   1. Main roofs:
      a. Specified type _____ Bonded _____
      b. Type installed per space _____ Tar and gravel _____
         Mineral surfaced _____ Aluminum paint _____
         Elastomeric _____
      c. Condition: Bubbles _____ Birds mouths _____
         Exposed tar _____ Evidence of heavy foot traffic _____
         General condition _____
   2. Flashing:
      a. Coping: Type _____
      b. Joints: Caulked _____ Asphalt _____
      c. Duct work: Collars covered with cap sheet _____
      d. Pipes: Cracks at penetrations _____ Collars adequate _____
   3. Mansard/decorative:
      Location _____
      Type _____ Materials _____
      Condition _____

gency numbers. The manual should also contain a lease information sheet for each tenant, listing pertinent data about each: total square feet of space; rental rate; costs charged for common area maintenance, insurance, merchants' association dues, utilities, and cost-of-living increases; percentage rent agreements; and lease terms, including options and lease restrictions. Exhibit 4.2 presents a sample lease information sheet, similar to what the manager might use in an operations manual.

The manual should also contain several *plot plans* that show the location of various essentials for the property: parking lot light controls, fire sprinkler valves, sewer cleanout, pumping stations, roof access ladders, fire extinguishers and fire alarms, and a complete list of utility meters at the center.

The manager should keep in the manual a separate list that notes all of the exclusives in effect at the center as well as all restrictions in effect. An *exclusive* is a clause in a lease that reserves the right for one tenant to conduct a certain business exclusively in the shopping center during the term of the lease. A list with these special provision prevents guesswork for the manager as new leases are being negotiated. The binder should also contain a list of employees and their home phone numbers and addresses and a list of maintenance contractors, with their addresses and phone numbers. Such a binder will provide a quick reference for as much as 90 percent of all situations that will arise. It will also serve as a guide to the rest of the staff when the manager is out of the office.

The property manager who takes over an existing center must be certain that the files contain tenant's leases and records, including copies of deeds of trust or mortgage papers; and covenants, conditions, and restrictions in the leases, if there are any. Any restrictive agreements that might apply to the center, a copy of current zoning laws in the area, former tax allocations, insurance records, tenant correspondence and payment records, sales records, and any communication from public officials should all be included in the files. Copies of contracts and employee records are also necessary.

Rent Analysis

Establishing a fair rent for all parties involved is critical for ensuring the investment's profitability. A low rent may attract tenants to the center but eventually will probably reduce the property's value. The following example may surprise readers, as

EXHIBIT 4.2. *Tenant Lease Information Sheet*

Project _____

Store No. _____

Prepared by _____

Date _____

Code _____

See Addendum _____

Tenant Information

Tenant name: _____   Lease date: _____

Trade name: _____   Commencement date: _____

Address: store _____   Termination date: _____

_____   Options: _____

Address: home office _____   Net leasable ground: _____

_____   Net leasable other: _____

Phone no: store _____   Net leasable total: _____

Phone no: home office _____   Gross leasable: _____

Phone no: manager _____   Front foot: _____

Manager's name: _____   Miscellaneous: _____

Miscellaneous: _____   _____

Terms

Monthly Base Rent

$ _____ effective for the period ___/___/___ to ___/___/___ _____ sq. ft.

$ _____ effective for the period ___/___/___ to ___/___/___ _____ sq. ft.

$ _____ effective for the period ___/___/___ to ___/___/___ _____ sq. ft.

% Rent rate (PRR) _____ %, PRR paid _____ on a sales breakpoint of $_____

($_____ per sq. ft.)

Base: _____

Options: _____

Security deposit: _____

Items deducted from % rent: _____

Merchants' association clause: _____

_____

Insurance requirement: _____

_____

Other pertinent data: _____

_____

_____

_____

Operating Expenses

	% of expenses	Billed directly to tenant	Reimburse landlord	Base year	Including above base year	Paid by landlord
CAM/reserves						
Maintenance escalation						
HVAC						
Real estate taxes						
Property and liability insurance						
Other insurance						
CPI						
Other assessments						
Other						

(Continued)

EXHIBIT 4.2. *(Continued)*

Tenant Information

_____
_____
_____
_____
_____
_____
_____
_____
_____

Terms

_____
_____
_____
_____
_____
_____
_____
_____
_____

Operating Expenses

_____
_____
_____
_____
_____
_____
_____
_____
_____
_____

they see how a "minor" reduction in rent can cut significantly into the investment's profits.

An owner decides to lease a 1,000 square foot store for an amount of 10¢ per foot per month less than the market would actually allow. That amount may seem insignificant, but it comes to $100 monthly, or $1,200 per year. With a conservative capitalization rate of 9 percent and a 10-year lease, the owner has actually reduced the value of the center by about $12,000. Multiply that amount by 10 stores in the center—and the lesson should be obvious: Any amount of reduced rent is likely to cut deeply into the investor's profits. (A *capitalization rate* is the percentage at which net operating income is converted into an estimate of value. It is discussed in greater detail later in this chapter.)

Yet, if rents are too high, leasing of space may be extremely difficult, and space may stand idle. Vacant space can give the entire shopping center a troubled look, compounding problems on the property. Setting a rent is thus a frustrating task, but there is a systematic approach that managers can take to set optimal levels of rent.

First, they should check with managers at competing centers and ask for rental rates. They may wish to check "for lease" signs at retailing spaces and request information about the rents that the owners are asking. This will provide an idea of the "going rate." After these figures are available, each manager must pursue other, more objective comparisons. The locations of the competing centers, the population in the immediate vicinities, and public transportation available in each area—each of these factors should be considered during the evaluation. The analysis should then move to specific factors within the subject center. Many prospective tenants will want to know about the retail mix, the aesthetics of the interior, the maintenance of the property, and the convenience of the location. The manager should also check the *vacancy rates* at competing centers, that rate being the ratio of vacant space to total rentable space.

After these items have been compared, the manager should prepare a grid that lists both positive and negative aspects of the subject property and competing properties. Such a grid will be presented in chapter 5, "Market Analysis." Many decisions about rental levels will depend on this final comparison. If small-sized shop space rents for $4.00 per square foot, and the subject center is new, the new space probably can command a rent of $4.50 or $5.00 per square foot. Other factors, however, will have to be considered. Space for a complete store, as opposed to a shell, will achieve a higher rent. A net lease will yield a lower base rent than will a gross lease. A *net lease* is one that requires the tenant to pay rent and all of the costs of maintaining the center, including costs for insurance, repairs, and taxes. A *gross lease*, on the other hand, requires the landlord to pay for these expenses, and the tenant pays only the rent.

Ultimately, the matter of rent is a subjective decision, but it should depend, nevertheless, on objective market conditions. The property, again, will suffer if rents are either too high or too low.

The total of rents will largely determine the value of the center, and the manager must understand how optimal rents will increase the value of the property. The owner may decide against the highest rents possible, but still the manager should know what those rents would be. Finally, once the manager has set a fair market rent, that rate should apply to only some of the spaces at the shopping center. Different types of businesses will command different rental levels. For example, most supermarket owners that operate on a high volume of sales with a low markup will have an overall rental that is one percent of their total sales, while jewelry store retailers, who operate on a low volume but high markup, will pay as much as 10 percent of their sales for rent.

Generally, smaller spaces rent for a higher rate per square foot than do larger spaces—as illustrated in the case study in chapter 3. The economic theory of supply and demand explains part of this, but smaller spaces also cost the owner more to build per square foot than do larger spaces, mainly because every space has certain set construction costs, regardless of the size of the space.

Variations in rent at a shopping center will depend on many other factors, and there are many examples that point to these differences. Kiosks, because of their high exposure, for example, rent at a higher rate per square foot; corner spaces, likewise—for the same reason. (*Kiosks* are small, freestanding structures where goods such as food, costume jewelry, or keys are sold.) Spaces in low visibility locations will be leased at a lower rent, and tenants located between the anchors will pay higher rents. If all spaces were leased at the same rental level, all tenants would seek the best locations, and the owner would have several vacant, less desirable spaces remaining to the several tenants paying average levels of rent. Only at the point where one or two spaces are left to be leased should the manager and owner begin discussing rent reduction. A strong tenant may add enough appeal to the center, such that the owner will agree to a lower rent. Extremely desirable tenants, who will attract consumers and other tenants to the center, may be well worth the lower rental rate.

Tenant Evaluations

The management plan should contain an analysis of each tenant. The lease summary will help in this evaluation, but the analysis must go beyond the lease agreement. A study of the tenants' past sales records offers a good point at which to start this evaluation.

After the past sales records have been analyzed, the manager can compare the tenants to similar merchants in the trade area. At this point, all of the analyses of the market and of the property will come together. A property analysis should indicate whether the property would satisfy the needs of the tenants, and whether the tenants would be suitable for the property.

The market analysis should indicate whether the tenant will succeed at the center, given the economic conditions and demands in the region. The manager should consider the possibility that the tenant may be unsuitable for the mix of the center. If so, the search for another, more appropriate tenant must continue. The manager should look carefully at the tenant's credit references, including statements about the tenant's promptness of payment, current assets and liabilities, and net profits. The manager and owner should also consider the tenant's willingness to maintain a well-merchandised, clean store, and to participate actively in advertising. They should consider the tenant's readiness to operate during normal center hours. Once the manager has evaluated the tenant on these criteria, the basic question emerges: Would this tenant be suitable, and ultimately, help to increase the NOI of the investment?

The manager may find that the center needs new tenants—perhaps to create a new image—so that it will be competitive with other shopping centers in the market. The manager, on the other hand, may find the contrary, that the center is actually out-performing the competition. Whatever the case, without this thorough analysis, the manager and owner may never know.

Analysis of Alternatives

Once the manager has gathered the information about the center and has evaluated the competition, the investment enters a new phase. Alternatives for the property become open for consideration. Through alternatives, a whole range of possibilities opens up for a property. The manager and owner can consider different options for a property, and, by weighing the costs of each, they can arrive at the best plan for the property.

Perhaps the owner purchased the property to develop it as an office building. After analysis of the property, the region, and the competition, however, both the manager and the owner may realize that the market demand for a shopping center is much stronger. It is unlikely that after office building construction has begun, the developer would halt the project and begin pouring money into a shopping center. Nevertheless, the property manager's assistance can come before the start of such a venture. The manager can offer valuable analyses, and ultimately prevent the owner from taking unwise risks.

As noted earlier in this chapter, in analyzing the alternatives for an investment, the property manager searches for what is called the *highest and best use*, which is a subjective determination. Highest use refers to economic factors, suggesting that the success of an investment depends purely on economic factors. Each developer has a different expectation of what the return on the investment should be. Best use refers to that which makes one use more appropriate than another. The investor may see that a shopping center, rather than a condominium development, would benefit the area commercially. If the center seems likely to prosper, the developer has chosen the highest and the best use. If an existing property is doing well financially, and it fits into the growth patterns of the area, then the property is probably functioning at its highest and best use, and its status quo, therefore, would be the appropriate "alternative."

Assume, however, that the property, at status quo, is operating at less than its highest and best use. The developer faces a major decision about the property, and the decision is whether to change it or to continue trying to optimize profits, even with its limitations. Basically, the shopping center owner has four options, and they are modernization, rehabilitation, conversion, or enclosure. Each alternative will have a different cost, and so it is understandable why investors analyze each alternative carefully. The text will discuss these four alternatives in detail.

Modernization. This is generally the least costly of all options. Modernization refers to the removal or upgrading of original or existing features to reflect technological improvements—for example, the installation of central air conditioning in a mall. The purpose of a modernization program is to replace items on the property that are outdated and are adding significantly to the costs of operations. Modernization should reduce loss due to changing modes of operations, a process referred to as *functional obsolescence.*

Many shopping centers built during the 1950s and 1960s were well planned and are still architecturally sound today, but their exteriors date them. A modernization program would benefit them greatly. Many early developers put large arches on the windows or pylon signs at the tops of the major tenants' buildings. These additions were attractive in their day, but now they appear to be dated. For a reasonable cost and minimum disruption, the property owner can conduct a modernization program that would improve the minor problems that age the center. The simple removal and replacement of obsolete signs can change the entire look of an older center. The owner can lease a new sign with little capital outlay, and greatly improve the appearance of the center.

In the past, shopping center owners generally imposed few restrictions on the use of signs. Each tenant tried to surpass the other tenants in size, brightness, or attractiveness of signs. That has also changed, however, and most centers now have guidelines that all tenants must follow in their use of signs. The idea that the center is a unit, and that tenants must plan all their promotional efforts in relation to the whole unit, is the basic purpose for such coordination.

The same philosophy holds true for all designs at the center, from the color of paint to sidewalks and lighting. The design must be coordinated, or the shopping center will look chaotic. Again, a modernization program can be inexpensive; in fact, it might cost virtually nothing. A simple request that merchants remove paper notices from their windows costs nothing, and yet it may greatly enhance the appearance of the center.

Other cosmetic changes will help to improve the appearance of the center and will probably be worth their relatively minor cost. New benches, new trash receptacles, new parking lot striping and sealing, new lens covers for the canopy lights—any of these will help to rejuvenate an aging center.

The manager can also remove items on the property that have lost their useful purpose. Old flag poles, bent roof drains, broken trash containers, and abandoned pipes all fit into this category. Many early shopping center developers scrimped with landscaping; they included only minimal landscaping on their properties. Today, most centers have extensive landscapes that surround the property. A modernization program might improve the property's landscape, although extensive changes to the landscape go beyond that of a modernization program.

Modernization alone can accomplish much, but such a program corrects only cosmetic problems. It will not change a poor layout of buildings, nor will it solve the problems of a center that has poor access or poor visibility. The manager must be able to distinguish between those problems that a can of paint can correct and those problems that require more extensive work.

Rehabilitation. Rehabilitation is a second alternative, and it refers to major structural changes on the property. A rehabilitation project might involve a complete removal or an addition of a building. It might mean a complete relandscaping. It might involve total remodeling of many of the tenant spaces. Whatever the changes, however, rehabilitation restores a property to its original condition, without changing its basic use.

Rehabilitation generally takes place in an operating center, which gives the manager the added concern that construction workers may disturb customers and tenants. The manager and owner must decide how much rehabilitation is needed at the property, a factor that will be determined largely by the competition in the area. A compromise on improvements might eventually mean that the best merchants will not lease space at the center, or that rents might be below the market rate. Market surveys should offer the best advice for what would constitute the proper amount of improvements to make the center competitive again.

Generally, rehabilitation becomes necessary either because of neglect of the property or because of major changes in the neighborhood. The underlying problem could be complex, and a single project—however extensive—would be unlikely to change the core problem. Many rehabilitations are also necessary because of changes in the shopping center industry and the retailing industry that cause centers to become obsolete. The real issue could be that the owner has little interest in seeing the investment prosper or has too little money available to see that it does. The professional manager must determine what the actual problems are and work around those issues. With an insufficient amount of money, however, even a well-prepared property manager will confront great obstacles in trying to turn a decaying property into a prosperous one.

In planning a rehabilitation program, the manager should consider every aspect of the shopping center—and ensure that each part of the program conforms to the owner's objectives. The manager, therefore, has many items about the property to consider.

The basic layout may be a detriment to the center. Some older centers have old-fashioned metal walkways held up by steel posts rather than attractive, architecturally integrated supports. An automatic sprinkler system might reduce insurance costs. An evaluation of each retail space, in a search for any such deficiencies, is appropriate. If the owner decides to improve the interior of the stores, the retailers affected should pay a higher rent. If clauses in their leases prevent such increases, the owner may be able to negotiate with them—and agree, for example, that if these tenants will pay a higher rent, the owner will rehabilitate the exterior of their stores as well. Both parties stand to gain something from such an agreement.

If the investor has obtained the necessary financing, and the improvements appear to be wise economically, the best advice would probably be to proceed with the plans as soon as possible. In an inflationary economy, the cost of construction will probably be higher in six months. Some property owners decide on phased construction projects, completing small tasks and gradually rehabilitating the property. Such plans, however, reduce the investment's earning power. They reduce the impact of an "all-new" shopping center, which can be promoted effectively to the public; they raise construction costs; and they delay increases in rent that come with the project.

Enclosure. The decision of whether to enclose the center with a mall has become a question today for virtually all shopping center owners. The public has grown accustomed to the conveniences of indoor shopping, and any owner of an unenclosed center must consider the possibility that the absence of a mall may be harming the investment. "Enclosure" can refer to a simple canopy, or it can refer to a million-dollar enclosure project. By definition, an *enclosure* refers to a project that converts part of the common area to a fully enclosed mall with a roof and walls. Most enclosures are also heated and air-conditioned.

The property owner will have many factors to consider in determining whether to enclose the center. Probably the most important consideration will be economic, whether the improvement will actually increase income enough to justify the cost. Once the center is enclosed, the owner will be justified in raising rents, but other considerations will also be important.

One matter would be whether the competing center or centers are enclosed. If the competition has an enclosure, but the subject property does not, gradually shoppers will turn away from the unenclosed center. The decreased customer traffic in many downtown areas, when enclosed shopping centers posed intense competition, is witness to this.

In an area with severe winters, an enclosure will probably improve business during winter months. An enclosure, thus, may produce greater traffic and increases in tenants' sales volume. Likewise, in extremely hot climates, air conditioning would do much to improve the shopping environment.

Strong communications provide one key to good management. The manager should meet with tenants at the center before an enclosure program, to learn if they have specific suggestions for the project. These merchants are in the center every day, and they would be aware of what goes on there daily.

When the plan is complete, the manager should again present it to the center's tenants. During the enclosure project, both retailers and shoppers may suffer inconveniences. Retailers must know just what the project will involve, and how long it will take. Only then can they respond honestly to customers' inquiries regarding the project. During most enclosures, however, sales will actually increase because of the interest that is generated by the work, the addition of new tenants during construction, and increased advertising by the merchants' association and retailers.

Change of Use. The change of use alternative is becoming more common for shopping centers. Many specialty centers have evolved from abandoned buildings that some creative developer noticed and saw great potential in. One example is an old warehouse that some innovative developer converted into a seven-story specialty center. Another developer converted an old movie theatre into a thriving center. One developer converted an obsolete railroad station into an indoor shopping mall. Conversions, in sum, provide developers with many possibilities.

To a large extent, the market survey will determine how the property should be altered. Yet, a change of use will demand efforts beyond a market survey, and ultimately, the manager will have to decide what would be the best use for the property. That decision will rest on the sum of the manager's experiences and best judgments. If the property owner is considering the change of a convenience neighborhood center into a discount center, the demographics in the region will indicate whether a discount center would better suit the area. The manager should also check with other discount stores in the area and try to find out how successful they have been, in financial terms. A check of the competition would also indicate whether the market is already saturated with discount stores.

Unless the manager and owner have data that show that there is a need for a shopping center in the area, they would be mistaken to proceed with the project. The demographics must be appropriate for the types of stores at the center, and there must be a need for the center. The property owner also must be able to locate both large and small tenants for the shopping center.

If the owner decides to change the use of the property, the manager must be certain that all the spaces can be filled. Throughout the country, success stories abound of developers who have transformed a property into a thriving shopping center. Ghiradelli Square in San Francisco, and Salt Lake City's Trolley Square are two such places. Both of these were old, industrial locations, until some insightful developers saw investment possibilities. Ghiradelli Square lies close to a tourist area, Fisherman's Wharf, which from the start provided it with a major consuming public. Yet, in spite of this obvious advantage, other developers could have built a shopping center in the same location and still failed. The developers of Ghiradelli Square knew that the tourist trade alone would be insufficient to sustain the property, and so they took special steps. They added shops to the tenant mix that would appeal both to local residents and to tourists. They included nice restaurants that would appeal to many people. Average San Franciscans probably do not do their daily shopping at the square, but nevertheless, when they do go there, they can purchase more than simple trinkets of their city.

Trolley Square sprang up from the trolley barns of Salt Lake City. The square is another successful specialty center, which is different from Ghiradelli Square, mostly in terms of the shoppers it attempts to attract. Trolley Square places its promotional efforts more on the local population than on tourists. The developers try to present the square as a practical but interesting place to shop.

Trolley Square and Ghiradelli Square are two success stories. Unfortunately, there are many other stories with less pleasant endings. The important point that developers must remember is that not every old industrial building lends itself for conversion into a specialty center. Some developers have built specialty centers for tourists, in areas where the tourist trade is too small to sustain such an investment. The demographics of the area, an analysis of trends, a study of the competition—in sum, a review of all considerations in the market analysis—must be part of the decision. The developer may look on an old, industrial building that has been converted into a specialty center as "charming" or "delightful," but unless the market will support the investment, the "charm" will probably not produce profits.

When the property owner decides to enclose an existing center, the manager must assume a special responsibility. The tenants naturally want business to continue uninterrupted. The manager, therefore, must take special steps to guarantee that that condition will exist. Construction workers should leave adequate space open for entrances. There should be signs posted, offering shoppers an apology for the inconvenience. During a period of construction, the management team should put special efforts into the public relations program. Consumers may stop going to the center if the inconveniences become too great. Tenants will be unhappy if their sales decline. If possible, construction should occur during the slowest retail months, which varies significantly, depending on the location of the shopping center.

Finally, the manager should keep tenants continually informed of timetables and of progress on the project. Practitioners have found that personal contacts, as part of the merchants' association's agenda, provide an opportunity to communicate these plans. (A *merchants' association* is a tenant organization present in most shopping centers that plans promotional, publicity, and advertising events for the center. Merchants' associations are discussed in detail in later chapters.) The manager may wish to distribute a newsletter that informs tenants of all developments, but almost always, some form of spoken dialogue is also necessary.

Financing

Many excellent real estate alteration projects never advanced past the first step because the would-be investor could not obtain financing. When this happens, it is generally more a statement about the project than about the marketplace. Funds are almost always available for commercial projects, but in some instances, the cost of the funds runs too high for the project to be feasible. The property manager should contact several lenders, explain the project briefly, describe current financing, and find out if the lender is active in the market. A loan broker may be quite helpful for carrying out this task. These calls should produce an alternative form of financing that will suit the project. Assuming that there will be more than one choice, the manager and owner then must select one that best meets the goals of the investment. However, financing is a very specialized subject, especially in relation to a shopping center, and the bulk of the responsibility should be handled by a professional mortgage banker.

Refinancing

Consider the following example. Mr. Smith has an existing loan that has a low principal balance and with improvements to the property, he has increased value such that he now owns a large equity of the property. Using the income approach for the improved property, the manager informs Mr. Smith that the improved value would mean new money at about 70 percent of the new value. Mr. Smith may pay off his old loan and use the "new" money to finance the improvements. In conditions of high interest rates, this might prove to be extremely costly for Mr. Smith. He is thus faced with a choice: He can either prepay the existing loan, with a penalty, or he can accept the new financing terms. Refinancing can be an expensive alternative, if the original loan had an interest rate of, for example, 8 percent— a rate that is virtually unheard of in a high interest rate market. Still, investors will consider the tax breaks that usually accompany real estate investments, the appreciation of the property, and the lower interest and small payments from the old loan— and they may indeed find opportunities.

To offset the loss of income potential, lending institutions have also established a policy of charging *points* in connection with loan placement. These points (each point is some percent of the loan value) are assessed to the borrower up front and are levied in addition to the rate of interest. For the lender, points significantly increase the rate of return on the loan. The points vary in percentage, depending on the cost incurred by the *mortgagee*, which is another term that describes the lender.

Before plans for an alternative proceed, the manager and owner must review the profitability of the property, in its present state. They will have to review current operating expenses

122   MANAGING THE SHOPPING CENTER

and expenses as they can be expected after the improvements have been completed. An enclosed mall will increase the operating costs of the shopping center, but it will also increase the amount of rent that the owner can collect from tenants. The manager and owner can establish the income and expenses for the completed project, deduct the current net operating income, and finally arrive at an estimate of what the investment's cash flow will be.

Basically, the manager and owner should be precise in their analyses as they weigh the alternatives for a property. They can follow a completely rational approach to decision making. To determine projected rental income, they can look at rents that owners of comparable projects in the area or in similar parts of the country are receiving. With these figures available, they should be able to set reasonable rental levels.

Valuation

Along with a clear statement of the rents that tenants will pay, the manager and owner should evaluate the financial outcome of the completed project. They should have an idea of what the value of the property will be after the completion of the project and the increase in value that they can expect. They can choose among three approaches to value, which can serve as cross-checks to each other. The three approaches to value are the *income approach*, the *replacement cost approach*, and the *comparable sales approach*. The text will discuss each of these approaches to value.

First, however, property managers must understand the two types of value that are used in investment real estate. They are *market value* and *investment value*. Market value is equal to the price for which a seller would be willing to sell the property, and the price that the buyer would be willing to pay, if neither side were acting under unusual pressure. The market value of a property is based on the implication that both buyer and seller are acting as "typical" participants in the interaction. The other type of value, investment value, is the price that an investor, bound by special circumstances and restraints, will agree to pay. Market value, therefore, is an objective measure; and investment value, a subjective measure. The two types of value will be equal only when the investor and the current economic conditions represent the prevailing features of the market.

Income Approach. Most sophisticated investors use the income approach to value. It is considered the most accurate way of arriving at a measure of value, even though the method does have certain problems. With this approach, value is determined on the basis of the property's ability to generate income.

Investors must consider all long-term replacements, such as roof improvements, even if the property has only recently been built. Managers will often prepare an income statement without accounting for vacancies or possible emergency maintenance requirements. Often the developer or former owner will agree to manage the property for an extremely low fee, which keeps expenses down for the new owner but only for a temporary period. The capitalization rate, better known as "cap rate," ultimately becomes the critical statement about the value of the property.

The cap rate is essentially an interest rate that puts a value on the net operating income. Capitalization is, therefore, the process of translating a property's estimated income stream into an estimate of value.

In real estate, the rate expresses the yield on the full purchase price that an investor might expect from the property. The cap rate is the cash flow return (the yield) that the investor expects from the equity. Ultimately, the market cap rate reflects the "typical" buyer's evaluation of risk. The higher the cap rate, the greater the risk, but the higher the return from the investment.

Cap rates change for many reasons, including the condition of the property, the safety of the investment, the rental levels of the property compared to those in the market, and above all, market conditions. If many buyers in the area are willing to buy property at a 7 percent cap rate, but one investor is only willing to buy at 9 percent, the more demanding investor—the investor who will buy only at a 9 percent cap rate—is unlikely to find many properties available. This means only that 7 percent is the current cap rate.

Replacement Cost. This method offers a crosscheck of the income approach. In reality, however, the result has little bearing on the value of a property. A single-use, concrete building may cost a great deal to replace, but on the market, it may actually have little value. Yet, in the context of other approaches to valuation, and assuming that the property is useful, the replacement method may reinforce a decision about the property. The property manager takes each element in the building and prices each part in the current market. The manager, therefore, may confer with architects, engineers, cost estimators, and developers to determine how much, at current prices, it would cost to replace the property.

Underlying the theory of replacement is the *theory of substitution*. This theory implies that a buyer will not knowingly pay more for a property than it would cost to build a new, identical property. If this were true, however, why would developers ever build shopping centers in the first place? They simply would not. Tenants occupy the center and thereby increase the income of the property. The property is therefore worth much more than the total of its "replacement" parts.

The manager must also include in the total any development costs and allowances for depreciation—all which affect the income of an occupied building. After considering all these factors, the manager should have a value that is close to what was obtained by the income approach. This is a greatly condensed description of the replacement approach, but it should give readers an idea of the basic concepts.

Comparable Sales Analysis. The main advantage to a comparable sales analysis, which compares the property to comparable properties, is that it directly reflects the market. No two properties—and particularly, no two shopping centers—are exactly alike, however, and this, in essence, is the basic problem with the method. If the manager does use this approach, special care must go into finding the comparison properties. Factors such as age, location, condition, layout, tenant mix, financing, surrounding area, and possibly even a personal problem of the seller—might all affect the final sales price. Therefore, property managers must learn as much as possible about each sale before they can use it as a comparison. In some cases, the seller receives favorable financing terms in exchange for a higher price, or higher financing terms in exchange for a lower price.

In sum, each approach to value has some inherent problems. Although most sophisticated investors use the income approach, it also is an imperfect method. Ideally, the property manager will use all three methods, and each method will then serve as a crosscheck for the others. Ultimately, only a willing buyer and a willing seller will decide on the real value of a property.

The main problem with all of these methods, however, comes with finding an accurate cap rate. Through the years, practitioners have used many different methods for obtaining the cap rate. This chapter will discuss only briefly some of the more common methods. This book's bibliography lists other useful references. In the early years of investment real estate, managers often obtained a rate from the comparable investments in the market. They divided the net income at the time of the sale by the purchase price, and what remained was the yield rate for each transaction. Unfortunately, there are many problems with this method, including the difficulty in finding comparable properties. Also, the purchaser's net income is often higher than the seller's, and the method ignores the cost of improvements. Furthermore, financing structures, which do affect the value of the investment, will change from one transaction to the next. In sum, rarely are two real estate transactions alike in all respects.

Another method that is used commonly to determine cap rate is the *gross rent multiplier*. The property manager divides the sales price by the gross rent roll at the time of sale. The quotient then is multipled by the gross rent roll of comparable properties, to arrive at a cap rate. However simple this method is, its problem is that it implies that a homogeneity exists among properties in the sample. There are actually too few comparable shopping centers to permit the development of a statistically accurate model. However, this method does reflect the market, which makes it a valuable crosscheck.

Another method, the *Ellwood tables*, is significant primarily because it was the first to figure in the importance of debt interest and debt amortization rates. The major problem with the method, however, is that it does not go far enough in factoring in these components.

The *band of investment method* paved a new road for investment real estate. It provided the first method that used elements of a first loan, second loan, and equity, and their relation to the cap rate. This method relies completely, however, on interest rates and does not take into account individual buyers' behavior.

Finally, there is the method that practitioners today consider the most accurate way to determine cap rate: the debt/equity band of investment method. This procedure combines two critical elements of investment real estate: specifically, debt constant and equity dividend. This method recognizes the principle that the market depends on financing, and that interest rates often change in time, and from one property to the next. This method also recognizes the notion that investors want to measure their equity cash flow. The debt/equity band of investment method takes into account both debt and equity components and assumes that the investment can and will be financed or refinanced at conventional rates with conventional terms.

Many factors in today's economy, however, frustrate attempts in arriving at an acceptable market cap rate. The cap rate reflects the relative risk of an investment. Under normal economic conditions, a new property with no deferred maintenance would have a lower cap rate than an older, neglected property, and the buyer of the new property could expect a higher rate of return.

In recent years, however, cap rates have been lower than interest rates, making most large loans imprudent. Cap rates may range from 7 to 9 percent, while interest rates may hover around 14 percent. Unless the down payment is extremely large, the cost of borrowing money is so high that the property will operate with a *negative cash flow.* A negative cash flow means that more money is going into the property than is coming out. As a result, the buyer of a clean, new property can no longer assume that the investment will yield a higher rate of return.

Another factor has entered the picture. Many foreign investors are entering the American marketplace, for a variety of reasons: American real estate prices are low compared to properties at home; some fear nationalization of their assets in their own countries; and some see the United States as the most stable market in the world. If a foreign investor will buy property at a cap rate of 7 percent, it brings down the cap rate for domestic investors also. If an analysis of the property indicates that 9 percent is a prudent rate, but the foreign investor is willing to buy at 7 percent, the domestic investor will be outbidded. Investors have been forced to bid for property on a competitive basis, regardless of what their own analyses indicate.

The cap rate can change dramatically if the investor obtains a large loan with attractive terms. The better the financing package, the more affordable the property. The terms of the purchase are better, and therefore, the purchase price will probably be higher.

In general, the old standards for determining cap rate by qualities of the marketplace have all but disappeared. The purchase price of a shopping center is more a function of external forces than of a preconceived cap rate.

Wraparound Financing

Wraparound loans ("wrap loans") have become popular in today's high interest rate economic climate. With such a loan, the investor retains the existing first loan before approving the new loan. The wraparound lender figures in the terms of the first loan with the terms for the new money and combines the two figures—wrapping them together—around an interest rate somewhere in between. The wrap lender then assumes responsibility for payment on the first loan, and the borrower pays the wrap lender.

Assume, for example, that a property owner has a current loan balance of $400,000 and decides that $100,000 more is needed for improvements to the property. Instead of writing a second mortgage, the lender writes a loan for $500,000, with a single payment, and the wrap lender pays the original lender.

Recasting an Existing Loan

For many shopping center investment situations, the recasting of an existing loan offers a logical means for obtaining funds. The lender is already familiar with the property owner, the project, and the financial arrangement and, therefore, the recasting of the loan closes faster. In recasting, the lender merely puts up the additional funds and renegotiates the interest rate. This is an efficient system for the owner to obtain funds and generally reduces the loan fees and possible penalty fees.

Once the owner and manager together have considered the possibilities for financing a loan, they must remember that the financing plan they discuss with a lender today may not be available in two months. A lender may agree to commit to a project, but it can almost be assured that the conditions of the market will dictate the final terms of the loan.

All of these considerations must be part of the management plan, since they are central to the success of a real estate investment. It is worth repeating, however, that owners vary considerably in the amount of responsibility they will grant to the property manager.

The Owner's Objectives

Until this point, this chapter has described the shopping center property as a sole entity, with little discussion of the owner's part in the project. Once an alternative becomes necessary for the property, however, an inspection of the owner will also be necessary. The property manager must know the owner's objectives. As discussed in chapter 2, investors hold income-producing property for many different reasons, and those reasons will eventually determine which alternative the property owner will decide on for a specific property.

If, for example, the owner is a single elderly woman, who expects the investment's cash flow to provide her with income during her retirement years, she will probably reject a plan to use the entire cash flow to modernize the center. The project would eliminate her income. Her interest is immediate. She will probably have little interest in the long-range prosperity of the center. Another owner might be a small syndicator, who seeks short-range tax benefits and long-range appreciation. In this case, cash flow generally takes on secondary importance. The manager here should look at long-term possibilities that will maximize the property's value. The appearance of the property and long-term appreciation will be primary concerns to this investor.

Whatever the owner's preferences, however, the manager, in all cases, should prepare a thorough management plan. The management plan is an integral part of the property manager's job. Whether information in the plan is eventually used should be of little importance to the manager. What is important is that the manager present a management plan, complete with management's programs and recommendations for the property. The property manager is a professional, an expert who knows the property from every angle. The management plan is the exhibition of that professional expertise.

The manager's responsibilities relative to such matters as the management, maintenance, and remodeling of a center remain unaltered, regardless of the owner's objectives. If positive steps are not taken at a center either to maintain or to improve its present position in the marketplace, the investment is likely to begin an economic decline. Ultimately, should the owner be unwilling to invest the necessary money, the manager may want to recommend that the owner sell the shopping center to an investor who will be willing to make the necessary improvements. Once a center has reached the latter stages of deterioration, it is very difficult and extremely expensive to turn the trend back to a positive investment.

What, again, is a management plan? For a shopping center, it is a detailed look at the property, the tenants, the neighborhood, and the market. It is a list of alternatives for the property. It is an indication of the property's value. It is a statement about the investor's means for financing. Ultimately, the management plan offers a great contribution toward understanding the property investment. As such, it is best that the manager make it a written document that all members of the center staff can refer to at any time.

This chapter noted the alternatives that are available for a shopping center: modernization, rehabilitation, change of use, and enclosure. The alternatives vary in the extent of their changes and in their cost. Each has the potential to put an investment back to prosperity, however, and bring the owner back to earning profits.

Information about the center and the forces affecting it will change constantly. This means that the management plan must be updated continually. Volatile economic times present property managers and property owners with difficult tasks. The times demand astute practitioners who can prepare a workable plan for the center. The shopping center is a complex operation, and many different parts of it will require different amounts of attention, at different times. This complex system demands a true professional—a professional property manager—who understands all of its intricacies.

Review Questions

1. What items should be contained in a management plan?
2. Why is the success of the major tenant important in a small shopping center?
3. Will freestanding pads generally command rents that are higher or lower than the rest of the center?
4. What factors will determine a capitalization rate?
5. What is a triple-net lease?
6. What is the primary trade area of a shopping center?
7. What effect does a natural or human-made barrier in the trade area have on a shopping center?
8. What spaces will generally rent for the lowest rate in a shopping center?
9. How frequently should the management plan be updated?
10. Indicate some sources where tenants' sales figures can be obtained.

5

Market Analysis

Plans for a shopping center should begin only when there is a sufficient demand from an appropriate market—a sizeable, consuming public. A developer would be ill-advised to move into a market and build a shopping center, or an investor to purchase a shopping center, without first conducting a market analysis that shows that there is a demand in the area for such a property. The market is what keeps the shopping center investment profitable; the market supports the venture. The market, therefore, must be studied on a regular basis. Neighborhoods change, the market changes, economic conditions change—and all of these factors affect the shopping center.

Market studies are a property manager's valuable guide in evaluating a trade area and the market potential for the goods that will be sold at the site. However, an important point must be remembered. A typical neighborhood center will not be developed unless a food supermarket company signs a lease. A typical community center will not be developed unless a discount department store or junior department store signs a lease, and a typical regional center will not be developed unless two or more major department stores sign leases. Tenants will carefully study the market before they commit to a shopping center lease. Shopping centers, in sum, are not built purely on the bases of the developer's market analyses and the developer's speculation. Several different parties will study the market.

As part of analyzing their own centers and tenants, property managers should stay informed of national economic events and be able to evaluate the impact, if any, that these events have on the retail industry. Many national developments eventually affect local consumers and the local market.

National trends—for example, inflation, family composition, federal guidelines and policies—often affect the local retail market. A change in any one of these might create opportunities for retailers and shopping center managers. For example, an increase in the number of single-person residences would probably improve the trade of retailers who cater to the needs and demands of singles. Managers and developers need not be situated in ideal economic conditions to find opportunities. Sometimes they can capitalize on the "negative."

For example, during the 1981-82 recession, unemployment was a nationwide problem, but in Detroit, with its ailing auto industry, the problem was a devastating one. Most people living in Detroit, dependent on the auto industry, did not have a great deal of spendable income. Realistically, at that time, a new superregional center in Detroit would have had a difficult time attracting a steady, sizeable public. Still, people must eat, they need clothes, they need basic household items—but during an economic slowdown, they generally need these goods at discount prices. and are generally willing to sacrifice quality for price. A discount center, therefore, may have done quite well, even during economically hard times.

Regional Analysis

Most market analyses begin with a study of the region. The property manager first must set the boundaries of the region. For the purposes here, a region will be defined as a large area that might have an impact on the shopping center. A center's region can be defined as a state, as a major metropolitan area (for example, the Twin Cities or Greater Cincinnati), or by a descriptive name (for example, the Sunbelt or the Los Angeles Basin).

The manager should identify the region's population and its growth rate, or its rate of decline. The manager might compare the region's current population to its population at some past date, which could help project a future total. The manager would probably also want to compare the region's growth rate with national and other regional growth rate averages.

In analyzing the region, the manager should also analyze its demographic breakdown. This profile should note the average

age of the population, the per capita income and income distribution, and the employment market. The region's natural resources and raw materials, its recreational and cultural offerings. its climate, its economy, and the tendencies of its government might all be useful data for the profile. Finally, the profile should contain a statement regarding the demographic future of the region.

Where can the manger obtain this information? The federal government, notably the Census Bureau, the Department of Labor, and the Department of Housing and Urban Development, can provide data for a regional analysis. Professional and trade associations, such as the Institute of Real Estate Management (IREM), and the International Council of Shopping Centers (ICSC), also publish information of this nature. State and local governments, local industries, utliltity companies, financial institutions, and the local chambers of commerce all study their own regions, and most of them publicize their findings. Some of these organizations, however, have a tendency to paint an overly bright picture of their own regions, and the manager should be aware of this possible bias.

Trade Area Analysis

The trade area represents the subject shopping center's drawing power, forming the boundaries from which a center can attract consumers. The type and size of the shopping center will largely determine the number of consumers that it can attract. The following summary will provide guidelines for estimating the sizes of trade areas for different types of shopping centers:

Type of Center	Minimum Population Needed to Support
Superregional	300,000 and up
Regional	150,000 to 300,000
Community	100,000 to 150,000
Neighborhood	5,000 to 40,000
Convenience	1,000 to 2,500
Discount/outlet	150,000 and up

Although helpful, this chart, again, establishes only general guidelines. Many factors can affect a shopping center, and standard-sized trade areas cannot be stated in precise terms. Intervening factors include competition or the absence of competition, the center's location, the condition of the property, the tenant mix, and barriers to access. This chapter will discuss all of these factors.

A trade area is generally divided into three market zones: (1) *primary*, (2) *secondary*, and (3) *tertiary*. The primary trade area is the area from which the center draws between 70 to 80 percent of its regular customers. Primary shoppers of a neighborhood center are within 2.5 miles, or a 5-minute drive from the center. A community center's primary trade area is larger, usually within a radius of three to five miles. Regional centers, because of their grand scale, can generally draw regular shoppers from as far away as 10 miles, or up to 20 minutes in driving time. In some rural states, the trade areas for all types of shopping centers are much larger. Normally, it is expected that the average consumer will travel about 1.5 miles for food, 3 to 5 miles for apparel and household goods, and 8 to 10 miles for goods when selection and price are particularly important.

The secondary trade area generates from 20 to 25 percent of the average shopping center's total sales. People who live in this fringe area generally shop at the center less frequently than do those in the primary trade area; most shoppers in this secondary trade area go to the center only when the center or individual merchants sponsor sales or promotions. Some customers may stop at the center en route to another location. These shoppers are not steady customers, however, and the property manager should not count them as steady customers.

The remaining customers come from the tertiary trade area. The tertiary area may be extremely large, but since shoppers who come from this area, in general, visit the center only sporadically on an annual basis, these tertiary shoppers account for only about 5 percent of all sales.

Boundaries of a Trade Area

The manager should draw a circle around the shopping center, on a geographical map of the region. An appropriate radius will represent the center's primary drawing power, which is its primary trade area. Once the trade area has been indentified, the manager should estimate barriers that block access to the shopping center. A river that runs through the middle of the trade area, for example, will interfere with a direct route for many potential shoppers. The manager must take into account both natural and human-made barriers—such as a mountain range, railroad tracks, a stadium, or a college campus.

The definition of the center's trade area is a subjective matter of determination. It will depend on, among other qualities of the area, the available transportation, the socioeconomic level of the population, and the tenant mix at the center. In some parts of the country, people will travel long distances to shop at the center; the primary trade area in these places will be quite large. In many suburban regions, however, a near-saturation of shopping centers has increased competition among shopping centers and retailers, reducing the size of many centers' primary trade areas.

The manager must remain objective in identifying both the primary and secondary trade areas, not exaggerating the size of either, or overstating the center's ability to attract consumers. Managers who discount the competition or ignore barriers to access inevitably will overestimate the buying power of the trade area. A manager may believe that a unique speciality center will draw from a 10-mile radius. Another manager may believe that shoppers will travel long distances to attend the shopping center's interesting promotions. Such presumptions, however, must be backed by evidence, showing that there is a sufficient population to support the center. Errors in estimating the size and strength of the primary and secondary markets, from which the majority of the center's sales will come, can lead to extensive development plans that the market cannot support.

Demographic Profile

After defining the boundaries of a trade area, the manager must explore the demographics of the trade area. Income growth or economic decline, racial and ethnic changes, future projections—all of these factors should be part of a demographic analysis. Specifically, a demographic analysis should contain data on the following key factors:

Population. The current population and noticeable signs of population trends, either growth or decline, is critical information. The size of the current population and a projection of a future total will essentially determine whether the market is large enough now and will be large enough in future years to support the shopping center.

Family Composition. The composition of the family describes the family's size and the ages of its members. The size of the family is one demographic factor that has experienced general changes during the past few years: Families have grown smaller. The average size of the family in 1979 was 2.78, compared to 3.20 in 1970. Although the drop may appear slight, statistically it is not, and a decline is evident. In many parts of the country, the singles' population has grown larger. As consumers, singles have different needs than do families; in general, singles seek smaller and less durable goods, although it is difficult to generalize about the buying habits of a particular group. Nevertheless, the property manager should know the primary family composition in the area since this often affects retailing business at the shopping center. Many young families with children are establishing themselves; they are accumulating household goods and appliances, and many are paying a home mortgage. These priorities will affect their buying behavior.

If most families in the area have children, the major age groups of the children would be useful information. The presence of many children in a trade area will increase the demand for toys and children's clothing. Families with teenagers generally strengthen the demand for items such as clothing, cosmetics, and sports equipment—to name only some of the goods desired by teenagers. Teenagers, as a whole, have money to spend, and they are eager and willing to become active consumers. Many merchandisers have capitalized successfully on this teenage market, stirring the want of a young, consuming public.

Empty nesters—either people whose children have grown and left or elderly couples or singles who have never had children—may demand and consume more goods for luxury or recreation, goods that they can enjoy in their retirement. On the other hand, many older people find retirement a much more financially limiting time and instead must shop at bargain and discount centers. The property manager should investigate the income levels of the empty nesters.

Number of Households. The property manager would want to know how many people in the trade area own their own homes, and how many people pay rent for their housing. New households will be forming each year: The manager should learn their numbers and composition. The number of apartment dwellers and condominium owners, the development of new subdivisions, the cost of housing in the area—any of these developments may indicate market trends. More homeowners today are decorating and repairing malfunctions themselves, primarily as a way to save money. For a shopping center, this trend might indicate the need for a change in the tenant mix, with the addition of, perhaps, a home decorating or hardware store.

Average Household Income. The property manager should compare the area's median income to the median income at the national level. The lower the disposable income, generally the higher the proportion that is spent on necessities such as food, and the less that is spent on nonessential items. In many households, two adult residents work outside the home, and the researcher should check the reasons why both are working. It may be due to financial need, to the need for supplemental income, perhaps for personal career enrichment, or it may be a combination of these factors. These reasons, in turn, can be important in predicting buying behavior.

Employment Data. The main sources of income in the area will affect the shopping center investor's ability to earn a steady profit. The manager should dissect the area by its primary types of employment; for example, industrial, domestic, professional, technical, managerial, clerical, or farming. In general, each of these groups has different buying habits, and the manager can use the information about the sources of income to identify the purchasing habits of people in an area.

The U.S. Census Bureau, regional planning commissions, or state and local agancies can provide this information. Commercial data services also have it available for a fee.

Physical Inspection

The property manager should also inspect the physical details of the trade area and of the shopping center's location in the area. The physical report should identify the site by its street address and by major intersecting streets that are at or near the location. It should also note the condition of highways or expressways that serve the center, because this information will indicate the accessiblity of the property. Likewise, access barriers, as noted earlier in this chapter, would be important information for the physical inspection. The manager should also take traffic counts at the project's cross streets, at major thoroughfares in the area, and, for comparison purposes, at other major intersections in the area.

The routes of local public transportation close to the center will also be valuable information to the property manager. If buses do not serve the center but do serve competing centers, the manager and property owner may want to exert political pressure locally to try to change the situation. The manager may want to suggest that the owner offer free shuttle service to the center from various locations in the city. The costs involved with such a service would have to be evaluated carefully to determine if the service would be cost-effective. The important point here is that accessiblity is vital to the success of a shopping center investment. The location must be one to which consumers can conveniently travel.

An important point that must be remembered—and a point that becomes especially important when discussing accessibility and location—is that most property managers are assigned to properties and have little or no voice in determining location. Location, however, will nearly always be a major consideration in determining the value of a property, and in particular, the value of a shopping center property. The manager's responsibility, then, would be to manage the center, given the limitations or advantages of the location that has been selected. Taking steps to improve public transportation to a location is an example of how a manager can work with the limitations of a given location.

The property manager should inspect the area's residential districts, checking the average prices of single-family homes and comparing these prices with home prices in nearby areas. Residential homes may be increasing or declining in value, which is often an apt indicator of the general prosperity of the surrounding area. In some cases, a residential neighborhood will slowly be changing into an industrial district. The manager, therefore, should also inspect new projects—residential or commercial—to determine whether this is a trend in the area.

The manager should also investigate the local government's attitudes toward growth and development. Local officials may have expressed public opinions about the area, which is information that would be pertinent to the property manager and the property investor. Areas such as Lake Tahoe or the California coast, for example, have commissions developed to preserve the wilderness. The resulting ordinances in such areas place strict limitations on commercial growth.

The manager should also inspect undeveloped land in the area, analyzing the impact that new projects might have on the trade area. The manager should check with local planning commissions to find if developers have plans for this undeveloped land. In a similar vein, it is critical that the manager find out if there are strict zoning regulations in effect in the area.

Every characteristic of the neighborhood that is studied should be described quantitatively, whenever possible, and complemented by qualitative remarks concerning each characteristic's possible impact on the shopping center.

Consumer Survey

Consumer data collection is ultimately directed at arriving at important conclusions about the region, the trade area, and the market. The data should finally answer the question, "Who is the consumer?" Will a demographic study answer that question? Not completely. A demographic study will probably lead to valuable quantitative data, but it does not answer questions on such matters as lifestyle and buying habits. Buying habits—power, preferences, and frequency, to name but a few—are major concerns for the property manager. People in the same income bracket but from different socioeconomic classes often display completely different purchasing habits. A college-educated banker who earns $25,000 annually, for example, will probably have different motivations for buying and will exhibit different buying habits than a plumber who earns the same salary.

The property manager, therefore, must interpret demographic data, compiling a profile of the "typical" consumer. For a new center, the manager will be attempting to determine the general quality and price range of merchandise that the center's tenants should offer. To do this—to translate quantitative data into a qualitative image—a consumer survey will be very useful.

Generally, between 300 and 500 shoppers must participate in a consumer survey if the survey is to be valid. For an on-site survey, the manager or members of the management staff can interview customers at the center. Properly prepared questions for an on-site survey will reveal a great deal about the people who shop at the center, including their intended purchases, their favorite stores, their usual hours of shopping, the radio stations they listen to most frequently, and the newspapers they read most often. Presented in Exhibit 5.1 is a sample on-location survey questionnaire. A survey allows the manager to zero in on a trade area. Another advantage to a survey is that it provides consumers with an opportunity to express complaints and problems about the shopping center and its tenants.

Two precautions are especially important in developing an on-location survey. First, the manager and owner should prepare the questionnaire with complete objectivity. To carry out

EXHIBIT 5.1. *Suburban Regional Center On-Site Survey*

INTERVIEWER: _____   I.D. # _____

DATE OF SURVEY: _____   TIME OF SURVEY:

(1)____10:00–12:00 p.m.
(2)____12:00– 2:00 p.m.
(3)____ 2:00– 4:00 p.m.
(4)____ 4:00– 6:00 p.m.
(5)____ 6:00– 8:00 p.m.
(6)____ 8:00– 9:30 p.m.

(INTERVIEW PERSONS 18 YEARS OR OLDER. IF A FAMILY OF GROUP OF PEOPLE ARE SHOPPING TOGETHER, INTERVIEW ONLY ONE MEMBER OF FAMILY OR GROUP.)

Hello. ABC Center is conducting a survey of shoppers to determine how we can best serve you.

Do you work in the mall?
(1) _____ YES (TERMINATE)   (2) _____ NO (CONTINUE)

Have you shopped here at least twice in the past year?
(1) _____ YES (CONTINUE)   (2) _____ NO (TERMINATE)

1 When planning your trip to the mall today, what items did you *intend* to purchase?

(1) _____ WOMEN'S CLOTHING   (10) _____ TOYS OR SPORTING
(2) _____ MEN'S CLOTHING   GOODS
(3) _____ CHILDREN'S CLOTHING   (11) _____ BOOKS
(4) _____ SHOES   (12) _____ FABRICS
(5) _____ FURNITURE   (13) _____ HOUSEWARES (i.e.,
(6) _____ LARGE APPLIANCES   SMALL APPLI-
(7) _____ PERSONAL CARE ITEMS   ANCES, POTS &
(8) _____ JEWELRY   PANS, ETC.)
(9) _____ STEREO EQUIPMENT   (14) _____ SNACKS OR FOOD
            OR RECORDS   (15) _____ BANKING
                                              (16) _____ BROWSING OR
                                                              NONE

WRITE IN OTHERS: _____

_____

_____

2 What did you *actually* buy?

(1) _____ WOMEN'S CLOTHING   (10) _____ TOYS OR SPORTING
(2) _____ MEN'S CLOTHING   GOODS
(3) _____ CHILDREN'S CLOTHING   (11) _____ BOOKS
(4) _____ SHOES   (12) _____ FABRICS
(5) _____ FURNITURE   (13) _____ HOUSEWARES (i.e.,
(6) _____ LARGE APPLIANCES   SMALL APPLIANCES,
(7) _____ PERSONAL CARE ITEMS   POTS & PANS, ETC.)
(8) _____ JEWELRY   (14) _____ SNACKS OR FOOD
(9) _____ STEREO EQUIPMENT   (15) _____ BANKING
            OR RECORDS   (16) _____ BROWSING OR NONE

WRITE IN OTHERS: _____

_____

_____

3 How many stores did you enter? _____ (WRITE IN NUMBER OF STORES)

(continued)

EXHIBIT 5.1. *(Continued)*

4 What stores were they?

(1) ___ DEPARTMENT STORE A   (7) ___ DRUGSTORE
(2) ___ DEPARTMENT STORE B   (8) ___ MUSIC STORE
(3) ___ JEWELRY STORE   (9) ___ BOOKSTORE
(4) ___ JEANS STORE   (10) ___ RESTAURANT
(5) ___ CHILDREN'S STORE   (11) ___ FASHION SHOP B
(6) ___ FASHION SHOP A   (12) ___ MEN'S CLOTHIER

WRITE IN OTHERS: _____

_____

_____

5 Did you eat while you were here?
(1) ___ YES   (2) ___ NO

6 In minutes, how long did your shopping visit last today? _____
(WRITE IN NUMBER OF MINUTES)

7 During which hours do you normally shop at ABC Center . . .

A. *On Weekdays?*   B. *On Saturday?*
(1) ___ 10–12   (1) ___ 10–12
(2) ___ 12–2   (2) ___ 12–2
(3) ___ 2–4   (3) ___ 2–4
(4) ___ 4–6   (4) ___ 4–6
(5) ___ 6–8   (5) ___ 6–8
(6) ___ 8–9:30   (6) ___ 8–9:30
(7) ___ NO SPECIAL TIME   (7) ___ NO SPECIAL TIME
(8) ___ DON'T SHOP   (8) ___ DON'T SHOP SATURDAYS
WEEKDAYS

8a Which shopping malls or areas, both here or elsewhere, do you shop?   8b How many times in the past six months?

(1) ___ ABC CENTER   (1) ___
(2) ___ EASTSIDE MALL   (2) ___
(3) ___ PLAZA SQUARE   (3) ___
(4) ___ FASHION CENTER   (4) ___
(5) ___ NORTHSIDE SQUARE   (5) ___
(6) ___ WESTSIDE MALL   (6) ___
(7) ___ SOUTHSIDE SQUARE   (7) ___

WRITE IN OTHERS:

_____

_____

_____

9 What department stores, both here and elsewhere, do you shop?

(1) ___ DEPARTMENT STORE A   (8) ___ DISCOUNT DEPARTMENT
(2) ___ DEPARTMENT STORE B   STORE A
(3) ___ DEPARTMENT STORE C   (9) ___ DISCOUNT DEPARTMENT
(4) ___ HIGH-FASHION   STORE B
      DEPARTMENT STORE A   (10) ___ HIGH-FASHION
(5) ___ DEPARTMENT STORE D   DEPARTMENT STORE D
(6) ___ HIGH-FASHION   (11) ___ DEPARTMENT STORE E
      DEPARTMENT STORE B   (12) ___ DEPARTMENT STORE F
(7) ___ HIGH-FASHION
      DEPARTMENT STORE C
WRITE IN OTHERS: _____

_____

(continued)

EXHIBIT 5.1. *(Continued)*

10 Excluding department and discount stores, what additional stores would you like to see added to ABC Center where you could purchase the following . . .

(PLEASE SHOW CARD A)	(IF GENERAL NEED INDICATED, CHECK THIS COLUMN)	(LIST SPECIFIC STORE NAMES— PROMPT)
(1) WOMEN'S CLOTHING	_____	_____
(2) MEN'S CLOTHING	_____	_____
(3) CHILDREN'S CLOTHING	_____	_____
(4) SHOES	_____	_____
(5) FURNITURE	_____	_____
(6) STEREO	_____	_____
(7) TOYS	_____	_____
(8) SPORTING GOODS	_____	_____
(9) BOOKS	_____	_____
(10) FABRICS OR NEEDLECRAFT	_____	_____
(11) CRAFTS/HOBBY EQUIPMENT	_____	_____

11 Is there anything about ABC Center that you do not like?

_____

_____

12 What daily newspapers did you read in the last two days?
(1) _____ RECORD   (4) _____ NEWS
(2) _____ TIMES   (5) _____ TRIBUNE
(3) _____ STAR   (6) _____ NONE
(WRITE IN OTHERS):_____

13 What Sunday newspapers did you read last Sunday?
(1) _____ RECORD   (4) _____ NEWS
(2) _____ TIMES   (5) _____ TRIBUNE
(3) _____ STAR   (6) _____ NONE
(WRITE IN OTHERS): _____

14 What weekly or bi-weekly newspapers did you read in the *past week*?
(1) _____ SHOPPER   (4) _____ TODAY
(2) _____ REVIEW   (5) _____ NONE
(3) _____ COURIER   (WRITE IN OTHERS): _____

15 Have you seen any ABC Center advertising supplements in newspapers during the *last six months*?
(1) _____ YES (CONTINUE)   (2) _____ NO (SKIP TO 19)
(3) _____ DON'T KNOW (SKIP TO 19)

16 In what newspaper did you see the supplement?
(1) _____ RECORD   (4) _____ DON'T KNOW
(2) _____ SHOPPER   (WRITE IN OTHERS): _____
(3) _____ REVIEW

17 In the *last six months*, have you attended a special event as a result of information provided by an advertising supplement?
(1) _____ YES   (2) _____ NO   (3) _____ DON'T KNOW

(continued)

EXHIBIT 5.1. *(Continued)*

18 In the *last six months,* did you make a purchase as a result of information provided by an advertising supplement?
(1) _____ YES   (2) _____ NO   (3) _____ DON'T KNOW

19 Would you participate in art workshops if they were offered here? (SUCH AS PAINTING, CLAY, MUSIC, DANCE, ETC.)
(1) _____ YES (CONTINUE)   (2) _____ NO (SKIP TO 21)
(3) _____ MAYBE (SKIP TO 21)

20 What types of classes would you like to see offered?

_____

_____

21 We're planning live arts events for ABC Center. Which of the following events would you prefer watching?
(1) _____ MODERN DANCE   (5) _____ GOSPEL SINGING
(2) _____ BALLET   (6) _____ FOLK MUSIC
(3) _____ FOLK DANCE/   (7) _____ BLUE GRASS MUSIC
       CHAMBER MUSIC   (8) _____ LIVE THEATER
(4) _____ JAZZ

OTHERS: _____

22 What radio station have you listened to in the *past week?* (PROBE AS TO AM OR FM)
(1) _____ WABC-AM*   (9) _____ WIJK-AM   (17) _____ WQRS-FM
(2) _____ WBCD-AM*   (10) _____ WJKL-FM*   (18) _____ WRST-FM
(3) _____ WCDE-AM   (11) _____ WKLM-FM   (19) _____ WSTU-FM
(4) _____ WDEF-AM*   (12) _____ WLMN-FM   (20) _____ WTUV-FM
(5) _____ WEFG-AM   (13) _____ WMNO-FM*   WRITE IN OTHERS:
(6) _____ WFGH-AM   (14) _____ WNOP-FM*   _____
(7) _____ WGHI-AM   (15) _____ WOPQ-FM   _____
(8) _____ WHIJ-AM*   (16) _____ WPQR-FM   _____

23 (IF RESPONDENT LISTENS TO WDEF, WHIJ, WABC, OR WMNO ASK)
You say you listen to _____ (SPECIFY STATION)
What time of day do you usually listen?
(1) _____ 7–9 a.m.   (4) _____ 5–7 p.m.
(2) _____ 10–2 p.m.   (5) _____ 7–10 p.m.
(3) _____ 2–5 p.m.   (6) _____ OTHER

24 Do you listen to that station in your home, in the car, at your place of work?
(1) _____ in   (3) _____ at work
home
(2) _____ in   OTHER: _____
car

25 How long do you usually listen? _____ (MINUTES)

26 Do you recall hearing advertising for stores you patronize on that station?
(1) _____ YES   (2) _____ NO   (3) _____ DON'T REMEMBER

27 (IF YES) What stores' advertising do you recall?

_____

28 What newspapers were delivered to your home in the past week?
(1) _____ Times   (7) _____ Shopper
(2) _____ Daily News   (8) _____ Review
(3) _____ Record   (9) _____ Courier
(4) _____ News   (10) _____ Today

(continued)

EXHIBIT 5.1. *(Continued)*

(5) _____ Tribune   WRITE IN OTHERS: _____

(6) _____ Star   _____

29 What is your home zip code? _____

30 What town is that? _____

31 In minutes, how long did it take you to reach ABC Shopping Center today? _____

32 What form of transportation did you use to get to ABC Shopping Center today?

(1) _____ Car (CONTINUE TO Q. 28)   (2) _____ Bus (SKIP TO Q. 34)

(WRITE IN OTHERS:) _____

33 What would encourage you to use the bus in the future?

(WRITE IN:) _____

_____

34 How many persons currently reside in your household? _____ (WRITE IN NUMBER)

35 How much did you spend at ABC Center today? _____ (WRITE IN $ AMOUNT)

36 (SHOW CARD C) Which number on this card most closely represents your total household income?

(1) _____ UNDER $10,000   (5) _____ $25,000–$50,000

(2) _____ $10,000–$14,999   (6) _____ OVER $50,000

(3) _____ $15,000–$19,999   (7) _____ REFUSED

(4) _____ $20,000–$24,999   (8) _____ DON'T KNOW

37 (SHOW CARD D) Which number on this card most closely represents your age group?

(1) _____ 18–24 YEARS   (4) _____ 45–54 YEARS

(2) _____ 25–34 YEARS   (5) _____ 55 + YEARS

(3) _____ 35–44 YEARS   (6) _____ REFUSED

Thank you very much for your time and have a good day!

(NOTE SEX): (1) _____ Male   (2) _____ Female

LOCATION OF SURVEY:

(1) _____ Department Store A   (3) _____ Mall entrance–East

(2) _____ Department Store B   (4) _____ Mall entrance–West

---

this task, a competent pollster, who can create a thorough, objective study and provide a detailed, statistical breakdown of results, may be well worth the cost. Another possibility is that the manager recruit a local college marketing class to prepare and conduct the survey project. Members of the management staff can prepare the questionnaire and conduct the survey, if this is what the owner desires, but they must be reminded of the importance of remaining completely objective. They must avoid phrasing questions, for example, such that they yield certain preferred results. A surveyor who asks a customer, "The center is always clean, isn't it?" is phrasing the question in a way that is likely to bias the respondent's answer.

Many people do not like to be approached or bothered while they are shopping. This is the second precaution that all on-location surveyors must remember. It is important that the survey be kept short. Any survey that takes more than 10 or 15 minutes for the customer to complete is probably too long. Survey employees should have detailed instructions on how to approach customers for survey purposes. Survey employees must also be made aware of the notion that they may be disrupting busy schedules.

Once the survey has been completed, the results should be evaluated carefully, and if possible, any necessary action be taken as soon as possible. Some problems may require immediate remedies, and many of these types of problems are relatively easy to cure. For example, several customers may indicate on the survey that the center's landscaping blocks their vision at the entrance. This is a matter of safety, and the manager, therefore, should see that this condition is corrected immediately. The solution may be simple, involving nothing more than the removal of trees. An added benefit here would be that when action such as this occurs promptly, customers who completed the survey are more likely to believe that the center's surveys are meaningful, and that the management staff actually listens to what the respondents have to say. These customers will be more apt to participate in future surveys at the center. A situation like this may also promote the public image of the center owner, as a concerned, responsible member of the community.

The shopper's survey should also provide the manager and owner with a distinct perspective of the center's "average" consumer. This will be valuable information for creating and maintaining an effective tenant mix. As noted earlier in this chapter, the profile of the "average" consumer in the trade area will change, which makes periodic research necessary.

As valuable as such on-location surveys are, however, they have certain limitations. One problem that may bias the results is that the person who agrees to fill out a survey may be quite atypical. The person who agrees to complete the survey may convey a more positive impression of the shopping center than might the shopper who declines to take the time to stop.

The other major problem with an on-location survey is that it provides little or no information about residents in the trade area who are not shopping at the center. This defeats one of the main purposes for such a study since it fails to reach the "unseen" market. Phone or direct mail interviews, therefore, may be more effective. With a random sample of people in the target area, in a direct mail survey, the manager can pose questions, such as the following: Where do you usually shop for groceries? Where do you go clothes-shopping? Why do you shop at a particular center? Here again, however, the sample of respondents—the people who agree to take the time to complete and return such a survey—may be composed of quite an unusual group of people and may not typify the people living in the trade area.

The manager who conducts both types of surveys—a direct mail survey sent to people in the trade area and a survey of on-site shoppers—may find some interesting results. A comparison of the two groups may reveal, for example, that the majority of residents in the trade area actually do shop at the center. The manager may learn that most of the customers fit into a specific income group; perhaps the average customer's income has declined since the center first opened. In this case, an eventual change in the tenant mix may be appropriate. An exclusive dress shop in a shoppng center in this area may be filling space where a variety store would probably do better. If several respondents claim that they rarely shop at the center, the manager should try to learn the reasons. Perhaps the tenant mix is inappropriate for the area and market; perhaps access to the center is difficult; or perhaps people prefer to travel to the enclosed mall, which in drive time, is an hour away. The results of the survey may be enlightening; they might also present the manager and developer with some difficult decisions about the direction of the investment plans.

A license plate survey offers another method for studying a center's consumers. For several days, an employee of the management staff can note license plate numbers of all cars entering the center. The manager then can match the numbers with home addresses, to find out from where the traffic is coming. Another possibility is to ask merchants to compile a list of addresses from credit card slips and personal checks that they accept at their stores. Most merchants will probably agree to cooperate in such an evaluation since the results would also be beneficial to their businesses. The property manager should tell merchants that they will receive a copy of the survey results. Both methods, however, produce information only about where consumers live and provide almost no other information about consumers.

As mentioned earlier, a trade area's profile and the preferences of consumers within the area can shift drastically during a relatively short period of time. For this reason, the manager should conduct a demographic analysis and consumer survey every two or three years. These studies will indicate shifts in the population, changes in average household income, and changes in consumer buying habits. The effects that new competitors are having on the center should also become apparent through the survey.

The property manager should stay current with community trends. A key question will focus on how consumers are spending their disposable income. Once the manager knows *how* the public is spending its money, the concern can turn to *where* the money is being spent. The manager then must focus on the competition.

Analysis of Competition

In analyzing the competition, the property manager must study both the primary and secondary trade areas. An evaluation of shopping centers in the area and a comparison of these centers to the subject center will be necessary. The property manager thus can obtain a complete summary—and if done correctly, an objective summary—of each center's comparable strengths and weakenesses.

Before the manager can begin to compare, however, a thorough description of the subject property is needed. The description should include not only the center's physical appearance but should also contain the following information:

A list of tenants, including the square footage and type of
merchandise carried by each tenant.
The size of the center and the advantages and disadvantages
regarding the size.
The type of the center and its relation to the neighborhood where it
is located.
Special site conditions.
Rental rate histories.
Past sales comparisons.
Potential maintenance concerns.
Access problems.
Management analysis.
Tenant mix weaknesses.
Vacancies.
Signage problems.

In short, the manager should note any factor that may have an impact on the project and the investment.

Again, only after the manager knows the subject property completely can attention turn to the competition. After this has been done, the manager should study the competing centers individually, gathering the same type of data about competing properties as about the subject property. The manager then can put this information into a comparative context. For example, a survey of competitor XYZ Center may reveal that its tenant mix suits the market, but that the center has poor access and less parking room available than does the subject property. This information can then be used to help lease the center to prospective tenants.

Lease information about the competition should also become part of the analysis. The manager should learn the lease terms, tenant improvements, and special terms that the competition is offering. If the competition's rental income per square foot is available, this would be valuable information for the manager and developer. Likewise, tenant improvements that the competing landlord provides and special terms of the leases would be useful information. Beyond these general items, the manager should learn of particulars about the competition: whether the landlord or tenant pays property taxes, common area costs, roof maintenance expenses, insurance premiums, and management fees. The manager should find out whether other owners are requiring cost-of-living increases in their leases, and if so, how often they are levying these increases and on what indices they are basing the increases. The manager should investigate how other owners are adminstering percentage rent clauses. It will also help the manager to know the terms of recent leases that were signed at competing centers. Management at a competing center may be quoting one rent but actually agreeing to leases at rates well below that figure, which is quite common in a shopping center with a weak marketing program.

The number of vacancies at other centers will also be valuable information for the property manager. The manager should determine the number of vacancies in each project, how long the store spaces have been vacant, and, if possible, the reasons for the vacancies. The causes may be hidden, and the manager may not arrive at any answers at all if the core of the problem is poor management.

Managers may find it difficult to obtain the competition's total leasing dollars and sales figures from retailers in competing centers. Yet, any such sales data that can be obtained will be helpful. Some property owners are willing to exchange sales data with competitors. Nevertheless, the manager's search for this data does not have to end with owners of competing centers. Tenants may offer general sales information. City officials, local chamber of commerce offices, or the marketing departments of local colleges also may be able to provide sales data. If none of these sources produce results, the manager may want to observe the competition to arrive at subjective measures. Personal observation can lead to some of the best insights into the competition.

Finally, in conducting the competitive analysis, the manager will want to determine the subject center's share of the market. The manager first should study the retail potential within the trade area. This potential—which can be stated in terms of potential sales—will be only an estimate. The manager can base these figures on historical data and on future projections—all of which is available from various federal, state, and local government offices. The manager then must review all retailers who are currently in business in the area. The following categories, called *GAFO*, generally serve as classifications for different types of retail sales:

G   General merchandise (such as dishware, kitchen appliances, and hardware).
A   Apparel (such as men's and women's clothing, shoes, and accessories).
F   Furniture (such as living room, kitchen, and bedroom furniture; and major appliances).
O   Other (such as books, toys, and food).

The shopping center manager should pay particular attention to the trade area's average per capita expenditures on various types of goods. Although the per capita consumption figure is only an average, the figure can provide the manager with an excellent basis on which to compare the gross sales figures of various retailers at the subject center. The quotient that results from the trade area's total sales in each category, divided by the trade area's total population, will serve as a basis for comparative purposes. The manager can determine the shopping center's share in the market by dividing the subject center's gross sales in each category by the total trade area expendtures. Likewise, the manager can use these sales figure for spotting weaknesses in the center's tenant mix.

For example, many neighborhood centers have a supermarket as the anchor tenant. If the manager and developer of such a center want to know what share of the market the supermarket is attracting, first they must determine the total supermarket sales potential in the trade area. This they can do by multiplying the per capita expenditures for food by the total population in the trade area. The U.S. Department of Labor annually publishes national averages of per capita expenditures. The surveys are adjusted for inflation and growth and are readily obtainable. Ultimately, the manager and owner should have an idea of the amount of funds in the area that could support all of the supermarkets in and near the area. To succeed, a supermarket must generate a very high volume, high at least in comparison to other retailers. If the manager divides the square footage of all supermarkets in the trade area into the dollars available for supermarket goods, it should become apparent whether the area can generate enough volume for all of the supermarkets.

After this, the owner and manager should evalute the supermarket in their center in regard to its share of the market. They should divide the potential food sales in the trade area by the store's sales volume. Then, by comparing sales in the market to one particular store, they can learn whether this store is attracting its share of the market.

If there are three grocery stores in the community, and the grocery store at the center receives only 20 percent of the total gross sales, the manager should begin looking for the cause of the problem. If the grocery store happens to be one of a chain, it will help the manager and owner of the center to know how successful the store is at other locations. The problem may be the shopping center, or it may be the store, and comparative data such as this will help answer the question.

When success is relative to the market, the manager must consider such factors as the subject center's size, age, suitability to the neighborhood, and the extent of the competition. If new facilities are being developed in the area, their impact will be greatest when they first open, because at that point they are novel, but the novelty usually does not last long. If the analysis reveal that certain stores in the center are not attracting a sufficient share of the market, a thorough inspection of the shopping center may be appropriate. The manager should determine if deficiencies in the tenants' spaces or in their services have caused the problems. Perhaps some of the stores are too small, or perhaps some of the retailers are not providing the vast selection that their competition provides. Many of the stores may be poorly stocked, poorly managed, poorly maintained, or in need of modernization. On the other hand, if the problem is that too many stores in the area are selling the same goods, the situation will be more difficult to cure.

Smaller merchants are harder to evaluate in such detail, mainly because there are more smaller tenants. Each small retailer, however, demands the same, thorough review required of the larger tenant. *Dollars and Cents of Shopping Centers,* a statistical study published every three years by the Urban Land Institute, contains average sales figures for different types of stores. The manager can compare these figures to the total sales of stores in the subject property. The book is a valuable reference, although some of the figures may require time adjustments. In evaluating smaller tenants' market shares, the manager should also weigh factors such as merchandise mix, sales trends, suitability to the trade area, store appearance, drawing power, and advertising efforts.

In general, then, the property manager must remain alert to each competitor that enters the trade area and project the impact that the store will have on other businesses in the center. When fish-and-chips restaurants first became popular on the West Coast, for example, the profit margin was excellent. People liked and supported these fast food restaurants. In a short time, however, it seemed that nearly every neighborhood center on the West Coast had a fish-and-chips restaurant. As competition grew, the desirability of these restaurants as shopping center tenants declined. Today, relatively few of these specialty restaurants remain in shopping centers.

Importance of Ongoing Market Research

Most changes in the trade area and in consumers' attitudes and buying power occur gradually. The property manager should stay informed of conditions in the region and neighborhood, thereby becoming qualified to advise the property owner of significant changes. An example should illustrate the point. A community center may be prospering, offering many fashion-oriented stores. Most of the tenants may be succeeding financially at the center, largely because they face little competition in the area. If a regional mall, filled with several fashion tenants, were to open in the same trade area, however, the situation could mean trouble for the community center.

As it has been discussed in other parts of this book, community centers, in general, have had difficulties in recent years. They confront problems in trying to compete directly with large regional shopping centers, and the example just noted speaks directly to this. The community center, in general, also does not have the selection that the regional center can offer consumers. Many community centers also lack a clear, focused identity. The manager of the community center noted in the example would probably want to learn, during the early stages of the regional center's development, about plans for the new center. Preventive measures may be possible. For example, the property owner and manager may agree, upon conferring with current tenants, that a change in the tenant mix is needed. Perhaps they will decide that an extensive expansion program would be beneficial. The community center owner may be able to avoid costly, possibly fatal, lapses in time. Both the retailer and the property manager may agree that a small fashion store would fare better in the regional center. The community center owner may be forced to take radical steps, perhaps creating a completely new image for the center, changing the tenant mix, or directing the center's promotional efforts to a new market.

In some cases, a change in the major tenant may be advisable. Many surveys taken over a period of years may reveal that the major tenant is no longer competitive. If this is the case, the center's management should begin discussions with the tenant, in an attempt to devise a solution to the problem. If the major tenant cannot solve the problem, the property owner and manager may want to encourage the tenant to move, although rarely does an owner want a tenant to vacate a space before a replacement tenant has been found.

A major tenant may be content with the location, even if this tenant is not an asset to the center. The tenant may not be willing to end its lease. This becomes an extremely delicate negotiating matter, and the situation may be impossible to change. Nevertheless, the long-range goals of the shopping center should always stand in the forefront of the property manager's priorities. Several years ago, a large variety store anchor stood in many small centers. This anchor tenant was a rather low-volume operation, and it did not draw the large crowds that other anchors did. Some property owners were extremely unhappy with the effects that these anchor stores were having on the centers. This particular tenant was earning a profit at many of its locations, however, and refused to cancel any of of its leases. In cases such as this, the manager and developer should encourage the anchor tenant either to attempt to improve sales, or to leave the center. This need not be a hostile confrontation between the owner and the tenant. It can be a businesslike discussion, where the two parties and the property manager discuss both the advantages and disadvantages of the anchor tenant remaining at the center. In many cases, if the anchor tenant, or for that matter, any tenant, is not earning a profit at the center, an opportunity to cancel the lease may be welcomed. If all negotiations fail, however, the property owner will be forced to wait for the tenant's lease to expire before a new tenant can move in.

Conclusion

A shopping center will succeed only if it can attract a steady, sizeable buying public. A consuming public is essential to the survival of a shopping center. Therefore, the characteristics of the market directly affect the center investment. The management team first must define the primary trade area and then conduct regular market analyses to study the variables in the area. Many demographic factors will affect an area; a demographic analysis of an area is constantly subject to change. The management team must stay in touch with trends—and, in turn, be able to estimate how these trends will affect the shopping center. The number and sizes of families, the average ages, the economic level of people living in the area, the percentage of homeowners—these are only some of the market variables and demographic data that must be continually reviewed.

The manager has many means available for obtaining information about trends and buyers' preferences. Center shoppers can be surveyed, car license plates can be studied, or a direct mail questionnaire can be sent to random households in the area. These are only some of the many possibilities. The manager also has a wealth of reference materials available. The manager and developer must use all of these tools to maintain the shopping center as a profitable real estate investment.

Review Questions

1. What information should the property manager obtain about the region in which the shopping center is located?
2. What is a trade area, and into what market zones is it divided? Describe these zones.

3. What items should be included in a demographic analysis?
4. Describe a consumer survey and the items that should be contained in such a survey. Approximately how many shoppers should take part in such a survey?
5. What are two precautions that on-site surveyors must remember? What are two problems with on-site surveys?
6. What is GAFO?
7. How can market analysis aid the property owner?
8. Why is ongoing market research critical to the success of the shopping center investment?

6

Building Operations: Maintenance, Life Safety and Security, Energy Conservation

A shopping center is a real estate property, and as real property, its structure and individual units demand ongoing care. Attention, therefore, must turn to the operations of the building. The property is a community of shoppers and tenants, and so it demands a considerable amount of maintenance—as does any property that people will visit daily. Life safety and security are also continual concerns, just as they are concerns in any community, and in particular, on property where many people gather. Finally, especially in an economy of high fuel costs, the consumption of energy on the property will almost certainly remain a high priority for tenants, property owners, and property managers.

The topics covered in this chapter are, by themselves, not unique to the shopping center. They are all part of owning and managing property, however, and all property investors and managers eventually must contend with them. Each of these topics has particular consequences for the shopping center, and each poses unique problems for the shopping center industry. For example, security creates different types of problems in a shopping center than it does in an apartment building. In an apartment building, attention is generally directed at residents' safety and the building's protection against robberies and vandalism. In shopping centers, however, the concerns are more numerous. Not only must the tenants' properties and the building itself be protected from robbery and vandalism, but also present are the potential problems of any retail area: among them, shoplifting, loitering, or friction that might arise between shoppers.

Profits are equal to the difference between the investment's income and expenses, and maintenance, life safety, and security are all expenses. Therefore, these expenses will affect the owner's bottom line directly. They will also sustain the value of the property. Likewise, energy conservation helps the property owner reduce the costs of operation, which, in turn, helps the owner earn a higher income. Maintenance, life safety, and security will also have an indirect effect on the owner's profits because these essential functions will affect the amount of income generated at the property. Consumers tend to stay away from a shopping center that has a reputation for being poorly maintained, or a center that is known to be poorly equipped for handling emergencies.

Who carries out the duties involved with the building operations? It will depend on the size of the center, the wishes of the property owner, the skills of the property manager and the management staff, and the demands of the tenants. In most small centers, the management staff must handle these operational tasks, but in these small centers, the job of operating the building is also less demanding than it is in large centers. Many managers of large shopping centers hire contracted services to perform the jobs necessary for operating the building. Whatever the specifics of the center's operating schedule, the need for excellent performance of every task involved with the building's operations is consistent for every type and size of shopping center.

Maintenance

Shoppers arriving at a center will probably first notice the general upkeep of the property. Maintenance thus lends a first impression, which may very well be a lasting impression. Shoppers are likely to notice if part of a fence that surrounds the property is blown down. They will notice whether the parking lot is clean, or whether the landscape is well maintained. They will notice if trash is scattered about the property, and they will take note of workmen's tools that have been carelessly left on the parking lot. Long-time patrons may stop shopping at a center if they begin to notice decay due to poor maintenance. Inside a mall, they will observe the cleanliness of the corridors, common restrooms, and eating areas. Quality maintenance will help keep occupancy rates high, sustain the physical value of the property, contribute to property appreciation, and help attract a steady stream of consumers.

The more shoppers that a shopping center can attract, the more prosperous the investment. On the other hand, the bigger the property, and the more people that visit it daily, the bigger are the tasks involved with maintaining the shopping center.

As real estate property, a shopping center has a limited life. What begins as a bright, thriving shopping center eventually will age and lose its vibrancy. The process of aging, however, can be deterred through excellent maintenance and property preservation. The property owner may opt to revitalize the property with an extensive rehabilitation, modernization, or conversion project. Astute practitioners recognize, however, that an effective schedule of daily operations does much to prolong a property's life. Ultimately, the goal of a program of daily operations should be to sustain the center's profits and present it to shoppers as a clean, attractive, and safe property.

Managers have an option. They can choose to operate their properties through "management by crisis," performing jobs only when problems develop. Most managers do not make a conscious decision to operate their properties by this "plan"— but because of time limitations or plain neglect, they fall into this trap. The problem is that if the manager is lax with equipment and the general features of the property, eventually far more costly and time-consuming maintenance tasks will be necessary. The other choice for managers is to carry out a planned maintenance program. The assumption of this chapter is that property managers prefer to follow the guidelines of a planned program rather than a haphazard one.

Shopping centers are relative newcomers to the real estate investment world. Only during the past 20 years have they been developed in all areas of the country. "Life cycle," therefore, is yet to become a major concern among center investors. Actually, many practitioners believe that the vibrancy of a shopping center depends more on external forces, such as the neighborhood, the highways, or the competition in the area, than it does on the general upkeep of the property. Nevertheless, as with any real property, shopping centers are susceptible to decay, and it is often poor maintenance that hastens the process of decay.

Maintenance Defined

Many people use the word "maintenance" interchangeably with housekeeping, conversion, modernization, and rehabilitation. All of these terms, however, represent different processes. Conversion, modernization, and rehabilitation, as discussed in detail in chapter 4, are structural changes that involve a basic transformation of the property. Maintenance, on the other hand, refers to steps that the management team takes to preserve the property and sustain its economic life. By that definition, the word still covers an enormous scope. It includes everything from repairing the parking lot to keeping the corridors clean, and managing the center's daily trash removal. Maintenances tasks range from simple to complex, with each job contributing to the smooth functioning of the center. Housekeeping—cleaning, dusting, sweeping, scrubbing—is only part of the maintenance job.

Maintenance Costs

Great variation exists in the types and sizes of shopping centers. Likewise, different-sized centers require different types of maintenance systems. Throughout this chapter, managers should keep in mind the particular demands of the shopping centers that they manage.

Most managers realize that a good maintenance program is essential to the success of the investment. They realize that the attractiveness of the center, the cleanliness of the public areas, the lighting in the parking lot, the appearance of the sidewalks and the landscape—that all of these factors affect the shopping center's ability to attract a steady flow of consumers. The problem that most managers confront, however, is how to control costs and still support a strong maintenance program. Maintenance will be the property owner's major expense.

In recent years, the necessary costs of maintenance have escalated greatly, forcing property owners to search for ways to cut back and to conserve. In contrast to the earlier years of shopping centers, conservation has become an essential part of operating and maintaining a property; today, it is a fundamental responsibility if the manager is to help the owner achieve a profitable investment.

Property management firms are taking steps to cut maintenance costs. Some firms have changed the custodial staff's work hours, from nighttime to daytime hours, thus lowering the center's electrical needs and expenses. Other management firms are reducing the size of their maintenance staffs. The manager should be assured that changes do not interfere with the shopping conveniences of the center's patrons, or with the demands of tenants at the center.

As will be discussed in chapter 8, "The Lease Document," most shopping center leases today have clauses that divide maintenance expenses between landlord and tenant, requiring tenants to pay their pro rata share of the common area maintenance costs of operating the property. *(Common area maintenance (CAM)* expenses are those costs involved with maintaining the boundaries of the shopping center that two or more tenants will use in common.)* Most property owners will take financial responsibility for costs involved with maintaining the physical structure of the building, the roof, and utility lines. Tenants will generally pay for all other items, including maintenance costs for the leased premises and a pro rata share for those of the common area.

Maintenance Employees

Probably the most important part of a maintenance program are the employees, the people who do the work. Regardless of how modern the equipment, how organized the management plan, or how excellent the supplies—the ultimate test of a maintenance program is focused on the people who do the work. This includes both the support and professional staffs. The property manager must hire skilled practitioners who know what needs to be done, and know how to do it.

Contract vs. In-House Maintenance

The advantages and disadvantages of in-house and contracted maintenance have long been a controversy in the property management field. Each approach has certain strengths and weaknesses, and the property manager must analyze each, determining which is the more efficient and economical for the particular property. A contractor has the advantage of expertise: The contractor will probably stay informed about the latest equipment and methods, and ultimately these modern techniques will be passed on for the smoother operation of the property. Also, maintenance is the contractor's only business, which forces the firm to be aggressive in controlling costs.

Furthermore, a contractor relieves the property manager of numerous responsibilities. The property manager need not be concerned with hiring, training, firing, or supervising employees. The manager also need not worry about purchasing equipment, nor must the manager be concerned with developing maintenance schedules or working on a particular maintenance problem. These jobs are all handled by the contractor.

On the other hand, a contractor tends to reduce the amount of control that the manager has over the property. By controlling the maintenance of the property, the contractor has control over a large part of the entire operation—and eventually might control more of the property than does the manager. Contractors are also not as familiar with the property as are employees who work there everyday. Employees on a permanent maintenance staff are likely to gain a familiarity with the property such that they can anticipate problems. When something goes wrong, these employees often know immediately where to spot the problem. These maintenance employees are also more likely to possess a basic pride about their work and the property.

There is yet another advantage to hiring a permanent maintenance staff: The owner can avoid the middleman costs that come with a contracted staff. Nevertheless, as noted earlier, there are advantages to hiring a contractor, and the decision of whether to use a contracted service will depend entirely on the particular maintenance needs of the shopping center.

Some maintenance is seasonal in nature or needed only on an on-call basis; this work should probably be contracted. Many local areas, for example, require the licensing of all pest control technicians. The center's budget could probably not support a full-time, year-round technician to take charge of pest control, when it is needed only monthly. A contractor could provide the same service, and the center owner would be required to pay only for those periodic expenses.

In practice, most owners of neighborhood and community shopping centers hire independent contractors to handle all maintenance work. Many large regional centers, because of the size of their operations, have their own maintenance staffs. The main factor that will determine whether the contract system is effective will be the amount of control that the property manager exerts in the relationship. If the manager establishes the guidelines and, in precise terms, states the job that must be done, there should be no misunderstandings, and the job should get done. Firms that specialize in parking lot sweeping, stripping, pest control, landscaping, and exterior lighting have experts to handle these jobs, but even these experts need the guidance of the property manager to advise them on the specific demands at each center.

Management's Selection of a Contractor

The manager, therefore, must select a contractor, and so must first define the work of the contractor. Once the manager has described the job, it should become open to the bids of appropriate contractors. Even if a contractor is known and offers past-proven competency, bidding is an essential step. All bidders will start on an equal ground. The purpose of the bidding process generally goes beyond an attempt to find the lowest price, although cost does play a major role in the decision. Nevertheless, the manager should also qualify each bid on the basis of references, quality of work, and past experience.

After the property manager and owner have selected a contractor, they should draw up a contract. The contract should include an exact description of the services that the contractor will perform, the cost for the services, a time schedule, and provisions that will judge the quality of performance. Many property managers have standard contract forms that they use for all such cases.

A typical contract that deals with the maintenance of the interior mall might include the following provisions:

1. Periodic cleaning of public areas.
2. Supervision.
3. Hiring and training of personnel.
4. Supply and application of equipment and materials.
5. Accounting and billing.
6. Extra work requested by tenants or building manager.
7. Detailed job specifications.

Many contracts also state the procedures to be used at the shopping center for handling various duties. Such provisions may be stated in the contract as follows:

Management supervision. The project supervisor will administrate the entire cleaning operation, but will report to the building manager.
Qualifications of project supervisor. The supervisor will have a business or educational background, excellent communication skills, and experience in supervising a janitorial program.
Hiring and training of custodial workers. The project supervisor will hire custodial workers, basing selection on experience, attitude,

and skill. The supervisor will acquaint the employees with the property through an intensive training program. All workers will receive written job descriptions during their training.

Cleaning equipment and materials. The contractor's cleaning equipment will be subject to the property owner's approval. The contractor will furnish restroom supplies and trash container liners.

Contact with tenants. The project supervisor will maintain open communication with tenants and respond promptly to their maintenance needs. The building manager will handle tenant demands that require efforts beyond items listed in the contract. The project supervisor will also maintain an updated list of each tenant's special needs.

Grading system. The supervisor will inspect the center each week, assigning a grade to each maintenance area. The property manager will post the grades in a place where they can be seen by members of the maintenance staff.

A cautionary note is in order. The provisions noted above are samples only. A contract with a maintenance contractor is similar to any other type of contract. In preparing and approving a maintenance contract, the manager and property owner should seek the advice of a legal counsel.

Management's Evaluation of the Contractor

The property manager should be available to offer the final word on problems that may arise. Ideally, the property manager will define the job so precisely that the contractor will know how to handle any possible contingency without further explanation. In reality, however, rarely is this possible, since so many unexpected events occur with most such jobs. The manager, therefore, should inspect all contracted work before, during, and after the contractor's assignment. The manager's time is limited, and it is impracticable, for example, that during a 3:00 a.m. snow removal, the manager could be on hand to inspect the results. Within a reasonable amount of time, however, the manager should try to evaluate all of the contractor's work—or have a responsible member of the management staff conduct an inspection.

Property Inspections

At some point in operating the property—whether the property is a new investment or an acquired one—the property must be thoroughly inspected. Such inspections must go beyond a cursory look at basic operations of the property. In general, every shopping center demands three types of inspections: (1) standard, (2) task, and (3) annual.

A person who knows how the property should look but does not come in daily contact with the subject property would be best for conducting the standard inspection. The owner, the chief property manager, perhaps an unbiased real estate practitioner—any of these people can provide a professional appraisal of the center's general appearance.

The person responsible for overseeing the day-to-day operation of the center, often the supervisor, should handle the task inspection. The task inspection involves judging details about the property's condition and deciding what needs to be done to correct problems that are discovered. This might include simple tasks, such as cutting the grass and sweeping the sidewalk, or more complex jobs, such as designing and installing a new sign or replacing a main water pipe. Task inspections should make any of these necessary jobs apparent.

Essentially, shopping center managers need to be concerned with two types of task inspections: an inspection of structural jobs and an inspection of tasks needed to maintain the common grounds. Exhibits 6.1 and 6.2 present, respectively, a detailed interior and exterior inspection form for a shopping center. Following are some items that should be inspected as part of a structural evaluation:

Caulking around the windows. Gaps in the structure can cause water leakage and eventually cause costly damage at the center.
Brickwork and siding. The inspector should examine the property for cracking, which is generally made apparent by loose mortar. A technician can repair this condition through a process known as *spot tuck pointing*, which refers to filling mortar joints in a cracked brick wall. Caulking will also seal wind leaks or weak joints that allow moisture and cold air to enter the building.
Mildew. The inspector should check for mildew, which is an indication of water leakage and poor ventilation in the building.
Painted exteriors. The inspector should evaluate the painted exterior. South and west sides tend to show the earliest signs of paint deterioration since these sides receive the most exposure from the sun.
Foundation. The inspector should evaluate the stability of the foundation and check for rotting at the bottom of the frame. As a

building settles, its position can shift, which can cause cracking in the parking lot and sidewalks.

Gutters and downspouts. The inspector should check for clogged channels. Blocks at the bottom of gutters may cause water to collect around the building's foundation.

Filters. The filters in the heating or air conditioning ducts should be changed several times each year. A dirty filter places great demands on the heating and air conditioning systems, ultimately increasing the center's fuel bills.

Sewer clean-outs. The inspector should check the locations of the sewer clean-outs and look for any problem sewer lines.

The other part of the task inspection—that concerned with the maintenance of the common areas in the shopping center—includes the following items:

The overall condition of the property, including the cleanliness of the common areas, restrooms, and corridors.

Parking lot and sidewalks. The inspector should check for cracks in the surface, spalling, or chuckholes. All such defects will eventually have to be repaired; it is best to correct them before they worsen, and the cost of repair rises.

Plumbing. Prevention offers the best protection against emergency situations. For example, in cold winter climates, it is a good idea to wrap water pipes with a heating wire and insulation for protection against freezing and possible breakage.

The third type of inspection is an annual property evaluation, which is a detailed review of major equipment on the property. The annual property inspection can be compared to the inventory that any business takes at regular intervals. The annual inspection will determine how fast the property and equipment are depreciating. The manager may want to hire an outside consultant to conduct this inspection, but all employees at the property can probably contribute their efforts to the evaluation.

All members of the maintenance staff should be aware that the property manager will inspect their work. With a strictly enforced inspection policy, employees are more likely to do their work promptly and correctly. The manager may want to grant substantial merit wage raises to employees who meet certain standards of excellence.

EXHIBIT 6.1. *Interior Inspection Report*

Project: _____ Date: _____
Address: _____ Inspected by: _____

Interior

Items	Condition	Needs	Est. Cost
I. Entrances			
1. Glass			
2. Doors			
3. Door hardware			
4. Sign (entry)			
5. Sign (doors)			
6.			
7. Comments:			
II. Vestibule (entrance hall, lobby)			
1. Glass			
2. Door			
3. Flooring			
4. Walls			
5. Furniture			
6. Lighting			
7.			
8. Comments:			
III. Mall			
1. Carpet			
2. Wood flooring			
3. Tile			
4. Stairs			
5. Elevator			
6. Escalator			
7. Benches			
8. Walls			
9. Columns			
10. Hand railings			
11. Fountains/pools			
12. Drinking fountains			
13. Telephones			
14. Sand urns			
15. Trash bins			
16. Fire extinguisher			
17. HVAC			
18. Hose cabinet			
19. Return air vent			
20. Light fixture			
21. Banners			
22. Windows			
23. Skylights			
24. Ceiling			
25. Fire detector			
26.			
27.			
28. Comments			

(continued)

EXHIBIT 6.1. *(Continued)*

Items	Condition	Needs	Est. Cost
IV. Landscaping			
1. Planters			
2. Sprinkler			
3. Hose bibs			
4. Ground cover			
5. Color			
6. Shrubs			
7. Trees			
8.			
9. Comments:			
V. Restrooms (men)			
1. Doors			
2. Door hardware			
3. Floors			
4. Base			
5. Walls			
6. Ceilings			
7. Partitions			
8. Watercloset			
9. Paper dispenser			
10. Urinal			
11. Counter			
12. Sinks			
13. Mirror			
14. Soap dispenser			
15. HVAC vent			
16. Fire detector			
17.			
18. Comments:			
VI. Restrooms (women)			
1. Doors			
2. Door hardware			
3. Floors			
4. Base			
5. Walls			
6. Ceilings			
7. Partitions			
8. Watercloset			
9. Paper dispenser			
10. Vending machine			
11. Counter			
12. Sinks			
13. Mirror			
14. Soap dispenser			
15. HVAC vent			
16. Fire detector			
17.			
18. Comments:			

(continued)

EXHIBIT 6.1. *(Continued)*

Items	Condition	Needs	Est. Cost
VII. Corridors			
1. Doors			
2. Door hardware			
3. Floors			
4. Base			
5. Walls			
6. Ceiling			
7. Lighting			
8. Signs			
9. Ventilation			
10. Vents			
11. Fire detector			
12.			
13. Comments			
VIII. Electrical Rooms			
1. Doors			
2. Door hardware			
3. Floors			
4. Base			
5. Walls			
6. Ceiling			
7. Lighting			
8. Signs			
9. Ventilation			
10. Vents			
11. Electrical panels			
12. Fire detector			
13.			
14. Comments:			
IX. Storage Room			
1. Doors			
2. Door hardware			
3. Floors			
4. Base			
5. Walls			
6. Ceiling			
7. Lighting			
8. Signs			
9. Ventilation			
10. Vents			
11. Lockers			
12. Cabinets			
13. Fire detector			
14.			
15. Comments:			

(continued)

EXHIBIT 6.1. *(Continued)*

Items	Condition	Needs	Est. Cost
X. Vacancies			
1. Storefront			
2. Doors			
3. Door hardware			
4. Flooring			
5. Base			
6. Wall			
7. Ceiling			
8. Sprinkler			
9. Thermostat			
10. HVAC vents			
11. Restroom			
12. Fire detector			
13.			
14. Comments:			
XI. Occupied Store/s			
1. Storefront			
2. Door			
3. Signs			
4.			
5. Comments:			
XII. Miscellaneous			
1.			
2.			
3.			

XIII. General Comments

1. Total cost of work needed: _____

_____

2. Capital expenditure anticipated: _____

_____

3. Special problems:_____

_____

4. Comments: _____

_____

Reporting Documentation

The project supervisor should submit a daily maintenance report to the center manager. The report will offer a brief statement on all maintenance tasks carried out on the property that day. In most smaller centers, the property manager must assume this

EXHIBIT 6.2. *Exterior Inspection Report*

Project: _____ Date: _____
Address: _____ Inspected by: _____

Exterior

Items	Condition	Needs	Est. Cost
I. Surrounding Area			
1. Neighborhood			
2. Access to project			
3. Street condition			
4.			
5. Comments:			
II. Signage			
1. Pylon signs			
2. Entry signs			
3. Parking lot signs			
4. Tenant signs			
5.			
6. Comments:			
III. Parking Lot			
1. Driveways			
2. Parking stalls			
3. Striping			
4. Parking bumpers			
5. Drainage			
6. Concrete curbing			
7.			
8. Comments:			
IV. Lighting			
1. Pole mounted			
2. Wall mounted			
3.			
4. Comments:			
V. Landscaping			
1. General appearance			
2. Ground cover			
3. Trees			
4. Shrubs			
5. Sprinklers			
6. Curbing			
7.			
8. Comments:			
VI. Other Items			
1. Walls and fences			
2. Sidewalk and ramps			
3. Bike rack			
4. Newspaper rack			
5. Trash bins			
6. Loading docks			
7. Electrical cabinet			
8. Meters			
9. Sprinklers (bldg.)			

(continued)

EXHIBIT 6.2. *(Continued)*

Items	Condition	Needs	Est. Cost
10.			
11. Comments:			

VII. Building Exterior

Items	Condition	Needs	Est. Cost
1. Walls			
2. Stucco			
3. Wood siding			
4. Wood beams and trim			
5. Columns/posts			
6. Storefronts			
7. Doors			
8.			
9. Comments:			

VII. Roofs

Items	Condition	Needs	Est. Cost
1. Soffit/overhang			
2. Main roof			
3. Flashing			
4. Drains/gutters			
5. Mansard/decorative			
6.			
7. Comments:			

IX. Vacancies

Items	Condition	Needs	Est. Cost
1. Storefronts			
2. Doors			
3. Door hardware			
4. Flooring			
5. Walls			
6. Base			
7. Ceilings			
8. Sprinklers			
9. Thermostats			
10. HVAC vents			
11. Restrooms			
12. Comments:			

X. Miscellaneous

Items	Condition	Needs	Est. Cost
1.			
2.			
3.			

XI. General Comments:

1. Total cost of work needed: _____

2. Capital expenditure anticipated: _____

3. Special problems: _____

4. Comments: _____

responsibility. Exhibit 6.3 presents a sample form that supervisors might use or revise for these reports.

The supervisor should use a similar report for items that are checked on a weekly basis, such as the following, and as presented in Exhibit 6.4:

1. Indoor landscape.
2. Outdoor landscaping.
3. Lighting in parking lot.
4. Parking lot repair.
5. Sewer system.
6. Roof.
7. HVAC system.

The general maintenance contractor—if hired—will not be directly responsible for all of these items. Yet, the contractor might inspect each of these items periodically, making note of problems and reporting them to the center manager.

This record also helps the property manager evaluate labor costs. The record offers an obvious indication, for example, of whether the results are justifying the cost, a decision that the owner and manager can reach together. Tenants would also be interested in these reports, since, as noted earlier, at most shopping centers, each tenant pays a pro rata portion of common area maintenance costs.

Maintaining the Physical Structure

All real property requires maintenance at many different levels. Preservation can refer to maintenance of existing components, or it can refer to the installation of components. The distinction between maintenance and other changes to the property such as conversion and modernization, in general, lies in the extent of the changes. In a maintenance program, the basic structure of the property is not altered. Physical maintenance comes basically in three forms:

Preventive Maintenance. The "ideal" maintenance job is one that never has to be done. Preventive maintenance is work that is done to "prevent" more serious problems from ever developing. Preventive maintenance generally covers two categories: the inspection of major equipment, such as the boiler and air conditioner; and the scheduling of major maintenance projects, such as painting and landscaping.

Preventive maintenance is considered one of the primary fac-

EXHIBIT 6.3. *Daily Maintenance Report*

Item	Location	Work Performed by	Inspected by
Mall lights			
Sidewalks			
Tenants' signs			
Trash areas			
Common area hallways			
Mall entry glass			
Thermostats			
Canopy lights			
Mall entry doors and locks			
Mall floors			
Music system			
Store lights			
Restrooms			
Drinking fountains			
Decorative fountains			
Other _____			
Other _____			

Inspected by _____

---

tors that will sustain the shopping center's life. Inspections should be conducted regularly and for most centers, on a daily basis—all as part of the preventive care of the property. Two important points about preventive maintenance should be borne in mind. First, the operations manuals of all equipment, particularly major equipment, must be followed concisely. If this is not done, the manufacturer may not consider the warranty valid, and the property owner runs the risk of paying for costly repairs. Second, to prevent possible misuse and consequent breakage of costly facilities, only skilled, qualified personnel should be permitted to work with the major equipment.

Curative Maintenance. When equipment malfunctions or parts become worn, someone must be available at the center to repair the problems. Even with the best preventive plans, malfunctions will occur at every type and size of shopping center.

For problems that can be relatively easily and inexpensively cured, the solution is obvious: The problem should be cured. However, at some point, the property manager will confront a decision between repairing or replacing a major item at the center that will not be so obvious. Physical items will wear out: They will reach a point where repair is no longer cost-effective. Although general rules cannot be applied to every situation, the

MANAGING THE SHOPPING CENTER

EXHIBIT 6.4. *Weekly Time Log*

Accounting Code	Job Description	Mon. RT	Mon. OT	Tue. RT	Tue. OT	Wed. RT	Wed. OT	Thurs. RT	Thurs. OT	Fri. RT	Fri. OT	Sat. RT	Sat. OT	Sun. RT	Sun. OT	Total RT	Total OT
	General bldg. maintenance																
	Roof																
	HVAC																
	Structure																
	Plumbing																
	Electrical																
	Other																
	Common areas																
	Interior landscape																
	Exterior landscape																
	Parking lot																
	Security																
	Lighting-interior																
	Lighting-exterior																
	Mall maintenance																
	Plumbing																
	Electrical																
	Snow removal																
	Trash removal																
	Sewer system																
	HVAC																
	Doors and windows																
	Equipment repair																
	Other																
	Total Hours																

RT = Regular Time   OT = Overtime

Week Beginning _____
Week Ending _____
Employee _____
Department _____

center manager can basically assume that replacement is preferable if it will cost at least half as much to repair an item as it will to replace it.

In most situations where major equipment is involved, the

manager must confer with the property owner, and together they should consider the many factors involved. Careful decision making on such matters may also give the manager the opportunity to operate the center more efficiently. For example, the replacement of an obsolete heating system ultimately could save the center owner thousands of dollars in fuel costs. Without a careful review of the current system, however, the owner and manager may never know of the costliness of the system, or even that the system is obsolete. On the other hand, careful deliberation is not required for each such decision that occurs at the center. At a certain point, "careful" decision making becomes wasteful. Many such decisions between whether to repair or to replace an item on the property should be obvious ones.

     Deferred Maintenance. Practitioners refer to tasks that are put off to some future time as deferred tasks. Deferred maintenance is often the consequence of a lack of effort, brought about by an incompetent manager, although in some cases, the center owner lacks the necessary funds to carry out important maintenance tasks. Nevertheless, property managers with tightly limited funds available should remember that in an inflationary market, a repair job will still cost less today than it will cost one year from now.

Standard Operating Procedures

A *standard operating procedure (SOP)* is a step-by-step course of action that states precisely how a particular system or policy is to be conducted. The property manager should develop a *standard operating procedures manual* for the shopping center. This manual will detail all the specific policies, procedures, systems, and job functions that relate to the property's operation.

     To prepare the manual, the manager first should inspect the property thoroughly, listing every item that requires periodic attention. The manual should state the specific standards that must be maintained for regulating the property's operation. After the procedures have been established, enforcement is of primary importance. The policies must be enforced for the proper performance of the maintenance staff, and in some cases, for the proper performance of tenants at the center. Generally, the property manager must assume responsibility for enforcing these policies.

     The following offers a sample SOP checklist, guidelines for

maintaining the roof of a structure ("The Worry-Free Roof," *Shopping Center Report* [New York: International Council of Shopping Centers], 1975). With preventive action, including regular inspections, the manager may be able to avoid what many real estate practitioners consider the most bothersome of all maintenance problems—roof repairs. The manager should develop the same type of rigorous checklist for every major item on the property.

1. Painted Surfaces. Check for rust, rot, or other deterioration.
2. Drainage Sumps. Check for any broken or plugged sumps.
3. General Roofing Surface. Look for surface abrasion, scuffing, tears, cuts, slits, holes.
4. Deterioriation. Inspect for alligatored bitumen, exposed laps of felts, dried felts, blisters, ridges, insufficient or nonexistent aggregate.
5. Sponginess. Walk on surface and check where it is not firm (should indicate moisture-filled insulation).
6. Debris. Remove it to prevent clogging of drains, gutters, downspouts.
7. Material or Equipment. Remove from roof and store elsewhere.
8. Other roof-related items that should be inspected:
   Interior ceilings.
   Areas around skylights.
   Cracked wall.
   Dampness (particularly around vent pipes or ducts leading from the roof).

Many shopping center managers face the constant threat that vandals will damage the property. Vandals might throw rocks through several windows or spray graffitti on the fences or walls. Managers can take preventive action against such acts. They might hire night security guards or install sophisticated alarm systems, but there will probably still be many events that they cannot control. That is why some shopping center owners carry crime insurance, which, as it will be explained in chapter 11, "Insurance, Risk Management, and Taxes" is another form of control.

Some problems become apparent only when something goes wrong. That is why property managers must be familiar with all the physical aspects of the properties that they manage, which does not mean that they must become experts on maintenance. They should find experts who are available and are willing to be consulted. They should have all the facts and proper procedures available for handy reference, perhaps in their own small libraries. Their resources should include plans and specifications, inventory lists, manufacturers' warranties, and maintenance and repair manuals. The manager then must delegate physical maintenance tasks to competent members of the staff.

Physical Maintenance

In many ways, a shopping center can be compared to other properties. The building—particularly if enclosed by a mall—demands the same type of constant care that any structure requires. This chapter will not attempt to offer readers a comprehensive guide to maintenance, complete with detailed instructions. The purpose here is to present an overview of the subject. The following is a brief description of some essential parts of maintaining the physical property. Many suggestions apply only to centers with enclosed malls. Others are appropriate only during the design stage, or should the developer undertake a major transformation of the property.

Exterior Building Surface. Polished stone—granite, stainless steel, or glass—offers an ideal exterior surface. All of these stones are easy to clean and durable. Marble is also an extremely firm and attractive—albeit expensive—stone. The manager should take special care with signs posted at the center on the exterior of the building. Most shopping center leases contain restrictions on the tenants' use of signs, and the manager should enforce these rules. Many centers display their own signs, and all too often, missing letters in these announcements give the entire commercial operation an amateurish image.

Floors. Some shopping center mall managers today recommend that carpeting be installed to cover the floors of the building. Real estate practitioners once considered carpeting prohibitively costly and impractical for a property such as a shopping center, which must endure tremendous wear and tear. Carpeting, however, offers certain advantages. It can be attractive, especially in the common area or at the entrance areas of a shopping center. Carpeting also soaks up mud, and it controls sounds. Nevertheless, carpeting requires considerable maintenance, it may emit foul odors, and spillage can stain and ruin rugs.

Washroom Facilities and Plumbing. Public washrooms are a necessity in a mall. Most states have laws that require a location that serves food also to provide public washrooms. A strip or community center may or may not have these facilities available for the public, but, in many of these centers, one tenant will provide a restroom that is open for the public's use.

If the center does have public washrooms, the management staff must put special efforts into maintaining them. Some shoppers may judge the entire center on the basis of the restrooms' cleanliness.

Plumbing pipes should be clearly identified, which is a way of saving time and money and of reducing the number of accidents. Many practitioners use a standard color code, established by the American National Standards Institute. The following color codes have been established for all buildings:

Fire protection—red.

Steam supply—orange.

Condensate return—aluminum.

Hot water—gold.

Cold water—dark green.

Chilled water—light green.

Condensing water—light gray.

Gas—light yellow.

Air—dark brown.

Drains—natural with walls.

Electrical—natural with walls.

Vacuum—beige (Edwin B. Feldman, *Building Design and Maintainability* [New York: McGraw-Hill, 1975], p. 153).

Each valve should be identified, as should the direction that each pipe leads, the location of expansion joints, and the location of anchor pipes. The property should also contain floor drains, wherever fluids might accumulate regularly, such as in a restaurant or restroom.

Electrical System. The section on energy conservation later in this chapter contains a detailed discussion of electricity. For now, suffice it to say that some developers err simply by not planning great enough electrical capacity for their properties. The manager should remember that products manufactured in the future will be far more advanced technologically and are likely to require greater electrical voltage.

Lighting. Lighting is also discussed in more detail under the section on energy conservation. A primary concern to the property manager is the accessibility of the lighting fixtures for cleaning and relamping. Accumulated dust and dirt on the fixtures can reduce total illumination of the lights by half. Ideally, lights for the mall area—not the individual stores—will be controlled from a central lighting panel. Outside the center, floodlighting might do a great deal to reduce vandalism on the property.

Housekeeping

Housekeeping is the job of keeping the entire property clean, and that is no small task. Excellent housekeeping is needed to maintain the investment's profitability. A small but meticuously clean center is more likely to attract a steady flow of consumers than is a larger but unkempt property. Housecleaning activities include sweeping the parking lot, cleaning the sidewalks outside the center, cutting the grass, caring for the mall floor, cleaning mall entry glass, emptying trash bins, and clearing snow-blocked lanes. Part of the task of housekeeping is preventive, since if it is not done at all or done haphazardly, the property will deteriorate fast.

In neighborhood and community centers, most of management's housekeeping tasks involve the exterior of the property, since the tenants at the center generally assume responsibility for housekeeping in their own areas. For interior malls, many additional maintenance duties become necessary, notably in each mall's common areas.

Cleaning techniques and equipment changed dramatically during the 1970s and early 1980s. Manufacturers took major strides in developing machinery that makes maintenance easier, faster, and more serviceable. On the other hand, the maintenance staffs in many smaller centers still use brooms, vacuums, and blowers—which actually are more effective along curbs and sidewalks. Nevertheless, the property manager should stay informed of new housekeeping products and procedures, in order to maintain housekeeping of the property at the highest possible level of efficiency.

Landscaping

Landscaping and lawn care can become major maintenance costs—although these costs will depend almost entirely on the amount of landscaped areas at the center, the city codes, and the climate of the region. A heavily landscaped garden at a shopping center requires more maintenance than does a small strip center with only a 10-foot-wide green belt that surrounds it. The garden center will demand the attention of an experienced horticulturist who supervises a full-time landscaping crew. The strip center manager can hire part-timers to mow the lawn two or three times each month during the growing season. Good landscaping, still, is very important in small shopping centers, as it is in all shopping centers. A pleasant landscape does much to enhance the physical attractiveness of both the large and small property.

Snow Removal

Snow removal is a concern only in some areas. A shopping center located in Phoenix, Arizona has no need for a snow removal budget. For a center in Minneapolis, Minnesota, however, snow removal might amount to 50 percent of the total common area maintenance budget. The manager must clearly explain the center's snow removal policy to maintenance workers or to a contracted maintenance service. Ultimately, it is timing, supervision, and excellent equipment that will determine the effectiveness of the center's snow removal plan. The business activity of merchants at the center will suffer if the parking lot is filled with snow and ice, or if entrances to the center are blocked.

For consumers, one of the distinct advantages of a shopping center is the convenience provided by a one-stop—in some cases, enclosed—setting. This factor becomes very potent in cold winter climates, providing another reason for an excellent snow removal program. The snow removal program must be geared to providing the greatest convenience for consumers and encouraging them to choose the shopping center over another retail setting.

The maintenance staff must have the proper equipment available and possess the necessary skills for conducting an efficient snow removal program. The maintenance staff, besides being highly skilled, must also have superior supervision.

The demands of a snow removal policy will vary from one region of the country to another. Shoppers in Minneapolis tend to be more tolerant of blocked snow roads and icy parking lots. They are generally accustomed to the winter conditions, and they realize that it takes time to clear the streets after a major snowfall. Once the streets are cleared, most Minneapolis residents will travel on the streets to wherever they have to go. In middle regions of the country, however, such as in St. Louis, Missouri, or Memphis, Tennessee, people generally do not expect major snowstorms, and when one does occur, the results can be devastating for retailers. Customers there might stay home for several days until they are convinced that the roads will be clear.

Ultimately, the basic objective of any shopping center's snow removal program is to keep the parking lot and entrances clear during business hours. The management staff should also take special care in keeping the sidewalks outside the center free of ice and snow. The manager may want to throw salt or chemicals on icy areas, to prevent shoppers from slipping on the sidewalks. If a customer suffers an accident on center property, the property owner may be held liable, which makes it even more important that these areas are always cleared.

The following is a list of the advantages and disadvantages of various abrasives that can be used to control ice (*Management I Institute Course Material* [New York: International Council of Shopping Centers, 1979], p. 2):

I.   Salt (NaCl)
   A. Positive—
      Very effective.
      Melts snow.
      Acts as an abrasive in cold temperatures.
   B. Negative—
      Useful only over a narrow temperature range—about 14° F to 32° F.
      Turns parking lot white, thus obscuring stripes.
      Shoppers track salt into building.
      Corrodes metal.
      Attacks concrete.

II. Calcium (CaCl)
   A. Positive—
      Similar properties to salt.
      Fairly wide temperature range.
      Not quite as damaging to concrete.
   B. Negative—
      More expensive.
      Not readily available in large quantities.

III. Sand
   A. Positive—
      Not damaging to concrete.
      Not damaging to vegetation.
      Inexpensive.
      Can be mixed with salt.
   B. Negative—
      Nonsoluble.
      Must be removed, plugs sewers.
      Not effective in extremely cold weather.

IV. "Miracle" Chemicals (Ureas)
   A. Positive—
   Melts faster than salt.
   Useful on a small scale.
   B. Negative—
   Cost extremely high.

Trash Removal

During the design stage, managers and owners tend to avoid the subject of trash removal, possibly more than any other maintenance concern. Trash removal is the headache that everyone would like to forget. Removal of trash, however, is an essential matter, especially in a structure that many people visit each day, and where merchants try to present a positive image to a buying public. By its nature, trash is a "problem," and most people want the "problem" removed, corrected, taken care of—and forgotten. Shopping center investors, architects, construction contractors, and property managers all tend to diminish the importance of trash collection. Trash removal is not one of the more enjoyable parts of planning and operating a shopping center, but it must be considered a critical part.

Property managers have various options available in setting up a trash removal program for a shopping center. Generally, it is not recommended that tenants be required to dispose of their own trash in a single location on the property. The tenants are likely to leave a trail of garbage scattered from the service corridors to the trash bins. A trash removal program, particularly in a large center, may demand the skills of experts in waste removal. The property manager will have to consider the needs of each center. One alternative may be to rent dumpsters from a waste management company and place the dumpsters at inconspicuous but convenient locations throughout the mall, still requiring tenants to handle removal themselves. With the dumpsters located in convenient places, trash removal is less likely to create problems.

Another possibility is for the management team to control all phases of trash removal. The tenants might put their trash at the back door each day, and someone from the staff would remove the trash daily. The manager must recognize the importance of cleanliness in trash collection. Flies and foul odors can permeate the entire center, especially in warm climates. The manager should purchase a disinfectant to keep this area sanitary. Also on the market today are simple granules that maintenance crews can spread at and near the trash bins to eliminate odors.

Restaurants, grocery stores, and large department stores present the center's trash removal program with special concerns. The manager should develop an individual trash removal plan with each of these tenants. Their disposal needs are greater than those of the average tenants, and the property manager may seek to charge these more demanding tenants accordingly.

Parking Lot Repair

The property manager should prepare written guidelines on the care of the shopping center parking lot. Properly installed and composed of quality materials, the lot should endure for the life of the center, requiring only minimal repairs.

Failure of a parking lot is generally due either to a water drainage problem or to improper installation. Water is the primary enemy of parking lot pavements. Water, by way of subsurface sources, seepage, ponding, icing, or melting, can cause the lot to fall. Generally, a good drainage system, along with quality paving, which will vary depending on the climate of the area, will help preserve the parking lot.

As with other aspects of maintenance, prevention of problems on the parking lot eventually will create the least number of problems for tenants, shoppers, and the management staff. A large part of prevention requires regular inspections. The management staff should inspect the lot, checking it for cracks, potholes, depressions, movements, or ripples, all of which are indications of problems, either as reactions to weather conditions or of problems occurring below the lot. If necessary, the property manager should hire a technical consultant who will know specifically how to handle these problems.

Life-Safety and Security Systems

In many respects, shopping centers are similar to cities, and in many respects, they must be managed as cities. They are places where shoppers can find the same goods and conveniences they would find at any central, urban location—including hardware, soft goods, food, household appliances, restaurants, entertainment, and professional services. Besides representing an exciting trend in retailing, however, shopping centers, as cities, have many safety and security needs, and all center owners must contend with these needs.

Just as cities demand effective fire and police protection,

shopping centers need the protection of effective life-safety and security systems. The two systems—life safety and security—are interrelated, but there is a difference. Life safety refers to the physical safety both of the people on the property and of the building itself. Security refers to measures that tenants, management, and the property owner must take to prevent theft, vandalism and other crime or disturbances on the property.

Preparation is the key for both systems. Consider life safety. Once the center opens, threats to safety will come in many different forms. A water tank may burst. A tornado may strike the area. A fire may break out on the property. Generally, the manager cannot prevent these occurrences, but the maintenance staff must know how to handle them.

Ultimately, it is human knowledge that will restore the center after an emergency. Any life safety system demands the quick judgements of human beings. A computer cannot replace a property manager who knows the proper action to take in the event of a fire or flood. Human intervention is an essential part of evacuation and crowd control. Many federal safety codes now require that selected people in the building be trained as fire safety directors. These people then work with the local fire and police departments.

Many consumers choose the shopping center over the traditional downtown retail area because the shopping center is considered to be a safer environment. This, then, becomes another reason why security at the center is of great importance.

Another security issue occurs with groups or individuals who wish to distribute political literature or collect money at the center for various causes. At one time, many shopping center owners insisted that their private property rights permitted them to decide who could canvass on the property, and who could not. In 1980, however, the U.S. Supreme Court laid down a ruling in the court case "Pruneyard Shopping Center vs. Robins" (447 U.S., 74) which, for the present time, has dramatically altered the handling of such matters at shopping centers.

In very general terms, the Supreme Court ruled that if a group or individual is using the property as a means for expressing an idea, and the public is not led to believe that the ideas are those of the property owner, then these parties do have the right to use the shopping center as a forum for public expression. The court noted that the property owner does not use the shopping center for private use. Rather, the court ruled, the shopping center is a public meeting place and is advertised to the public as such.

In an event such as this, however, the property owner must be urged to seek the advice of an attorney. The particular circumstances of this case may not apply to another similar situation, and the statutes vary in different states. The owner would be well advised to use a legal counsel in preparing specific guidelines that can be followed for all cases involving similar types of public use of the property.

Life-safety and security systems often overlap, and the center's lighting is one example of how they can overlap. Lighting has consequences for both the safety and the security of the center. Good lighting keeps traffic at the center moving; lighting also keeps people from bumping into one another and into merchandise. A power blackout could create havoc. A mall may have a battery-operated lighting system or an emergency back-up electrical system. Imagine the damage that could be caused in a china shop if a blackout suddenly occurred, and there were no emergency lighting. Security, on the other hand, could also become a major concern during a blackout. The blackouts in New York City a few years ago are evidence of what can happen when the electricity fails. Looting became rampant, and for a few hours, the city was terrorized. Most shopping center owners would want to prevent a situation such as that, at any cost. A back-up lighting system, thus, is a preventive device, against both safety and security problems.

Generally, the larger the center, the greater the requirements for sophisticated life-safety and security systems. Many large centers maintain a separate department for each function. Smaller centers may be able to function with much less, perhaps training one person or hiring a contracted service to handle all life-safety and security matters. Any safety and security program will include some or all of the following:

1. Guards, either in-house employees or by contract.
2. A patrolled parking lot.
3. Video security, including cameras and monitors.
4. Fire management systems, alarms, monitoring, and fire safety organizations.
5. A lighting system.
6. Two-way radio and telephone systems.
7. Electronic and computerized systems which permit only preprogrammed card holders to enter the premises during certain hours. (This concept has worked effectively for after-hour access

to the mall or to tenants' spaces, and for use of the center's parking lot. Once the card has been validated, an electronic door lock releases, allowing entry. Many of these systems also have video cameras. For many properties, these security systems have eliminated the need for an employed security guard.)

8. Lock control.
9. Burglar alarms and monitoring stystems.
10. Public and safe training; evacuation plans.

The notions of safety and security at the shopping center raise the issue of social responsibility, the center owner's and the tenants' responsibility to provide a safe and secure environment for people who work and shop at the center. The property owner is sometimes held responsible for accidents that occur in the common areas; and tenants, for accidents that occur in their stores. This will be discussed in more detail in chapter 11, "Insurance, Risk Management, and Taxes." Both the owner and tenants are forced, by the pressures of society, and more concretely, by the laws of its government, to conduct life-safety and security programs.

As discussed in the maintenance section of this chapter, shoppers will notice if safety matters are handled haphazardly. They will notice how strenuously the center enforces security measures. Customers want a sense of well-being wherever they shop. If they do not have that feeling, they will probably shop elsewhere, which, in the end, will cut into the property owner's earnings. The owner, in sum, has every reason to ensure that the shopping center is both a safe and a secure environment.

Safety and security mean protection from risk. Every shopping center, indeed every type of property, is filled with risks. Insurance helps reduce the cost of risk, but it cannot prevent it. Merchants can attempt to hire competent and honest salespeople—to help reduce risks. The property owner can install efficient fire-fighting equipment to reduce risk. The main responsibility for the control of risk, however, falls on the people on staff who must carry out the daily operations of a risk management program.

The property owner and tenants are responsible for financing the life-safety and security programs. Safety and security programs may be costly, but the owner and tenants will probably make up these costs many times over. Customers or employees who suffer injuries caused by the property owner's neglect are likely to turn quickly to legal action, which can amount to excessive costs to the owner. Damage to the property or to the tenents' merchandise or crime against tenants or shoppers eventually will reduce the owner's earnings. The responsible and profit-conscious owner should be willing to spend money to reduce these threats.

Energy Conservation

An effective energy conservation program requires that the property manager regularly communicate plans to the tenants on various methods that will be used to conserve energy and reduce energy costs. Tenants' cooperation and involvement with such programs will be necessary. The next section of this chapter will discuss a topic that continues to beset the shopping center industry—namely, energy shortages and rising energy costs. This chapter, however, will assume a positive stance: It will focus on the solution, namely energy conservation.

Energy conservation has become a necessary task in all types of investment property. Rising fuel and electrical costs have put great strains on the profits of property investments. Property managers, therefore, must have basic information about energy use before they can begin planning conservation programs for their properties. This chapter does not offer a detailed guide to the necessary steps for an effective conservation program at a shopping center, but if offers general guidelines and some helpful suggestions.

First, the manager should collect information about anticipated and current energy consumption at the center. This information audit will offer some bases for comparisons with other properties in the area that use the same type of fuel, and it will provide a comparable for measuring the effectiveness of a conservation program. The manager can arrive at a performance ratio through the following calculation:

Performance ratio = fuel consumption + square feet ÷ (total
heating + cooling degree days)

The lower the performance ratio, the lower is the amount of energy consumed on the property per square foot. Thus, a conservation program can be directed at reducing the performance ratio. The ratio gives the manager a quantitative definition of the program's goals.

Energy conservation at a shopping center can be divided into four major categories: building skin, HVAC system, economizer system, and lighting and electricity.

Building Skin. Basically heat loss occurs two ways—by *infiltration*, which is the conduction of air through the skin of the building; and by way of air leaks, which occur when air seeps through small holes in the building's structure. Infiltration is a costly problem to cure, since it involves a change in building material. Such problems are best prevented during the planning stage, a reminder that does little for the manager who assumes responsibility for an existing center. All property managers, however, can take steps to stop air leakage. A building structure gradually develops cracks at joints where the surface materials meet. Cracks also develop through dry rot caused by moisture, fungus, vibration, poor maintenance, poor construction, or shrinking due to temperature changes. The manager can use caulk to fill these gaps and to fill other holes where cold air seeps.

The other problem involves cooling the structure, which becomes more costly when a hot summer sun puts excessive strains on the air conditioning system. The management staff can install awnings and screens to reduce the hot rays.

HVAC System. The property manager should maintain the temperature in a mall at a moderate level—neither too hot or too cold—and hold the temperature at a consistent level during the center's hours of operation. This will help to reduce costs, although managers should not depend on thermostat controls to cure their energy cost problems—nor for that matter, should they depend on any energy conservation program to solve all of their energy expense problems. Property owners and property managers must remember that the costs for fuel and electricity have risen. If the center has not wasted energy before a plan goes into effect, an energy conservation program will probably not create savings. Yet, a simple rule that managers can follow is to start the heating, ventilation, and air conditioning units each day as late as possible, and turn them off as early as possible.

There are other ways to conserve energy through the HVAC system. The maintenance staff can reduce or turn off heat or air conditioning in unoccupied spaces or storage rooms. Estimates are that this practice can reduce energy usage by as much as 10 percent. Maintenance workers should continually check heating and air conditioning units or registers to ensure that these systems are completely free of obstacles.

Hot water pipes in the building should be turned off at night, except in extremely cold temperatures. A frozen water pipe might burst, creating innumerable problems, including costs that would far surpass any "savings" that would result from shutting off the pipes. The hot water temperature in public washrooms should not exceed 140° (60°C). For every 10° F that the water temperature is raised above 140°, hot water costs, on the averge, increase by 3 percent.

Economizer System. A more radical conservation alternative is an *economizer system*, which is used effectively in many parts of the country. An economizer system uses outside air through a refined distribution system. The system provides large amounts of outside air that either heat or cool the building, without using fuel or electricity. The system can produce several weeks of "free" heating and cooling, mainly by reducing the operating hours of the HVAC machinery. Nevertheless, the ability to install and use such a system depends on the geographic location of the center.

It is often more efficient to re-circulate inside air rather than use outside air, which then passes through the equipment. This concept is based on the use of air that is heated by means other than outside air, including light radiation, body heat, and heat from equipment on the property. Hot air rises, and sophisticated equipment collects and re-circulates the air to the rest of the property.

Property managers have reported great success with a combination of an economizer and re-circulation system. In many cases, the existing HVAC system can be converted to accomodate. both methods.

Lighting and Electricity. Lighting and electricity are among the most costly energy uses in a shopping center; property managers, therefore, generally direct considerable attention to this area. The shopping center should present an aesthetically pleasing atmosphere, and attractive lighting is often part of the design. Many property owners, however, are cutting back in this area. In past years, the Christmas season meant the highest lighting costs of the year. Managers and owners are now more conscientious about conserving energy—for example, by limiting the number of Christmas lights. Some centers are changing the hours that the maintenance staff works, changing the work hours from night to day hours.

Many major retail chains are taking active steps to save energy. Some retailers are lowering the requirements in their leases for minimum parking lot illumination, from 1.5 footcandles to one footcandle. For safety reasons, extremely busy parking lots still require more light, but for most neighborhood and community lots, one footcandle will suffice.

The property manager can take many other steps. All interior and exterior lamps and light fixtures should be kept clean. The manager can limit parking lot lighting to actual hours that the lot is used. Another trend has been to purchase higher lighting poles for parking lots: They illuminate farther and more uniformly. Whenever possible, the manager should provide the center with fluorescent rather than incandescent lighting, since fluorescent lighting emits twice as much light, at a lower cost. The maintenance staff should also remove lenses and shields over light fixtures, where glare and mechanical damage are not a problem. Shields can reduce light output by 50 to 75 percent.

Developers can plan center malls such that the walls are bright-colored, accented with skylights, thus reducing the light requirements during day hours. Some center managers have eliminated the use of all mall lights during daylight hours, but this should only be done when the light is quite obviously not needed.

Finally, at the end of each day, the maintenance staff should run through a checklist, to ensure that lights, elevators, escalators, and business machines—in sum, all electrical utilities—are shut off when the center closes. Some centers have automatic controls that turn off electrical power systematically at specified hours, thus eliminating the risk of human error.

In a shopping center, whatever affects one tenant eventually has consequences for all tenants, the owner, and the property manager. A community spirit of conserving and reducing energy costs ultimately will benefit everyone at the center. Any conservation program demands all tenants' cooperation and continuous efforts. Tenants should be informed of specific methods they can use to conserve. The Institute of Real Estate Management has sponsored numerous seminars throughout the country on conservation methods, and has published handbooks that offer suggestions on conserving energy in income properties, such as *No-Cost/Low-Cost Energy Conservation Measures for Multifamily Housing*. The property manager may want to provide tenants with this or a similar type of conservation manual.

It is interesting that many of the major energy-saving ideas actually rely on common sense—for example, cleaning lamps and lighting fixtures regularly; reducing light when possible; cutting air leakage by weather stripping; and caulking. Energy conservation need not be an extremely complex or highly technical program in order to be effective. Above all, conservation demands cooperaton and active assistance from all of the tenants at the center.

Conclusion

Undoubtedly, maintenance, life safety, security, and energy conservation will continue to be significant topics throughout the decade of the 1980s, although all but energy conservation have always been of utmost concern to property owners. Energy conservation became a major topic during the 1970s, when fuel shortages first became apparent, and energy costs shot up dramatically. Competent handling of the operations of the building has both a direct and indirect effect on the owner's earnings. Energy conservation and reduced operational costs will reduce the property owner's costs; safety and security on the property will help to give shoppers a sense of well-being; and the general upkeep of the property will keep patrons pleased with the surroundings and willing to continue shopping there.

Managers and owners have many options to consider as they establish effective operations for their properties. "In-house" versus "contracted" service is a controversy that has been around for many years among shopping center practitioners. Each service has certain advantages and disadvantages, but the general conclusions are not definitive. As with many aspects of the shopping center, the choice rests on the specific needs of each property. If the work is needed only periodically, for example, hiring a contracted staff may be well advised.

In many ways, the shopping center is unique among properties. Continual upkeep of the physical plant is necessary to assure a steady steam of shoppers, and a steady stream of shoppers is necessary to assure a profit for the tenants and the property owner. In few income properties will the building operations have such a direct impact on the property owner's income.

So, once again, the responsibility for the 1980s falls on professional property managers—managers who know the technical aspects of real estate; who know the overall workings of the property; who understand the essential purposes of life safety and security, and who know how to carry out effective programs for both; and who know how to reduce energy costs at a time when it seems those costs will only continue to increase. Shopping centers of the 1980s will demand management by experts, people who have an astute understanding of the shopping center's physical plant. As fuel shortages and higher prices become more expected than feared, property managers can be ready to deal with the changing demands.

Review Questions

1. Why are maintenance, life safety, security, and energy conservation related functions of property management?
2. What control does the individual tenant have in monitoring rising common area maintenance costs?
3. Does a 100,000 square foot shopping center require its own parking lot sweeping staff and equipment, used solely for cleaning the parking lot? Why or why not?
4. You operate 12 small shopping centers in a four-state area. All maintenance and security services are contracted. Your budget does not permit on-site management staffing. How do you control the quality of service?
5. Which maintenance costs are typically the responsibility of the landlord, and which are typically the responsibility of the tenants?
6. Parking lots and roofs seem to cause property managers a good number of maintenance problems. What steps can be taken to alleviate some of these problems?
7. What is the difference between preventive maintenance and curative maintenance?
8. As a representative of the property owner, do you have the right to restrict political groups from campaigning at the shopping center? Discuss the rationale.
9. What are three inexpensive actions that the property manager can take to reduce energy costs?
10. Do you think security guards at a shopping center should be equipped with firearms? Why or why not?

Tenant Mix

Plans may appear ready for the development of a new shopping center. The design, location, construction plans, and leased anchors at the center may be ideal. The center's merchants may have exciting promotional plans. Market studies may show a strong demand in the area for a retail center. Nevertheless, a critical component—an effective tenant mix—may be missing, which could become a void that would offset even the best conditions. The tenant mix at the center must be appropriate to the area's socioeconomic levels.

The choice of tenants for the center is actually one of the most important features that distinguishes a prosperous shopping center from one that is failing. Every shopping center must have a basic identity. It needs to attract a steady, consuming public. Its identity serves as the basis for setting up a proper mix of tenants. Therefore, developers must consider the basic requirements of their communities and establish an identity and tenant mix based on those needs.

Property managers, however, have little or no control over the tenant mix that is finally selected. That decision is generally left to the property owner. Managers can try to develop the best mix for the center, perhaps advising the property owner on what types of tenants would be most suitable for the property. Furthermore, much of the "control" over tenant mix selection is actually a consequence of demand, of how many prospective tenants seek space at the center. The property manager and the property owner cannot always control selection of tenants; selection is often a function of the market.

Chapter 5, "Market Analysis," discussed the factors in the market that the property manager and developer should study. These factors include location, competition, income level, and family size. Only after the demographics, the strength of retail sales in the area, and the competition have been analyzed can steps proceed to define the trade area in both geographic and demographic terms. Only after the manager and developer know their market can they develop an appealing tenant mix.

Tenant mix is an extremely important factor in regional and superregional shopping centers and important, but less so, in community centers. Tenant mix becomes even less significant in nieghborhood centers; and in convenience centers, with only two or three tenants, tenant mix is virtually not a factor. The degree of importance of the tenant mix factor depends generally on the number of tenant spaces at the center.

Tenant Placement

Tenants pay a price for their locations at a shopping center. As in a downtown district, the more central the location at the shopping center, the higher is the rental level. Some tenants seek a prime location, whatever the rent, because they consider their location at the center one of the most important factors that will determine their success. By the nature of their business, some tenants must demand this prime location. Most anchor tenants in a regional center, as it will be discussed in more detail later in this chapter, obtain the locations with the greatest exposure because of the appeal these tenants add to the entire shopping center. Some tenants are willing to settle for secondary locations at the center, and their businesses will not be harmed in these locations. They too will be discussed in more detail later. Ideally, the layout at the center will generate a sufficient amount of business for all tenants.

A kiosk is an example of a tenant that demands a prime location at the center and pays for that location through a very high rent per square foot. As noted in chapter 3, a kiosk is a small, ancillary shop commonly found in shopping malls. Kiosks, ranging in size from 150 to 300 square feet, might sell anything from costume jewelry, keys, insurance, and fruits and nuts to caricature drawings and fast foods. Shopping center managers generally agree that kiosks are a great boost to the tenant mix in a shopping mall. A strong kiosk is not parasitic but draws customers and repeat shoppers to the mall, as can any strong tenant.

The landlord has a major interest in the proper placement of all tenants at the center. If all tenants can benefit from the layout, the profits of each—and of the property owner—will be higher. The placement of tenants, therefore, becomes a decision-making concern for all parties involved with the success of the property. The specifics of what constitutes a strong or a weak location at the shopping center is discussed later in this chapter.

The anchor tenant sets the tone and image of the shopping center. Consumers, in general, come to the center because of the anchor, whether the anchor is a major department store, a supermarket, a discount store, a large home center, or a catalogue showroom. In many respects, the success of the center rests on the anchor tenant or tenants. The anchor should lie in a central, convenient location at the center. For example, if the anchor is a food market, people should be able to move easily in and out of the store. It should offer an assortment of goods that attracts a steady stream of shoppers. In any center with an anchor grocery store, customers should have ample parking available near the market.

The tenants that draw customers to the center should be strategically located so that an even flow of traffic moves along the shopping area. In well-planned centers, all tenants have an equal opportunity for high sales; there are no bad locations.

In many regional centers, two anchor tenants stand at each end of the shopping area. This layout encourages customers to walk by the smaller shops that are distributed between the anchors. The implication is that the greater the flow of pedestrian traffic, the more potential customers there will be walking past the other stores. Some centers have anchorless ends; one end of the center has no major tenant. Most of the merchants at the barren ends cannot match the high sales of those merchants located closer to the major tenant, but tenants located in the less central spaces also pay lower rents.

The developer or manager should plan parking and center entrances in a way that best serves the center. Ideally, in a mall the entrances will be located so that customers must walk from the entrances to the major tenants or to points of interest past the smaller stores. Likewise, in a smaller center, parking must be convenient, and close and accessible to the entrances.

In establishing a tenant mix, it may help the property manager to think of a shopping center as a large department store, with each retailer representing a separate department. Each store complements and depends on the others. Broad selection and cooperation—as in a department store—are essentially the goals that should result from an effective shopping center tenant mix. A well-designed, properly merchandised shopping center will probably lead to higher sales for all merchants. For example, a men's clothing store, a sporting goods store, and a men's shoes and accessories store can complement one another. The stores do not compete with one another directly; rather, they offer different goods to service the customer.

Even if the stores are direct competitors, they support one another by offering customers a wider choice of merchandise. Together, competing and noncompeting merchants increase traffic at the center and bring in more people to all of the stores.

Some types of stores have special placement needs, or, by their location at the center, they may offer certain benefits to other tenants. Clothing stores and boutiques, for example, must be highly visible because they require heavy customer traffic. Some service and convenience merchants, such as a movie theatre or dry cleaner, by themselves can draw consumers, and in many centers, they do act as traffic builders. Banks and beauty salons, which depend far less on impulse shopping, do not need high-traffic locations; they are more concerned with easy access and plentiful parking. For this reason, it is common for service tenants to stand in secondary locations within a center.

Above all, the manager who establishes a tenant mix and places tenants should seek to optimize the center's income-producing ability. Service tenants (for example, banks, insurance companies, travel agents, hairdressers, and dry cleaners) not only meet customers' needs, they also enhance the center's appeal. The manager can plan the location of food services (for example, a supermarket, restaurant, bakery, liquor and wine store, and cheese shop), such that shoppers can satisfy all of their grocery needs in one convenient location. Many recent developments have restaurant facilities with common seating provided in the mall, giving the customer a large selection of fast foods in one location.

Tenant Types

Next, the property manager asks: What tenants are available for the center, and which should be selected? To answer this question, the manager should begin with an analysis of the anchor tenant.

The anchor may be a full-line department store, a junior department store, a grocery store, a discount department store, a home center, a catalogue store, or a small convenience grocery store. The choice of the anchor should depend on the needs of the shopping center and the demands of the market. The anchor may sell exceptionally high-quality goods (for example, Saks Fifth Avenue, Neiman Marcus), or it may offer popular-quality goods (for example, J.C. Penney, Sears Roebuck and Company). The anchor might be a local department store with a highly localized identity, or it might be part of a national chain (such as K Mart).

Attention then must turn to the other tenants. The manager first must identify the appropriate merchandise categories. These general categories, called GAFO, were presented in chapter 5, "Market Analysis."

Before starting the leasing process, the manager must take a thorough survey of the tenants already in the marketplace. The manager then must decide whether to duplicate what already exists in other centers or to aim for a totally different image.

Many questions will arise:

What is the competition doing?

How are competitors succeeding? How are they failing?

What categories of merchandise not represented could the trade area support?

What is the position of the anchor tenant in the marketplace? Is its primary competitor in the near vicinity?

What national and regional chains are represented in the trade area? What is the image and personality of each? What are their space requirements?

What local tenants can the center attract?

This last factor is extremely important. Local tenants may be hard to locate and difficult to persuade, either to open another location or to relocate, but they can distinguish a center and give it a basic identity. Independents generate repeat business through personalized service, which few national and regional chains can offer the consumer. The more interesting the tenants in a center, the greater the center's edge over the competition. Asking the questions noted above, the property manager can determine which tenants will most effectively enhance the tenant mix: the best local, independent merchants; the best non-competing stores from outside the market; the best merchants in competing centers. With this information, the manager can begin to merchandise the center.

Merchandising the Center

Merchandising begins with a leasing plan, whether the plan is for a new center or an existing center. A *leasing plan* is the formal statement of the shopping center's rental rates and the types of tenants that would be suitable for specific spaces at the center. The plan must contain a layout of the property, drawn to proportion; and a measurement of the center's rentable area. The manager then must analyze the trade area to determine the types of merchandise most in demand and the amount of space that should be allotted for each category.

If the center has been in operation for an extended period of time, an analysis of different tenants at the center is necessary as part of the merchandising process. The analysis will point out the weak tenants and the weak locations within the center. The manager should list tenants' lease expiration dates to identify opportunities, and examine tenants' leases, noting conditions that might require renegotiation before the leasing plan can go into effect. In older centers, some tenants may occupy more space than they need. Other tenants, at the same time, may stand cramped for space. A thorough evaluation of tenant space will indicate to the property manager whether this appears to be the situation at the center.

Some leases may contain certain clauses that must be renegotiated. The manager may see that a variety store can be divided into a number of smaller stores. To compete in today's market, the supermarket, on the other hand, may require additional space. If every store needs all the space that it occupies, perhaps the center itself can be expanded. In preparing a leasing plan, the manager must consider all of the possible ways to fill or recapture space and present many different ideas to the property owner.

Merchandising a new center requires a different approach than merchandising an existing center. In general, the new center is less secure as a venture but offers the manager a greater chance to serve as the property owner's consultant and to offer recommendations from the start of the project. The manager in this situation is entering the project closer to the design stage and thus is working with fewer limitations than the manager who is charged with an existing center. The property manager of the new center may attempt to find how the merchandising mix can be developed to stand apart from other shopping centers.

The manager of an older center generally does not have this opportunity. Long-term leases at low rents burden many older shopping centers. Some of the tenants there have no incentive to give up their spaces or their low-rate, favorable-term leases. For this type of property, the manager's best approach is to establish both long- and short-term goals. On a short-term basis, for example, the manager might plan only the termination of old leases that are not adding to the center's profitability and may actually be contributing to the center's dated image. The retail merchants may be resisting renovation programs or the property manager's suggestions to improve displays in their stores. With retailers who are resistant to any type of change, the manager's best advice to the property owner may be to seek the fastest possible termination of their leases. In regard to more long-term goals, the manager can help the property owner plan more profound changes, such as enclosing the center or updating existing facades and storefronts.

Exhibits 7.1 through 7.3 provide general guidelines for selecting appropriate merchandise categories for various-sized centers

EXHIBIT 7.1. *Neighborhood Shopping Centers—Tenant Classifications*

	Percent GLA	Percent Sales	Ratio: Percent Sales to Percent GLA	Percent Total Charges	Ratio: Percent Total Charges to Percent GLA
General merchandise	6.6	3.6	.55	3.9	.59
Food	27.8	57.9	2.08	23.0	.83
Food services	8.6	6.5	.76	12.7	1.48
Clothing	5.3	5.1	.96	8.3	1.57
Shoes	1.1	.8	.73	1.5	1.36
Home furnishings	2.2	.8	.36	2.1	.95
Home appliances/music	2.0	1.2	.60	2.4	1.20
Building materials/garden	3.1	1.3	.42	2.1	.68
Automotive supplies/service station	2.4	1.1	.46	1.8	.75
Hobby/special interest	2.6	1.8	.69	3.3	1.27
Gifts/specialty	2.6	1.7	.65	4.2	1.62
Jewlry and cosmetics	.6	.7	1.17	1.3	2.17
Liquor	1.5	2.0	1.33	2.1	1.40
Drugs	9.3	9.9	1.06	7.6	.82
Other retail	3.5	1.5	.43	3.7	1.06
Personal services	5.4	2.1	.39	6.7	1.24
Recreation/community	3.4	.7		2.4	.71
Financial	4.3	.1		5.7	1.33
Offices (other than financial)	3.2	.7		4.3	1.34
Other	4.5	.5		.9	.20
Total	100.0	100.0		100.0	

EXHIBIT 7.2. *Community Shopping Centers—Tenant Classifications*

	Percent GLA	Percent Sales	Ratio: Percent Sales to Percent GLA	Percent Total Charges	Ratio: Percent Total Charges to Percent GLA
General merchandise	35.4	25.6	.72	21.0	.59
Food	14.9	34.3	2.30	14.6	.98
Food services	4.7	4.5	.96	8.2	1.74
Clothing	7.4	7.1	.96	12.1	1.64
Shoes	2.0	1.8	.90	3.4	1.70
Home furnishings	2.5	1.4	.56	2.5	1.00
Home appliances/music	1.8	1.8	1.00	2.8	1.56
Building materials/garden	2.2	1.6	.73	1.8	.82
Automotive supplies/service station	2.1	1.2	.57	1.5	.71
Hobby/special interest	2.2	1.9	.86	3.2	1.45
Gifts/specialty	2.1	1.5	.71	3.8	1.81
Jewelry and cosmetics	.8	1.5	1.88	2.2	2.75
Liquor	.6	.4	.67	.7	1.17
Drugs	4.6	5.9	1.28	4.6	1.00
Other retail	2.8	1.6	.57	3.1	1.11
Personal services	2.5	1.1	.44	3.5	1.40
Recreation/community	3.3	.8		3.3	1.00
Financial	3.0	5.4		4.0	1.33
Offices (other than financial)	2.1	.2		3.0	1.43
Other	3.0	.4		.7	.23
Total	100.0	100.0		100.0	

EXHIBIT 7.3. *Regional Shopping Centers—Tenant Classifications*

	Percent GLA Mall Shops	Percent Sales	Ratio: Percent Sales to Percent GLA	Percent Total Charges	Ratio: Percent Total Charges to Percent GLA
General merchandise (excluding department stores)	15.1	10.0	.66	7.0	.46
Food	14.2	27.3	1.92	9.7	.68
Food services	7.0	6.7	.96	9.8	1.40
Clothing	16.6	18.6	1.12	23.4	1.41
Shoes	4.4	5.5	1.25	7.4	1.68
Home furnishings	2.4	1.5	.63	2.1	.88
Home appliances/music	2.8	3.5	1.25	3.9	1.39
Building materials/garden	2.0	1.2	.60	1.1	.55
Automotive supplies/service station	1.9	.8	.42	.8	.42
Hobby/special interest	3.1	3.2	1.03	4.0	1.29
Gifts/specialty	3.8	3.7	.97	6.0	1.58
Jewelry and cosmetics	1.6	3.8	2.38	4.2	2.63
Liquor	.7	.6	.86	.6	.86
Drugs	4.9	5.6	1.14	3.4	.69
Other retail	3.2	2.1	.66	3.4	1.06
Personal services	2.8	1.6	.57	3.2	1.14
Recreation/community	4.3	1.3		3.1	.72
Financial	3.5	2.2		3.3	.94
Offices (other than financial)	2.4	.5		2.5	1.04
Other	3.3	.3		1.1	.33
Total	100.0	100.0		100.0	

(*Dollars and Cents of Shopping Centers: 1981* [Washington, D.C.: Urban Land Institute, 1981], pp. 295–296). The categories are guidelines only, however, and should not be taken as established rules. Every center is in some way unique, and each stands in a different position in the marketplace. Changes in consumer populations, in lifestyles, and in income levels will all affect retailers; the center's tenant mix, in turn, may have to be altered as the region changes. Consequently, what is appropriate for one shopping center may not be appropriate for another.

Once the manager has determined an optimal mix and proportion of tenant categories, the center should be planned in ideal form before tenants have had a chance to veto or approve the layout. The manager can implement changes to turn the ideas into a workable plan.

Old and new centers, regional, community, or neighborhood—in any type of shopping center, the same basic principles of leasing and merchandising will apply. For every type of center, the property manager must study the market thoroughly. The demographics, the center's position in the marketplace, the image of the anchor tenant—all must undergo a thorough and ongoing reveiw. Research cannot stop when a new center opens for business. Studies may indicate that customers are staying away from a center because of a problem that is within the management staff's power to correct, such as poor maintenance.

Identifying and Evaluating Tenants

After determining the types of merchandise that would be most appropriate for the center, the manager must begin to search for retailers that sell this merchandise. The manager then must evaluate the retailers' financial stability and their suitability to the center's image.

First, the manager must identify the ideal types of tenants for the center: national, regional, or local. As the name indicates, national tenants own stores throughout the country, or throughout several major regions of the country. Most of these tenants have in-house real estate staffs or outside brokers to represent them. Most have specific space requirements and well-defined expansion plans. Many national tenants also have extremely slow, in-house decision-making processes—but for center managers, it is worth the extra time that will probably be needed to negotiate with these larger tenants. Well-known national tenants will strengthen the center and help attract other tenants to it. Nationals also help the property owner obtain a financing commitment.

National tenants operate their individual stores in one of two ways: The parent company might own and operate the store, such as Petrie, Inc., with its Marianne and Stuarts women's apparel stores. Or the store will be owned and managed by an individual who uses the company name, such as Tandy Company's Radio Shack.

Regional tenants have store locations in several neighboring states, or they trade in a major section of the country (for example, the Northwest, Southwest, or Midwest). Financially, regional tenants may be as strong or stronger than national tenants, and may have more drawing power within a trade area. The difference is that nationals own stores nationwide; regionals do not. For example, Caldors, Inc., a discount tenant located in several New England states and in New York state, in its own area draws a market as good as or better than a K Mart.

Throughout this book, the importance of the anchor tenant has been stressed. Yet it would be a mistake to think that a shopping center could prosper without small independent tenants. Small tenants are essential to the success of the investment. As discussed in other chapters, independent retailers help create a more interesting tenant mix and bring with them loyal customers and an established identity within the community.

To expand into new markets, a retailer typically requires three outlets, since three is the minimum needed to spread advertising distribution and administrative costs efficiently. Astute property managers will stay informed about local merchants' plans, checking with many of them periodically to determine if the shopping center could meet these retailers' needs.

Many center managers, especially those who are given responsibility for a new center, must eventually ask the question, "How do I find tenants for the center?" There are no simple solutions. Finding tenants demands that the property manager observe the community to find out what merchants appear to be most successful, which merchants have soon-to-expire leases, and what general types of products consumers are demanding.

References such as *Chain Store Directory* are readily available and can be extremely useful for locating new tenants. Most reference books will list, by merchandise category, the name of the tenant and the number of units that the tenants owns, providing the name of a person to contact at the retail store. Most of these publications, however, list only retailers that own five or more units. Therefore, these reference books can often help the manager identify national and regional tenants that operate within the area, but the directories would list few of the local tenants.

Other potential sources for locating retail tenants for a shopping center include the following:

The Yellow Pages of the local telephone directory.
Department store managers and sales personnel.
Buyers and sales representatives of major suppliers.
Local newspapers.
Advertising agencies.
Community leaders.
Other tenants' referrals or word of mouth.

Of all these sources of new tenants, probably the most beneficial are the referrals from other tenants. Current tenants, in general, can offer the most credible evaluations of the shopping center. Most tenants that are doing well in a center will eagerly recommend it to other retailers, who will complement current tenants' trades.

Most merchants want to be located in a center that has a strong reputation. They want a center with a good management team and a tenant mix that will produce a high sales volume. Once a mutual interest develops—that is, the manager and property owner are interested in the retailer, and the retailer is interested in the center—steps can begin to determine if the tenant would be appropriate for the center.

The property manager confronts numerous concerns in evaluating a prospective tenant. Although the process is taxing both in time and effort, if the center is to be a successful one, the tenant evaluation process is essential. Again, to a large extent, a shopping center's success lies in the hands of the people who establish the tenant mix. Professional leasing agents must concentrate their efforts on filling space, but they must also consider the total environment at the center. Selection of tenants goes beyond finding merchants who are willing to accept the rental rate. Frequently, the wisest decision will be to break a lease, sacrificing a minimum rent in order to preserve a good tenant mix. The hope is that high percentage rents will yield higher profits later. Concerns in nine areas will occur:

Space Requirements. Every retailer has different requirements for space. However, most tenants want as much frontage space with as little depth as possible. A store depth is usually four to five times the length of its frontage, yet a retail store has limits to the depth that it can absorb. Basically, it is difficult to move customers into a store more than 70 to 80 feet. Therefore, the rear areas of most stores contain dressing rooms or storage areas. An "ideal" store size will be about 70 feet × 80 feet. Most small retailers in neighborhood centers prefer stores between 1,200 square feet to 1,800 square feet (about 40 feet × 40 feet).

Although many retailers seek a great deal of frontage space, most smaller-scaled merchants (under 6,000 square feet) agree that merchandising storefronts of over 40 feet is unrealistic and generally not successful. It is difficult to make such a large display area attractive, and more than two entrances add security problems. Managers should learn of the tenant's space requirements at the outset. They will save a great deal of time, and the information will help them in determining whether the tenant would be suitable for the center and if so, what location would be best for the tenant.

Business History. How long has the merchant been in business? Generally, the retailer who has been in business longer is in a stronger position financially. Nevertheless, the length of time in business is only one criterion that the property manager should use to judge the retailer's financial strength. Probably more important than the number of years is the success of the business, and whether the retailer has and will continue to have the financial means and expertise needed to handle other locations. This is all part of the retailer's business history. The responses to these can be placed on a scale: very successful; successful, marginal, or poor. The manager should also try to learn the retailer's future business plans, beyond those of locating at the center.

The manager should check the retailer's trained personnel and be assured that the staff is capable of handling a new unit. Knowledgeable merchants know the types of problems that arise in a new store. They carefully build their organizations such that expansions will be handled efficiently. Many tenants of all types—local, regional, or national—have expanded too quickly, have overextended themselves, and a short time later, have been forced into bankruptcy. High interest rates have cut deeply into retailers' cash flows, just as they have cut deeply into property owners' profits. The property manager must evaluate the merchant's financial capabilities to expand into the shopping center.

Type of Business. As noted earlier, the property manager must evaluate whether the merchant would be appropriate for the tenant mix and for the market that the center is attempting to reach. The shopping center should project an image, and the store should fit that image. For example, an amusement game operation placed in the center would almost certainly affect the shopping center. The question then turns to whether such an operation would benefit or harm the center's image.

The Merchandise. The manager must be certain that the store's merchandise is appropriate for the center. The merchandise might appeal to a certain type of shopper—young, old, tall, husky, or petite. Or the price range might be limited to a certain market—popular, moderate, or top of the line. The style, taste, and selection of goods must appeal to the type of consumer that the center's management is attempting to attract. The methods that the retailers use to promote their merchandise should suit the market and the rest of the center.

Merchandise Compatibility Presentation. In evaluating a retailer, the manager must look at the manner in which the merchandise is presented—store concept, displays, product presentation—and its compatibility with other merchants. The methods that the retailers use to promote their merchandise must appeal to the market and the balance of the tenant mix.

The store's concept is another important consideration in determining whether a prospective tenant is compatible with the shopping center. The store might aim to project an ultramodern image, its walls covered with chrome, glass, and electric colors. It may seek an early American touch, designed with a solid, conservative decor. The manager should evaluate how effectively the store's concept is tied to its merchandise. A children's store, in general, should be bright and colorful. A high fashion boutique should lend an expensive, sophisticated air. The store's image must be consistent, all the way from the display windows, to the interior, and its employees. The ultimate test of whether the store is projecting itself successfully, however, is whether customers are clear about what it offers. A retailing operation will not stay in business long if it fails to attract a steady stream of suitable customers.

Any well-run retailing store puts a strong emphasis on product presentation. The marketing world is one of visual stimulation. Today's shoppers are package-oriented; they go for the prettiest wrapping. Manufacturers and retailers spend hundreds of millions of dollars each year trying to convince consumers that one product is better than another. Packaging is one of manufacturers' primary means of appealing to a buying public. Therefore, the retailer's presentation of the product is as important as the product itself. The presentation should arouse the buyer's interest—not only for one item, but also for all the accessories.

Some products have such a strong appeal that consumers will travel long distances to purchase them. The merchandise must look tempting: fresh, crisp, and clean. It must be seasonally appropriate. Some merchandise has a fast turnover. If the retailer sells goods that stay on the shelves for several months, the manager should inspect the merchandise to see if it appears to be fresh. The manager should also observe the general upkeep of the store. Perhaps no other store in the area carries a certain brand of an item. The manager should inspect the supply and selection of that item. To repeat, a store's merchandise compatibility with other tenants is always a consideration in deciding whether the retailer would be appropriate for the center.

Although perhaps an extreme example, an auto supply store in a specialty center would be inappropriate. But what about a dress shop in a service center that contains several professional offices, a hardware store, a grocery store, but no other soft-good stores. The dress shop would face numerous obstacles, since customers shopping at the other stores would probably not have an immediate interest in shopping for dresses. Likewise, the dress shop probably would attract few customers to the hardware store.

Promotion. Tenant promotion refers to what merchants do to advertise their own stores, as opposed to their contributions for all-center advertising. Generally, a merchant spends between 2 and 2.5 percent of gross sales for advertising and promotion. If a merchant is first entering the market or is opening another location, the percentage that promotional dollars will represent of total expenditures will probably be higher. Some merchants may want to develop their own advertising; others may rely on the center for most of their promotions. Essentially, all advertising attempts to encourage the consumer to buy. Tenants must bring the consumer not only to their own stores but also to the stores of other tenants. The concept of a shopping center, again, is that tenants depend on and complement each other.

Tenant advertising begins with the store's exterior, notably its identifying sign, which is most visible. The manager should take note not only of the prospective tenant's current exterior sign but also of interior signs and displays. Preferably, the signs in the windows and on displays will be professionally painted. Some store owners may hang handwritten cardboard signs to advertise their merchandise. Most such signs are crudely drawn and, in the end, only harm the shopping center's image. The center should strive for a consistent, professional approach to promotion, a topic that is discussed in detail in chapter 10, "Advertising, Promotion, and Publicity."

Likewise, the tenants' promotional programs should be consistent with one another. All tenants need not follow the same promotional route, but whatever form they take—newspaper, television, radio, direct mail, special events, window displays, or circulars—it should complement, not interfere with or harm, the other stores' trades. Many retailers develop imaginative ideas that draw attention to the center. One merchant might sponsor an annual blood drive. Another might support a local Little League team each summer.

Some merchants may be reluctant to take part in all-center promotions. Some tenants—national or local, large or small—may not want to contribute money for group advertising, which can cause a number of problems for the property manager. This subject is covered in depth in chapter 10; suffice it here to say that a retailer's willingness to participate in all-center activities should be a consideration in tenant selection. The property manager can obtain this information perhaps by asking the prospective tenant or perhaps by requesting the information from retailers who are currently doing business near the tenant.

Customer Service. The importance of customer service begins with the premise that part of a retailer's purpose is to provide conveniences to customers. This includes shopping conveniences, such as store hours, credit arrangements, collection policies, sales services, and return policies.

Store hours should be set for the shopping conveniences of the consumer rather than for the conveniences of the merchant. While most national and regional merchants always operate this way, some small retailers may prefer that hours meet their own personal needs. Where several retailers are operating on the same property, such as in a shopping center, it is important that all stores—with the notable exceptions of a cinema or restaurant—stay open during the same hours. The public shops at a center expecting to take care of all of its planned shopping errands. The public expects stores, at the very least, to be open during normal shopping hours. Tenants in the same shopping center should be open during the same hours, on both a daily and a seasonal basis.

The center manager should investigate each retailer's customer services. Merchants will vary in the services they provide: for example, alterations in a dress shop; lessons in using a home computer; waxing lessons for cross country skiers; and, decorating assistance with the purchase of furniture. Likewise, some merchants will provide these services free, and others will charge a fee. Any of these services will be an added benefit that can be derived from the tenant's presence at the center.

Credit services are another important concern. Stores will differ in the credit cards or financing methods that they offer to customers. They might have in-house credit cards, accept national credit cards, or offer a lay-by plan. Each store with a credit plan also needs a collection policy for handling bad debts. Some stores might repossess merchandise; others may turn collections over to an agency that specializes in these problems.

An important service that the property manager should consider in evaluating the retailer is the store's return policy. A merchant who prohibits all returns and exchanges could create bad feelings with consumers, which consumers might, in turn, generalize to the entire center. Nevertheless, there are some very successful high-quality discount stores that set such "no-exchanges, no-returns" policies. They post the warning prominently, however, and in some cases, salespeople remind anybody who buys merchandise of the store's strict policy. The customer has been forewarned in this case, and this is usually sufficient to avoid problems. Whatever return policy the store has created, that policy should be posted clearly somewhere in the store, perhaps even printed on the customer's receipt.

In general, the buying public considers all of these items important. The sum of retailers' customer service policies helps create either a negative or positive impression of the individual retailers and of the shopping center as a whole. If too many tenants in a center offer little customer service, the public is likely to turn to other retail locations, where more serviceable retailers can be found.

Sales Performance. The merchant's sales volume, the number of store locations, the established clientele, the merchant's expense structure, and the merchant's profits all become

MANAGING THE SHOPPING CENTER

important concerns to the manager. These criteria will determine which tenants to pursue, and they provide the basis for determining percentage rents. Essentially, they indicate the rental income that the property owner can expect to receive from each tenant. This, in turn, determines whether final leases are signed.

Each merchandise category operates on different gross and net profit margins. A supermarket, for example, operates on a 19 to 21 percent markup, with a net profit of 1 to 1.5 percent before taxes. A supermarket's high volume makes up for this relatively low profit margin. The clothing industry, on the other hand, operates on a 49 to 53 percent markon, and profits before taxes are generally between 5 and 6 percent. (*Markon* and *markup* refer to the same thing; they are the difference between the retailer's purchase price and selling price. Retailers have traditionally used the *keystone markup*, which is 100 percent of cost, or 50 percent of the retail price.)

Sales volumes vary greatly from one type of merchant to another. Therefore, a specific sales volume per square foot may be excellent for a dress shop but insufficient for a supermarket. Most supermarkets must gross at least twice the volume of a dress shop, per square foot, just to survive. The profit needs of each tenant are critical in putting together the center's tenant mix.

Most major retailers can quote sales volume per square foot, totalling their costs and profits per sale to within pennies. The smaller merchant may be able to provide only total sales per store, not thinking in terms of earnings per square foot. This does not mean that smaller retailers are not successful; rather, their accounting systems are just not as sophisticated.

Most experienced retailers can estimate their potential in a new location, but many prospective tenants want the property manager to quote or estimate sales potential. Then, if those projections are not met, the retailer may try to blame the manager. Managers, therefore, should take the offense; at the outset, they should offer the retailers an estimated projection of sales. If sale figures for the center are available, the manager can quote average sales per square foot. If the center is large enough, sales by merchandise category can also be provided. Next, however, the manager must warn the retailer that such projections are only estimates, and precise sales projections cannot be determined.

Qualifications of the Merchant. The merchant's personal qualities become a factor for the property manager to consider. Intelligence, aggressive marketing abilities, community spirit, sales skills—these can all affect the store's prosperity and suitability to the rest of the center. Does the retailer hire good employees and train them properly? The center manager should check for consistency between the store's concept and its personnel. The manager, in sum, should inspect all factors that indicate whether the merchant is capable of maintaining a well-run, well-stocked store.

The combined financial strength of all tenants is basic to the success of the entire shopping center investment. Nevertheless, the owner and manager may select a tenant based not on financial strength but rather, because of a merchandise void that the tenant would fill. They might think that the new merchant shows promise of growth. In establishing a tenant mix, the property owner generally completes the process with a balance between strong credit tenants and some tenants who are weaker financially.

A tenant data sheet, as shown in Exhibit 7.4, can help during the qualification process. Such a form provides a ready record of factors that will help to evaluate a merchant. The formal procedure outlined here may not be necessary for all tenants, but is recommended that the manager maintain a record for any merchant that might benefit the center, and that, realistically, might be interested in locating at the center. Although the center may not currently have space available for a particular tenant, or the tenant may not be ready to relocate or expand, again, plans can and do change. This tenant information should be on record for future use in leasing center space.

The Practice of Placing and Qualifying Tenants

The procedures for determining what types of tenants should be located at the center, where they should be placed, and qualifying individual retailers are essentially the same for all types of centers. Yet, there are subtle differences, enough so to warrant a discussion of each type. Recommendations for developing leasing plans for regional, community, neighborhood, fashion, and outlet centers thus follow.

Regional Center

Many shopping centers have become not only places to shop but now also serve as entertainment, recreational, babysitting, and public meeting centers. Today, most of these all-purpose shopping centers are sheltered, indoor shopping malls.

EXHIBIT 7.4. *Tenant Data Sheet*

Tenant category_____

Trade name _____ Locations _____ Telephone_____

Name: Parent company_____ Contact_____

Square feet_____Frontage_____ Telephone_____

Merchandise_____ Quality_____

Price range_____ Size range_____

Expansion plans_____ Units per year_____

Concept (anything unusual, clearly defined, image)

_____

_____

_____

Merchandise (target market, product lines, cleanliness, seasonal variations)

_____

_____

_____

Sales personnel (general helpfulness, enthusiasm, consistency)

_____

_____

Promotion (describe promotional program)

_____

_____

The changes have made successful "glamour centers" out of many regional locations. As a result, many regional and superregional shopping centers have become very valuable properties. Yet, only a handful of companies built and now own these prime shopping areas.

Regional centers must draw from a large, diversified trade area. A regional center tenant mix, therefore, must appeal to a broad range in price, quality, and interest. A J.C. Penney or a Sears Roebuck and Company typically anchors the regional center. One or more full-line department stores might also lease anchor locations in a mall. The objective is to appeal to several socioeconomic groups by offering a variety of merchandise, yet avoiding the dangers of overextending.

In selecting tenants for a regional center, the manager must choose tenants that will be appropriate to the general areas and the specific spaces of the center. In an enclosed mall, tenants regard *center court*—the midway point between the anchor tenants—as a prime location for satellite tenant spaces. Fashion-oriented merchants traditionally stand in these spaces. The main or central mall area lies on either side of center court, between the anchor tenants. Merchants with a variety of goods—shoes, books, toys, food—will lease this space. Tenants should stand in positions that will stimulate consumer interest in their products. The manager should generally try to prevent a concentration of one merchandise category in any one area, although, in some cases, such a concentration may be beneficial. As noted earlier, several different types of restaurants clustered together in one area has proven to be successful in some modern malls.

Selection of the tenants that will lie closer to the anchors demands special attention. This is especially true of the tenant in an adjacent position to the entrance of the anchor. Some retailers have mistakenly assumed that this is a good location for fashion merchandise. Actually, however, many stores get lost there—they are easily overshadowed by the awesome anchor. Generally, the best type of tenant to locate in this area is a *destination retailer*. A destination retailer is a tenant that sells goods that a customer will make a special trip to purchase, such as furniture, stereos, and valuable jewelry—as opposed to items that shoppers tend to buy on impulse.

Mall entrances or off-mall locations should also be reserved for destination retailers. Sit-down restaurants or service tenants (a bank, hairdresser, travel agency, or cinema) are destination retailers that usually do well in these locations. In sum, a properly designed regional or superregional mall, although extremely large, will have few poor locations. The property manager must take special care in helping the property owner find the appropriate tenant for each space, and in helping tenants find the appropriate space within the center. Exhibit 7.5 shows a typical, detailed layout for a regional mall.

Community Center

In some areas, community centers have replaced the role of a regional mall. Community centers, like regional centers, can be open or enclosed, depending on climate and design. A junior

EXHIBIT 7.5. *Detailed Regional Mall Layout*

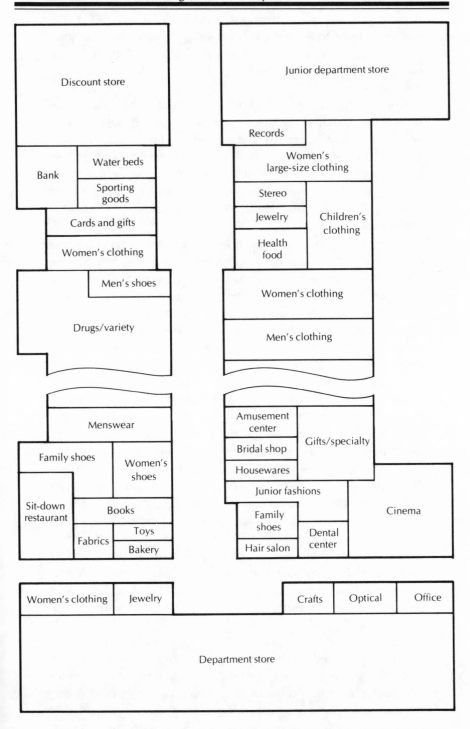

department store, a relatively small but full-line department store, a variety store, a discount department store, or a supermarket is likely to anchor the community center. Some community centers have several national chainstores in their tenant mix; others have a much higher proportion of local or regional merchants.

Community centers, in general, confront two major problems. One is that most lack a national tenant. A national tenant tends to add strength and appeal to the tenant mix. The second problem occurs when a large national tenant does decide to build in a community center. If the development focuses on the demands of the major tenants, many of the smaller tenants, whose needs are very different, will probably suffer as a result.

When a discount store anchors the community center, the manager should pay special note of the store's merchandising program. The store may promote soft lines, hard lines, or both. The manager should observe the amount of space devoted to nonselling functions—customer service, hair salons, restaurants, offices, and storage areas. In general, the more items the discount store carries, the more limited the assortment of each line.

Problems may develop if the center has both a supermarket and a discount store. A supermarket demands a high concentration of people, within a 1.5 mile radius or five-minute drive time. A discount store, on the other hand, draws from a much larger trade area. Therefore, the two types of stores have different needs, and they will attempt to attract different markets. The supermarket would want to concentrate its promotions, for example, in the immediate area; the discount store would have to expand its efforts far beyond this. One site will probably not meet the needs of both, and if the two stores are in the same center, one of them will probably suffer. A shopping center such as this is trying to accomplish too much; it is trying to satisfy immediate, neighborhood-type needs, and at the same time, it is trying to promote the discount center, with its vast assortment of goods.

Despite these problems, which are preventable, many more discount-anchored community centers succeed than fail. As with all types of shopping centers, merchandising the community center depends on the demographics, customer profile, and competitive conditions within the marketplace. A tenant that complements rather than competes directly with the discount store will work best for this type of center. Typical tenants at a discount-anchored community center sell costume jewelry, hardware items, household appliances, food, and some lower-priced clothing and shoes.

Still, there is no typical tenant mix for a community center. Generally, a tenant mix that complements rather than competes with a discount store anchor will work best in this type of center. In a community center that is anchored by a junior department store, the merchandise mix will lean more heavily toward soft goods and clothing. A fashion-oriented community center closely resembles a regional mall mix; it is only on a smaller scale.

Today, there is a trend toward developing 50,000 to 100,000 square foot "home decorating centers." Their size and market area place them in the community center category. As their name indicates, home centers sell everything for "do-it-your-self" homeowners and carry products ranging from plumbing and lighting fixtures to paneling and lumber. Some tenants may sell carpeting and floor coverings, paint and wall coverings, unpainted furniture, and stereo and audio equipment. Other home centers contain specialty retailers that carry decorator accessories for the home. Some of these centers contain catalogue showrooms.

The interest in community centers appears to be increasing, largely because of their possibilities to be redeveloped and expanded. That, however, is not to detract from the problems that many of these centers are facing. As noted in earlier chapters of this book, the community center, in general, offers neither the simple conveniences of the neighborhood stop nor the grand assortment of a regional center. Yet, community centers present developers with many alternatives. This chapter will present a case study, illustrating an encouraging investment alternative—the remerchandising of the community center.

The center being studied is the only shopping center in the immediate trade area. The city where it lies, population 30,000, is a suburb of a major metropolitan area. There is a regional mall 20 minutes away, and the main metropolitan district lies more than 50 minutes away. Although the suburb has a small downtown area, the center provides the community with most services and merchandise. It fills many of the buying voids in the community; the center contains one high-quality department store, a movie theatre, three restaurants, a nightclub, a four-screen cinema, several soft- and hard-line stores that sell both full-price and discount goods, and one lawyers' office and five doctors' offices. The layout of the center is presented in Exhibit 7.6.

The suburb has a young, high-density, upwardly mobile population. There are many families living in the region. About half of the residents own their own homes. The average annual income here for a family of four is $25,000.

The shopping center has two distinct sections. One side (Side 1 in Exhibit 7.6) contains a discount store and many service-oriented tenants. The small strip area of Side 2 contains professional offices and other service tenants. Side 3 is geared to clothing and accessories.

A review in 1980 of impending lease expirations revealed opportunities, mainly in the fashion-oriented area, for recapturing space. Following that examination, 2,900 square feet were recaptured in 1981; 5,386 square feet in 1982; and 2,550 square feet were planned to be recaptured in 1983. In Side 1 of the center, the variety store, occupying 21,000 square feet, had a lease that was about to expire. This tenant's sales volume, $39 per square foot, fell substantially below national sales averages for variety tenants.

The developer believed that the professional space was well located, taking up rental area that stood a long distance from the anchor tenant—space that may have been unworkable for a retailer. The professional tenants also helped draw more consumers to the retail stores that were located on that side of the center. As noted, service tenants already occupied a large amount of space; therefore, the property manager discouraged the addition of any more service tenants. The manager also evaluated the sales of these service tenants to determine if their income justified the amount of space that they occupied.

Two small shoe stores in the center were both struggling with low sales volumes. This apparently had more to do with the types of shoes the stores carried (low quality at low prices) than with the category of merchandise. Another shoe store that sold quality, high-fashion shoes was prospering at the center. The center contained only a few women's clothing and accessory shops.

The center contained a variety of tenants, in terms of merchandise sold, including a natural foods store, an aquarium store, and a stereo store. After talking to store owners and obtaining some sales figures, it was evident that well-merchandised stores, particularly well-merchandised, fashion-oriented

EXHIBIT 7.6. *Older Community Center Leasing Plan—1980*

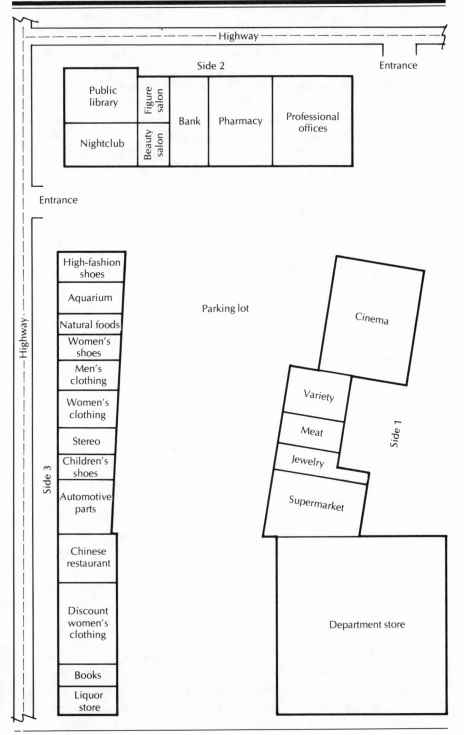

stores, were yielding high sales volumes. Profitable tenants were reporting sales of over $100 per square foot. In fact, the high-fashion shoe store and clothing store each were yielding more than $150 of business per square foot. The study also evaluated the quality of the merchandise in each store, the store's general upkeep, and the demand for its products. The manager and property owner, in turn, used all of this information to determine which tenants to keep and which to relocate.

They finally offered the following recommendations, as illustrated in Exhibit 7.7. The owner implemented fifty percent of the plan immediately; the balance was to go into effect during 1983 and 1984.

1. Increase rents to between $6.50 and $8.00 per square foot.
2. In future leases, require the reporting and payment of sales.
3. Relocate the liquor store, stereo store, and automotive parts shop to Side 1 of the center.
4. Eliminate the weak tenants—aquarium, natural foods store, variety store, Chinese restaurant, meat shop, jewelry store, and bookstore.
5. Transform Side 3 into a fashion center by adding more stores that offer, among other related goods, discount linen, men's discount clothing, children's clothing, leather goods, and hosiery.
6. Expand the supermarket to 30,000 square feet, thus reducing the size of the liquor store location, since the liquor store had done only marginally successful business.

Neighborhood Center

The neighborhood center is perhaps the easiest of all centers to merchandise, since its size limits the number and variety of retailers that can lease space within it. Most neighborhood centers are less than 100,000 square feet, with a supermarket and drugstore occupying 50 to 60 percent of the total space. In addition to the anchors, service tenants, such as hairdressers, banks, travel agencies, office space users, and variety of food stores, such as delicatessens, bakeries, and restaurants, often occupy the neighborhood center.

Fashion Center

The fashion center is a newer type of shopping center, first developed in the 1970s, mainly in high-income areas, notably resort locations. These centers, many of which do not have a major anchor, range in size from 150,000 to 500,000 square feet.

Fashion centers concentrate on high-fashion, high-quality

EXHIBIT 7.7. *Older Community Center Leasing Plan—1981 to 1983*

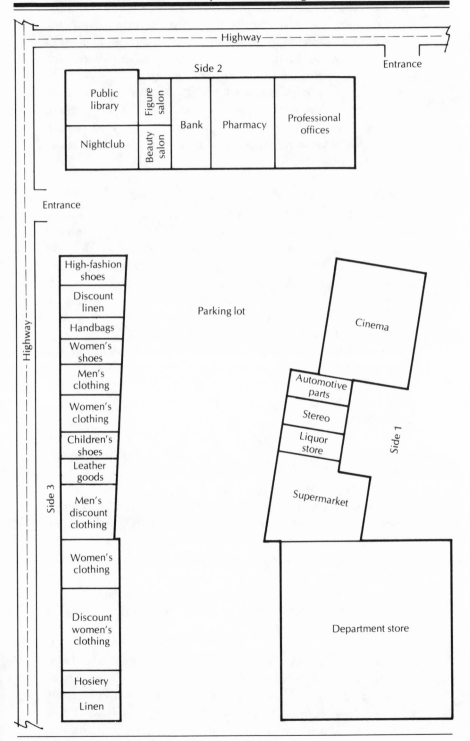

merchandise. The architecture in many of these centers is striking, providing an attraction by itself. Also, as in any shopping center, there is a need in a fashion center for ample parking or easy access by public transportation. Many fashion centers are similar to specialty centers, and some centers, such as Water Tower Place, are both a specialty and a fashion center. However, in a fashion center, the clear emphasis is on fashion, which need not be the case in a specialty center. Most fashion centers also have some quality restaurants, and gourmet, wine, cheese, or candy stores.

Outlet Center

Outlet centers are still quite new. They are not to be confused with discount-anchored centers or with typical discount tenants such as K Mart or Loehmann's. There are two types of outlet centers. One is the pure manufacturer's outlet, with retail stores owned and operated by the manufacturer. The other is the outlet center that takes many different types of merchandise on consignment, buys factory overruns and seconds, and sells them all at discount prices.

Probably the country's most famous outlet area, and the place where the concept started, is Reading, Pennsylvania. Customers from New York, Philadelphia, Washington, and Baltimore for years have traveled to Reading to shop at its outlet stores. Today, outlet centers are being developed all over the country, particularly in suburban, middle-class areas. The centers range in size from 75,000 to as much as 1,000,000 square feet.

Most outlet centers do not have an anchor, although some of the larger outlet operations, such as the Burlington Coat Factory and the Great Factory Store, occupy up to 40,000 square feet. Typically, however, tenants range in size from 800 to 8,000 square feet. The outlet stores demand easy access and an abundance of parking to handle a high volume of traffic. The design appears to have little effect on whether the center succeeds. Instead, success depends much more on the quality and price of the merchandise.

Outlet centers have been developed in, among other places, old factories and warehouse buildings, and have also been developed as strip centers. Some of the layouts would have spelled failure for any other type of shopping center. Merchants and developers now realize, however, that consumers will travel long distances, and are willing to accept modest shopping surroundings for quality merchandise at low prices. Reading, Pennsylvania, proved it. Still, increasingly, developers are working toward sophisticated displays and pleasant surroundings.

Outlet centers carry all types of clothing, luggage, books, linens, home decorating accessories, and kitchenware. The price range among these center tenants is great, but the typical outlet tenant seeks a low rent and a high consumer volume. These tenants will generally rule out a location that generates first-year sales of less than $150 per square foot. Many of the outlet tenants want to locate only with merchants that complement their own businesses. They then turn to the developer or manager to coordinate promotions.

Conclusion

Shopping centers of the 1980s will depend on strong, astute property management. The need for excellent management becomes particularly great in establishing and maintaining an effective tenant mix. Varying forces—many of them out of the manager's and the investor's control—will affect the shopping center. The selection and placement of tenants, however, are factors that can be controlled. Consumers will come to the center because it has stores that are pleasant to shop at and carry appealing merchandise. The tenant mix is a changeable determination. There is no formula that can determine an ideal mix that will last for the life of the center. Therefore, ongoing research is an essential part of the property manager's job. The market will change, and, with it, the tenant mix must also change.

The shopping center manager operates on a delicate balance, always sensitive to the changing needs of consumers and tenants, yet ever aware of the property owner's objective for a profit. The demands of consumers, tenants, and investors often stand in conflict to one another. In establishing a tenant mix, the property manager confronts all of these forces. The tenant mix is a clear reflection of the property manager's expertise in balancing the needs of all parties.

Review Questions

1. What are the necessary steps for developing an effective tenant mix? Why are these steps necessary?
2. How is a customer profile developed, and why should such a profile be necessary?

3. What is the most effective way to evaluate the success of a tenant mix?
4. In evaluating the tenant mix of an existing center, what factor should be analyzed first?
5. What are the primary considerations in merchandising a discount center?
6. In evaluating a prospective tenant, what features should a leasing agent consider?
7. What are outlet centers, and what does the future appear to hold for them?
8. Discuss the fashion center and its importance to the shopping center industry.
9. Why is a retailer's return and collection policy important to a shopping center community?

8

The Lease Document

A real estate lease is a founda-
tion. It serves as the legal document that states the rights,
duties, obligations, and liabilities of the parties involved. The
nature of a shopping center investment limits the amount of
vocal communication that can occur between the developer
and the tenant. Leases offer written statements, written communication, about matters that will concern the tenant and the
landlord. Leases are essential documents for a shopping center
development.

Yet, for shopping centers, the term "lease" is actually a misnomer. A shopping center lease is unlike any other type of real
estate rental contract. With other rentals—offices, apartments,
townhouses—a lease binds the landlord and tenant to a few
basic items: the amount of rent per square foot, the size of the
space, the length of the lease, and, in most cases, the amount of
the security deposit. A shopping center lease goes beyond these
essentials, and such a lease might more accurately be called a
long-term commercial arrangement. The length of the average
shopping center lease runs for many years, much longer than
most other real property leases. In many cases, the center structure has not even been built or developed when both parties
sign the lease. Finally, both the landlord and the tenant are
seeking a profit from the center; therefore, both are concerned
with conveniences offered to shoppers at the center and with
the center's tenant mix. Both parties have similar concerns
about maintaining the center and making it attractive to customers. Although most commercial office tenants seek a profit,

few are affected as directly by the building's environment. Also, although other retailers may rent space in downtown areas, they need not worry about all the variables that might affect a single development. Nevertheless, because the term "lease" is so common, this chapter will use it throughout, although the reader should be aware of the term's limitations.

In setting up a lease, all parties must remember that a lease is a legal document and should be prepared by an attorney. Property managers should understand the details of these contracts, but at some point, all managers must turn to a lawyer to prepare the final document.

Identification of the Parties

Most leases involve two parties—a landlord and a tenant. In recent years, the descriptions "landlord" and "tenant" have acquired negative connotations. To some people, the words suggest an unfair class distinction. "Landlord" suggests a member of a ruling class; "tenant" implies a second-class citizen. Those uncomfortable with the terms have chosen to use the more objective words, *lessor,* for landlord, and *lessee,* for tenant. But actually "tenant" and "landlord" more accurately describe the relationship between one person who owns and another person who pays rent for occupying land or space in a building. People can pay rent for goods—office equipment, televisions, furniture—and thus be lessees. Only the word "tenant," however, suggests that the person is paying rent to occupy space. The terms "landlord" and "tenant" will be used throughout this chapter and are used throughout the book.

Most leasing arrangements require other identifications—including a guarantor, assignor, assignee, subtenant, prime tenant, and licensee. All of these terms have legal definitions, a situation that demands that they be used precisely. The term "prime tenant," for example, is not legally identical to "anchor tenant," and using the two terms interchangeably may lead to legal complications. The term *prime tenant,* as discussed in earlier chapters, refers to an assignment or sublease situation, distinguishing between a tenant who has signed a contract directly with the landlord (prime tenant), and a "successor-in-interest" tenant (assignee) who may or may not have agreed to a direct contract. *Anchor tenant,* on the other hand, refers simply to a tenant that occupies a substantial amount of rentable space.

The landlord generally provides the lease form, except when

negotiating with some anchor tenants. The landlord or manager has the time and expertise to prepare an appropriately named "boilerplate" lease form. This document serves as a basis for all the matters that must be settled between the two parties. By providing the form, the landlord has the advantage of knowing in advance which lease clauses are subject to negotiation.

The leasing agent who assists with negotiations should understand the legal status of each party. This status will determine the manner of preparing the document and will indicate who assumes responsibility for the obligations of the lease. Both landlord and tenant also need to know the other's status, as a corporation, partnership, or proprietorship. Some locales also require that the parties note any distinction between a proprietorship and an individual tenant.

The corporate tenant executes the lease by declaring the name of the corporation and the state of its incorporation. Two corporate officers may sign the lease on behalf of the corporation, although one signature is generally acceptable. Most landlords and property managers will require that each tenant's signature be notarized, even if notarization is not a legal requirement. The use of the individual or large corporate guarantor is most common where the tenant enjoys the limited liability of corporate status, especially where it has been formed for the specific business venture contemplated by the lease. The same rules apply to the corporate landlord. A corporate resolution will also state that the person signing the lease has the authority to do so.

The lease should specify whether the partnership is general or limited, as discussed in chapter 2. A limited partnership restricts the limited partners' liabilities of partnership debts. A general partnership, on the other hand, represents a shared pooling of capital, profits, and liabilities. In either case, at least one of the general partners must sign the lease to bind the partnership to the agreement. The lease should note the state in which the partnership originated, if it is different than that of the leased premises. By their partnership accords, all partners have agreed to pool their personal assets. Therefore, whether they are general or limited partners, they must abide by any of the partnership's binding contracts. Limited partners incur personal liability only to the extent of their capital contributions to the partnership.

Proprietorships and individual tenants present the fewest number of problems in lease preparation. Each person who signs the lease incurs personal liability to the extent of the lease.

A contract can be valid, even if one party has inadvertently forgotten to sign it. This holds true if the lack of signature is shown to be inadvertent, and both parties, by conduct, have treated the agreement as effective.

If the tenant will use a trade name ("dba"—"doing business as"), this information should appear in the lease document. This general rule should apply regardless of how the tenant is legally organized.

Description of Leased Premises

As with any real estate lease, the lease for shopping center space must first establish a description of the property. This description must offer enough details such that a "reasonable" person could understand it. A lease that describes the specifics of the leased premises will prevent future misunderstandings. This description supports the idea that the lease offers the ultimate statement on any possible contingency.

For most shopping centers, a site plan attached to the lease offers a description of the rented property. Most of these plans show the building that houses tenants, with the leased portions hatched in black. The building and store number further specify the premises. Both should initial the plan. Although usually covered in the body of the lease, a disclaimer in some site plans states that the drawing is not to scale and is meant only for locating the premises. Another disclaimer should state that the site plan is subject to change at the landlord's discretion.

Descriptions can also be by street or mailing address or by the center's geographical boundaries.

The Lease Term

Most shopping center leases state the tenant's term of occupancy in number of years. With a fixed term, the developer enjoys the benefit of a tenant committed for a specific period of time, and the tenant has the benefit of knowing what the financial obligation will be each month. Circumstances may alter the commitment of either party. The tenant may demand a lease term of some minimum length, in order to "buy time" and eventually obtain financing and operating capital. On the other hand, the lender might request a longer term, to assure a repayment of the loan amortized over the length of the lease.

If the property manager anticipates that the lease starting date will not coincide with the first day of the month after the tenant opens for business, the lease should contain an amendment that specifically establishes the commencement and termination dates of the lease. One approach to fixing the commencement date is to state that the lease will begin a fixed number of days after the lease is executed, or on a fixed date, whichever occurs first. This protects the landlord from a delay by the tenant, either on the opening date, or on the rent commencement date.

The lease term must be specific. Should the lease fail to mention a term, most states require that the contract run month-to-month, or the tenant hold only periodic rights to the property. Should there be a question as to when the tenant can complete work in the demised premises and consequently open for business, the manager should address the problems as follows:

1. The manager should estimate the date that the tenant will open for business and consider adding 30 more days to that date. The words "on or before" the starting date might then be added to the lease.
2. The manager should also negotiate the rent starting date, so that the tenant will be obligated to pay rent, even if the retailer is not yet open for business.
3. The manager should negotiate the proper construction to be granted to the tenant from the date that possession of the space is tendered.
4. The manager should reach an agreement with the tenant to amend the lease as stated above.

The termination date might become an issue of dispute if either the landlord or tenant has an option to end or renew the lease. Options are discussed in chapter 9, "Lease Negotiations."

Types of Shopping Center Leases

Shopping center leases may be classified by the method of rent payment. By this standard, there are four main types of leases: (1) flat- or fixed-rent leases; (2) percentage-only leases; (3) fixed-minimum-plus-percentage leases; and (4) step-up leases. The following discussion covers each type of lease in some detail.

Flat- or Fixed-Rent Lease

The *flat- or fixed-rent lease* sets the tenant's rent for the entire term of the lease. The tenant has one unchangeable sum payable as rent to the landlord. The owner cannot increase or decrease that amount during the term. Few shopping centers offer fixed leases, because, with them, inflation would quickly erode the profits of the investment. Shopping centers that do offer these leases, however, generally do so in one or more of the following circumstances:

The tenant has just begun in business and is looking for a way to experiment in the retail market.

The leasehold term is extremely short (for example, six months), and the lease states that the tenant may extend or renew the term, subject to the landlord's right to adjust the rental schedule.

The shopping center will benefit from the tenant's general retail appeal, which makes the owner more willing to grant concessions. Most landlords in this situation, in turn, charge the smaller tenants proportionately more for rent. The landlord hopes that these higher rents will counter the concessions—and that the smaller tenants will oblige because of the consuming public that the anchors will draw to the center. As noted in earlier chapters, however, with costs spiraling and consumer buying power dwindling in today's economy, major tenants stand in a less favorable position for obtaining such concessions. Smaller tenants are also objecting more vehemently to these arrangements. As a result, these types of concessions are becoming more rare.

The shopping center has a high vacancy factor, is under construction, or has just been built. Immediate tenant occupancy becomes more critical than concerns about whether rents are up to fair market value.

Each of these situations symbolizes bargaining strength between the landlord and tenant. In general, the owner suffers from the financial outcome of a fixed-rent arrangement. A fixed rent assumes that the manager and owner have estimated all future costs, such as maintenance, insurance, taxes, depreciation, and advertising; that they have accounted for inflation; and that they have included all these costs in the rent. The market is changeable and unpredictable, however, and property owners can never be certain that fixed rents will cover their costs sufficiently. Tenants also suffer some of the consequences since the center owner may lack the necessary income to maintain and promote the property.

Most fixed-rent leases do not require that the tenant pay directly for the center's operating expenses or participate in the merchants' association. Nevertheless, the landlord may consider these costs in developing the fixed-rent schedule.

Finally, some tenants agree to a fixed rental rate that is higher than current rental values, hoping that over the long term, they will be in a better position than if they had agreed to a percentage lease.

Percentage-Only Lease

The *percentage-only lease* bases the amount of rent payable each month on the tenant's gross income from the preceding month or months. Thus, rent fluctuates according to the amount of business that the tenant generates. A percentage-only lease requires no fixed-minimum rent. The lease has strict reporting standards, granting the landlord the right, if necessary, to audit the tenant's records. In this arrangement, the tenant's ability to market its merchandise relates directly to the rent structure. Both parties have similar concerns about whether the retailer will succeed.

Besides paying a percentage rent, depending on the lease, the tenant may be subject to one or more of the following obligations:

Payment of a pro rata portion of taxes, insurance, and common area dues.

Required membership in and dues payment to the merchants' association.

Payment of utilities. Most landlords, if they provide utilities through meters or submeters, will provide that each tenant pay only for actual consumption.

Some percentage-only leases arise in distress situations, notably the landlord's. Although some tenants may have sales volumes high enough to benefit the landlord, generally the percentage-only lease works in the favor of the tenant. The tenant's profits control the amount of each rent payment.

Percentage-only leases require strongly worded and enforceable clauses demanding that the tenant's business be of a continual nature. Most such leases also state the precise hours that the tenant must stay open for business. Again, it is in the landlord's interest that the merchant generate a high volume of business, and clauses that dictate various matters regarding the tenant's business are likely to improve the volume.

Finally, many percentage-only leases require that each tenant pay an estimated sum each month to apply toward the total obligation. If the percentage rent depends on gross sales from the preceding month, the tenant will be required to compute gross sales. Because of the time involved, if the lease does not stipulate that the tenant pay an estimate, the landlord will not receive the rental payment until the following month. Most such leases also require that the tenant submit a monthly statement of gross income for the preceding period and, in turn, pay any balance due. If the tenant has a refund coming for an estimated percentage rent paid in advance, most landlords use this credit to offset the tenant's next rent payment.

Few percentage-rent leases tie payment to net sales or net income. It is difficult to define the scope of each tenant's net income, and, with varied operating expenses, many tenants would find it harder yet to define their net income.

Many real estate practitioners use the terms "gross income" and "gross sales" interchangeably, but the words are not synonymous. *Gross income* refers to the receipt of all funds from any source. *Gross sales* refer to income generated by sales of merchandise or services. Problems can arise if a tenant sublets a portion of its premises. The sublease rental may be "income," but not necessarily a "sale." The lease should clarify the distinction between these two terms and also specify which will be used to settle matters between the tenant and landlord.

Gross income can be defined as broadly as both parties agree it should be identified. Gross income may include any or all of the following items:

Gross sales, receipts, charges, and revenues of every account, including sales and services for cash or charge, over the counter, telephone or mail order, collected or uncollected, and including charged-off accounts.
Income from vending machines, licensees, concessionaires, or transactions on the demised premises.
Service, finance, and interest charges on open accounts, receivables, and notes generated by the business.
Deposits for merchandise that are not refunded.

Most landlords and tenants agree to deduct the following items from gross sales to arrive at a base, or net sales total:

1. Sales taxes, use taxes, gross receipts taxes (but not income taxes, property taxes, or any other tax not directly levied on sales volume).
2. Refunds and allowances offered by tenants to their customers.
3. Exchanges of merchandise between tenants' stores.
4. Credits received in settlements of lost or damaged merchandise.
5. Workroom charges, such as for alterations and delivery, provided

that customers actually receive the services, and that they do not pay for them in the sales price.

6. Sales of trade fixtures, after the tenant has used them in its business operation.
7. Returns to shippers, distributors, and manufacturers.

Landlords have different methods for treating lay-by sales. Some consider the full purchase price as income on the date of the transaction, regardless of any payment or collection schedule. Others consider each payment that the customer makes as part of gross income, when the actual payment occurs. Still others follow the same method that the tenant uses to account for each sale.

In arriving at a gross income, the tenant and landlord might negotiate to exclude any of the following items from the total:

1. A percentage of sales to employees, for whom most retailers offer a discount.
2. A percentage of sales from major credit card sales. The credit card company charges the retailer a fee; the retailer, in turn, can receive credit from the center by presenting these charge slips.
3. Gift certificates, which the retailer might include in gross income at the time that the customer uses them, rather than when they were issued.

All percentage-rent leases state not only a fixed rent but also contain a clause regarding the landlord's auditing rights. The landlord must have open access to the tenant's books of account, including vouchers, receipts, checks, checking systems, cash register totals, tally sheets, bank accounts, salesbooks, and deposit slips. The tenant, therefore, would pay the cost of the audit, plus any percentage rent due. Some leases contain a clause that states the means for dealing with tenants who do not submit their monthly gross income reports in the appropriate format, as set out in the lease. Generally the tenant pays for the audit, regardless of the outcome.

Fixed-Minimum-Plus-Percentage Lease

Most shopping center owners use a lease that combines the two forms just discussed: the fixed-minimum rent and the percentage rent. It is called the *fixed-minimum-plus-percentage lease*. This type of lease, in conjunction with other rent provisions regarding common area maintenance, taxes, insurance, and merchants' association dues, is based on the premise that the shopping center is an attractive property and has few major problems. The retailer can assume that the center will offer an adequate market that will provide sufficient volume to offset rental payments.

Most shopping centers employ a system whereby the tenant pays a monthly fixed-minimum rent. On reaching a *breakeven point* in its business—the point at which the tenant's fixed rent is equal to its percentage rent—the tenant must assume the obligation of paying a percentage rent. In this context, the percentage rent could be called "overage rent," since it is rent paid in excess of a fixed minimum. The percentage rent is based either on gross income or gross sales; regardless of which total is used, the percentage always ties in with the fixed-minimum rent.

For example, assume a lease requires the tenant to pay a fixed-minimum rent of $12,000 annually and a percentage rent of 6 percent of gross income. The tenant does not have to begin paying percentage rent until gross income reaches $200,000— since 6 percent of $200,000 equals $12,000, which would be the annual fixed rent. For this tenant, therefore, $200,000 would be the breakeven point. The tenant pays the percentage rent only on the amount of gross income that exceeds $200,000 in the lease year.

Some landlords require that the tenant pay a fixed-minimum rent and a percentage rent without regard to a breakeven point. Usually with this arrangement, the fixed rent is quite low, and the gross income is flexible—notably for seasonal retailers.

The method for paying percentage rent varies. Most leases provide a monthly, rather than an annual, breakeven point. Thus, in the example above, instead of concentrating on an annual gross income of $200,000, the landlord and tenant would concern themselves with a monthly total. If one month the gross income exceeds $16,666.67 ($200,000 ÷ 12), the tenant would be obligated to pay a percentage rent of 6 percent on the excess amount. The tenant pays that percentage when the overage occurs rather than at the end of the year. If the gross income never again reaches the monthly breakeven point, the tenant does not have to pay the percentage rent. If, by year's end, total annual gross sales fail to reach the breakeven point of $200,000, the landlord must grant the tenant a refund or a credit for the overage in the one month it was paid. The landlord has had the tenant's money available to invest during that period.

To avoid accounting complications, the total amount of percentage rent is often determined at year's end, after the tenant has provided an annual statement of gross income or sales.

The tenant and landlord generally base the fixed-minimum rent on a fair rental value per square foot. Location within the center, tenant mix, and competition within the center's trade area will all influence the price of rent. A "fair" rent may be higher for one tenant than for another, although both may occupy the same number of square feet. For example, as noted in an earlier chapter, in an enclosed regional mall, a tenant occupying 100 square feet in a kiosk located in the center of the mall with maximum exposure to traffic would pay higher fixed-minimum and percentage rents per square foot than a tenant less strategically located.

Step-Up Agreement

Under the terms of a *step-up lease agreement* (also called a *graduated* or *graded lease*), the rental rate goes up or down, either in predetermined amounts or in accordance with a specified economic index, at specific times during the term of the lease. Retail tenants that are opening a new business or relocating into an untested market will probably find the graduated lease most beneficial for them. The property owner may set the initial rent low for the period when the retailer is establishing business and increase the payments as the tenant's business volume increases.

The property owner of a shopping center where rental rates are at market level and the space is highly sought after stands in the best position to demand graduated rental leases. Space at the center is highly marketable, giving the owner an advantage during lease negotiations. If the tenant will not accept the step-up rate, there will probably be another tenant that will accept it. Graduated leases may also help a center that has begun to decline in value. If the owner is trying to re-establish the center, offers of graduated leases may lure new tenants to the center. When the center reaches its optimal income level, the owner can increase rents, and with the increased rental income, the owner may be able to add improvements to the property.

Net Leases

The lease terms "net," "net-net" and "net-net-net" describe an allocation between landlord and tenant of the property's operating expenses.

A *gross lease* obligates the landlord to pay for real estate taxes, insurance, and exterior and structural maintenance expenses; the tenant pays none of these costs. The landlord can charge the tenant for some of these costs indirectly, through the fixed-minimum rent or a percentage-rent obligation. The landlord, committed to such an arrangement, must be careful in setting rents because inflationary costs are essentially unknown at the time of the lease's signing. Research could help determine what a reasonable rent would be.

A *net lease*, on the other hand, shifts the burden of property taxes to the tenant. The landlord retains the other, basic obligations of ownership.

A *net-net lease* shifts two burdens to the tenant: the real property taxes and the landlord's insurance costs. The landlord retains the obligation to pay for certain maintenance, repairs, and management fees.

Finally, a *net-net-net,* or *triple-net, lease*, shifts all financial burdens to the tenant: real property taxes, insurance, maintenance, and repair costs. Most landlords will pay expenses for maintaining the roof of the building and, in some cases, for repairing any of the building's structural flaws. Most net-net-net leases in a shopping center shift common area maintenance obligations (in addition to building maintenance) to the tenants. If the landlord is paying for some repairs, the lease is actually not a pure triple-net lease. Most shopping center leases are modified triple-net leases, where the landlord assumes responsibility for roof repairs and building structural repairs. Most landlords also continue to pay management fees.

Definitions of Measurements

Both the landlord and tenant must concern themselves with measurements, basically for two reasons: (1) to describe the square footage of the leased premises, and (2) to determine the tenant's pro rata share of operating and common area charges.

For the discussion here, the tenant's pro rata obligation for real property taxes, landlord's insurance, maintenance, repairs, and common area charges will be referred to collectively as "additional rent." Practitioners, however, commonly use the term "pro rata" to refer to each tenant's obligation.

A fraction (A/B) generally identifies the tenant's additional rent: the numerator (A) is the gross square footage of the tenant's premises (also called gross floor area); the denominator (B), the gross number of leasable square feet in the shopping center. The practitioner then multiplies this rent-adding fraction by the total cost of each item on an annual basis to determine the tenant's pro rata share of that cost. For example, a tenant occupying 5000 square feet of a 500,000 square foot shopping center would pay 0.010, or one percent, of the total cost of each item of additional rent.

Property managers define *floor area* as the total square feet of floor space in all store areas. Floor area measures from the exterior faces of outside walls to the center line of individual tenants' walls. The floor area thus defines the denominator in the pro rata fraction. Managers include in this total all outside selling or display areas as well as columns, stairs, escalators, elevators, dumbwaiters, conveyors, and loading docks and ramps. Tenants want the denominator to be as large as possible, since this reduces the fraction and their proportional share of additional rent.

Some property managers define the denominator as the total number of square feet in the retail center that is actually leased. In a center that consistently has many vacancies, therefore, a smaller denominator results, and so the tenant's pro rata share is greater. In effect, the tenant in this case is paying a share of the operating expenses for those store areas that are not occupied. This system is generally not acceptable to the tenant, since it reduces the landlord's incentive to locate more tenants for the vacant areas.

Some landlords reserve the right to separate the retail sales and service areas, and alter—up or down—the center's total area. Thus, they exert control over the denominator of the fraction, which implies that the tenant's rent may fluctuate. Likewise, a lease that does not specifically grant the landlord the power of control essentially prohibits the landlord from altering the total space. Many anchor tenants insist on the right to restrict the landlord from changing the denominator. Or they might demand that the landlord have their consent before any change goes into effect, even if the change means a reduced rent, or an increase in the denominator.

The total area in the leased portion is a gross area in a shell condition, which means that it includes all space, including that taken up by fixtures and displays. This total is the numerator of the fraction.

Most landlords add a provision to their leases that states that no measurement of the property will be taken unless the tenant requests it. Even then, the measurement will be in the "landlord's standard manner," that is, by the definition of floor area noted earlier. Some leases hold that if the tenant wants the floor area of the premises verified, that check must occur before the execution of the lease. Otherwise, the tenant's acceptance of the premises implies an approval of the measurement.

The property manager must be able to compute the total floor area of the center according to industry standards. Gross leasable area has been adopted as a measurement of the total floor area designed for tenant occupancy and their exclusive use. The gross leasable area differs from *gross floor area*, which includes space that is not used and occupied exclusively by individual tenants. This space, called the center's *common area*, includes public washrooms, corridors, stairways, equipment rooms, management offices, storage areas, lobbies and mall areas and parking areas. Common areas are not leasable to tenants, but these areas are essential to the operation of the center.

Tenant Improvements and Finish Allowance

Negotiations between landlord and tenant—to work toward an agreeable contract—begin. Chapter 9, "Lease Negotiations," will discuss this subject in detail. Among the first issues that the tenant and landlord will probably address if the center is still under construction will be the condition of the structure and the progress of construction.

For an established shopping center, the easiest transition occurs when the tenant agrees to accept the premises "as is." The concern will turn to improvements that the tenant will request. Therefore, most tenants must provide the property owner with specifications that show proposed changes before physical changes to the space begin. The two parties also should concur on a letter agreement (sometimes called a "Consent to Alterations Letter"), which specifies the terms and conditions on tenant changes done to the property. The letter should demand the following items:

1. The tenant should bear the costs of construction, although some landlords will agree to pay the tenant a fixed allowance fee.
2. The tenant will take every precaution to avoid a mechanical lien or a claim against the property as a result of the work. The tenant may be required to provide a completion bond for this purpose.
   (A *completion bond* is a bond obtained from a bonding or insurance company. The bond provides assurance to the property owner that if the general contractor or tenant exhausts its financial resources to pay for improvements on the leased

premises, the bonding company will step in and pay to complete the job.)

3. The tenant will notify the landlord before work begins so that appropriate notices can be posted at the center.
4. The tenant will provide waivers of mechanical liens on demand. This assures the landlord that the tenant is paying contractors, laborers, and material suppliers.
5. The landlord has the right to approve materials and contractors and to discharge contractors, laborers, or employees, for due cause.
6. The tenant agrees to hold the landlord harmless from losses or damages that might result from the improvement work.
7. The tenant agrees to purchase workmen's compensation and liability insurance. Also, the tenant's contractor will name the landlord and the property management firm as additional insured.
8. The tenant assumes liability for defects in construction.
9. If the work requires the use of the owner's facilities, the tenant will pay a reasonable fee, plus the actual costs for those services.
10. The tenant's contractors and laborers must not interfere with other workers who may be on the property. Some centers also require only union labor.
11. The landlord will designate times when work may and may not be performed and, within reason, has the right to change these times.
12. The agreement should restrict loud construction (for example, core drilling, heavy installation), and should contain a provision stating that no one can enter the premises without being accompanied by someone from the management staff.
13. The landlord reserves the right to revoke any of the terms should the tenant fail to meet any such terms of the agreement.
14. The agreement should include a disclaimer, stating that the landlord is not the tenant's agent or partner and in no other way— but as a landlord—is participating in the work.
15. A breach of any of the terms of the letter agreement will be considered a violation of the lease, and the landlord will have the same rights as in the event of default.

If the tenant does not accept the premises in their "as is" condition, the concern turns to the landlord's obligations regarding improvements. The situation can take on two forms: (1) The tenant provides all plans and supervises construction. The landlord acts only as a financing agent, either by paying for the improvements up to some maximum or by serving as the tenant's construction lender. (2) The tenant provides the specifications, but the landlord controls construction. Most landlords in this situation pay for all construction, with no ceiling. Some practitioners call this arrangement a turn-key operation since the tenant, except for providing displays and inventory, can simply "turn the key" and open for business.

Many problems occur in preleasing, when space is leased in a center under construction. Tenants must plan the opening of their businesses around at least a partial completion of the center. Problems often arise when the developer lacks experience, or has little control over the general contractor. Staggered rent obligations are usually the result.

For example, the lease may require that the tenant pay only percentage rent until the center becomes 80 percent leased, at which time the landlord can charge the tenant the accrued, fixed-minimum rent. Some landlords charge tenants for the percentage rent, without any fixed minimum, up to the time that the anchor tenants open for business. This arrangement requires a clear definition of an anchor tenant. It is best to define the anchor tenant quantitatively, by a certain number of square feet, rather than by name. This avoids any borderline controversies should the originally scheduled anchor back out of the deal. Also, if negotiations break down with one anchor tenant, and the owner finds a substitute to occupy the same space, the satellite tenants' obligations to pay a fixed-minimum rent would stay the same.

Some tenants may demand the right to cancel their leases without penalty if the center is not 80 percent leased by a given date. In a situation such as this, the developer will be under considerable pressure to ensure that the contractor will complete construction by the due date; the leasing agent will be pressured to find a sufficient number of suitable and stable tenants.

Many leases defer all rental obligations during the so-called fixturization period. A typical clause would read as follows:

Within _____ days after delivery of possession of the demised premises to tenant by landlord, tenant will, at its own cost and expense, install such new fixtures and equipment in the demised premises as are reasonably required to equip and operate a store for the purposes in Article _____ (the "use" clause) and within _____ days after delivery, tenant will open and operate its business, regardless of whether such date is the actual commencement date of the lease. Notwithstanding any other provision to the contrary, tenant's obligation to pay fixed-minimum rent and additional rent (except utilities) shall be deferred until the _____ day after said delivery or until tenant opens for business, whichever is first to occur.

The landlord can modify this clause to guarantee that the tenant will not open for business before the official starting date, without the landlord's consent. Should the store open earlier than the stipulated date, the lease would become effective immediately, although the terms would not change.

The owner must be extremely careful whenever a tenant receives a finish allowance. The landlord should reimburse the tenant for all expenses, but only after the tenant has shown the landlord copies of paid invoices and mechanics lien releases. The landlord should also request from the tenant a list of all contractors, subcontractors, and laborers, who might acquire mechanics lien rights during the improvement project. The landlord should ensure that each tenant has issued a release. The landlord should also reserve the right to pay construction costs through checks made payable jointly to the tenant and the appropriate recipient.

Provisions Unique to Shopping Center Leases

As discussed earlier in this chapter, the shopping center investment stands apart from any other type of property investment. The shopping center contains retail stores, and the stores stand interdependently to one another and to the structure. The leases for space in the center, therefore, demand clauses not found in other real estate contracts. Following is a discussion of some provisions that are unique to shopping centers.

Store Hours Clause

A well-managed shopping center should present a unified image, and to maintain consistency, all stores should be open for business during the same hours. A lease should contain clauses that pertain to minimum and maximum hours of operation. Yet, the clause for minimum hours must not be too specific; retailers need a certain amount of flexibility in their operating hours, especially during peak seasonal periods. There are three variations for this, and they are as follows:

1. The tenant will remain open at least during the same hours when specific anchor tenants are open.
2. The tenant will remain open for business at least during the period when retailers who represent more than 50 percent of the gross leasable floor area choose to stay open.

3. The tenant will remain open for business during all hours that the landlord decides are necessary, and those hours are often stated in the lease. For example, the hours may be Monday through Friday, 10:00 a.m. to 9:00 p.m.; Saturday, 10:00 a.m. to 6:00 p.m.; and Sunday, noon to 6:00 p.m.

If the tenant fails to comply with the store hours provision, the landlord faces an awkward situation. The tenant has actually violated a part of the contract. Yet, compared to other possible offenses, this is a minor breach. If the tenant pays rent regularly and is otherwise an excellent tenant, most landlords would hesitate before spoiling an otherwise good relationship. In some leases, the parties agree that in the event of this kind of violation, when the landlord does not want to use full legal means to cure the problem and yet is entitled to some retribution, the court can issue an injunction ordering the tenant to comply with the minimum hours clause. Even if both parties agree that an injunction would be appropriate, however, the court may decline to issue one, especially since the landlord does have another legal option—namely, eviction.

It is extremely difficult to translate the tenant's breach into monetary terms. The tenant's failure to comply might reduce the amount of percentage rent that the landlord would receive, but it would be extremely difficult to put a dollar figure on the amount. Moreover, there are negative effects that one tenant's breach may have on the shopping center operation as a whole and on the owner's ability to impose regulations on the other tenants. Complying tenants might complain that the owner is taking no action against the resistant tenant.

At the other extreme, as noted, are maximum hours. There may be a seasonal tenant who desires to stay open beyond the normal hours of the center's operation. Most leases do not deal in terms of maximum hours of the center, and a landlord probably cannot force a tenant to close at a specific hour if the lease contains no such provision. The landlord will not want to pay any additional operating costs that result from only one or two tenants staying open beyond the normal operating hours of the center. The lease should cover this contingency. A common example of this is a restaurant tenant in an enclosed mall; most such tenants must stay open beyond normal mall hours.

Continuous Occupancy Clause

In order to maximize the level of percentage rents, the lease should require the tenant to occupy the premises continuously throughout the term of the lease. This is the function and purpose of the *continuous occupancy clause.* Vacancies and store closures have an extremely negative effect on the rest of the center. Even if a tenant continues to pay a fixed-minimum rent, common area dues, taxes, and insurance, the center owner will confront numerous problems in this situation. When tenants leave space vacant, the shopping center loses its sense of vibrancy and prosperity. The center comes to resemble a downtown area filled with abandoned buildings. The public becomes less inclined to shop there, even if the shopping area still offers other convenient and well-stocked stores.

A tenant who agrees to the terms of a lease that permit continuous occupancy of store space has an obligation to fulfill those terms. Should a tenant vacate the space, the landlord has rights beyond eviction and lease cancellation. With the aid of an attorney, the landlord can obtain possession of the space, cancel the lease, and obtain either a total rent acceleration or payment for damages.

The practical problem arises over enforcement of the continuous occupancy clause. The landlord would not want to evict the tenant, if this would mean losing the amount of rent that is being paid. Most landlords handle the situation by trying to learn the causes for the tenant's actions, accepting whatever rent is possible, and above all, actively seeking a replacement tenant.

Continuous Operation Clause

Related to the minimum hours and continuous occupancy provisions is the *continuous operation clause.* Many leases include the three clauses as a single paragraph or article and refer to the clause as the ongoing business clause.

In general terms, the continuous operation clause requires the tenant to keep the store fully stocked at inventory levels equal either to: (1) those when the tenant first opened for business; (2) the inventory of like stores that the tenant operates in other locations; or (3) similar stores in the area. The clause also may impose requirements regarding staffing, service, and managerial supervision.

Common Area Charges Clause

The *common area charges clause* stipulates the amount that tenants and the landlord will pay for the maintenance of the common area. A shopping center's *common area* can be defined as any area within the legal boundaries of the shopping center that one or more tenants will use in common. This area includes one or more of the following:

1. Parking lots, driveways, malls (open and closed), and access and perimeter roads.
2. Loading platforms and underground passageways.
3. Service corridors, stairways, elevators, arcades, and exterior walks and balconies.
4. Directory equipment.
5. Subsurface storm and sanitary sewers and drains and utility lines.
6. Landscaped areas.
7. Washrooms, comfort rooms, drinking fountains, toilets, and other public facilities.
8. Bus stations and taxi stands.

Most landlords insist on their right to add or delete areas from the list of common areas in their centers. Many shopping center leases classify maintenance costs for common areas as additional rent.

The agreements between the parties and the landlord's ability to recognize all maintenance costs, therefore, are the only limitations to the costs and overhead that the tenants will pay.

Within this context, common area maintenance includes any one or more of the following items:

1. General maintenance and repairs, resurfacing, painting, restriping, cleaning, sweeping, and janitorial services.
2. Maintenance and repair of sidewalks, curbs, signs, roof, sprinkler systems (both fire and landscaping), planting, landscaping, directional signs, mall and other directories, and other markers and bumpers.
3. Maintenance and repair of any fire protection system, lighting system, storm drainage and sewer systems, and any other utility systems.
4. Cost of personnel, including requirements imposed by a collective bargaining agreement or by federal or state employer regulations.
5. Real and personal property taxes and assessments on the improvements and land contained in the common area.
6. Depreciation of costs involved with operating machinery and equipment, if owned, or rent paid for such machinery and equipment. The standard in the industry is to limit this cost to the value of the item's useful life. Therefore, tenants generally are not required to pay the entire price of equipment in the year acquired.

MANAGING THE SHOPPING CENTER

7. Adequate public liability and fire and extended coverage insurance for the common area, including broad form all-risk coverage, or other casualty insurance considered appropriate by the landlord.
8. Costs of trash receptacles and trash removal.
9. The costs of auditing total common area maintenance expenses.
10. An allowance for the supervision of the common areas, usually expressed as a percentage of the total annual expenses.
11. The right of the landlord to arrange with independent contractors to provide any of these services.

Enclosed shopping malls impose additional expenses. These costs include those for maintaining the roof, beams, walls, storefronts, doors, and automatic doors; HVAC costs; and expenses for replacing plate glass that is part of the common area mall. Most leases allow the landlord to estimate all common area maintenance expenses on an annual basis; each tenant then must pay a monthly pro rata portion of the estimated costs.

This charge will be readjusted when a year-end audit shows the preceding year's actual costs. A tenant who has paid more than necessary receives a credit in the amount of the excess for the next rent installment. The tenant receives a refund only if it occurs at the end of the lease term. For underpayment, the tenant will pay the shortage within 30 days after receiving the audit.

Ideally, the manager will estimate the annual costs such that tenants will not underpay more than 5 or 10 percent. This requires careful cost planning, however, and the manager should project adjustments for anticipated cost increases.

Many anchor tenants try to obtain the right to approve any change that would increase the amount of common area. The less space, the lower the common pro rata maintenance costs. For example, if the landlord wanted to add a kiosk retail operation for the benefit of the mall area, the anchor tenant would seek to obtain a veto right against such actions. The property manager and owner must take extreme care, however, in granting the anchor tenant any control of the common area.

The landlord should attempt to retain control of access, use, and cost of the center's parking lots. Those rights will include the following: (1) an ability to restrict access to certain parking lots during given hours of the day to prevent center employees from parking in choice slots; (2) the right to alter the total number of available spaces, subject to any local governmental regulations regarding minimum spaces; and (3) the right to control the amount of any parking charge. Most centers that do charge a fee for parking combine the fee with a validation system so that the store where the shopper purchases an item will offer a reimbursement for parking.

Brokerage Clause

Many shopping center owners hire their own staffs, including their own leasing agents, who handle the job that would otherwise be handled by a broker. Nevertheless, there are some owners who hire brokers, and when brokers are involved, the landlord wants a guarantee, through the *brokerage clause*, which states that the broker is paid only if the tenant takes possession and pays rent. In the lease, the landlord generally tries to gain assurance that only one broker will be paid, and at that, will be paid only in accordance with the specific arrangements that have been made with the broker.

There are two purposes for a brokerage clause. First, the landlord wants the tenant to identify all brokers with whom the tenant has been dealing. In most cases, the tenant has dealt with only one broker, and that broker is the same broker that the landlord has agreed to pay. In some situations, however, more than one broker may contact the landlord about the same tenant, and the landlord may be pressured to pay two brokers. The brokerage clause will protect the landlord against this possibility.

The second objective in the brokerage clause involves an indemnity purpose. Through this clause, the tenant is asked to indemnify the landlord from liability against brokers that might arise out of the transaction.

Merchants' Association Clause

Many shopping centers set up a merchants' association, which handles the publicity and promotion of the center. This is the reason that most landlords request a *merchants' association clause*. The success of these associations depends largely on the support of the tenants at the center. Most such associations are organized as nonprofit corporations. The landlord may donate funds, but the tenants generally contribute most of the association's operating income.

The merchants' association has its own bylaws, which dictate the tenants' monthly membership dues. The association provides retailers with a means for promoting their own goods and the shopping center. Many shopping center leases require membership in the merchants' association.

The characteristics of a merchants' association clause include the following:

1. The tenant agrees to join the merchants' association and to participate in its activities throughout the term of the lease.
2. Either the board of directors of the merchants' association or a majority approval of the tenants is necessary for requesting participation by all tenants in a specific program. Most leases define "majority" in terms of the number of tenants, rather than by the total number of square feet that the tenants occupy.
3. The requirement that the association will pay for promotional employees, most of whom work for the landlord, is included in the clause.
4. Tenants must agree to advertise in association circulars, publications, and newspaper advertising. If the tenant fails to submit the required copy, the landlord may prepare it and charge the tenant for the service.

The landlord should try to maintain control of the association's promotional activities. Large shopping centers may sponsor many grand-scale promotions, but any type of center can be effective in its promotional efforts. Promotion might include sidewalk sales, annual clearance sales, seasonal sales, fashion shows, or novelty sales. Most leases limit the tenant's obligation to participate in advertising campaigns—such campaigns can become quite a time and cost burden for the tenant. Most landlords insist on the right to vote on matters regarding the association. Nevertheless, in most shopping center leases, the property manager or the owner is given veto power over activities in the common area. The property manager may veto an activity that appears to present too great a risk; for example, hot-air balloon rides.

Some tenants may demand a clause that provides that the merchants' association's bylaws will not affect the tenants' rights as stated in the lease. However, it is rare that such a clause will flatly prohibit changes in the bylaws that may affect merchants' association dues.

Advertising, Signs, and Graphics Clause

Every tenant's involvement, in some way, affects the end product, which is a smoothly functioning, prosperous real estate investment. Therefore, most landlords put controls on tenants' advertising and on their use of signs and graphics, through an *advertising, signs, and graphics clause*. Some landlords will insist, for example, on controlling the use of display signs or on approving the content of advertising materials. This is done such that all promotions will be consistent with local zoning ordinances. Restrictions might include any of the following:

1. Sign locations. The landlord must approve the posting of any exterior advertising sign. In most cases, the landlord will also want to approve the format and content of any sign.
2. Sign format. Most landlords retain the right to approve the posting of any permanent sign outside the tenant's premises. This assures the landlord that the development's design will be uniform. Some landlords even establish limits on size, location, and means of illumination.
3. Sign removal. The tenant agrees in the lease to remove any sign, at the landlord's request. If the tenant refuses to do so, the landlord has the right to enter the premises and remove the sign. Exercising this "right," however, may invite legal problems. Confronted with a noncomplying tenant, the landlord may be able to obtain a court injunction—which would make such an entrance legal.
4. Seasonal sign. The landlord may require each tenant to bear the cost of displaying signs that relate to seasonal sales. The landlord must approve or veto the use of these signs within a short period of time; for example, 48 hours.
5. Reputation. Most landlords retain control of the content of advertising, to prevent slanderous statements that could harm the reputation of the landlord or of the shopping center.

In sum, the lease gives the landlord the right to review each tenant's advertising signs and advertising programs. The bases for review include quantity, quality, type, design, color, size, style, composition, material, location, means of illumination, and appearance.

Parking Regulations

Asked why they prefer shopping centers to other business districts, consumers invariably will say something such as this: "Because the center has free and convenient parking." "Convenient" is nearly always true; "free" is true in most cases. Some centers offer free parking only if the customer makes a purchase at the center. Whatever the case, the landlord must maintain almost unlimited control of parking. Shopping centers—from major regionals to local strip centers and specialty centers—all rely on automobile traffic for exposure and easy access.

Most shopping center leases include the following controls in regard to parking:

1. Restraints on the terms and locations of tenants' loadings and deliveries.
2. Controls on center employees' parking, regarding location within the lot.
3. Parking restrictions, in regard to time (for example, two hours) and use (for example, handicapped only, loading zones).
4. Many landlords reserve the right to charge a fee for parking. As mentioned, some require customers to purchase an item at the center before they can park for free.
5. The landlord generally has the right to obtain the license plate numbers of all of the tenants' employees. When parking is congested, the management staff must try to determine whether all of the cars in the lot belong to employees or shoppers, or if many of them are unauthorized to park there. Often, the landlord may levy a fine against a tenant whose employees violate the center's parking rules.
6. The landlord has towing rights. In nearly all cases, the right to tow away a car that is illegally parked in the center's lot requires clearly posted notices and coordination with the local police.

Notice Clause

The proper notice procedure is often a central issue in determining whether the tenant has defaulted. The purpose of the *notice clause* is to establish the proper method for the tenant to give notice. Nearly all such clauses state that only a written notice will be sufficient. The clause should state that the notice will be valid only if sent by U.S. mail and then, only if mailed by certified or registered mail, return receipt requested.

Some parties want the notice to become effective on the date that the notice is written; others, on the date that the notice is received. The party giving notice should specify which date is intended. However, it is suggested that the clause state that notice will be considered given on the delivery date specified on the mail receipt. This way, the notice date will not be altered because of possible mishandling by the postal service.

Holdover Clause

The *holdover clause* defines appropriate action to take when the tenant fails to vacate the premises by the last day of the leased term when a lease renewal has not occurred. This situation, which may seem unusual, actually occurs quite often. Without the clause, the rights and obligations of both parties would be left to conjecture.

The landlord or property manager should make it clear to each tenant, from the very start, that neither will ever assume that a tenant wants its lease renewed. When the lease expires, and it has not been renewed, the tenant's occupancy is over. Only a written amendment or official extension of the lease can guarantee the tenant's right to remain in the space. If the tenant is maintaining occupancy through month-to-month rent payments, the landlord has the right to end the tenancy by giving appropriate notice, which is usually 30 days.

Many holdover clauses state that a tenant illegally remaining in a space agrees to pay the landlord monthly rent plus additional rent, equal to twice the amount paid during the last month of the term. The clause might also provide that as long as the tenant remains in the center, it must continue to abide by the terms of the lease, except for the amount of rent—which may be increased or decreased.

The general rule is that the landlord can start proceedings to evict the holdover tenant, provided that the landlord does not accept further rent from the tenant. Once the landlord has accepted rent from a tenant, a tenant-landlord relationship has been created—even if the basis of that relationship is month-to-month. Once the tenant has paid rent, however, the landlord may lose the right to evict the tenant.

Mode of Rent Payment Clause

Some tenants may want to pay rent from a checking account that lies in the name of a different business. The landlord, in this case, faces the dilemma of accepting payment from an unknown third party. Yet, the tenant might claim that the landlord is indirectly attempting to evict the tenant by refusing to accept the rent payment. The lease, therefore, should contain a clause that states that the landlord can refuse any rent payment that does not come directly from the tenant, and that the landlord can return the check from a third party, demanding payment from the proper account. Should the tenant refuse to submit a new check or another acceptable payment, the landlord can take appropriate action for nonpayment of rent.

Some clauses in a shopping center lease serve only a restrictive function, restricting in some way, the tenant's business operation. The *use clause* is one of four such restrictive covenants that will be discussed here.

Leasing techniques have become an art. In the past, the attitudes "rent it and forget it" and "lease at any cost, just keep it full" prevailed. Today, practitioners know much more about the subject. Studies have shown that a strong tenant mix is one of the most vital elements to a successful shopping center, and landlords have become far more discerning in determining to which tenants they will lease space.

Shopping center tenants need not stand in complementary positions to one another. Two retail shoe stores can coexist; each can offer a wide selection, and ultimately, both will help to create a more desirable shopping location. The range in price, quality, and selection within one structure serves as an ideal promotion of the shopping center. This concept, however, can apply only to certain types of merchandise.

How the tenants use the leased premises, therefore, is an essential part of a strong tenant mix. The use clause limits the type of business that a tenant can conduct on the premises. The clause might also prohibit the tenant from changing its trade name without the landlord's consent.

To be effective, a use clause must be specific. Such general phrases as "assorted accessories," "related items," or "high quality" can lead to problems of interpretation in the event of a dispute. The manager should be aware of the *general construction rule* of any written document, which holds that the person who drafts the document will be held responsible for ambiguities in the language of the document.

The manager and owner must establish a standard for any limitations on multiple uses or on direct competitors. For example, a jeweler may want to sell costume jewelry along with a line of diamond pieces. Yet the owner's main purpose in leasing to the jeweler was to add a diamond dealer to the tenant mix. The lease may limit the amount of costume jewelry that this particular tenant can sell, limited by a percentage of the total inventory. Or the lease may put limitations on the total display space in the premises that can be used for the less expensive lines. Here again, both parties should avoid vague terms, such as "limited amount of" or "some" costume jewelry.

The tenant's breach of the use clause can result either in a court injunction or an action to evict. The landlord would have great difficulty in placing a monetary value on the tenant's violation.

Exclusive Use Clause

Leases apply to the specifics of each case. Yet one general rule should prevail in all leases: The landlord should resist granting exclusive uses of the property to any tenants. Another restrictive covenant, an *exclusive use clause*, prohibits the landlord from leasing space in the center to any tenants whose "primary business" is the sale of specified merchandise or services. The tenant's motive is to restrict competition. For the landlord, however, granting an exclusive use clause—especially to a long-term tenant—greatly hinders leasing progress. Ultimately, such clauses can adversely affect the marketability of the shopping center.

For example, assume that the tenant—a men's ready-to-wear clothing store in a newly developed center—obtains, in its 20-year lease, an exclusive right to sell this merchandise. The tenant could obtain the clause because construction has not been completed, the center is not entirely leased, or the landlord is pressured to fill space. Five or 10 years later, however, the market for men's ready-to-wear clothing expands: Several new businesses enter the area, and the demand for clothing increases. The local economy is prospering. The exclusive use clause would prevent leasing to other stores that would compete directly with the tenant holding the exclusive.

If the landlord does grant an exclusive to a tenant, it is best if the clause states that no other store in the center may sell *primarily* a specific item. Many tenants may sell the *same* items. From a practical standpoint, department stores are not granted exclusives, nor do they want them, because of their fear of restraint of trade litigation. One product per tenant may work successfully with few problems in neighborhood centers, but a community or regional project could not proceed beyond the planning stage with this approach.

Actually, shopping center practitioners have found that competition in the retail shoe industry increases customer traffic. Shoppers tend to "comparison shop," especially when they buy items such as shoes—which explains why, in many centers, retail shoe tenants are located together in the same part of the center. Many shoe store retailers, on the other hand, are unaware of this effect or do not believe that it actually occurs, and prefer to be located apart from other shoe retailers.

In some instances, exclusive clauses can help both the landlord and tenant. In agreeing to lease in an uncompleted center, the tenant may deserve a benefit for taking the risk of locating in the new development. However, the following guidelines should limit such an agreement:

1. The exclusive should be in effect for only a limited period; for example, it should expire on the last day of the fifth year of the leasehold term.
2. The exclusivity stated in the clause may be gradually reduced; for example, at the end of three years, the landlord may lease to one new restaurant; at the end of five years, to two new restaurants.
3. The exclusive may be defined by square feet; for example, restaurants occupying less than 1,000 square feet would be permitted but not restaurants larger than 5,000 square feet.
4. The exclusive may be limited by scope; for example, table service would not exceed 30 tables and could not serve liquor, except beer and wine.
5. The exclusive may be limited in distance; for example, no restaurant would be permitted within 1,500 feet of the existing tenant.

These restrictions are critical additions to an exclusive clause. Without them, the relationship between the landlord and tenant is likely to suffer. Many landlords will agree to an exclusive clause, then regret it, and eventually try to break the lease or hold the tenant in default. If the tenant has otherwise benefited the center, the landlord would not want to be forced to resort to these means.

Radius Clause

The *radius clause* is another restrictive covenant. It prohibits a tenant from opening and operating another business, whether competitive or not, within a certain radius of the shopping center. There are two main reasons for such a clause: (1) It restricts competition that might take away sales from the center, reducing the tenant's gross income and percentage rent; and (2) It removes a tenant's urge to refer business to another, less expensive location, using the center location primarily as a way of keeping out competition.

Both landlord and tenant must be careful that they are not violating a state or federal antitrust law. Exclusive and radius clauses restrict business activity, and federal and state laws attempt to control any agreement that lessens competition.

Use clauses—with their basic purpose of guaranteeing a beneficial tenant mix—cause the fewest number of antitrust problems. The general attitude is that any restraint caused by these clauses is either insignificant, or its effects impossible to measure.

Exclusivity and radius clauses, however, have far more profound consequences, and such clauses have been the frequent subject of litigation. The obvious purpose in these clauses is to restrict competition—and that stands in direct conflict with antitrust legislation.

Yet, whether an exclusive clause actually violates an antitrust statute will depend on the size of the shopping center and the area's retail market. Generally, the larger the center and the more expansive the terms of the exclusive clause, the greater the likelihood that an antitrust law has been violated.

The radius clause also makes the landlord and tenant susceptible to violations of antitrust laws. The risk depends on the radius restriction stated in the lease and the extent of the tenant's market control. A nonchain retailer with a radius restriction of five to 10 miles has little effect on competition. However, the larger the store and the greater the radius, the higher the risk.

Escalation Clause

The *escalation clause* is the fourth restrictive covenant. In today's inflationary economy, the escalation clause offers some relief for landlords, who are greatly burdened with cost increases on all items. Tenants resist the clause, but today they would have a hard time finding a lease that does not contain one.

The clause allows flexibility in what otherwise would be a fixed rate for rent throughout the lease term. One of the benefits of a long-term lease is that the rights and duties of each party remain fixed throughout the term. Both landlord and tenant benefit from the arrangement—since it helps to bring stability to the entire operation. On the other hand, once the fee is set, the landlord could get caught in an upward price spiral.

Likewise, should the business community suffer a severe economic slowdown, tenants would be burdened with extremely high rents. The escalation clause is designed to work both ways and actually can benefit both parties. Both parties would suffer if the rent were either too high to be affordable for the tenant, or too low to be profitable for the owner.

An agreement that permits the landlord to raise the fixed-minimum rent unilaterally during the term needs a basis on which to determine the increase. The *Consumer Price Index (CPI)* is often used for that purpose. The Consumer Price Index, a figure constructed by the U.S. Bureau of Labor Statistics, measures consumer purchasing power by comparing current costs of goods to those of a selected base year. An escalation clause allows changes in the tenant's rental payments, coinciding with any increases or decreases in inflation. In practical terms, changes in the economy may not directly reflect actual operating expenses. The CPI, for example, during one year may show sharp increases in medical care and food costs. These increases would not have a direct impact on the shopping center's expenses, yet the tenant would be required to pay a higher rent because of them. The implication is that any cost increase eventually will have an effect on all prices.

The full economic theory behind the indices goes beyond the scope of this chapter. Therefore, the text will describe only the most common types of escalation clauses: (1) an increase tied to an established index, generally published by the Bureau of Labor Statistics of the U.S. Department of Labor; and (2) an increase tied directly to operating expenses passed on to the tenant.

Index Escalation Clause

An *index escalation clause* is a lease provision under which the rent rate is adjusted to reflect changes in a specified cost-of living index. The clause has the following characteristics:

1. *Definition of the index.* The landlord generally selects the index. That index should reflect the most accurate measure of the cost of living in the center's metropolitan area. For example, in the Los Angeles area, the "Consumer Price Index Specified for All Items for All Urban Consumers for the Los Angeles—Long Beach Area as Published by the Department of Labor's Bureau of Labor Statistics" will be applied. It is possible to use another category in the same CPI index—for example, "Urban Wage Earners and Clerical Workers," instead of "Urban Consumers"; or "Housing (Rent),"

instead of the broader "All Items" category. Other variations are possible. The CPI also contains information on increases for "All Items Less Shelter" and "All Items Less Energy." The exclusion of any one item will probably result in a lower percentage increase and ultimately a lower increase passed on to the tenant.

2. *Replacement index.* The clause also notes an alternative index—the replacement index—to be used should the specified index be altered or the Department of Labor change the statistical base of the index. The clause may indicate a conversion formula, provided by the Department of Labor, should the index be converted to a different standard of reference. If the index ceases to be published, the landlord and tenant may agree on another reliable publication that presents the same information.

3. *Percentage increase.* Most percentage increases are fractions, with a numerator that indicates the index figure in December of each calendar year and a denominator that indicates the figure in the month in which the tenant will begin to pay rent. The parties may agree that the increase will come only at fixed periods during the term. In this case, the numerator of the fraction would be limited to the figure published in December of the fifth lease year, tenth lease year, or any time interval. The percentage increase in the CPI multiplied by the fixed-minimum rent will reflect the landlord's increase in dollar income, less any prior, cost-of-living increase.

4. *Comparative statement.* Most landlords prepare an annual comparison between the numerator, denominator, percentage increase, and dollar increase in fixed-minimum rent. Upon receiving the statement, the tenant is obligated to pay one-twelfth of its share of the total amount, with each monthly payment of rent, until the next CPI determination is made.

Pass-Through Escalation Clause

The *pass-through escalation clause* has the following characteristics:

1. *Operating costs defined.* Operating costs include all wage and labor costs, whether workers are employed by the landlord or an independent contractor; increases in hours of employment, insurance taxes, and fringe benefits; and costs of utilities, fuel, building supplies, insurance, service contracts, and common area maintenance.

2. *Percentage increase.* A fraction expresses the percentage increase: The numerator is the total square feet in the tenant's premises, and the denominator is the total square feet in the whole center. Either gross floor area or gross leasable area can express this total. The

tenant's pro rata share then equals the amount of the increase multiplied by the fraction.

3. *Payment.* The landlord uses a comparative statement approach, which works much like the index method. Here again, the tenant each month must pay one-twelfth of the total annual pro rata increase, until the landlord provides a new comparative statement.

Some landlords combine the cost-of-living adjustment along with a pro rata share of operating expenses. For example, a tenant may be required to pay a pro rata share of common area maintenance changes, landlord's taxes, and insurance, plus any increases based on the CPI.

Security Deposits

A *security deposit* is a sum of money that the tenant pays to the landlord, protecting the landlord from the tenant's possible default. The security deposit ensures the tenant's performance of certain obligations under the lease. The deposit presumes the possibility of the tenant's breach of the lease.

Specifically, the *security deposit* clause states the following guidelines:

1. The landlord may use the deposit for any tenant breach, which is most often for delinquent, or unpaid rent.
2. The landlord may use the deposit only in the amount needed to cure the problem; otherwise the landlord must return the money to the tenant. Many states prohibit the use of nonrefundable security deposits in commercial and residential leases.
3. If the landlord does use the deposit, the tenant's failure to replenish it will be considered a breach of the lease.
4. When the landlord returns the deposit, it comes without interest. The landlord also reserves the right to commingle the deposit with its own funds.
5. If the center is sold, the tenant agrees to deal with the new owner for return of the security deposit.
6. The tenant must not assign the security deposit to a third party.

A variation of the security deposit is the "execution" bonus. Here, the tenant agrees to pay a one-time, fixed deposit, as an additional incentive to encourage the landlord to sign the lease. There is no security deposit. However, the execution bonus relates directly to the execution of the lease and therefore is equivalent to additional rent; it is not refundable. Some landlords have found that this arrangement works more smoothly than a security deposit.

When the landlord has used all or a portion of the security deposit, it is good practice (in some states, it is required by law) that the landlord provide the tenant with a complete accounting for the expended portion. Copies of paid invoices or rent statements should accompany this statement.

Conclusion

All real estate investments demand leases that bind tenants to the property. Without signed and enforceable leases, the real property owner has no guarantee that tenants will continue to pay rent. The lease is the owner's guarantee of an ongoing income. The lease also serves as the legal basis for any claims, either to money or to property, by the tenant or the landlord. This is true of all leases written for all real estate income property.

Although the agreement between the parties in a shopping center is called a "lease," here the word is actually a misnomer. In a shopping center, the two parties' interests and their commitment to each other is much stronger than in other tenant and landlord agreements. In a shopping center, both are concerned with the long-term prosperity of the structure. The landlord is not merely "renting out" space, and the tenant is not simply finding a suitable space to lease.

In shopping centers, the importance of a binding contract intensifies. In no other real property are tenants as dependent on one another and on the structure itself. Therefore, some clauses become necessary, exclusively for shopping center leases. For example, the landlord of a shopping center cannot be content with simply collecting rent when the tenant is not actually occupying the space. Empty space in a shopping center signals problems, and in an older center, it marks one of the first signs of decay.

Basically, shopping center owners use four types of leases: flat- or fixed-rent; percentage-only; fixed-minimum-plus-percentage rent; and step-up, or graduated rents. In general, the fixed-minimum-plus-percentage rent lease works for the benefit of both parties. For the landlord, it produces a regular, minimum income, plus any gains that the tenant earns, a condition that actually reflects the center's success. For the tenant, if the store does not achieve a profit, no percentage rent will be required.

Today most shopping center owners insist on leases that fluctuate with some aspect of the economy—either with the overall prosperity of the store, as just mentioned, or by some index that measures the condition of the nation's economy.

Both the tenant and landlord have much at stake through lease negotiations. The lease sets down the tenant's obligations to the landlord. Likewise, it establishes the landlord's responsibilities to the tenant. Ultimately, the document stands as the foundation for the center's prosperity.

Review Questions

1. What special considerations go into a lease when one of the two parties represents either a limited or general partnership?
2. What is required in most states, should a lease fail to state a specific term?
3. What are the four major types of shopping center leases?
4. What items are included, and what specific items are excluded, in the identification of gross income?
5. What factors are considered in establishing a fixed-minimum rent for a percentage rent agreement?
6. Define net, net-net, and net-net-net lease agreements.
7. Why will computation of the square footage of center space be necessary in some cases?
8. What is a completion bond?
9. What precautions should a property manager take when a tenant has received a finish allowance from the landlord?
10. Describe some of the provisions that are unique to shopping center leases. Why are these clauses unique to shopping centers?
11. What are the major characteristics of a merchants' association clause?
12. What is a holdover clause?
13. Discuss the clauses in a shopping center lease that serve a restrictive function: use clause, exclusive clause, and radius clause.
14. What purpose does a security deposit serve, and what provisions should be contained in a clause requiring such a deposit?

9

Lease Negotiations

A lease represents numerous compromises between the tenant and the landlord, compromises that are often settled only after many hours of negotiation. The *lessor* (landlord) and the *lessee* (tenant) bargain for numerous provisions that will enhance their own positions in the agreement. Ultimately, the signed lease contract represents each party's deference to the other party on certain points.

This, however, does not imply that a lease cannot favor one party over another. Many leases do favor either the landlord or the tenant. For example, the landlord may seek a major tenant whose presence, it is believed, would greatly enhance the shopping center. The landlord, in this case, would probably have to concede certain items that work for the benefit of the tenant but against the landlord's own interests. With prospective local tenants who are anxious to lease space at the center, however, this same landlord would stand in a stronger bargaining position.

Many small tenants believe that they cannot negotiate a lease on any terms. They want to lease space in a shopping center, and they are willing to accept any terms requested by the ownership. The landlord's terms, however, are usually not so fixed—and a small tenant should recognize its right to negotiate.

The tenant will probably receive the initial lease in the mail, packaged in a thick, bound book. A note with the lease may say, "sign and return," which is an instruction that the tenant should not adhere to. The landlord does not expect the tenant to sign and return the lease immediately. The lease must be

259

negotiated, no matter how strong the tenant's wish is to lease space at the center. The tenant should employ the services of a lawyer, who will become the tenant's continual reference during negotiations.

A leasing program for a shopping center that is to be constructed takes top priority at the start of the center's construction. During the construction period, which usually takes from 10 to 18 months, leasing efforts should accelerate. Once the center is completed, if the leasing plan has not yet been effected, the project may be in deep trouble. The degree of trouble can only be measured by the amount of vacant space that remains at the time of the center's opening. An acceptable vacancy level for a new center ranges from 5 to 15 percent. After the first six months of the center's operation, an acceptable vacancy level can be established for each particular property.

The property owner places great trust in the agent who negotiates leases for the center. That person is most often the property manager, although many shopping center owners entrust the responsibility to specifically hired leasing agents, whose primary responsibilities are to find tenants and negotiate leases. In many cases, the property manager hires and trains all of the center's leasing agents. The agent's job is to find tenants and ensure signed leases for the center. To avoid the cumbersome phrase "property managers or leasing agents," this chapter will refer to both simply as "leasing agents." When property managers work to negotiate leases, they are, in effect, acting as leasing agents. Readers should understand, however, that in practice, either the property manager or the leasing agent might assume the responsibility.

Chapter 8 dealt with the lease document, noting a few of the many important clauses contained in a typical shopping center lease. This chapter will focus on the art of lease negotiations, the process that comes before a lease is signed. This chapter will discuss some of the commonly negotiated clauses in shopping center leases. An understanding of lease negotiations will aid the leasing agent in developing the best leases for both the tenant and the owner.

Human Behavior

"Lease negotiations," as the term implies, are a form of "give and take." As in any situation where people interact, some people will be more inclined to lead, and others will be more inclined to follow. Whatever role each assumes, the tenant and landlord must also exchange words and ideas. Leasing agents, therefore, must also be effective communicators. Agents who have all the other qualities necessary to be successful in shopping center leasing—an astute knowledge of the market, an understanding of the prospect's business, and of course, a well-located and desirable property—might prove themselves inadequate for the job if they lack basic communication skills. Over and over again, they will probably find themselves forgetting critical points, being misunderstood, and losing prospective tenants. The prospective tenant may balk at the amount of base rent per square foot. The leasing agent must be able to explain the reasons for the rent and convince the prospect that the rent coincides fairly with others in the market.

During the early stages of negotiations, the successful leasing agent also must be able to distinguish between terms that are essential to the prospect and those that are negotiable. Once these priorities have been established, the leasing agent will know when to accede to the prospect's demands, in order to arrive at an optimal lease.

That involves a significant amount of skill. The successful leasing agent must be knowledgeable not only about the subject property, the neighborhood, and the area, but also about each tenant's business. That information ranges from information about each space, to data about the tenants, including specific leasehold information and the financial position of current tenants. The skilled leasing agent will know how to present the full lease package effectively.

Improvements on Premises

In order to negotiate a lease, the manager must know the tenant's required leasehold improvements, especially the cost of these improvements. If, through additional rent, the tenant plans to amortize these costs over the term of the lease, the leasing agent should be familiar with construction costs and current interest rates.

Assume that the cost of the improvements will be included with the base rent for a retail tenant. The lease requires a base rent set against a certain percentage of business sales. The leasing agent, in this case, should remember that the base rent for reaching a breakeven point, as discussed in chapter 8, should not include that portion of the base rent that applies to lease-hold improvements.

The following example describes just such a case: A lease clause holds that leasehold improvements will not be included in the base rent. Rent is $10,000 annually, against 5 percent of gross income. The base rent divided by 5 percent is $200,000, which is the amount of sales that the tenant must generate before the 5 percent charge goes into effect. If the tenant plans to amortize improvement costs over the term of the lease, the total extra cost per year amounts to $2,000, which brings the annual rent to $12,000. The tenant's sales now will have to reach $240,000 per year before the landlord can begin collecting a percentage rent. The tenant essentially is saving 5 percent of the difference between $200,000 and $240,000, or $2,000. In a different lease, this would have been income for the owner.

This example is much simpler than most situations that actually occur. Yet, it points to a common trap into which leasing agents fall: They end up conceding items that reduce the property owner's income. An uninformed leasing agent works as a hindrance to the property owner, who ultimately stands to lose thousands of dollars by sacrificing income from similar-type percentage-rent agreements.

The Purpose of Leases

Leases do not provide guarantees that tenants will pay rent. Once a lease is signed, it is used to settle disputes between the owner and the tenant, and if necessary, it is used by their attorneys or in a court of law to settle disputes that might arise between the two parties. Before a lease is signed, both the owner and the tenant must agree to become business associates in the shopping center. The owner and the tenant should have a mutual respect for each other and be able to assume that each will accept numerous responsibilities during the tenant's occupancy. This mutual effort will result in an improved shopping center, which ultimately should yield a higher profit both to the tenant and to the shopping center owner.

Lease Document

Most landlords use their own lease documents in negotiations. Not surprisingly, therefore, many real estate practitioners refer to these documents as "landlord leases." This means that the shopping center owner's attorney or legal staff has prepared the lease document and has included clauses that are important to the landlord, with little thought given to what might be important to the tenant. The exception, however, comes with large tenants, whom the landlord depends on for the success of the entire project, whether the development is a neighborhood center or a superregional center. Most anchor tenants develop their own lease forms. They design these leases to protect their own interests, which often puts the leasing agent in a difficult position. It becomes the agent's responsibility to negotiate a lease document that both parties will accept. A great deal in negotiations, therefore, depends on the size of the prospective tenant's space requirements and on the tenant's importance to the success of the shopping center development.

National Tenant vs. Local Tenant; Large vs. Small

A "large" tenant is an anchor tenant—local or national—that occupies space at a shopping center. A "small" tenant is a satellite tenant, which can also be local or national.

Many landlords very much need the large tenants for their shopping centers and are forced to accept many of the anchor's demands. However, owners are generally not forced to accept small tenants' demands. The agent who represents the anchor tenant may insist that every clause in the lease be negotiated; small national tenants will probably not insist on negotiating every term, but they are generally more knowledgeable about leases than are small local tenants. Large and small national tenants and their leasing agents are not unsuspecting parties, eager to yield to the wishes of the property owner. Instead, they are sophisticated, adept practitioners who know what they want from a lease and will do everything they can to ensure that the lease satisfies these demands. Many lease negotiations with major tenants represent a power struggle. Nevertheless, in recent years, with continued cost increases on nearly all items, coupled with many smaller tenants' protests of the inequitable arrangements, many landlords are resisting extremely large concessions to national chains.

Many small tenants, particularly small local tenants, come to negotiations with fewer demands—and generally they carry less weight during negotiations. Most small local tenants have certain expectations for rent, leasehold improvement allowances, the length of the lease, common area maintenance charges, and tax and insurance escalation requirements—and have few expectations beyond these. Smaller tenants are generally forced to be more amenable to the landlord's terms than are larger tenants. The smaller tenants, again, are important but not as critical to the success of the shopping center, and the owner's profits do not depend heavily on one small tenant.

Rent

One of the most important parts of the lease concerns the payment of rent. *Rent* is a periodic payment due by a tenant to a landlord for the occupation of space and the use of improvements. By the terms of the lease, the tenant agrees to pay the stipulated rent to the landlord according to the schedule as stated in the lease. The tenant should be held liable for rent, even in the event of default. Should there be litigation on an issue, the landlord can sue the tenant for the total rent covered under the lease, rather than for only the portion that is required on one payment date.

Rent is nearly always subject to negotiation. The leasing agent must take care in establishing a landlord posture for these negotiations. On the one hand, the leasing agent should be firm in negotiating the base rent, and yet the agent must also consider the eventual consequences. The leasing agent must remain flexible throughout negotiations. Many anchors will insist on a certain rental level, which the leasing agent may be required to accept, particularly if the landlord considers a specific tenant extremely important to the success of the investment. Rent will be a factor that almost all prospective tenants will consider. The rental level ultimately may determine whether the anchor tenant, or any tenant, agrees to join the development.

Term

The length of the lease and related options produce another broad area for negotiations. In many cases, as it will be discussed later in this chapter, the lender imposes requirements on the property owner regarding the terms of the shopping center's leases. The leasing agent, in this case, stands in a far more restrained position than when these requirements are not established. Most property owners seek a longer initial lease term from the anchor tenant than from the small tenant: The owner seeks a more permanent and stable relationship with the anchor tenant. During inflationary times, a property owner should generally try to limit lease terms to a maximum of three years. If the tenant demands a longer term, the landlord should require a rent increase, which would begin in the fourth year of the tenant's occupancy.

Options

An *option* in a lease grants the tenant the right to obtain a specific condition within a specified amount of time. Most landlords look upon options as "one-way streets"—terms that grant much to the tenant and offer the landlord little in return. The tenant gains an advantage over the landlord, for example, by remaining on the property longer than the two parties originally agreed. Many landlords define an option as a "tenant's privilege," and so it should not be difficult to understand why landlords try to avoid granting such rights. As with many other terms of the lease, many options are granted to anchor or restaurant tenants because of these tenants' desirable effects on the entire center. However, any tenant in a strong negotiating position may insist on an option. There are many different types of options, ranging from a simple clause to one of such complexity that an attorney must interpret it. The most common options will be discussed here.

Option to Renew. The option to renew grants the tenant the right to renew the lease on the same terms and conditions. This option, however, in many cases implies a renegotiation of rent or the execution of a new lease. Many options to renew contain elements of increased rent, based either on a stipulated amount of rent or an amount related to an economic index.

Option to Extend. An option to extend is similar but not identical to an option to renew, although many leasing practitioners use the two terms interchangeably. An option to extend implies an extension of the lease term, without renegotiation or execution of a new lease. Landlords have little to gain from granting a tenant this option, and in recent years, the option to extend has become quite rare. Both options—to renew and to extend—do give the tenant some flexibility, especially a tenant who does not want the liability of a long-term lease and essentially seeks a re-evaluation of the space and the lease at the end of a certain period of time.

In an inflationary economy, however, an option to extend harms the property owner possibly more than any other option.

The tenant's rent will not change with inflation, and since a dollar today, in an inflationary economy, will be worth less to the investor in 10 years, the investor stands to lose a significant amount of money.

The landlord faced with either an option to renew or an option to extend basically lacks sufficient forecasting abilities. Even with fixed rent increases, cost pass-through clauses, and cost-of-living adjustments, no one can predict the future value of the space with absolute certainty. Yet the tenant, in order to evaluate the lease, will want to know the costs that will be imposed by the lease.

Option to Cancel. Some owners may want a ten-year lease, and a highly sought-after tenant may accept only a five-year lease. The great uncertainties involved with setting up business in a new location or in a new market prompt many tenants to take such cautious routes. Both parties may agree to an option that allows a cancellation. For example, the lease might have a ten-year term, and with proper notice and perhaps a penalty fee, the tenant may hold the right to cancel the lease at the end of five years.

Option to Expand. Some tenants may believe that their business will expand in the future, to the point that, in a few years, they will need more space. These tenants may ask for a clause that gives them the right to expand into adjacent space. They would then be ready to accomodate a growth in their business. Nevertheless, agents should be wary of such options. An option to expand puts restrictions on space that the tenant might use later for expansion. The leasing agent either would have to keep the space vacant or enter into leases that expire on the same date that the option to expand becomes available.

Option to Purchase. Some large tenants seek clauses in their leases that give them the option to purchase the building that they occupy at a specified time during the lease term. Options such as this demand that the leasing agent carry out a considerable amount of research. The future price value of the property and the terms of sale that the property owner might accept represent only two of the many issues that the leasing agent will be required to address.

There are parameters that the leasing agent should consider in handling any type of option negotiations. If the owner obtains the preferred rental rate, the agent should be more flexible in negotiating options. On the other hand, should the owner be forced to accept less than the preferred rental rate, then the agent can be less amenable to options.

Whenever possible, the lease should require that the tenant pay the owner an additional fee for any type of option. Again, as mentioned earlier, options tend to favor the tenant; the landlord, in turn, should receive some compensation for granting these options.

Option to Sublease and Assign. An *assignment* signifies the transfer of all of one tenant's rights, title, and interest in the property to a new tenant, with the latter assuming all of the obligations of the lease. Generally, the landlord (assignor) and the new tenant (assignee) establish a direct contract with one another. The original, or *prime tenant*, is no longer part of the relationship, except as a guarantor, should the assignee default.

A *sublease* is the transfer by the prime tenant of only a portion of its rights, title, or interest in the leased estate, limited by the amount of leasehold area transferred or the length of the sublease term, or both. The subtenant and the landlord do not establish a direct contract. The prime tenant collects rent from the subtenant and, in turn, pays the landlord. Should the landlord breach the lease, the subtenant cannot take direct action against the landlord but must rely on the prime tenant to do such.

Nearly all leases will maintain that a tenant cannot assign or sublease without the landlord's consent. The landlord clearly has a strong interest in preserving both the tenant mix and the quality of tenants.

The lease also provides for any one or more of the following:

1. If the prime tenant defaults, the landlord may collect rent directly from the sublessee without releasing the prime tenant from the lease obligations.
2. No assignment or subletting will release the prime tenant from its monetary obligations under the terms of the lease.
3. Consent to one assignment or sublease does not serve as automatic consent to subsequent assignments or subleases. Each case requires the landlord's consent.
4. The landlord will not unreasonably withhold consent. However, the landlord can terminate the lease rather than accept the proposed assignment.
5. The landlord has the right to charge the prime tenant a processing fee for each such assignment.
6. The assignee or sublessee agrees to abide by all of the terms, conditions, and provisions of the prime lease.

Although the landlord may not withhold consent "unreasonably," the clause should specify contingencies that would be "reasonable," such as the following:

1. If the assignee's or sublessee's proposed use of the premises is not consistent with the character of the shopping center as a whole.
2. If the proposed use conflicts with existing exclusives of current tenants.
3. If the proposed use violates the use clause in the existing lease.
4. If the character, reputation, and financial responsibility of the assignee/sublessee is not satisfactory or does not match that of the prime tenant.

Another common restriction relates to the tenant's "moral stability"—a criterion that is difficult for the landlord to determine.

Some tenants may reserve the right to withdraw a requested assignment or sublease from the landlord's consideration if the landlord intends to terminate the lease rather than consent to it.

Finally, a written document, executed by all parties, should contain the terms of the assignment or sublease. This document should restate the obligations of both the prime tenant and the assignee or sublessee. If the agreement does not release the prime tenant from monetary obligations, the landlord should not be required to give notice of default to the prime tenant, should the assignee default.

Anchor tenants must be handled on an individual basis, and they often must be granted options before they will rent space at the center. The settlement that will be most acceptable to both parties should be sought. An anchor tenant generally has an in-house policy established, and the property owner may be forced to accept that policy. Difficult negotiations are usually necessary to keep options for large anchor tenants to a minimum, but most owners realize that some options will have to be granted to the large tenants.

Concessions

A *concession* refers to a reduction or allowance in rent granted in order to lease new space on a property or to retain an existing tenant. As mentioned earlier, the anchor tenant and landlord will be forced to negotiate many terms of the lease. This is not true, however, with most small tenants. Of about 30 clauses in the average small-tenant's lease, only 4 or 5 clauses are likely to be negotiated. If the positions of the landlord and the anchor tenant stand at fairly even grounds, the landlord may consider granting the tenant one or two concessions. A concession could be the factor that determines whether or not the anchor prospect agrees to join the project.

The leasing agent can evaluate certain items in deciding the extent to which concessions should be granted. First, the agent should consider the degree to which the prospect desires to relocate in the center, or, in the case of a new business, how quickly the tenant wishes to get the business started. Next, the leasing agent should find out how many similar retailers already do business in the same market. Finally and probably most important is the property owner's financial position. If it is weak, the need for a signed lease will be more urgent, and the owner may be forced to provide more concessions. The landlord who stands on sound financial footing generally does not have to concede as much to prospective tenants.

As with options, concessions take many forms. One concession might be one or two months of free rent. Another concession may hold that the owner will pay for a portion of the leasehold improvements.

Leasing agents should remember that all concessions have a dollar price. The property owner, obviously, does not want the agent to negotiate costly and excessive concessions.

All concessions should be negotiated on an individual basis. Not all tenants will demand concessions before they agree to sign a lease. Yet, concessions granted to one tenant often move other tenants or prospects to request the same concessions. The leasing agent actually can expect to confront this problem quite often. The agent should remain firm, however, in maintaining that the manner of one lease negotiation does not necessarily affect another. For the property owner, the end product of any concession is a reduced income, and with too many concessions, the investment may reach a point where the owner can no longer afford any concessions at all.

The leasing agent must be careful to avoid granting *favored nation clauses*—lease clauses that offer a large concession to one tenant but not to any other tenant. For example, the agent should not waive for one tenant the requirement that all tenants pay merchants' association dues; the concept of the association rests on monetary contributions from all tenants. One tenant's inactivity could lead to discord among the remaining tenants and could do great harm to the merchants' association and eventually to the shopping center as an investment.

Up to this point, the discussion of lease negotiations in this chapter has focused on negotiating leases with new prospects. Two other situations, however, will require lease negotiations, and they are the following: (1) *renewal*—negotiating the renewal of a lease before it expires; and (2) *replacement*—negotiating with a prospect for a space that has become vacant.

Lease renewals generally require the least amount of negotiations of any type of lease negotiations. Any shopping center that is more than three years old and is at least as large as a community center has almost continual lease renewals. In many cases, the signed renewals are nearly automatic, and yet the leases still must be prepared and signed. The leasing agent needs to establish an organized system for keeping records of these changes. The system must be accurate and current. Each tenant's file should include the specific lease term, a realistic knowledge of negotiating conditions, and some words on the tenant's negotiating position. The leasing agent must also keep in mind the shopping center owner's long-range plans and objectives.

When the time comes to negotiate a renewal lease with a current tenant, the property owner and leasing agent together should review several items. Some of these are discussed below:

Gross Volume. Most tenants in a shopping center are retailers, and therefore, many of their leases call for a base rent plus a percentage of gross sales. The leasing agent, therefore, needs complete records of the retailer's yearly gross income. The agent should analyze the retailer's business thoroughly, comparing it to the volume of competing merchants in the same trade area. The agent should inspect whether the tenant's business is growing faster than the rate of inflation. If it is not, the tenant's business is actually not growing at all; the volume is only keeping pace with inflation. Such an analysis can help the leasing agent and property owner arrive at a fair renewal rent.

Current Base Rent. The leasing agent should also compare the lease rent with rents that competitive merchants in the same trade area are paying. This review, along with a study of the tenant's gross business volume, are two of the most efficient ways of arriving at a new base rent. As discussed in chapter 5, "Market Analysis," shopping center owners will determine a market rent based on their lease negotiations with tenants.

This includes negotiations both with tenants who have signed leases for space and with tenants who ultimately decline to become tenants at the center. The manager of the center will discover very quickly the point at which the market rent has stabilized. In extending a current tenant's lease, the property manager should make every attempt to increase the rent to the level that has been established in the marketplace, the level that is known as the "market rent."

Common Area Maintenance. The agent should analyze not only the amount of money that the tenant contributes for the common area but also how much the tenant's business enhances the need for common area maintenance. For example, a supermarket increases the need for common area maintenance more than does a bookstore or clothing store. The nature of the business, the kind of people it attracts, the type of products that it sells—but most important, the size of the space—all of these will determine how much the tenant adds to the deterioration of the common area and the tenant's subsequent expense for common area maintenance.

Lease Term. The length of the term stirs up considerable conflict during renewal negotiations. A retailer who is earning a substantial income at the center will probably seek to renegotiate a long-term renewal lease. The tenant doing only marginal business, on the other hand, will probably want to negotiate an exceptionally short lease, in many cases with an option to renew. The tenant seeking an option to renew will seek flexibility, should business fail to improve within a certain amount of time. It becomes the leasing agent's job to decide on a realistic and acceptable lease term for each tenant and a lease term that will also serve the property owner's best interests.

Real Estate Taxes. Another factor that leasing agents should consider in establishing a new rent for the renewal lease is the amount that the tenant has paid under the real estate tax clause, especially if there have been several tax increases since the original lease took effect. In many cases, the agent and the tenant will agree to use the current year as the basis for computing the tenant's obligations for future tax increases. If this is the case, then the amount that the tenant paid during the last year of the original lease is added to the new base rent. This way, the total annual rent that the tenant will pay under the new lease will not be diluted by a change in the base year. The trend, however, is for tenants to pay for taxes on their leased premises. For the tenant's benefit, each tenant's real estate taxes should be based on *leased* and not *leasable* space. If the lease says leasable space, and the center is only half-filled, the tenant will end up paying for the empty portion also. Tenants should also be certain that they are entitled to a rebate should the assessed value of the property go down.

When the property owner refuses to renew the lease of a tenant, the leasing agent can probably assume that there is a demand in the market for the vacated space. The property owner would be unlikely to refuse a lease renewal, were there not first some assurance that the vacated space could be filled promptly. It is the leasing agent's task, however, to locate the suitable tenants.

Replacement leasing occurs in three situations. One, the lease expires and the tenant chooses to vacate the premises. Two, the tenant vacates the premises because the property owner refuses to negotiate a new lease. Three, the owner evicts the tenant as a result of noncompliance to the terms of the lease. In the first case, the property owner has little control over the tenant's decision other than possibly offering a more attractive renewal lease package.

Replacement leasing might occur when the leasing agent suggests that a current tenant vacate a space in the shopping center. The tenant may be detracting from the appeal of the shopping center, or the tenant's business may not be contributing sufficiently to the center's consumer drawing power. When a replacement tenant has been found, the agent will probably have to reassure the new tenant that the problems with the former tenant did not represent inherent problems at the center or with the location of the space. The center owner will probably also wish to be assured that the replacement tenant will suit the shopping center, and that the new tenant will be compatible with the rest of the tenant mix.

Replacement leasing in many ways presents the leasing agent with the same circumstances as an initial lease. The agent must seek prospective tenants through assorted marketing techniques—including advertising, cold-call canvassing, direct mail, and referrals. As with new leases, the agent will be looking for retailers that complement other merchants at the center. As it was discussed in chapter 7, "Tenant Mix," together the owner and the property manager or leasing agent must select an appropriate mix of tenants for the shopping center.

The leasing agent must be prepared to negotiate clauses such as leasehold improvements, base rent, percentage rents, common area maintenance charges, and real estate tax escalations.

Whether or not leasing agents get involved in renewal leasing or replacement leasing, they will be responsible for continual monitoring of the market. They will probably be required to compile files of market statistics, gathering data about rental rates in competitive shopping centers and the gross business volume of other merchants in the trade area—if it is possible to obtain that information. Agents should also try to obtain the names of these merchants and their lease expiration dates. They may be able to call on these merchants at some time when replacement leasing becomes necessary.

Lender Requirements

As mentioned earlier in this chapter, the leasing agent must be aware of leasing requirements that the lender or mortgage holder might impose and the effects that these requirements will have on the lease terms.

Almost all investment real estate lenders prefer that the mortgage on the property take priority over tenants' leases. Mortgage holders generally do everything they can to avoid a foreclosure on a property. They do not want to discover later that their claims come secondary to a tenant's lease.

The lender will probably require that the tenant sign a statement that sets forth the rent in the lease and states that the amount constitutes the full and entire rent that the tenant will pay for the premises. This statement is called an *estoppel clause*. Estoppels are required for must new shopping centers during the initial lease-up of the property. The purpose of such a statement is to assure the lender that the property owner is receiving nothing other than contract rent from the tenant. The tenant will probably also be required to sign a statement that says that no rents have been prepaid. The lender often seeks this guarantee to ensure that the property owner has not collected prepaid rents, which would hinder future mortgage payments. Finally, the property owner probably will require that all tenants sign a statement acknowledging that the premises have been completed satisfactorily and in accordance with the lease agreement. This statement serves as confirmation to the lender that the borrower has used all of the construction loan for its intended purpose.

The lender, in sum, is taking every possible step to guarantee that the property owner will be able to collect rent and thereby be able to meet mortgage payments as they become due. Many lenders also request the right to approve all of the shopping center's lease forms.

Both the tenant and the landlord will probably be forced to consider the requirements of outside lenders. The following may be some of the specific requirements that the lender providing permanent financing for the center investor will demand:

1. The lender may demand that the lease be subordinate to the security interest.
2. It may be demanded that tenants avoid mechanics liens. (A *lien* is a charge against a property, making the property security for the payment of a debt. A *mechanics lien,* specifically, is a charge against labor, materials, or service of a property.)
3. The lender may demand the right to terminate the lease should the center's mortgage or deed of trust face foreclosure.
4. The lender may refuse to allow the recording of the lease or an attachment to it because of potential problems in clearing title to the property.
5. It may be demanded that the owner deny tenants the right to encumber the leasehold, especially if the landlord pays for improvements with borrowed funds.

The tenant's lender, on the other hand, may demand the following requirements:

1. This lender may insist that the length of the lease term allow sufficient time to repay the loan intended to furnish and improve the premises.
2. A lender may demand ownership of the improvements and inventory during the term, especially if the lender wishes to retain a security interest to protect its position.
3. A lender may demand ownership of the improvements at the end of the lease term, or should the tenant breach the contract before the end of the term.
4. The lender may demand that the landlord not be granted arbitrary termination rights.
5. The lender may request that the lease include options to renew or extend the lease.
6. The lender may seek guaranties from financially sound third parties as further support for performance of the terms.
7. The landlord's acknowledgement of the lender's interest in the leasehold improvements is often required; for example, the lender may be granted the right of entry to take possession in the event of the tenant's default.

Default by Tenant

Both the property owner and the prospective tenant have high stakes in the wording of the default clause in the lease, and so this clause often becomes important during negotiations. The *default clause* states the rights of the landlord, should the tenant fail to meet any of the terms, covenants, and conditions of the lease—for example, if the tenant does not pay rent on time; if the tenant converts the use of the premises without the property owner's prior approval; or if the tenant subleases all or part of the premises with the property owner's consent.

Should the tenant fail to pay rent when due, the landlord legally has the right to declare the tenant in default. The lease would terminate, and the landlord could assume possession of the space. As discussed briefly in chapter 8, however, many landlords are reluctant to take such drastic action, especially when the offense is not too serious. Nevertheless, in the event of default, many states allow the landlord to re-enter the premises and take possession of the property. Some leases do not even require the landlord to give the tenant notice of such termination. In some states, on the other hand, the owners of shopping centers are prohibited by law to enter the premises and take possession of the tenant's premises. For example, in Illinois, if a tenant defaults in the payment of rent, the law requires that the owner grant the tenant a 5-day written notice to cure; the state of Wisconsin requires a 10-day written notice.

The Process of Lease Negotiations

Many real estate practitioners mistakenly believe that lease negotiations can be compared to a game. They believe that one party comes out the winner, and the other party comes out the loser. This, however, is not the case.

For the real estate transaction to be successful, both parties must "win." Both parties must be satisfied with the results and be willing to cooperate in the shopping center development. The tenant who is unhappy with the landlord's terms, or the tenant that does not have the financial means to meet them, ultimately will harm the investment.

Unlike a game, in lease negotiations, there are no rules. There are no "secret" formulas for success. Each leasing situation brings with it unique circumstances. What is most important in any negotiations is that both parties come to an atmosphere of honesty and trust. Many smaller tenants will lack the experience necessary to comprehend a complicated lease. The leasing agent must explain the terms to them to ensure that there are no misunderstandings. Many shopping center tenants have paid several times over for their lack of knowledge about legal contracts. Ultimately, in these cases, the property owner also loses.

Before leasing agents can begin to negotiate leases, first they must find prospective tenants. Probably one of the most effective ways—albeit one of the most frustrating ways—of finding prospective tenants is cold-call canvassing. Little can take the place of the leasing agent actually calling on retailers in the trade area and obtaining first-hand information from them. During these visits, the leasing agent can learn about new retailers in the community, and about community retail trends, changes in products, and changing tastes. In the end, the more the manager knows about the community, the more effective is the leasing effort.

During the first meeting with a merchant, the manager would be well advised to keep the interview at a low key, staying away from high-pressure selling techniques. These are fact-finding, not active-selling interviews. Most merchants enjoy talking about their businesses and will be willing to offer the necessary information. At this stage, the manager will be seeking a great deal of general information: space requirements, price range, and type of merchandise. The interviewer should try to determine if the merchant has an interest in expanding, specifically in locating at the center. At this point, talk of company profits or of leasing dollars should be avoided. The manager's aim in the first meeting should be to arouse the retailer's interest in the center—and little more than that.

The manager is trying to sell an expensive proposition, and the job will take time. It might be a good idea to invite the prospective tenant to the shopping center for an afternoon. Any meeting with a retailer gives the manager an added opportunity to gain more information. Most merchants would be pleased to learn that a center owner has sought them out and is interested in their presence at the center. Most merchants probably will not have plans to expand or relocate at the time of the interview, but leasing agents must remember that plans often do change quickly. Without prospective tenants, again, there are no lease negotiations.

The leasing agent also must find an effective personal style of negotiating. People develop their own style. Some use an extremly aggressive approach—which can be effective, if they have the personality that goes along with it. Others would appear unnatural and uncomfortable in that role. Again, there are no rules that govern the best approach. Each leasing agent must make that a personal choice.

The leasing agent has worked through a long process with the prospect. The agent has sought out each prospect, studied the specific needs of each, and reviewed how the business would complement the other tenants at the center. The agent has prepared a lease document, and the two parties have debated and finally settled their differences. What remains to be done? The most important step of all: a successful close.

There are different ways that the leasing agent can expedite a close. The leasing agent at a shopping center is generally dealing with sophisticated, knowledgeable people who know their trade. Most of these prospective tenants also know just what they want from a lease. Still, every agent needs to be familiar with the basic tools in lease negotiations. Whether the tenant is leasing 200 or 20,000 square feet of space, basic principles of psychology can guide the leasing agent to obtain the final signature.

Approaches to the Final Close

One method for approaching a final close is called the *interim close*, so-called because the agent assumes a final close. Therefore, an interim close is a temporary close. The leasing agent realizes that the prospect is leaning toward accepting the lease. The agent asks a question which presumes that the prospect wants the space; for example, "What type and color carpeting do you want installed in the space?" Many prospects will accept the assumption. The interim approach can provide the final push that convinces the tenant to sign.

The agent might try the "Ben Franklin" approach, named after the statesman's analytical approach to problem solving. The agent would say, "We can list all the reasons why you should lease the space on one side of the page, and all the reasons why you should not on the other side." Ultimately, the tenant should see all the reasons to sign.

The leasing agent should also learn how to handle prospects' objections. First, however, the agent must understand that an objection is a normal reaction to a threat—and lease negotiations for space in a shopping center are threatening. Sometimes the prospect is only asking a question; if so, the agent should just answer the question. Or, the prospect may try to delay a decision. If this is the case, the agent should be honest with the prospect and yet try to create a sense of urgency: "If you wait two weeks, this space may not be available. I have a couple prospective tenants who are very interested in this space."

Probably the most common prospect objection relates to budgetary concerns. As mentioned earlier, most prospects will question the rent and ask that it be reduced. Leasing agents must bring their prospects to a rational assessment of the rent. Perhaps the agent can show the prospect comparison figures with the rents at other centers or present total sales volumes that tenants at this center have reported. During the final stages, as throughout the entire negotiation process, the agent will be selling the shopping center. The agent should point out all of the center's good features—including its excellent location, its major anchor tenants, and the large buying public that the center attracts.

Conclusion

The property owner has much at stake during lease negotiations. The leasing agent is responsible for seeking stable, rent-paying tenants—and that is a difficult, challenging job. With solid planning, research, record keeping, sales ability, and follow-up, however, the job will usually produce beneficial results.

The leasing agent should refrain from granting too many options and concessions to tenants during negotiations. Anchor tenants are more likely to demand them than are the smaller tenants. Most anchor tenants have sophisticated, knowledgeable representatives who know just what their clients want in their leases. Leasing agents must remember, however, that any concession or option ultimately means a reduced income for the property owner.

The ultimate tests of whether lease negotiations have been successful are the number of tenants that eventually decide to lease space at the center and the number of tenants that decide to renew their leases. A new tenant's acceptance of the terms of a lease suggests a satisfaction with the lease negotiating process and a generally positive impression of management and the property. A lease renewal, likewise, suggests a satisfaction with the center, management, and the particular space. These are all excellent indications to the center owner and manager that the property investment will continue to prosper.

Review Questions

1. In lease negotiations, how must the leasing agent represent the landlord?
2. Why is it necessary for the leasing agent to have a strong knowledge of construction costs and current interest rates?
3. Why are some leases referred to as "landlord leases?"
4. Who presents the greatest challenge to the leasing agent, the large tenant or the small tenant? Local or national? Why?
5. Why do landlords look on options as being beneficial only to the tenant?
6. How should leasing agents handle the granting of options to tenants?
7. What major problem does an option to expand present to the property owner?
8. What are the two types of leasing other than new leasing? Explain both.
9. Explain the rights of the landlord in a typical default clause.
10. Explain why the mortage lender has a strong interest in well-negotiated leases for the center property.
11. Define the term "interim close."

10

Advertising, Promotion, and Publicity

$\mathbf{A}$ shopping center will survive only if it can attract a steady flow of consumers. An elegant, multiservice shopping center is worth little to the investor unless it brings in a steady stream of shoppers. The buying public, therefore, must know of the center's existence, its location, and the various goods and services that tenants at the center offer. Advertising, promotion, and publicity—or any combination of these three programs—will help to build traffic and increase sales for all of the stores in the center.

Most property managers must fill innumerable roles, performing many tasks, all geared to a smoothly functioning center. This chapter introduces another of the property manager's many responsibilities: administering the center's promotional programs. In the shopping center industry, "promotion director" often refers to the property manager. Most regional and super-regional centers have sufficient funds to hire a full-time or possibly a part-time promotion director who reports to the property manager. Many community centers also have such a director. In most neighborhood centers, however, it is the property manager who functions as the promotion director. Therefore, besides knowing the accounting systems and the budgetary aspects of the investment, performing and understanding market studies, negotiating and helping to prepare lease documents, recognizing the owner's objectives, and gaining awareness of fundamental principles of retailing, shopping center managers must also be knowledgeable about basic principles of promotion—whether they have control of the center's advertising and promotion program or not. Even if the manager has little voice in determining the center's promotional programs, a basic understanding of these programs is important. In this chapter, when the text refers to "promotion director," it may actually be referring to the property manager. Again, the function that the property manager serves will depend on the particular needs of the shopping center.

The amount of promotion that a manager or promotion director should arrange for a shopping center will depend on the size and nature of the development. Promotion directors in smaller centers will have a smaller budget with which to work and fewer stores to promote, but still they must use the available funds to promote the center. These directors will be required to use their creative abilities to find inexpensive but effective ways to attract a consuming public to the center. Although there are fewer stores to promote at such a center, an advertising and promotional program will still be necessary. Each director should study the market and the particular demands of the market to determine what type of promotional programs would be most effective.

Well-conceived promotional programs, in sum, should be considered essential for all sizes and types of shopping center investments. The ability of the center manager to stage special events and get them properly publicized can eventually determine whether the investment succeeds or fails.

The image that a center projects does not come about because consumers shop there. The process works in reverse. The image that the center projects should encourage consumers to shop there. Just how does a shopping center create an image and present it to the public? Who makes the decisions, and who carries out those decisions? What sales, news stories, and special events best serve the needs of a particular development? All of these are questions that can be answered only in relation to the marketplace and with a clear knowledge of each tenant's financial stability.

Promotion and Cash Flow

Regular promotions are an excellent way to create public awareness of a shopping center, attract new customers, and generate additional sales. The tenants, in turn, benefit from the added traffic, and, in most cases, the retailing business at the center improves. The center owner, however, has many other reasons for staging promotional events on a regular basis.

Many leases require that the tenant pay a percentage of sales to the owner. The extra income generated by successful promotions, therefore, will increase the property owner's cash flow. Similarly, the property manager, who is paid on the basis of a percentage of the property's gross income, has a financial interest in staging regular promotions.

The property owner and the property manager should strive to maintain the center's economic well-being through whatever promotional efforts are necessary. The owner has a major investment to protect; the property manager, a reputation. Advertising and special promotions are among the most effective means of maintaining the center's profitability.

Merchants' Association

The main purposes of a merchants' association are to increase tenants' sales potential and to advertise and promote the center as a whole. The merchants' association is a nonprofit corporation, which files its bylaws with the state. Ideally, the merchants' association will be formed during the development of the shopping center. The property manager, thus, can draft and record bylaws that will protect the landlord and the merchants' association. The association's bylaws, which are included with each tenant's lease package, establish the specific purposes, organization, and requirements of the association. The bylaws of a merchants' association appear as a sample in Exhibit 10.1.

The manager should serve as an officer on the association's board, as the owner's representative, which usually means that the manager holds the office of secretary. As a member of the board, the manager should be in a position to offer suggestions to the association, and to be an influencing factor in the planning of these activities. The property manager may wish to recommend that the merchants' association hire a director to handle its affairs. The duties and responsibilities of the person handling the affairs of a merchants' association are generally quite extensive and time-consuming.

Most shopping center leases require tenants to belong to the merchants' association. The bylaws of the association state the specific requirements to which all tenants must agree and abide. Many associations, for example, elect a board of direc-

EXHIBIT 10.1. *High Mark Mall Merchants' Association Bylaws*

ARTICLE I — NAME

The name of this organization shall be High Mark Mall Merchants' Association, Inc., a nonprofit corporation organized in the Village of Mainsville under the laws of the State of Illinois.

ARTICLE II — PURPOSE

Section 1. General. High Mark Mall Merchants Association, Inc. is organized for the purpose of furthering the general business interest of High Mark Mall, and all of the merchants in this shopping center, and, in the furtherance of such purpose, to engage in and conduct promotional programs and publicity, special events, decoration, cooperative advertising and other joint endeavors in general interest, and for the general benefit of the center and its merchants; to encourage the maintenance of high business standards and a spirit of cooperation among its members; and to compile and distribute business information to its members for their benefit.

Section 2. Nonpartisan/Nonsectarian. The Association shall be at all times conducted as a wholly and completely nonpartisan and nonsectarian entity. The Association shall not at any time or in any way act in behalf of, either directly or indirectly, or in any other way show any partiality to any religious, political, racial, national, ethnic, or gender group or individual of such group. Nor shall it in any way or at any time discriminate against any religious, political, racial, national, ethnic, or gender group or individual of such group.

Section 3. Not for Profit. The Association shall be conducted at all times as a not-for-profit organization which shall not engage in any function, plan, design, or any other activity intended for the profit of the Association, or for any officer, director, or member(s) of the Association.

ARTICLE III — MEMBERSHIP

Section 1. Class. This Association shall have one class of member with equal rights, duties, and privileges. Each tenant in the Shopping Center and the owner, whether individuals, partnerships, co-partnerships, associations, or corporation shall be entitled to membership in the Merchants' Association. Membership in the Association shall continue so long as the respective members continue as tenants or owners in the center or as otherwise provided herein.

Section 2. Termination. The resignation, withdrawal, or expulsion of a member shall result in termination of membership. The termination of membership shall constitute forfeiture of all interests of the member in and to the property of the Association, and the member shall thereafter have no right thereto or any part thereof.

ARTICLE IV — GENERAL MEMBERSHIP MEETINGS

Section 1. Annual Meeting. Commencing with the year 1983, the Association shall hold an annual meeting with the general membership on the third Wednesday in October of each year, or on such other date as may be fixed by the Board of Directors. Said annual meeting shall be for the purpose of election of directors for the ensuing year, and the transaction of any business within the powers of the Association. Any business of the Association may be transacted at an annual meeting without being specifically designated in the notice, except such business as is specifically required by statute or by the charter to be stated in such notice. Failure to hold an annual meeting shall not, however, invalidate the corporate existence of the Association or affect otherwise valid corporate acts.

(continued)

EXHIBIT 10.1. *(Continued)*

Section 2. Regular or Special Meetings. At any time in the interval between annual meetings, regular or special meetings of the members may be called by the President whenever it may be considered necessary or desirable, or may be called by a majority of the Board of Directors, or may be called by the written request of a majority of the general membership of the Association. This provision shall not affect any of merchant's other obligations pursuant to its respective lease with the owner/developer, its successors and assigns.

Section 3. Notice. Not less than five (5) days before the date of any meeting of the general membership, the Secretary shall give to each member written notice. Said notice shall state the time and place of the meeting, and in the case of a special meeting, the purposes for which the meeting is called. Such notice shall be delivered, either personally or by mail to the latest address of the members recorded in the books of the Association. Any meeting of the general membership, annual or special, may adjourn from time to time to reconvene at the same or some other place, and no notice need be given of such adjourned meeting other than by announcement.

Section 4. Quorum. A quorum shall consist of a majority of the entire general membership present at the meeting, either by person or by proxy. In the absence of a quorum, the Secretary shall be directed to send notice as herein provided of another meeting, and at said meeting a simple majority of those members in attendance will constitute a quorum.

Section 5. Proxy. Any member may vote either in person or by proxy or by representative designated in writing by such member. All proxies shall be in writing and submitted to the Secretary of the Association prior to any meeting of the general membership.

Section 6. Voting. Each member of the Association shall be entitled to one vote, plus an additional vote for each five hundred dollars ($500) that such member contributes to the Association in dues. Each member shall have the right to attend and to participate in all meetings of the members.

ARTICLE V — BOARD OF DIRECTORS

Section 1. Powers. The business and affairs of the Association shall be managed by its Board of Directors, all of whom shall be members in good standing of the Association. The Board of Directors may exercise all the powers of the Association, except such as are by statute, charter, or bylaws specifically reserved to the membership only.

Section 2. Number of Directors. The number of Directors of the Association shall be eleven (11). Three (3) of the Directors shall be permanent Directors, namely the manager of X Mart Department Store, the manager of Mann's Department Store, and the manager of High Mark Mall or a representative appointed by the owner/developer. The remaining Directors shall be elected by the members for one-year terms.

Section 3. Election of Directors. At each annual meeting the members shall elect Directors to hold office until the next succeeding annual meeting or until their successors are elected and qualify. The President, not less than thirty (30) days prior to the annual meeting for the election of Directors shall appoint a nominating committee of three (3) or more members of the Association to nominate from the general membership the Directors to be elected. Said committee shall file a list of the nominees recommended with the Secretary not less than ten (10) days before the election. Other nominations than those recommended by the nominating committee may be made by any member by petition

(continued)

EXHIBIT 10.1. *(Continued)*

signed by not less than five (5) members of the Association and delivery of said petition to the Secretary not later than five (5) days before the date set for such election.

All voting for the election of Directors shall be by written ballot. Every member shall have the right to cast its vote(s) in person or by proxy, or by representative, for as many members as there are Directors to be elected. The number of nominees corresponding with the number of Directors to be elected who received the highest number of votes, shall be declared elected.

Section 4. Vacancy. Any vacancy occurring on the Board of Directors for any cause, including the transfer of an elected Director, will be filled by a majority of the remaining Directors within ten (10) days after such vacancy occurs. The Directors elected by the Board of Directors to fill any such vacancy shall be elected to hold office until the next annual meeting of the general membership or until their successors are elected and qualified.

Section 5. Meetings. Regular and/or special meetings of the Board of Directors may be called at any time by the President or by the Board of Directors by a vote at a meeting or by a majority of the Directors in writing with or without a meeting and shall be held on such dates and in such places as may be designated by the Board of Directors. The Board of Directors shall keep minutes of its meetings and distribute copies same to the membership within thirty (30) days following any regular or special meeting of the Board of Directors. The Board may adopt such rules as may be necessary for the proper conduct of the business of the Association.

Section 6. Notice. Not less than five (5) days before the date of any regular or special meeting of the Board of Directors, the Secretary shall give to each Director written or personal notice stating the time and place of the meeting, and in the case of a special meeting, the purpose for which the meeting is called. Such notice shall be delivered or sent by mail to the latest address of the Director recorded on the books of the Association. Any meeting of the Board of Directors, regular or special, may adjourn from time to time to convene at the same or some other place, and no notice need be given of any such adjourned meeting other than by announcement.

Section 7. Quorum. At all meetings of the Board of Directors, a majority of the entire Board of Directors shall constitute a quorum for the transaction of business. Except in cases in which it is by statute, by the charter, or by the bylaws otherwise provided, the vote of a majority of such quorum at a duly constituted meeting shall be sufficient to elect and pass any measure. In the absence of a quorum, the Secretary shall be directed to send notice as herein provided of another meeting and at said meeting a simple majority of those members in attendance will constitute a quorum.

Section 8. Removal. Any elected Director of the Association may be removed by two-thirds (2/3) of the general membership whenever, in their judgment, the best interests of the Association will be served thereby.

Section 9. Compensation. In no event shall the Directors of the Association receive compensation for their services to the Association.

ARTICLE VI — OFFICERS

Section 1. Executive Officers. The Board of Directors shall elect from among the members of the Board, a President, a Vice President, a Secretary, and a Treasurer, and any other officers as shall be deemed necessary to carry out the affairs and business of the Association. Each officer shall hold office until the first

(continued)

EXHIBIT 10.1. *(Continued)*

meeting of the Board of Directors after the annual meeting of general members next succeeding the officer's election, or until a successor shall have been duly chosen and qualified or until the officer shall have resigned or shall have been otherwise removed.

Section 2. Vacancy. Any vacancies in any of the above offices shall be filled by a member of the Board of Directors for the unexpired portion of the term, elected by a majority of the remaining Board of Directors within ten (10) days after such vacancy occurs.

Section 3. The President. The President shall preside at all meetings of the members and of the Board of Directors at which the President shall be present. The President shall have general charge and supervision of the business of the Association. The President shall perform all duties as, from time to time, may be assigned by the Board of Directors. The President shall be an ex officio member of all committees.

Section 4. Vice President. The Vice President, at the request of the President, or in the absence of the President, or should the President be unable to complete the duties and exercise the functions of the job, and when so acting as President shall have the powers of the President. The Vice President shall have such other powers and perform such other duties as may be assigned by the Board of Directors or the President.

Section 5. Secretary. The Secretary shall keep the minutes of the meetings of the members and of the Board of Directors in books provided for the purpose, and shall distribute same to the membership as required. The Secretary shall see that all notices are duly given in accordance with the provisions of the bylaws or as required by law and shall be custodian of the records of the Association and in general shall perform all duties incident to the office of a Secretary of a corporation, and such other duties as, from time to time, may be assigned by the Board of Directors or by the President.

Section 6. Treasurer. The Treasurer shall have charge of and be responsible for all funds, receipts, and disbursements of the Association, and shall deposit or cause to be deposited, in the name of the Association, all monies or other valuable effects in such banks or other depositories as shall, from time to time, be selected by the Board of Directors. The Treasurer shall render to the President and to the Board of Directors, and to the membership, whenever requested, an account of the financial condition of the Association, and in general, shall perform all duties incident to the office of a Treasurer of a corporation, and such other duties as may be assigned by the Board of Directors or the President.

Section 7. Executive Committee. The officers of the Association, as herein provided, and the manager of High Mark Mall or a representative appointed by the owner/developer shall constitute the Executive Committee, which shall be empowered to act on behalf of the Board of Directors when the Board is not in session.

Section 8. Subordinate Officers. The Board of Directors may from time to time appoint such subordinate officers as it may deem desirable. Each such officer shall hold office for such period and perform such duties as the Board of Directors or the President may prescribe. The Board of Directors may, from time to time, authorize any committee or officer to appoint and remove subordinate officers and prescribe the duties thereof.

Section 9. Removal. Any officer of the Association may be removed by three-fourths (3/4) of the Board of Directors or by two-thirds (2/3) of the general

(continued)

EXHIBIT 10.1. *(Continued)*

membership whenever, in their judgment, the best interests of the Association will be served thereby.

ARTICLE VII — DUES AND ASSESSMENTS

Section 1. Dues. Regular annual dues shall be paid by each member to the Association as provided by lease or other agreement. The annual dues shall be payable each calendar quarter in advance as billed or as otherwise provided. Payment of dues shall be paid to the Association in care of High Mark Mall Merchants' Association, Inc., which will be responsible for depositing same to the account of the Association; the address is 124 Main Street, Mainsville, Illinois 60101.

Section 2. Delinquency. Whenever a member shall be in arrears in payment of dues or assessments for a period of more than thirty (30) days, the member shall be notified in writing by the President or Secretary of the Association that if such dues or assessments or both are not paid within thirty (30) days, the member shall be deemed as delinquent.

Section 3. Suspension. Upon certification by the Treasurer to the Board of Directors that a member is so delinquent, by a majority vote of the Board of Directors, such member may be suspended from membership in the Association.

Any member so suspended shall not be entitled to vote, participate in Association affairs, be a member of the Board of Directors, and in the event such member is a director or an officer, the member shall be automatically removed from such office upon suspension. Upon certification by the Treasurer to the Board of Directors that a suspended member has cured delinquency, the member shall be automatically reinstated to membership in the Association on the date of such certification. However, such reinstatement shall not entitle such member to regain previous membership on the Board of Directors nor any previous office held prior to the suspension unless re-elected in accordance with the applicable provisions of these bylaws.

Section 4. Expulsion. Members may be expelled by a majority vote of the entire Board of Directors for cause or nonpayment of dues or assessments as provided herein. In the event such member is a Director or their natural person representative an officer, the member shall be automatically removed from any such office upon expulsion. However, no member may be expelled without opportunity of a hearing before the Board of Directors. An expelled member shall have the right to appeal within thirty (30) days from the date of expulsion by the Board to the entire general membership and, upon written request, must be allowed to make such an appeal at the next annual meeting or at a special meeting called for the purpose within thirty (30) days of such a request.

A member may be reinstated by a majority vote of the general membership. A member so expelled, may, at any time after the expiration of thirty (30) days from the date of expulsion, petition the Association for reinstatement. Said petition shall be in writing and submitted to the Board of Directors. Within thirty (30) days of such a petition the Board of Directors, by a majority vote of the entire Board, shall act upon said petition, subject to ratification by a majority vote of the general membership.

In the event of reinstatement, the member shall not be entitled to regain previous membership on the Board of Directors nor any previous office held prior to the expulsion unless re-elected in accordance with the applicable provisions of these bylaws.

ARTICLE VIII — SUNDRY PROVISIONS

Section 1. Contracts. The Board of Directors may authorize any officer, agent, or employee of the Association to enter into any contract or execute and deliver

(continued)

EXHIBIT 10.1. *(Continued)*

deliver any instrument in the name of and on behalf of the Association, and such authority may be general or confined to specific instances.

Section 2. Borrowing. The Association shall not make any loans to any member, officer, or Director either individually or as a group.

Section 3. Deposits, Checks, Drafts, etc. All funds of the Association shall be deposited from time to time to the credit of the Association into a special account to be designated by the Board of Directors; and disbursements of said funds shall be made with the approval of the Board of Directors.

All disbursements shall be made by check, and all checks, drafts, and orders for the payment of money, notes, and other evidences of indebtedness, issued in the name of the Association shall, unless otherwise provided by resolution of the Board of Directors, be signed by the President or Vice President and countersigned by the Secretary or Treasurer, who shall be bonded to the extent deemed necessary by the Board of Directors.

Section 4. Bonds. The Board of Directors may require any officer, agent, or employee of the Association to give a bond to the Association, conditioned upon the faithful discharge of duties, with one or more sureties and in such amount as may be satisfactory to the Board of Directors.

Section 5. Budget. The Board of Directors shall prepare annually, with the commencement of each new fiscal year, an annual operational, promotional, and advertising budget, which shall be presented to the general membership for their approval. Once approved, this budget shall govern the financial affairs of the Association for the fiscal year.

Section 6. Annual Financial Report. There shall be prepared annually under direction of the Treasurer, a full and correct statement of the financial affairs of the Association, including a Balance Sheet and a Financial Statement of Operations for the preceding fiscal year, which shall be submitted to the general membership.

Section 7. Annual Corporate Report. The Secretary of the Association shall cause to be prepared and filed annually any corporate reports required by the laws of the State of Incorporation for not-for-profit corporations.

Section 8. Annual Tax Return. The Treasurer of the Association shall cause to be prepared and filed annually any Federal, State, or Municipal tax returns required for not-for-profit corporations.

Section 9. Fiscal Year. The fiscal year of the Association shall be determined and fixed by the Board of Directors.

Section 10. Committees. The Board of Directors shall authorize and define the powers and duties of all committees. All committees so authorized shall be appointed by the President, subject to confirmation by the Board of Directors.

Section 11. Insurance. The Association shall hold harmless and indemnify the owners from all injury, loss, claims, or damage to any person or persons or property while within or upon the center premises, occasioned by any act, omission, neglect or default by the Association or by any member or group of members while acting for on behalf of the Association. As a result, the Association shall effect and carry and pay for, and keep in full force and effect, insurance issued by reputable companies authorized and qualified to do business in the State of Illinois which companies are satisfactory to owners, if coverage is not provided in any other insurance policy carried by owner/developer. In addition, the Association shall furnish a certificate issued by the Industrial Board or other appropriate agency in the State of Illinois showing that the Workers' Compensation and Occupational Disease insurance is in full force and effect if said Association has any employees.

(continued)

EXHIBIT 10.1. *(Continued)*

ARTICLE IX — AMENDMENTS TO BYLAWS

Any and all provisions of these bylaws may be altered, amended, or repealed and new laws may be adopted by a two-thirds (2/3) vote of the membership at any annual meeting of the Association without notice, or at any special meeting of the Association, provided that at least ten (10) days written notice is given of intention to alter and amend at such special meeting. Further, any proposed amendments to these bylaws shall be submitted to the Board of Directors thirty (30) days in advance of any meeting at which said amendments may be presented. The Board of Directors shall make available to the membership the proposed changes in said bylaws fifteen (15) days prior to the meeting at which said bylaws will be considered.

tors, which is generally composed of tenants who are active in the association. The board then acts as the authority that exercises all powers for the association, except those related to charter or those specifically denied in the bylaws. If an existing center does not have a merchants' association, the property manager should organize a voluntary merchants' association.

In most shopping center leases, members of the merchants' association are also required to pay dues on whatever payment formula is established. Most anchor tenants' dues are a negotiated amount and are not based on a dollar-per-square-foot formula. Retailers who fail to pay membership dues or who refuse to participate in association activities—if these are stated as requirements in the lease—are in violation of their leases and actually risk eventual eviction from the property. This, however, is a very delicate matter, and few property owners would want to take this extreme action against a tenant.

The amount of dues collected by the merchants' association determines the extent to which advertising and promotional activities can be staged during the year. This treasury is, in effect, the organization's operating budget. At one time, merchants' associations devoted a large part of their budgets to circus-type promotions. In recent years, however, many merchants' associations have directed more of their funds to advertising and promotion.

Most small associations establish a system that bases the size of monthly dues on the specific needs of the center and of the association. In larger centers—those of 300,000 square feet or more—most leases specify the minimum amount of membership dues, including an initiation fee. Many such leases become extremely detailed in establishing the extent that tenants must participate in the merchants' association. They might specify, for example, how many times a retailer must advertise in shopping center circulars and the required size of these ads. Many leases allow the landlord to submit advertising copy on the tenant's behalf and charge the tenant for the costs involved, should the tenant fail to meet this advertising requirement. A sample lease clause pertaining to merchants' advertising obligations—a promotional fund clause—appears in Exhibit 10.2.

Since promotional activities will benefit the shopping center's tenants, the owner, and actually the entire community, it is important that all parties are represented in the association. Some property managers and property owners try to avoid involvement with the merchants' association because they fear that the association will be used only as a forum for tenants to voice complaints to the landlord. This can be prevented, however, if the manager reminds tenants that the discussion of matters other than the promotion of merchants and the shopping center is inappropriate at this meeting and contrary to the association's purpose.

Association Leadership

Most property owners or managers assume the responsibility of organizing the association. Eventually, however, a merchants' association should provide its own leadership. Whoever forms the group might also plan at least the first year's calendar of events. In a shopping center with a board of directors, the leases generally bind tenants to abide by all decisions of the board.

At one of the first meetings of the year, the association should elect a president; the president and manager then can work together to plan all future sessions. The association should hold its meetings before business hours, during lunch, or at any other mutually agreeable time. The important point is that these meetings be held regularly. Most associations hold monthly board of directors meetings and either monthly or quarterly general membership meetings.

Each tenant should receive a written agenda at least 24 hours before the meeting. The meeting then should follow the agenda strictly. A sample agenda appears as Exhibit 10.3. Business meetings have a way of meandering, of becoming too long, but if the members follow the agenda, they can deal with the business at hand quickly and efficiently. After the meeting, in most cases it is the property manager's responsibility to provide a full report to tenants who were unable to attend the meeting. These

EXHIBIT 10.2. *Promotional Fund Lease Clause*

Promotional fund: (i) Landlord will promptly establish a Promotional Fund for the Shopping Center. Tenant agrees to pay to Landlord the Promotional Charge, payable in advance on the first day of each month, as Tenant's contribution toward the advertising, promotion, public relations and administrative expenses related thereto. The Promotional Charge payable by Tenant to Landlord will be subject to adjustment by a percentage equal to the percentage of increase or decrease from the base period (as hereafter defined) of the "Consumer's Price Index for Urban Wage Earners and Clerical Workers, U.S. City Average All Items, Series A (1967 = 100)," issued by the Bureau of Labor Statistics of The United States Department of Labor in the Current Labor Statistics Section of the Monthly Labor Review (final publication only), provided that said Index has increased or decreased by at least ten (10%) percent or more from the base period. The term "base period" as used herein shall refer to the date on which said Index is published, which is closest to the date immediately preceding the formation of said Fund. In any event, however, and notwithstanding any decrease in such Index, the Promotional Charge payable by Tenant to Landlord shall at no time be less than the amount set forth under Paragraph 1 (t) hereof. (ii) If Tenant shall open or be required under the terms of this Lease to open for business in the Demised Premises at any time before or within ninety (90) days after the date of the grand opening of the Shopping Center, Tenant also agrees to pay to Landlord in addition to the foregoing Promotional Charge, an initial contribution in the amount of the Grand Opening Charge, for the purpose of defraying the advertising, promotion and public relations expenses to be incurred by Landlord (or to reimburse Landlord for advancing such expenses) in connection with the pre-opening and grand opening promotion of the Shopping Center; such Grand Opening Charge shall be paid to Landlord by Tenant within ten (10) days following the presentation of a bill to Tenant therefor. (iii) Tenant also agrees to advertise Tenant's business in the Demised Premises in special Shopping Center newspaper sections or tabloids sponsored by Landlord for advertising by merchants of the Shopping Center; and in connection therewith, Tenant agrees to purchase, not less than but limited to six (6) times during each Lease Year, advertising space hereinafter specified. Tenant agrees to purchase in each instance advertising space in minimum amounts based upon the Gross Leasable Area of the Demised Premises as follows: (a) Six Hundred (600) square feet or less of Gross Leasable Area—sixteen (16) column inches; (b) Between 601 and 2000 square feet of Gross Leasable Area—Forty-eight (48) column inches; (c) Between 2001 and 3000 square feet of Gross Leasable Area—eighty (80) column inches; and (d) 3001 square feet or more of Gross Leasable Area—one hundred sixty eight (168) column inches. If Tenant shall refuse or neglect to timely submit its copy of such advertising, Landlord, at its election, shall have the right (but not the obligation) to submit copy consisting of Tenant's Trade Name and address to the printer for inclusion in such printed advertising media on behalf of and for the account of Tenant. If Tenant shall refuse or neglect to pay for such advertising, Landlord may pay such sum or sums of money by reason of the failure or neglect of Tenant to perform; and in such event, Tenant agrees to reimburse and pay Landlord upon demand, all such sums so expended which shall be deemed to be additional rent for the purposes of enforcement and collection. (iv) Landlord agrees to contibute not less than twenty-five (25%) percent of the total amount of promotional charges paid to said Promotional Fund by the tenants of the Shopping Center, provided, however, that Landlord's contribution will in no event exceed Ten Thousand ($10,000.00) Dollars during any Lease Year. However, Landlord, at its option, may elect to contribute all or part of the services of a Promotion Director and/or Secretary and their respective offices, as a part of such cash contribution. The Promotion Director shall be under the exclusive control and supervision of Landlord and Landlord shall have the sole right and exclusive authority to employ and discharge such Promotion Director. In lieu and instead of the Promotional Fund, Landlord shall have the right and option to form a Merchants' Association; and in such case, Tenant shall become a member of the Merchants' Association (as soon as the same has been formed) and Tenant agrees to remain a member in good standing of said Association and Landlord agrees to promptly pay to said Association Tenant's Promotional Charge and/or the Grand Opening Charge, as and when actually paid to Landlord by Tenant.

tenants should understand new obligations that the association may have imposed on them in their absence.

Lack of tenant participation is perhaps the single greatest problem a manager will encounter with a merchants' associa-

EXHIBIT 10.3. *Merchants' Association Monthly Meeting Agenda*

I. Call to order.

II. Approval of new vice president, John Doe, X Mart manager.

III. One volunteer needed for promotion committee.

IV. Outdoor mall signs.
Estimate received from Best Signs of Mainsville.
Sign will border along the top of our building.
Two feet high letters, individually lit.
Cost—approximately $300 each—exact price will be known in one week.

V. June tabloid—Dads, Grads, and Brides.
Issue deadline is May 20 for June 3 edition.
WE URGE ALL MERCHANTS TO REMEMBER THESE DATES AND ABIDE BY THIS
DEADLINE!

VI. Promotional calendars.
All merchants will receive a calendar to place in their stores for
upcoming promotions, merchandising events, and tabloids.
You will be notified of changes.

VII. Upcoming May events.
Televac computer date changed to May 21-31.
"Shop Smith" May 4-10 at High Mark.
"Just for Mom" at High Mark—FREE makeup and facial classes . . .
courtesy of Mary Kay cosmetics. Tell your customers about it.
Joe Frisco's petting zoo . . . May 12-21. Discount tickets will be
distributed to all mall stores, to be given free to all children under the
age of 12.
Shelby American Auto Show.

VIII. Sweepstakes Winner!
Cindi Trump of Edgemore. Picture will be taken today at 2:30 p.m. in
General Optical. The winning ticket was written in General Optical,
and NEWS PUBLICATION will photograph the winner with the manager of
General Optical, Paula Short.

IX. Review statement.

X. Adjournment.
REMEMBER OUR NEWSLETTER:
Please inform the mall office if you have any news, information, or
special employee discounts/sales that you would like to announce in
our mall newsletter, *The Navigator.* The newsletter is issued at the
middle of each month.

---

tion. This is unfortunate, since such an association is so important to the individual successes of the retailers and to the center as a community. Many retailers fail to see the need to cooperate with their fellow tenants. They prefer to spend their time concentrating on their own businesses and their own promotions.

The manager cannot force a retailer to participate in the merchants' association. Yet, through persuasion, which demands excellent communication skills, most merchants will come to realize that whatever benefits the center as a whole also aids the individual merchant.

An Alternative to the Merchants' Association

In recent years, many property managers, property owners, and retailers have questioned the usefulness of a merchants' association. Many developers are questioning whether they want to turn their modern, efficient shopping centers over to a group of tenants, who often have little interest in or knowledge about promoting the property. The tenants in such associations can become so embroiled in disputes that they lose sight of their real purpose, which is to promote themselves and the center. Critics of the merchants' association claim that the association often wastes large amounts of time and money through frivolous promotional spending and many hours of bickering between tenants. Today, many real estate practitioners advocate that promotion be the job of a few professionals and not the combined efforts of several tenants. The merchants' association might be replaced by the property manager, who would plan how advertising and promotional funds would be spent. If this arrangement is used, it is important that the property manager keep tenants regularly informed of plans that are being considered and being developed.

The center manager may hire an advertising agency to develop ideas and create advertising material. Generally, this material is also subject to the approval of the merchants. The costs of hiring an advertising agency are extremely high, and generally only the most prosperous shopping centers can afford to hire an agency. The most common alternative either to a merchants' association or to property managers or owners who do not have the time, expertise, or money to establish a promotional campaign is to hire a consultant. For example, an outside marketing director can devise a campaign of special activities designed to draw consumers into the shopping center and into the individual stores throughout the year.

The Promotion Director

Many businesses and individuals specialize in planning and staging advertising and promotional events for shopping centers. Their services are costly, but in many cases, well worth the expense. These companies or individuals can offer their expertise to those retailers, shopping center owners, and managers who do not have specialized training in communications. Whether or not a center can hire a promotion director generally depends on the size of the development and its operating budget.

Most major shopping centers of 400,000 square feet or more have a promotion director on staff. The property manager of a center ranging from 100,000 to 400,000 square feet may hire a part-time marketing director. As mentioned earlier, in most small developments, 100,000 square feet or less, the merchants' association, or a committee established by the merchants' association, will handle the promotional activities of the center.

Most full-time advertising and promotion directors handle large budgets and stage numerous advertising and promotional events, such as antique auto shows, musical concerts, and art fairs. The massive amount of details involved and the need to communicate with many retailers demand that such promotion directors be present at the center almost each day of the week.

A company or individual hired on a part-time basis probably has several different clients and therefore may be able to spend only a few days each month at any one location. Centers with part-time promotional personnel generally have modest, tightly controlled budgets—and events that are less ambitious and less time-consuming. That does not mean, however, that their events are any less effective than the larger events staged in larger centers.

Property managers who act as their center's sole promotion director must be able, with a small amount of money and a strictly limited amount of time, to develop imaginative, traffic-generating events. Tenant participation, therefore, becomes especially important in assuring that the center's promotional program will be a successful one. Unfortunately, many property managers ultimately plan and stage events alone, with little assistance from the other retailers.

If the center has sufficient budgetary funds to hire a full-time or a part-time promotion director, it should be quite easy to find a qualified one. One way would be to check the local Yellow Pages under "Public Relations" or "Promotion." Many cities also have professional communication organizations, many of which have excellent job referral services. Retail trade publications also run ads for promotional and marketing services, or managers of other area shopping centers may be able to suggest names for referral.

Any prospect who interviews for the position should be made aware of the particular needs of the shopping center and of any of its financial constraints. The promotion director may hold accreditation from the International Council of Shopping Centers. The designation "Certified Marketing Director" (CMD) is given to people who meet specific guidelines and have demonstrated a practical knowledge of advertising and promotion, specifically for the shopping center.

The promotion director may be responsible either to the president of the merchants' association or to the owner. In either case, the director must have assurance that all events are approved by the owner, who may veto plans that seem too expensive or do not fit the image of the center—regardless of the amount of merchant support there is for such events.

Planning and Budgeting Promotions

Merchants' associations first determine their budget and then develop their advertising and promotional plans based on their budget. If the lease states the required amount for merchants' association dues, the operating budget cannot be altered. However, if the merchants decide on the dues among themselves, then only retailers' ability and their willingness to pay will limit the extent to which the center can sponsor events.

Generally, the promotion director develops a budget and a calendar of events and then presents them to the merchants' association. Many factors about the projected budget will affect the initial plan: the current operating budget, the director's past experience in dealing with similar shopping centers, the activities of other developments in the area, a marketing study that indicates why people shop at this center, the tenant mix at the shopping center, and the demographics of the area. Such a plan will indicate not only the time and nature of the events but will also present an advertising plan and a breakdown of costs.

The director usually draws up this preliminary calendar during the fourth quarter of each year and finalizes it before mid-December, thereby avoiding delays at the start of the new year. As noted earlier, the property owner will study the calendar and ultimately has final authority to approve or veto it.

Most budgets include a reserve fund for unscheduled events and advertisements. Such a reserve can be very helpful after a major snowstorm, a fire, or any situation that discourages people from visiting the center. The size of the reserve fund depends on the size of the center and the average amount that is spent annually to advertise the center.

The property manager of a small center may manage adequately by holding only $200 or $300 in reserve. A superregional shopping center, however, may demand that several thousand dollars be available for emergencies.

Whatever the amount of the reserve fund, the merchants' association must spend the full amount by the end of the year, or it runs the risk of losing its nonprofit status. Quite surprisingly, a surplus of money can be a hindrance: The retailers may be forced to stage promotions just to rid themselves of surplus cash. Nevertheless, more merchants' associations face the problem of a shortage of funds than the more desirable problem of having too much money on hand.

Most events require at least two months of preparation time. If the retailers will participate directly, such as in a sidewalk sale or centerwide "Dollar Days" promotion, the merchants should be reminded at least 30 days in advance to begin preparations.

Exhibit 10.4 shows one way that a property manager or promotion director might handle this communication or any communication that relates to the center's promotional program. Ads for these events should be ready at least two weeks before the date of the event and should appear in the newspaper for about three continuous days before the event.

The promotion director should check to see that no retailer conducts its own promotion that might conflict with the center's plans, and that all retailers coordinate their advertising and sales' efforts with the center's programs. A full-year calendar of events, sent to all tenants, will help prevent this, but only regular communication with store owners can guarantee that such problems will not occur. If a conflict does arise, the center's promotion should always take precedence over the individual tenant's scheduled promotion.

When the promotion is over, a consensus of retailers will determine whether or not the event was a success. If shoppers came to the center, and sales increased, then the event probably is worth repeating the following year. But if sales were sluggish, or the promotion brought in less money to the owner than the event cost, then the idea should be dropped the following year or, in some way, revised.

In a similar vein, managers need not surrender an idea because the idea fails once. Many factors that cannot be controlled, such as the weather or the condition of the economy, can turn even a "safe" promotion into a disappointment. In

EXHIBIT 10.4. *Sample Merchants' Association Newsletter*

THE NAVIGATOR

DEPEND ON 1983 TABLOIDS TO POWER YOUR STORE'S SALES!

In this day and age of heavy competition, *every shopping center requires a vehicle to make it go,* to bring shoppers to the mall, to provide identity for its merchants, to promote merchandise, *to produce sales and profits for its stores.*

At High Mark Mall, we do have an outstanding vehicle that has generated traffic and business for our merchants .... tabloid sections *in all three* newspapers in our areas—NEWS PUBLICATIONS, FRINGE TRIB, AND NEWSTIME. Since our opening last March, the High Mark Mall tabloid has done an *excellent job.* By every measure or standard, it is *your most economic, efficient, and effective advertising vehicle.*

Make your 1983 plans based upon 10 High Mark Mall tabloids:

Your merchants' association has approved the schedule below, so *you can make your advertising plans accordingly.* Remember only *this tabloid section delivers 51,000 circulation,* reaching the households in Rosewood, Ambridge, Falwell, plus numerous other suburbs. *In our three newspapers, your advertising cost is lower than in any other vehicle.*

HIGH MARK MALL 1983 CALENDAR OF TABLOID SECTIONS

Issue	Promotion	Sale dates	Deadline
Jan. 14	Sidewalk Sale	January 15-18	January 2
February 11	Dollar Days	February 11-16	January 31
April 1	Spring/Easter	April 1-18	March 20
June 3	Dads, Grads, and Brides	June 3-16	May 22
July 15	Christmas in July	July 16-19	July 3
August 12	Back to School	August 12-17	July 31
September 16	Septemberfest	September 16-21	September 4
October 14	First Anniversary Sale	October 14-17	October 2
November 18	Holiday Sale	November 18-30	November 6
December 9	Christmas Gift Guide	December 9	November 27

Dates and events are subject to change by your merchants' association.

We have gained considerable experience over the years, and we know now that it takes a *lot of promotions to bring a continuous flow of shoppers to High Mark Mall* .... *promotion through advertising, promotion through shows and events, promotion through merchandising.* PROMOTIONS ARE WHAT YOUR MERCHANTS' ASSOCIATION IS ALL ABOUT!

Getting more "mileage" for your advertising dollars

Since the basic vehicle for your mall promotions is your mall tabloid, it deserves your full cooperation and support. *You get more mileage out of your advertising dollars when you promote and work together with your fellow mall merchants.* You should be included in at least seven of the ten tabloids scheduled, though many of our aggressive merchants will *advertise in all ten tabloids!*

Contact Joe Smith at News Publication—999-1199. Let's all participate to make 1983 a successful year for all our High Mark Mall Stores!

most cases, the merchants' association must look beyond the economic results to determine if a program should be discontinued.

The Role of Advertising

Advertising promotes the image of a shopping center and attracts the public to special events. Because advertising involves the purchase of media time or space, usually by contract, it gives the center owner and the merchants direct control over the promotional message.

It is difficult to establish standards for the frequency and type of advertising that should be developed for a shopping center because these needs, and the funds that are available, will vary widely. The property manager, property owner, promotion director (if there is one at the center), and the individual merchants must decide how much and what types of advertising and promotion are necessary to attract the public to the center. The decision makers must also determine specifically which media will be most effective for promoting the center.

Since most specialty centers, for example, are relatively small, many of the property managers of these centers give short slots in their advertisements to each tenant. Small neighborhood centers rarely offer attractions beyond what is available from the individual merchants. These small centers, therefore, should probably focus on the merchants at the center and the goods and services that they offer.

Many types of advertising are available. The range of media open for a merchants' association depends on the amount of money available and the size and specific qualities of the primary market area.

Newspaper Advertising

Most shopping center merchants' associations advertise heavily in newspapers—in fact, more there than in any other medium. Newspaper ads are relatively inexpensive, can communicate a great deal of information, and have wide distribution. People buy newspapers because they want to; the medium is not forced on them. Newspapers reach their readers daily, which makes newspapers effective for any type of build-up publicity. Newspapers can be read at the readers' convenience and leisure, which is something that the medium of radio cannot match. Once a radio or television message airs, most listeners cannot retrack the program to refer back to it. (The advent of videotape players has changed this situation somewhat.)

In general, though, a newspaper ad must be repeated many times. A full-page ad in the local newspaper at least once every two weeks is needed to increase the public's awareness of the center. The content of the ad probably should alternate between promotion of the center itself and messages from the stores within it. Any centerwide event requires a full-center promotion.

A major development in newspaper advertising occurred little over 20 years ago, largely in response to growing competition from television. That was when big-city newspapers first began to offer zoned editions.

Daily newspapers in large metropolitan areas emphasize to their advertisers the value of their zoned editions. The newspaper that residents in the city buy contains a section with news and advertising intended specifically for the city's residents. The papers that are distributed in the surrounding area, however, contain a different section that deals primarily with local issues and contains only local advertising. The newspaper's circulation department generally studies the people who live in each zone. The socioeconomic level of the residents, their interests, their buying habits, and the distance they will travel for goods and services will all be of interest to potential advertisers.

Advertisers, therefore, can reach specific markets by placing their ads in localized editions of the newspaper. It is a simple idea, and, for newspapers, it has been a tremendously successful idea. Nevertheless, shopping center managers must remember that it costs a newspaper staff time and effort to localize a page, and the advertiser eventually pays for that cost. Although a center may draw from a small market, it may be more expensive to place an ad in only two or three local editions than to run the ad throughout the city. Naturally, small community and weekly neighborhood newspapers do not have zoned editions—and these are newspapers in which many merchants' associations do advertise.

Many centers use color ads. Color attracts readers' attention, and it has been proven to be effective as an advertising tool. Unfortunately, the cost of printing color is high—and not all newspapers have the equipment to be able to offer a high-quality colored product. Before the owner or manager commits the shopping center to a costly contract, the quality limitations must be considered. Many well-designed, black-and-white layouts are equally effective and cost much less.

Many newspapers will agree to combine one center's ad with a number of other full-page or multipage advertisements to form an insert or circular. These are popular because they are easy to remove, and they need not be clipped from the rest of the paper. Anyone comparing prices or interested in checking store offerings will notice the insert. The cost of purchasing this type of advertising generally covers a share of the bulk mailing costs. Extra copies can be distributed at the center, which many customers appreciate, especially if the ad contains money-saving coupons. A shopping center larger than 100,000 square feet should plan to develop a newspaper circular at least four times yearly, and, in particular, whenever a special promotion is planned.

Newspapers, however, do have limitations for the purposes of advertising. The average reader reads only a portion of the entire newspaper; in fact, the typical reader spends 30 minutes reading only one-fifth to one-fourth of all editorial content—and, at that, it remains questionable whether the reader will notice any single ad. Many practitioners mistakenly assume that if an ad appears in print, readers will see it. Even if readers do notice the ad, however, as with any type of advertising, there is no guarantee that they will act on the message. The promotion director must try to attract attention to the center's ads—and then arouse the public's interest so that people will visit the center. The ad, therefore, needs to be well designed, which is where an advertising agency might be especially valuable.

Direct Mail Advertising

Direct mail is a good way to convey messages to the public. The advertiser does not have to cooperate with the competition, as is necessary with newspaper circulars. Another advantage is that the recipient is likely to scan the literature, especially if the piece is personalized.

Unfortunately, mailing costs, even bulk rate, are high, especially when a distribution involves several thousand individual pieces. Combined with printing charges and the costs for appropriate mailing lists, the expense can exceed the means of a small merchants' association. Another problem with direct mail is that many people are so inundated with it—leaflets, flyers, letters, brochures—that many essentially "tune out" all of these messages. Some immediately discard any direct mail pieces they receive; some have even requested that the post office not deliver any direct mail to their homes. Direct mail experts constantly search for ways to hold their audience's attention, studying specifics such as colors, phrases, and letter size, as they try to determine what features will capture the eye.

Still, direct mail as a promotional option should not be dismissed lightly. It can be effective, and for some types of campaigns—such as sending discount coupons to potential customers—direct mail can be the best route. The owner or manager should account for all projected expenses before recommending such a plan. One compromise might be to print circulars to distribute at the shopping center. Such an effort can move traffic into the stores, although it does little to attract customers to the center.

Another alternative is to deliver door-to-door circulars. Many communities have professional delivery services that specialize in this form of advertising, or the center can hire local high school students to distribute circulars around the neighborhood. One caution is that direct delivery must not interfere with the United States Postal Service. Circulars cannot be placed in mailboxes. They can be slipped under doors, hung on doorknobs, or placed on doormats, but federal law prohibits any item other than mail delivered by the U.S. Postal Service to be placed in mailboxes.

Radio Advertising

Radio is a part of daily American life. People depend on their radios to wake them up; they listen to the radio at the breakfast table, on their way to work, in the bedroom, and at the beach. Radio is a flexible medium, and it is one of the most effective advertising means in today's market.

Considering the size of the market and the wide geographic area that it reaches, radio can also be very inexpensive—especially when the advertiser wants to target in on a specific part of the population. Radio stations gear their programming to attract certain age groups and demographic types. They, therefore, can guarantee their advertisers a concentrated percentage of a specific type of consumer. Moreoever, most radio commercials hold the listener's attention for the length of the spot. The listener—riding in a car, for example—cannot idly pass up a commercial and move on to the next program element.

Yet, it is radio's narrow-casting feature that makes it less than ideal for a shopping center's messages. A shopping center promotion aims to reach many markets. Unless a specific promotion is geared toward one group of people—teenagers, elderly persons, or business professionals—it will be difficult to find one or even two stations that will reach all potential customers.

The practical use of radio advertising, therefore, depends on the station's range and the size of the market. Most small-town stations offer attractive rates, and their audiences include the entire city. Many strip neighborhood shopping centers in low-density areas depend almost entirely on radio for their advertising messages. In large cities, on the other hand, stations tend to sell air time at a premium, broadcasting to thousands of people, few of whom have interest in a localized message.

Many shopping centers can take advantage of the smaller suburban radio stations. Most such stations offer low rates and a limited market coverage—both factors that a local center owner will probably desire. Owners with shopping centers that lie in the hearts of big cities, however, do not have this option available, making radio an attractive but unrealistic means of advertising for them.

Television Advertising

Television is easily the most powerful and persuasive communications medium in America. Its audience is large and remarkably loyal. To an advertiser, however, buying TV time means joining the big leagues. TV advertising can be extremely costly.

A merchants' association may be able to afford one or two commercials to be broadcast during a desirable time slot, but for TV advertising to be truly effective, the greatest number of potential buyers must view the ad, and so the ad must be repeated often. For many merchants' associations, this type of costly, concentrated campaign goes beyond budget realities.

Still, in smaller communities, as with radio, television advertising can be relatively inexpensive. Its wide exposure and visual impact make it a natural for small-town shopping centers and their special events.

Television permits the use of the printed word, spoken word, pictures in motion, color, music, animation, and sound effects—all blended into one message. In one decade—the 1950s—the size of its audience surpassed any other communication medium in the country. From national news to advertising and popular programs, the power of television to influence public behavior and thinking is demonstrated over and over again.

Because television has such a great impact, promotion directors should explore the possibilities of TV advertising, before ruling it out on the basis of cost alone. Directors should contact local TV sales departments to find out the rates and determine if the station might arrange a special advertising package. Some local TV stations have advertising "wheels" that carry the written words of continuous advertising messages, with music and news reports in the background. They work much like a radio station but still offer some of TV's visual effect. Although their impact is not as great as a regular TV ad, and there is often no sound to the ad itself, the rates are quite low, and they can be effective. For a special promotion, especially if it is community-oriented, this type of station might offer the shopping center a free spot. In many cases, then, TV is within the financial bounds of shopping centers, if the practitioners use initiative and imagination. The rates charged by a TV station might be surprisingly affordable.

Billboard Advertising

Billboards and other outdoor advertising have the advantage of being local. For a large center of 200,000 square feet or more, billboards can be used to identify the location of the center. Shopping centers smaller than that, however, probably cannot justify the relatively high cost of purchasing billboard space. The billboard advertiser is spending advertising funds in a way that will attract consumers to the shopping center. The basic function of a neighborhood center, which is to serve the daily needs of the immediate community, diminishes the need to attract new customers.

For a larger center, however, an excellent idea may be to develop a basic logo that will act as a permanent identifying sign for the property. An advertising agency can probably create the most effective identifying logo. This logo can then appear on all billboards, as well as in all print advertisements, center notices, and direct mail pieces. As drivers approach the center, therefore, they will see small signs, perhaps appearing with only the logo and an arrow. The more familiar that the logo becomes to consumers, the more effective it will be as an advertising tool. The logo can be incorporated into the center's letterhead, forms, and print ads. The use of a logo, therefore, goes far beyond outdoor billboard advertising.

For use of billboards beyond directional purposes, however, property managers must consider the limitations of such advertising. A single billboard will reach many people who travel by it daily, which means that although large, the audience generally stays very much the same from day to day. In a short time, people will adjust to the message, and the billboard will lose much of its impact. Another drawback to billboard advertising is that environmental groups today are pressuring businesses to limit their billboard promotions, and many companies are complying, a trend that is driving up the cost of the remaining billboards.

Finally, most billboard space is rented for set periods of time, generally a minimum of three to six months, and therefore, billboards are generally impractical for promoting special or short-term sales.

Nevertheless, given their limitations and the suggestion that they be used only for large properties, billboards can effectively advertise the name, image, and location of the shopping center.

Transit Advertising

Mass transit has become a popular means of transportation in many communities, and transit advertising is being used for some shopping center messages. Most transit ads are attention-grabbing signs, posted in city buses, trains, and taxicabs. The medium is localized, ads can carry a substantial amount of copy, and little interferes with advertising for only a short term. Furthermore, in most cities, transit advertising rates are quite reasonable. The promotion director should contact the local transit office for information on such advertising. The merchants' association may wish to request that a promotional expert be hired to create a professional ad that can be used for the transit space.

Advertising Agencies

Advertising agencies may be the answer for some merchants' associations in creating ads and buying advertising space. As noted, for special designs and one-time assignments, such as creating an advertising logo for the center, an advertising agency may be well worth the cost. The talent and production facilities in these agencies are generally several steps beyond the means of most merchants' associations and beyond what a newspaper or radio station advertising department will provide.

For most shopping centers, however, the retainers and service fees charged by advertising agencies are above what merchants' associations' budgets can support on a regular basis. Although an agency may be able to create a more professional product, the average merchants' association—restricted by a limited budget—should plan to use the art and copy services of the media in which it will advertise. Still, the manager or director might wish to investigate the fees and services of local advertising agencies.

Promotional and Special Events

Promotional and special events are successful ways of promoting a community's awareness that a shopping center exists and, in turn, of informing the public of the goods and services that are offered at the center. Promotions come in many forms and in a variety of prices. The events can range from a sidewalk sale to a professional circus. The types and frequency of promotional events will depend significantly on the size of a center, its operating budget, and the economic level of its clientele.

Frequency of Events

Shopping center merchants should plan to stage special events throughout the year—but again, the timing and frequency of these events will depend on the specific needs and the general nature of the development. Many merchants' associations try to hold their promotions in conjunction with major holidays, such as Christmas, Labor Day, and the Fourth of July. In this way, the excitement created by the holidays spills over into the promotion. Some shopping centers might base a promotion on a little-known ethnic holiday. If the event is well planned and well promoted, the public will bring a general holiday spirit to the celebration, along with a basic curiosity about the holiday.

Types of Promotional Events

Promotion directors of superregional shopping centers, with large operating budgets available, generally are in the best position to offer a wide range of promotional activities. Property managers of smaller centers, on the other hand, are wise to keep the price of their events low, aim for good press coverage, and try to tie their events into other community activities.

A good promotion is one that attracts many potential customers and moves them into the center's individual stores. Volume alone, however, is not the only criterion for success. As noted earlier, an event that attracts people once—people who do not become regular customers—must be called a limited success, no matter how large the response. The ultimate goals of promotion are to increase awareness of the center's existence and to increase customer traffic during the promotion and after the promotion, encouraging visitors to become loyal center patrons. All promotional events, therefore, should keep with the image of the shopping center. They should also be easy to stage and draw people who are eager to spend money. The ideal event is one that becomes so regular that customers wait in anticipation for it each year. Here are some ideas for effective and easy-to-stage events:

Bike-a-thons and marathons. Use a shopping center as the starting or stopping point for a community bike race or a marathon run. Entrants can be charged a nominal fee that can be turned over to a local charity. Shopping center merchants might donate prizes to the winners.

Charity bazaars. Volunteer the shopping center as the site for a local charity sale or auction.

Sidewalk sales. Select a day when all shopping center merchants will move their sale merchandise to the walks in front of their stores. This is a good event to hold during summer months, and in enclosed malls, the idea is workable for any time of the year. Alternatives to the summer-end clearance sale may be successful. The buying public is overwhelmed at the end of each summer with "one-day only," "special," "summer clearance" sales. The events may go by different names—"Crazy Daze," "Sidewalk Days,". "Maxwell Street Days"—but the basic idea is the same. It is an "outdoor," summer clearance sale, and it can be a very effective promotional activity.

Arts and crafts sales. Invite local artists to display and sell their arts and crafts at the shopping center.

School art fair. Contact area schools and have them select the best work of student artists for display at the shopping center.

Science fair. Arrange with local schools to have science exhibits displayed.

Used books sale. Ask customers to donate old books that can be resold at the center; the proceeds can be donated to charity.

Fire and police exhibits. Contact the local police and fire departments and arrange for special exhibits and demonstrations. Most fire and police departments have their own public relations departments that will be more than eager to cooperate.

Psychic fair. Invite local psychics to read palms, gaze into crystal balls, or interpret tarot cards—all at a public festival held at the shopping center.

Sports clinic. Ask area schools, country clubs, and health clubs for names of health and fitness experts who can conduct public demonstrations of various sports activities, such as golf, basketball, weightlifting, or billiards.

Fashion show. Stage an afternoon fashion show with merchandise displayed from the shopping center's stores.

Many events are pointed to particular seasons. Here is a calendar of promotions tied to various months and holidays:

January. Merchants can sell their remaining Christmas merchandise by holding a "Dollar Days" clearance sale.

February. The center can stage a "Hearts and Flowers" Valentine's Day sale, tying other events—perhaps a dance—into the Valentine's Day theme.

March. The manager can plan a centerwide sale with a St. Patrick's Day theme. If Easter should fall in March, the center could have an Easter Bunny roving through the center, greeting children and distributing chocolate eggs. The center could sponsor an Easter egg hunt or hold a raffle for a free ham. Each store might offer its own prize, or each store might have an entry box for a single-center drawing.

April. Enclosed malls can hold high-and-dry "April Showers" sales. Spring cleaning can provide another April promotional theme.

May. A Mother's Day essay-writing contest for area children might attract publicity, or possibly a raffle for a weekend vacation at a local hotel would generate excitement about the approaching summer.

June. Brides, dads, and new graduates provide popular themes for June promotions. A center also might hold drawings for free baseball tickets.

July. Sidewalk sales, cooking and barbeque demonstrations, and water safety programs are all timely events for midsummer.

August. Events with a back-to-school theme are appropriate at this time of year. Many centers will give away pencils or notebooks. Some centers may sponsor back-to-school, free dances for area teenagers.

September. The back-to-school theme can overlap into this month, and autumn-based promotions can also begin.

October. Halloween is in the air, and costume parties for local children are crowd-pleasers. Again, any type of autumn promotion could be effective during October.

November. With Thanksgiving approaching, a turkey raffle is appropriate. Here again, as with an Easter promotion, each store should sponsor a drawing, thus encouraging the public to go into each shop. Following Thanksgiving, the arrival of Santa Claus and Christmas dominates promotional activities.

December. Christmas lends itself to hundreds of commercial promotional events. A center can sponsor an ornament-designing contest or take photos of children with Santa Claus. Charity groups can decorate trees and have the public vote on which is most original. Children can display their drawings, or senior citizens can sell their crafts.

In all cases, effective advertising is needed to publicize the events. Most such events require a lead time of only two or three weeks, although some promotional activities require preparation on the part of the public (a costume contest or a bike-a-thon), and the center should begin its advertising efforts several weeks in advance of the event.

Arranging Promotional Activities

The shopping center manager, promotion director, or promotional committee should coordinate the shopping center's promotions. The complexity of the event and the size of the merchants' association budget will essentially determine whether the center should retain an outside organization to stage the promotion or carry out all necessary tasks in-house. Many companies specialize in staging events for shopping centers, but very few small centers can afford such services.

Many promotional events are related to the season. Promotion directors might plan promotions that focus on the heat or on the snow, or perhaps on the arrival of spring. There are numerous possibilities. As indicated by possible promotions that are appropriate for different months of the year, many promotions can be based on a holiday theme. Whatever the event, the property manager or the promotion director should ensure that any props, costumes, and decorations are stored securely so that they can be used for several years.

Special Problems

A center may be planning a sidewalk sale, and the manager may discover only days before the event that the city has an ordinance that levies a high fee for enterprises that stage more than two such sales per month. The major purpose of such an ordinance is to discourage garage sale enthusiasts from becoming commercial enterprises, but it also affects retail businesses, including shopping centers. Before committing to a promotional plan, therefore, the merchants' association—or whoever holds the responsibility for promotions—should check to see if any city ordinance will affect the promotion.

The shopping center manager or promotion director should also check with the local fire and police departments to arrange for special protection and security. Finally, if an outside organization will be retained, the manager should check the organization's credentials and ask for credit references.

Shopping Center Publicity

Publicity involves the coverage of planned events by the legitimate news media. Unlike advertising, where media print space or air time is bought for a price, publicity cannot be purchased. And unlike promotion, publicity cannot be expertly planned and controlled. If the editors of the local newspaper believe that a shopping center's promotion warrants public attention, they will probably cover the story. That decision, however, rests purely on individual judgements—and the property owner and manager have little voice in the matter. A newspaper story lends an objective touch to an event. It is this objectivity that gives an article of "news," however short the article, power and believability—something that advertising and promotion cannot equal.

Many publicity stories about a shopping center qualify as "news." Local business editors, for example, may welcome news about the signing of a major tenant's lease or of a new store's opening. A promotion that has a community twist—a charity bazaar or a fire prevention exhibit—stands a good chance of being covered in the newspaper. Shopping center managers need to be creative in finding ways to attract the attention of the media. Any such news event requires that the manager prepare a news release, such as the release that is presented in Exhibit 10.5.

Many newspapers will publish stories that spotlight individual stores, although managers should be wary of leaning too heavily in this direction. Such pieces often appear to be self-serving, unless the article includes consumer tips or some type of service information. For example, a shopping center bank official can explain the advantages and disadvantages of various types of savings accounts and savings certificates. A pet store can offer advice on how to shop and care for a dog or cat. Although these items take time and effort to plan and hold, the newspaper is more likely to print them than a story that simply praises an individual merchant.

EXHIBIT 10.5. *Sample News Release*

HIGH MARK MALL
Mainsville, Illinois

NEWS RELEASE
Contact: Buck Lindley
124 Main Street
(312) 222-0000

January 25, 1983

For immediate release

HIGH MARK MALL ANNOUNCES EXPANSION PLANS

Owners of High Mark Mall, Mainsville, Illinois, announced plans today for a 100,000 square foot retail space expansion that is expected to be completed by the spring of 1984.

"We're very excited about these plans," said John Brown, an owner and original developer of the five-year-old shopping center. "We believe that the program at High Mark Mall will provide the community of Mainsville with significant commercial growth and great possibilities for an even more prosperous Mainsville."

The plans were announced at a 10:30 a.m. press conference held on Tuesday, January 25, in the High Mark Mall conference room. At this time, few specific plans about the expansion have been announced, but Brown did indicate that one of the new retail tenants will be Olson's, a major discount chain that owns several stores throughout the Midwest.

Construction of the addition will begin in early May. Brown indicated that negotiations are currently underway with two tenants, and that at least five additional tenants have agreed to join the center. He declined to elaborate on the identities of these tenants.

-30-

Either the shopping center manager or the promotion director can carry out the publicity programs. Public relations agencies exist to do this type of work, but, similar to advertising agencies, their costs usually go beyond the means of the small-sized or medium-sized shopping center.

By definition, publicity is free. As such, if handled by inside personnel, publicity projects require only a small part of an association's operating budget. Some amount of money should be set aside for such expenses as typing, duplication, mailing, and photography.

Publicity, in many respects, means contriving stories, which is quite easy to do. It is not difficult to come up with ways to attract public attention to the shopping center. The problem however, is gaining attention that the public will view as positive, and motives that it will accept as honest. Believability is a top criterion in judging any publicity effort.

A creative manager can find many ways to publicize the shopping center. For example, when one community center celebrated its 25th anniversary, the property manager urged the local newspaper to republish several articles and pictures from the center's original opening. The center also sponsored a dress contest, and many people came to the center dressed in costumes of 25 years earlier. The contest and the items in the newspaper created quite a stir in the community. The center's anniversary promotion, in sum, became a community event. Many people in the community got positively involved with the event, and the media in the area were therefore more willing to publicize the activities.

Yet, the ultimate aim of publicity is to give an institution character. Practitioners must realize that exposure alone will not necessarily lead to a public image of integrity and good character. That type of reputation may take years to develop. Practitioners trying to build a solid image for a shopping center are likely to find that they cannot control all of the news that is generated about the property. The media might get a "scoop" about the center or about one of the tenants at the center, and the news could be extremely detrimental. The public, on the other hand, may not believe and certainly does not notice all of the news, nor will the public retain all of the information that it observes.

The Role of the Merchant

Promotion, advertising, and publicity are proven ways of drawing people to a shopping center. Once the customers are there, however, it is the responsibility of the individual retailers to make the merchandise attractive and desirable to buy.

A single promotion cannot keep customers coming back to a store with unreasonable prices, poor-quality merchandise, or shoddy service. Shopping center tenants themselves, not the merchants' association, the property owner, or the property manager, must provide their customers with motivations to buy. Each tenant must take care to keep its own space properly maintained, especially during special promotions. It is during promotional events that the increased traffic flow not only increases the store's volume but also increases the need for excellent maintenance.

Regular communication between the merchants' association and the individual tenants is necessary to ensure that merchants' advertising does not conflict with overall shopping center promotions. The property manager should try to coordinate the timing of individual retailers' promotional events to the merchants' association's events. If a junior department store is sponsoring an annual moonlight sale, for example, the entire center might join a centerwide moonlight sale. The themes of the merchants' association should constantly stress consistency and unity.

As noted earlier, the tenant's lease will outline most of each merchant's promotional responsibilities. As long as the merchant conforms to the requirements of the lease, few problems should develop. If a tenant refuses to cooperate, legal action is possible, although simple pressure from other retailers can be effective.

Emergency Situations

Occasionally, the merchants' association will be called on to tend to unexpected situations. A major snowstorm, a flood, or a fire that destroys one or more stores can devastate the entire center's business unless the merchants' association takes action quickly. Such an emergency can mark an ideal time for special sales or advertisements, such as a "Blizzard's Over Sale" or a "Fire Won't Stop Us" promotion. In any case, the center should take out notices in the newspaper explaining that merchants are still open for business and inviting customers to take advantage of special discounts created especially because of the situation.

The attention that a fire or snowstorm will bring to a center is attention that a creative promotion director can turn to the merchants' advantage. Most newspapers will cover this type of story anyway—so it becomes an opportunity to earn additional publicity.

Other Factors that Attract a Buying Public

Other factors beyond those discussed above play a role either in attracting or in discouraging the buying public.

Maintenance is essential to the success of a shopping center. This was discussed in detail in chapter 6. Suffice it here to say that merchants have an obligation, generally stated in their leases, to keep their stores clean, attractive, and well stocked. The manager should also be certain that common areas are always clean and attractive, that snow is shoveled during the winter, and that litter is removed regularly. The property manager may be forced to discuss housekeeping problems with individual merchants who are falling below the center's standards.

The availability of parking is another factor that customers will consider in deciding to go to a shopping center. Convenient parking is, in fact, a distinguishing feature of the shopping center. Virtually all types and sizes of shopping centers must provide some form of parking for their customers. Unless special lots are provided for employees at the center, merchants and their employees should use the farthest parking spaces, leaving the closer spaces for customers. If a parking lot is too small to handle an average day's traffic, the owner may be forced to expand the lot, and in turn, charge tenants for the expense, possibly in the form of higher rents.

Finally, security is a constant problem at all shopping centers. Security was discussed in detail in chapter 6. In general, customers should always feel safe at a shopping center, unafraid that loiterers will bother them, that pickpockets will steal their money, or that their cars will be tampered with while they are shopping.

Conclusion

Several factors will determine a shopping center's success in attracting the buying public. Foremost among these are a center's location and its tenant mix. Second is the willingness of individual merchants to keep their stores clean, attractive, well stocked, and well serviced. After these conditions have been met, the property manager and merchants can begin to advertise, promote, and publicize the attractions of a particular shopping center.

If the center's merchants decide to employ advertising, the messages should run frequently and reach the greatest number of potential customers at the lowest possible cost. The ads should alternate between messages for the center as a whole and those for individual merchants. The size of the development should determine specifically how these ads should be alternated. The medium that is used will affect the way that messages are presented.

Special events are effective ways to draw the public to the center. The events should be staged regularly—depending on the needs of the center—to attract new customers to the center and to build traffic. The events should be inexpensive, easy to conduct, and ultimately attract consumers who are likely to become regular patrons of the center. Community or charity promotions, tied in with an all-center promotion, can be effective in attracting the public. Special sales that carry the theme of an upcoming holiday should also build sales and increase tenants' and the property owner's income.

Publicity draws attention to the center and, if successful, gives the center a positive image in the public eye. The promotion director can circulate legitimate news items and prepare feature stories for the local news media. Maintaining the center's name in a positive light will help build a reputation for the property and sustain consumer interest.

The person or organization charged with promoting a shopping center—whatever the size of the center—has an extremely difficult job. But by using all the "tried and true" promotional techniques—or one or some combination of them—the job can be done effectively. Every shopping center must be backed by a sizeable consuming public that will support the property on a regular basis. Promoting the center to the public, therefore, is essential to the development's success.

Review Questions

1. Plan a basic marketing program for a shopping center for an entire year. Evaluate it in terms of its flexibility. Are alternatives planned in case of possible cancellations?
2. What types of special events are appropriate for the shopping center that you manage?
3. Discuss the major types of advertising media and describe the advantages and disadvantages of each.
4. How can current community events in your own community be tied into center services?
5. Are you familiar with local organizations' annual activities calendars? How can you align your programs with the activities that are planned?
6. What unique features are contained in the shopping center that you manage? What features might be created that could be used for publicity purposes?
7. What efforts are you taking to acquire free publicity for the center?
8. How are you encouraging merchants to get involved in promotions and other merchants' programs?

9. When is a good time to request a budget increase for promotional programs?
10. How should each advertising or promotional program be evaluated for its overall effectiveness?

11

Insurance, Risk Management, and Taxes

Fundamentally, all shopping center investors seek a profit from the money that they invest. Two functions that are vital to a successful shopping center investment and to the investor's continued profits are an effective insurance and risk management program and an effective real estate tax program. An insurance and risk management program helps to protect the property against the risk of financial loss. Probably as important as earning a profit and preserving capital are the many tax shelters that become available to real estate investors. The property manager, however, is not an expert on either of these subjects—and most clients will not expect such expertise from the property manager. Still, the manager should have an understanding of the subjects and be able to assist the owner in preparing and administering these plans for the shopping center. These two general topics—insurance and taxes—and the property manager's responsibilities regarding them are the subjects of this chapter.

Insurance and Risk Management

The shopping center contains hundreds of risks, which are often referred to as *loss exposures*. Risks are scattered from each tenant's space to the common areas and the structure itself. Wherever people gather in one location, as they do in a shopping center, the number of risks increases. A shopper can suffer a bodily injury, for which the center may be held liable. Vandals might deface the common area at the center, or a windstorm might blow down a fence that surrounds the parking lot. Even a federally imposed guideline can be considered a risk, if it means that the owner must abide by it or face the danger of litigation. If there were no risks, there would be no need to worry about safety or loss. Risks are realities, however, and every shopping center investor must contend with them. An insurance policy is one way to protect against economic loss.

Insurance companies do not prevent losses; they offer financial protection against the consequences of such losses. Insurance is based on the probabilities that events will occur in various climates, regions, areas, or neighborhoods. Through a statistical review of many factors, rates can be determined for a given exposure. The insurers pool together the insureds' premiums and thus have funds to pay for claims as they occur.

There are two basic ideas that readers need to keep in mind. First, insurance and the management of risk are both very general topics. This chapter does not attempt to present an all-encompassing guide to the subjects. Instead, it offers an introduction. Readers who need more information can turn to other sources, some of which are listed in the bibliography of this book.

Second, readers should remember that risk management is a primary issue that will confront center managers. Shopping center practitioners take many steps to manage and control the risk on their properties—and insurance is one of these steps.

Definition of Risk

Defined broadly, risk represents uncertainty, and many uncertainties affect the shopping center daily. Insurance serves as a financial shield against risk. Risk management prepares the owner for the financial demands of claims arising from accidents and lawsuits, and it gives the center owner and manager and their creditors protection against these claims and peace of mind.

In shopping centers, insurance can provide financial protection against loss from, among other things, fire, tornadoes, theft, and bodily injuries. Center owners can manage risk and thereby directly and indirectly increase their profits. Direct protection comes in the form of financial support when damage occurs. Risk management also produces indirect benefits. A property that the manager has inspected rigorously for loss exposures will probably be better controlled and managed than one that has not been so scrutinized. Risk management, thus, in many ways, prevents and prepares the firm for the financial demands of unexpected accidents or litigation.

Managers should avoid thinking of insurance as protection against inept business practices. Insurance offers safeguards against loss from uncertainties. Bad business practices are usually preventable.

A well-insured property is one that is prepared for loss. Likewise, a well-insured shopping center is one that is prepared for loss. Shopping centers, however, are generally larger and costlier investments than many other types of property investments. Many shopping center developers, therefore, are more interested in protection against major risks on the property than they are about minor losses. Generally, the larger the deductible, the lower the insurance premium. Because of the lower insurance premiums that come with high deductibles, many investors concentrate almost totally on major coverage.

An effective risk management program offers peace of mind, and that is an advantage that investors do not take lightly. It affects so many aspects of the investment. With an adequate amount of insurance coverage, the investor might try to reduce the loss from various hazards, insure the balance, then take the risks—and ultimately succeed. Risk management can also improve the quality of investment decisions. For example, an investor can identify all of the potential loss exposures involved with locating in a region with a high crime rate, be unable to find reasonable insurance coverage, and ultimately decide that the project is unwise.

Insurance also offers protection against financial loss, tying together insurance and the management of risk. Insurance reduces financial risk; it offers safeguards against unexpected losses. Shopping center managers need to understand both, since insurance against many of the hazards that could produce financial loss is essential for a profitable shopping center.

The insurance policy is a legal contract, which is prepared by an underwriter and issued by an insurance company. The property owner's insurance agent should negotiate the insurance contract, and an underwriter will also review the contract. The center owner will confront a basic question almost immediately: How much and what type of insurance should be carried for the property? The amount of insurance carried will vary greatly among centers. It will depend on, among other factors, the value of the property, the types of stores at the center, and the types of consumers that the center attracts.

A shopping center owner obtains insurance coverage basically the same way that any business does. The procedure is the same, whether the owner or the manager has the responsibility for obtaining the policy.

The person charged with finding insurance coverage for the shopping center should look first at the reputation of the insurance company. A proven track record, a wide selection of policies, prompt processing of claims, and thorough service— these are all factors that the decision maker should consider in evaluating the insurance company. The decision maker at the property can turn to an annual publication that insurance practitioners recognize as the only independent source for such data, *Best's Reports: Property and Casualty Edition*, which is published annually by A. M. Best Company, Olwick, New Jersey.

The property manager should find a reputable insurer and an astute insurance agent. The property manager should seek the services of an insurance agent who specializes in writing policies for income properties. The qualities of a good insurer have been noted. Next, how can the manager spot a good agent? An insurance agent should review the loss exposures at the property with the owner and manager, offer suggestions, answer questions, review the owner's objectives, and propose a solid, precise insurance program that will suit the risk management plan. Ideally, the property manager's job in insurance matters will be reduced to informing the insurance agent of the particular sources of loss at the center, and the agent will handle most of the work from there. Let us now take a closer look at the agent.

The Insurance Agent

In this discussion, *insurance agent* refers to the person who negotiates insurance. There are many professional designations that insurance agents can earn. Perhaps the most prestigious in property and casualty insurance is the CPCU, which signifies a Chartered Property Casualty Underwriter. Insurance agents act either as independents, or they represent one company, and as such are called direct writers or exclusive agents. Yet, more important than this distinction are the credentials, experience, and training of the agent. The manager should expect the agent to offer solid advice on the insurance plan for the center, to be knowledgeable on all aspects of risk management and insurance, and to have access to any number of resources.

The property manager should consider three activities of an insurance company: *coverage, capacity,* and *claims.* Coverage involves the insurer's ability to provide the appropriate contract for the exposures. Capacity refers to the insurer's ability to offer insurance policies and limits that meet the needs of the buyer. Finally, claims involves the insurer's capabilities to process claims quickly and efficiently. The manager should also assess the means that the insurance company uses to handle sales, underwriting, loss control, policy issuance, claims records, and policy renewals.

As part of the decision-making process, the property owner should assess property values first on a replacement cost basis. If the policy states the insurance value on an "actual cash" value basis, the depreciation that can be charged must be considered. Some newer package policies will provide replacement cost coverage if insurance is at eighty percent of value at the time of loss. Another plan might penalize the insured when a loss occurs and cover only the original cost of the item—which becomes a penalty because of inflation. This is discussed in more detail in the section in this chapter on coinsurance. Suffice it now to say that in an inflationary economy, all businesses must take extreme care before they approve any coinsurance plan.

The manager and owner must decide on the amount of coverage to purchase for the center. They also must decide on the type of policy. They should understand the exact coverage provided under each policy being considered. If some coverage will be limited, these statements ultimately could have major effects on the center's profits. A loss may not be covered.

After an insurer has been selected, and coverage begins, at least one person must evaluate the insurance company's performance on a continual basis. That person will assess factors such as whether the agent and insurer have provided the expected services, and how quickly the firm has processed claims. The person evaluating the insurance company also may take into account the comments of other insureds. If a center is having problems with its insurance carrier, and service does not improve, the manager may be forced to request bids for a new program. In some cases, a simple warning that the policy may be dropped is enough to stir the agent and insurer to action.

All real estate practitioners must understand the factors that can affect rates and premiums. The practitioners, in turn, may be able to suggest changes for the property that ultimately will result in lower insurance costs.

Essentially, property insurance rates are based on four factors: *construction, occupancy, protection,* and *exposure.* The following offers a brief discussion of each of these:

Construction. An insurance inspector will evaluate the materials that were used in building the shopping center structure, including whether the structure is composed of brick, masonry, or fire-resistant materials. The layout and design are also evaluated, as are the interior materials. The susceptibility of the materials to fire; whether or not the building has a fire sprinkler system; and other perils found on the property—these are some of several factors that will affect insurance rates, which, in turn, will affect premium costs.

Occupancy. The inspector reviews the types of tenants in the center. Typically, in a shopping center, tenants are retailers. Increasingly, however, service tenants, such as doctors' and lawyers' offices, movie cinemas, and dry cleaners, are leasing space in shopping centers. The insurer who develops the rate will probably take into account the greater exposure of one tenant (a restaurant) than another (a women's clothing store). The greater the risk, the higher the premium.

Protection. The adage that "prevention is the best medicine" is an appropriate reminder for shopping center managers. There are many ways to protect the property and reduce its exposure to loss. Sprinklers, parapets, fire doors, and fire divisions are some devices that are used and used effectively, ultimately reducing premium and underwriting problems. Prevention activities might include fire drills, meetings with tenants to discuss fire safety, and periodic store inspections. Ultimately, any of these techniques might reduce both the threat of fire or other losses—and insurance rates. Any type of preventive program is also likely to contribute to the center's longevity.

Exposure. External hazards that increase the dangers to the property fall under this heading. These are generally physical hazards, created in many cases by nearby structures. One example might be a shopping center located near a chemical plant, where the risk of explosion is compounded. An explosion in the plant would probably leave the shopping center owner with damaged property and possible liability claims. Weather conditions can create additional hazards to the property. Insurers take into account, for example, the vulnerability of the area to tornadoes, earthquakes, hurricanes, or hailstorms.

When underwriters review a property for coverage, they often look at the losses that similiar businesses in the area have suffered. Some rating plans also offer rate credits to those businesses that take active loss prevention measures. Property managers that press for preventive measures often can receive rate credits for their centers.

Property Insurance Penalty Clause

Probably best known among penalty clauses is the coinsurance clause, mentioned earlier in this chapter. The coinsurance clause states that the insured must carry insurance equal to a specified percentage of the value of the property at the time of the loss, or suffer a penalty. Should the insured carry less, the insurer is responsible to pay for only a percentage of the loss. The clause encourages purchasers to buy insurance to value.

For example, if a policy contains an 80 percent coinsurance clause, to avoid the operation of the clause, the insured must have coverage equal to 80 percent of the replacement cost of the property at the time of the loss. Otherwise, there will be a sharing of coverage between the insurer and the insured. The insurer agrees to a rate reduction if this clause is included. The clause provides that if the amount of insurance in effect at the time of loss is less than a certain percentage of the value of the property at that time, only a fraction of the loss will be paid. Some policies require the inclusion of such a coinsurance clause. The following example shows how a coinsurance plan works:

Building A is worth $100,000. Because of an 80 percent coinsurance clause, owner A purchases $80,000 coverage. As long as the value at the time of the loss remains at $100,000, the policy will cover 100 percent of the losses, up to the policy limit. The formula thus reads as follows:

$$\frac{\text{Amount carried}}{\substack{\text{Amount required at} \\ \text{the time of loss}}} \times \text{Loss} = \$ \text{ Amount received}$$

$$\frac{\$80,000}{\$80,000} \times \$10,000 = \$10,000$$

But if the amount of insurance the holder carries remains at $80,000, and the property value increases to $150,000, the insured will suffer a penalty:

$$\frac{\$80,000}{\$120,000} \times \$10,000 = \$6,666$$

In this case, the insured is a coinsurer for $3,333 ($10,000 − $6,666).

Or consider the case of a total loss. If, in the first example, the entire building were destroyed, the insured would receive only the policy limit. The formula would read as follows:

$$\frac{\$80,000}{\$80,000} \times \$100,000 = \$80,000$$

Today, insurers are trying other approaches that are similar to, although not exactly the same as, coinsurance clauses. Some contracts, for example, offer coverage with no deduction for depreciation, if the center owner carries a specified amount of insurance to value. If the property is insured for 80 percent of the replacement value at the time of the loss, for example, then a loss will be settled at replacement cost up to the face amount of the policy. If not, the holder will obtain a settlement at actual cash value, which is the cost of the replacement, minus depreciation.

Coinsurance is now used far less frequently than it was used in the past. Today, many investors insure the property for the actual replacement cost.

Another form of insurance is known as an *agreed amount endorsement*. This is where the insurance company and the insured agree that the property will be insured for a specific amount for a specific period of time, and that the insured need not worry about being uninsured so long as this amount of insurance is carried. The insurance company, in this case, will always honor the full amount of the loss up to the face value of the policy. Many insurance policies contain an inflation clause, which automatically increases the amount of insurance on the property by a predetermined percentage at periodic times during the policy period. Often, if it is an annual insurance policy, the inflation factor is figured at every quarter during the year.

Regardless of the method that is used to determine the amount of insurance that will be carried, it is recommended that all insurance policies be reviewed by the property manager and the insurance company at least annually.

Insurance records represent only some of the many files that the property manager will probably be required to maintain. Again, the manager should be able to place great trust in the insurance agent. A fully qualified insurance agent will also handle insurance records, informing the property manager of policy expiration dates, premium payments, inspection reports, and loss history. Many management agreements specify whether the owner or the manager will take charge of maintaining insurance records and coverage. Even if the insurance agent holds such files, the property manager should also keep insurance records for the property, thus allowing the manager and agent to provide a check of one another's accuracy. In practice, most management agreements require that the property manager obtain and monitor insurance coverage. Ideally, the insurance agent will serve as the property manager's highly valued consultant.

Systems that shopping center managers use for record keeping vary, depanding largely on whether the manager or the owner obtains the policy. In general, if it is the manager, the center can probably avoid a great deal of confusion. The manager has firsthand experience with the policy and can easily cross-index it by the renewal date and any follow-up dates.

In some cases, however, the owner obtains coverage and pays for it, and the manager has the responsibility of monitoring the program. Here, the manager must alert the owner to new risks that occur at the center during the policy term. The manager will also have to prepare renewal data for the owner at least 90 days before the term expires. The property owner will probably ask the manager to monitor records of losses and inspections. If the center follows this system, clear communication between the manager and owner is critically important.

Ultimately, some real estate practitioners believe that property managers should handle all insurance matters, including the decision-making process. It simplifies matters. The manager is knowledgeable about what happens on the property, and the manager can usually maintain a more thorough and efficient insurance program. Another general rule that most real estate practitioners concur on: The party that makes the premium payment should also decide on the general policy that applies to all insurance matters for the property. Many managers are in charge of their center's budget operations, and they stand, therefore, in a position to take on both responsibilities.

Risk can be *static* (pure) or *dynamic* (speculative). Speculative risk refers to the uncertainties involved in any business decision, results that lead to either a financial gain or loss. Many call these entrepreneurial risks. The decision to buy or build a shopping center is a dynamic risk. As soon as a "buyer" becomes an "owner," however, dynamic risk becomes static risk. Static risks create loss, or premium costs, but no gains, other than insurance payments for actual damage claims. Static risks are created by the center's construction, its tenancy, maintenance, and location.

Shopping centers cannot escape static risks. They are everywhere in the property. They are, in fact, a part of any real estate investment. Yet, careful planning can minimize loss exposures, and this is where astute management can be very helpful. Location, design, leasing, and operations may affect the amount of risk at the center; and these are factors that managers can try to control.

Managers can use a risk management decision-making model to develop their programs. The model has three modes: planning, action, and decision making. The risk management model presented in Exhibit 11.1 sets forth these steps. Each step is discussed here in detail.

Planning

The first mode, planning, involves three stages, and the first of these is an identification of all possible loss exposures on the property. The manager can study blueprints of the property and make a physical inspection of it and define all of its risks. Identification is followed by the second step, a thorough analysis of risks that the manager has named. An analysis should estimate the probability that the event actually will occur (on a scale from zero possibility to absolute certainty, with only a few events falling at either extreme). The analysis should also estimate how frequently the event will occur. Generally, frequent losses have limited financial effect. However, the property manager must also consider loss exposures that could cause severe loss. These are the rare but very costly losses. An earthquake is one example. Managers have a hard time anticipating earthquakes, and so when a destructive one occurs, many centers have no insurance to cover the damage.

The third step in planning, selection, begins after the man-

EXHIBIT 11.1. *Modes of Risk Management*

Planning mode

Identification

Analysis

Selection

Action mode

Decision mode

Decide (which risk management techniques to use)

Implement (put into use)

Monitor (review performance)

Evaluate (determine effectiveness)

---

ager has analyzed the probability that an event will occur. The manager must evaluate all of the loss exposures at the center.

Action

The next mode in the risk management model is action, and at this point, the manager can choose from four options. The choices are avoidance, control, retention, and transfer. Each of these will be discussed.

Avoidance. Generally, the owner selects this technique when it is possible to avoid a risk, and the rewards of eluding it outweigh those of assuming it. For example, anybody can avoid automobile casualty losses simply by refusing to own a motor vehicle. Likewise, a business can handle a risk simply by avoiding it; either it can withdraw from a plan or it can never assume the risk. Clearly, however, the tradeoffs must be considered. A firm that decides to sponsor a baseball team may learn that not only must the firm pay for the uniforms and equipment, but it must also assume responsibility for injuries. The avoidance decision for the company would be not to sponsor the team. Or a business that does not want to concern itself with potential losses to a building can relieve itself of these risks by never acquiring interest in the building. The company also must consider, however, the money that might be lost because of the company's unwillingness to accept the risks involved with owning property.

Control. Through the technique of control, the center manager takes active steps to reduce loss exposures. One method is called *loss control*; this involves activities with people, such as employees and customers, to protect them from injury. A second method is *property preservation*, which involves measures aimed at protecting physical property from loss. An important part of the manager's work with people involves a knowledge of how to instruct and supervise them in matters of safety and protection.

Who takes responsibility for loss control and the preservation of property? Primarily three different groups—the government, private associations that specialize in loss prevention, and individual firms, or, for the purposes here, each shopping center owner or property manager. The government becomes involved because it establishes standards, and because it has public funds available to provide services.

In 1970, Congress passed the Occupational Safety and Health Act (OSHA), which is one of the most significant items of federal safety legislation to be passed in recent history. OSHA places safety standards on all private employers—and these guidelines affect many aspects of the operation of a shopping center property. The following are some of the areas that affect shopping centers:

Walking and working surfaces.
Means of entering and exiting.
Powered platforms, handlifts, and vehicle-mounted work platforms.
Hazardous materials.
Personal protective equipment.
General environmental control.

Medical and first aid.

Fire protection.

Compressed gas and compressed air equipment.

Material handling and storage.

If an inspector discovers that the center or a tenant at the center is violating an OSHA requirement, a citation will describe the violation, and the employer or owner, within a specific time frame, must remove the hazard or correct the condition.

Many private groups also get involved with risk control. One is the well-known National Safety Council, which compiles and distributes survey data on home and business accidents. The Council also publishes materials on preventive activities. Insurance companies are also loss-control oriented. The insurance inspector will look for hazards on the property that can be corrected. Insurers also supply many types of safety materials.

Finally, the property manager must take responsibility to control losses at the shopping center. Some center owners give the property manager extensive responsibilities in loss control; others have only minimal duties in this area.

An active retention implies that the risk manager consciously decides that the center owner will pay the consequences of a known exposure. This can occur when the chance of loss is so low that it can essentially be ignored. A loss exposure is often retained by ignorance. Assumption through ignorance occurs when the risk is unknown or unobserved; for example, an old mine shaft under the property.

Loss exposures can be transferred in two ways. One is a non-insurance transfer, such as a hold harmless agreement. For example, a service station can be sublet, with an agreement that the tenant will assume responsibility for potential losses. The other form of transfer is a transfer to an insurance company. Transfers may also be combined with some form of retention and control.

Decision Making

The third mode in a risk management program is decision making. In this final step, the manager reviews the selection criteria and assigns the appropriate techniques to treat the loss exposure.

In many cases, such decisions require the approval of several people. The manager may have to convince the property owner that the risk management program will be an effective one, particularly if the program is costly, or if a less costly insurance plan would mean less coverage for the property. The management agreement should set forth the limits of the manager's authority and the approvals that are needed for major decisions regarding insurance matters.

With the selection criteria approved in advance, the manager will understand the parameters for planning the program. Following decision making, the manager can begin to implement the risk management program. The purchase of insurance will involve the advice and assistance of the insurance agent. Control activities generally require that the insurance company employees work continually with the center staff and tenants. Retentions must be monitored, and notes regarding various risks that will be avoided and eliminated must be processed. The plan, similar to all decision-making models, must be monitored to ensure that it is effective; and evaluated, to seek ways to improve it.

Types of Insurance Coverage

The person charged with obtaining an insurance policy for the center has many factors to consider. Those considerations will include the following:

The size and type of the center.
The center's location.
The center's physical characteristics.
Local ordinances, financial institutions, and insurers.

For a center still in the design stage, either as a newly constructed building or a renovated building, the decision maker should solicit the advice of all experts involved with the project. However, property insurance underwriters will generally not review architectural drawings or make suggestions on how they might be improved. The liability is too great. Most casualty loss control experts will make suggestions only after the structure has been completed. Boiler and machinery inspectors are concerned solely with the safe functioning of the boiler and machinery once it is installed and functioning, and these inspectors usually will not address the subjects of design and installation at all. Architects and engineers, on the other hand, may recommend any of the following items:

A more resistant structure.

Adequate fire escape exits and fire-fighting access.

A structure with heating, cooling, and other protective controls.

A physical layout that moves customer traffic safely and efficiently.

An automatic sprinkler system.

Whatever the recommendations, again—they must be suitable for the center. Furthermore, coverage, capacity, and claims—as discussed earlier in this chapter—should serve as the decision maker's guidelines. The two parties—the insurance company and the purchaser—are actually negotiating a program. As during any form of negotiations, both parties must give and take. The buyer may not necessarily want everything that the insurance agent suggests.

The insurer, in turn, may require certain changes in the design, space allocation, or location. Underlying their discussions, however, the overriding goal should be to create a shopping center that is safe for shoppers and employees. Center managers need to concern themselves essentially with two types of insurance: property insurance and liability insurance. Property insurance is available to protect the owner from direct and indirect losses to the property; liability insurance offers protection for claims made because of injury to others and for which the owner is legally and financially responsible. In recent years, the distinction between property and liability insurance coverages has faded. The two are often packaged into a single contract. Many businesses now purchase a Special Multiperil Policy (SMP). This policy offers the insured both property and liability insurance as needed in one convenient package, as well as optional crime insurance and boiler and machinery insurance. The SMP simplifies the administration of insurance. The insured can make several insurance decisions at one time and enjoy a common renewal date for all coverage. Lapses in coverage are thereby avoided. Finally, with an SMP plan, the insurer can provide coverage far more economically, since the costs for servicing and administration are reduced considerably.

Property Insurance

Basic coverage for property is often established under a fire and extended insurance policy with an extended coverage endorsement that covers not only damage from fire and lightning but also damage caused by windstorms, civil commotions, vehicles, aircraft, hail, explosions, riots, and smoke. Property policies can also cover consequential losses—income losses that occur because of the insured damage—and so-called specialty losses. These will be discussed in this section.

A standard fire policy offers only limited coverage; it essentially provides the insured with coverage only for damage caused by fire, lightning, and the removal of property from the premises. Claims under a standard fire policy are paid on an actual cash value basis. Again, actual cash value means that the person who handles the claim must determine the replacement cost with materials of "like" kind and quality and subtract an amount for depreciation.

The text first will discuss the provisions of a standard fire policy and move on to the other types of coverage that a shopping center investor can purchase to broaden coverage.

Fire is a constant threat on any type of property, and it is one of the main reasons that property owners buy insurance. Fire kills, and it puts people out of work. It destroys property. All property owners need protection against the financial consequences of fire.

Lightning—a natural, electrical charge—strikes properties less frequently than do fires. Nevertheless, when lightning does strike, it can destroy property. Most insurance policies provide coverage for damage to property caused by lightning and consequent fire.

Most states require that specific information be provided in the fire insurance policy, such as the following items:

Terms of the policy.

Description of the property.

Losses covered. The standard fire policy protects the center owner from losses caused by fire or lightning. The insured may choose and pay for coverage for other items. No insurance policy covers damages caused by war or nuclear attacks.

Amounts covered. A fire insurance policy is intended to pay the insured for the amount of the damage—no more and no less. The standard fire policy attempts to put the insured back in the same financial position as when the contract was signed or when the loss occurred.

Suspension. The standard fire policy's suspension—not cancellation—occurs in either of these situations: (1) a hazard increases in some way, with the insured's control or knowledge; or (2) during any period that the center, for any reason, stands vacant for more than 60 consecutive days.

Cancellation. A standard fire insurance policy holds that both the tenant and the landlord have cancellation rights, provided that both parties adhere to the specific guidelines that are stated in the contract.

Subrogation. Most insurance companies insist on this clause in their contracts. Basically, the clause states that the insurer assumes all rights to recover amounts paid to the insured for damage caused by a third party.

Apportionment. This is the pro rata distribution over several policies held by the same insured.

Extended Coverage

Extended coverage provides the insured with coverage beyond the perils of fire and lightning. This includes the perils of windstorms, hail, riots, civil commotions, vehicles, explosions, aircraft, and smoke. Intentional, destructive acts of vandalism done to the property can be insured under a vandalism and malicious mischief endorsement. There are many other property insurance coverages that can be considered to provide as broad protection as is needed.

Crime Insurance

The crime rate continues to rise, yet it is estimated that only about 10 percent of all crime that occurs is insured. Some center owners, or individual tenants in the center, may want to obtain coverage for burglary, robbery, theft, and employee crime. As with other types of insurance, coverage for crime should be tailored to the needs of the center. The high cost and limited availability of insurance coverage might prevent many owners from buying crime insurance. Shoplifting and theft are major problems, especially in large shopping centers, and insurance companies cannot afford to cover all losses covered by crime. Shopping centers have limited crime exposure, but many tenants have high exposure. Therefore, tenants are generally more concerned with crime insurance than is the property owner.

Special Coverage

Shopping center owners can also purchase insurance that covers specific risks in their areas. Flood insurance is an example. A *flood* is an overflow of water that comes from a lake, river, or ocean. Floods can devastate regions and destroy properties. A business located in an area susceptible to such water overflows should have flood insurance and may be required by law to obtain such coverage. Flood insurance is available from the federal government.

Earthquake insurance is another example of special coverage. Earthquakes occur because of movements in the earth's surface. They are possible in almost any region but mainly in those areas located along a geologic fault. Most centers do not carry insurance for earthquakes since, compared to other risks, the probability that a destructive earthquake will occur is low.

Specialty Contracts

Basically, the shopping center owner and the retailer should consider four types of specialty policies. One type is *accounts payable*, which covers risks associated specifically with the destruction of payment records. A *valuable papers* contract provides protection, should the owner lose important papers, such as a blueprint or a lease. Third, many shopping centers have large plate-glass windows, and to provide recovery from loss, the owners or tenants purchase insurance. A *glass insurance* policy provides coverage for accidental glass breakage and the subsequent board-up service. This coverage also insures against possible damage caused by the application of an acid or chemical. Finally, some property owners carry *rent loss insurance*. Most leases provide that a tenant's rental payments will abate during the period that a building is being restored from a casualty loss. Rent loss insurance will pay the contract rent to the property owner during the restoration period.

Business Interruption Coverage

Many businesses also purchase insurance to cover *indirect damages*, which are the loss of profits resulting from direct damage. It takes on many different forms.

For one, the operation of the shopping center may be interrupted, and tenants would lose business as a result. In this case, retailers will measure their damages in terms of their losses in sales volume. Insurance, then, would cover not only the profits that have been lost but also all of the expenses that have occurred because of the interruption and efforts to reduce the loss.

Another form of consequential loss coverage is *contingent business interruption*. This occurs when one supplier's product is so important that, if interrupted, the insured also suffers a loss. An example might be an insured bakery at the center, well-known for its bread. If the bakery buys the bread from a factory, and the factory burns down, the bakery would be entitled to recovery from its own contingent business interruption.

A third form of this coverage is called *extra expense insurance*. As the name implies, this insurance provides coverage to the insured for extra expenses that are the result of continuing business in the event of damage. For example, should there be a fire in the elevator of a two-level mall, specialty parts may have to be flown in from another city, and the maintenance workers would probably have to work overtime. These extra costs would be paid by the coverage.

Liability Insurance

When the owner or an employee of the center acted negligibly to cause injury to a customer, or causes damage to the property of another, the center may be held responsible for monetary damages.

The person who makes the liability claim is the "third party," and for this reason, many insurance practitioners refer to casualty insurance as "third party" insurance. Shopping center owners purchase liability coverage, not only because the costs of paying for a possible legal suit are high but also because increasingly the courts are awarding damage claims to injured parties.

Crowds of people, a large structure where numerous problems can occur, exposure to many risks—all of these characteristics of the shopping center are reasons why owners need liability insurance.

Boiler and Machinery Insurance

Some shopping centers, in particular shopping malls, have entensive heating and cooling systems, which are insured under boiler and machinery liability coverage. A boiler and machinery policy usually provides protection for damage to the operating machinery in the building, including air conditioning units, generating systems, heating systems, and electrical control panels. Coverage includes repairs to the unit, any costs up to $1,000 that will expedite the repair process, coverage of any damage to others' properties for which the insured is liable, and automatic coverage for new equipment. Such policies do not cover damage caused by wear and tear, corrosion, and erosion.

Workers' Compensation Insurance

The theory behind *Workers' Compensation Insurance* is that an employer must assume responsibility for injuries that arise out of or during the course of a worker's employment. Workers' Compensation Insurance provides the insured with unlimited coverage for death benefits, medical expenses, lost wages, and disability. The premium cost to the employer will depend on the size of the employer's payroll, individual job classifications, and the claims experience of the insured.

A shopping center owner will need to carry Workers' Compensation Insurance to cover the centers' employees. The individual retailers will also obtain it, as will the center's merchants' association, if the association hires its own employees. In sum, any entity that employs a certain number of employees—a standard established by each state—must meet the requirements of the law regarding Workers' Compensation Insurance. The injured worker's direct employer is responsible for the payments set by law, but the employer may pass on this responsibility to the property owner.

General Liability Insurance

The term *general liability insurance* refers to liability insurance other than automobile, workers' compensation, employer's liablility, aviation, and other specific coverages. A typical general liability policy provides for one or more of the following three coverages:

1. Bodily injury liability.
2. Property damage liability.
3. Medical payments.

Because most general liability policies are similar, many companies use a single policy to cover different hazards. The policy then is written so that coverage applies specifically to the scheduled hazards. A scheduled general liability insurance policy often is used for owners, landlords, and tenants' liability; contractual liability; medical payments insurance; and personal injury liability. Also available is comprehensive general liability insurance.

Owners, Landlords, and Tenants Liability. A shopping center can be insured under an owners, landlords, and tenants (OLT) policy form. With this policy, the insurer provides coverage for problems that arise from ownership, maintenance, or use of the insured premises and all operations necessary and incidental to it.

Contractual Liability. Contractual liability is created when there is a signed contract through which, under specific conditions, one of the parties agrees to assume the liability involved. A lease, for example, may include a hold harmless clause that shifts the liability of the landlord to the tenant for building defects or acts of neglect by the tenant or by any other person, including the landlord. Because of the serious problems raised by contracts, requiring one party to assume liability for another party's conduct, coverage for contractual liability is common in shopping centers and is strongly recommended.

Medical Payments Insurance. Medical payments insurance may be added to certain liability policies. This insurance coverage reimburses members of the public who are injured on the premises, regardless of liability, for medical, hospital, and funeral expenses that result from their injuries. This coverage is characterized by two features: It surpasses the medical payments provision in the general liability contract, and it imposes no prerequisites of negligence on the insured's part.

Personal Injury Liability. Many owners choose to add personal injury liability to their general liability policy. Personal injury includes libel, slander, invasion of privacy, false arrest or imprisonment, and wrongful eviction. In most shopping centers, where shoplifting and subsequent arrest occur frequently, personal injury liability insurance is important. Many shopping center tenants also carry personal injury liability insurance.

Comprehensive General Liability. A comprehensive general liability policy provides the broadest protection against liability claims. It provides for premises/operations, elevators/escalators, products, completed operations, and owners' protective liability insurance coverages. Also, many endorsements can be added for the broadest possible liability insurance.

Taxes

At some point, the shopping center and manager must direct their attention to real estate assessments and taxes. Taxes represent a large part of the operating costs for all types of shopping centers. According to the 1981 edition of *Dollars and Cents of Shopping Centers*, real estate taxes represent a significant part of all operating expenses: about 30 percent in neighborhood centers, 27 percent in community centers, and 20 percent in regional centers. In fact, in the percentage of total operating costs that they represent, taxes come second only to total maintenance costs for the property. Remember that maintenance is an all-encompassing job that involves everything from cleaning the parking lot to maintaining the common areas and the building structure. The portion that this huge job of maintenance involves hovers around 40 percent. The great part of operating expenses that taxes represent, thus, becomes even more apparent.

Demands from citizens that local governments provide them with basic services will almost certainly continue. Therefore, the high cost of taxation will probably also continue. Since the major source of revenue for local governmental services comes from property taxes, the demands on real estate practitioners will probably remain high.

Today, many shopping center owners expect the property manager to become involved in all phases of the investment. They expect the manager to be able to exercise sound, independent judgements. They expect help from the manager in key investment decisions. Since taxes are central to the shopping center investment, if property managers are to satisfy these new expectations, they must have a working knowledge of both taxes and value assessments.

Taxes have always been a primary concern to the property investor. At one time, investors themselves handled the administration of taxes. They may have asked an accountant to handle specific tax problems or to file the final tax forms, but generally, they managed their own tax programs. In today's complex market, however, as in other matters of property operations, investors are more inclined to turn over the total administration of taxes to a property manager. Many investors today seek a skilled real estate professional—who not only understands the management of the property but also has a sophisticated understanding of taxes. Still, this depends on the investor and for managers who are employed by property management firms, on the demands of their employers. It is generally the manager's responsibility to know how taxes affect the investment, and to be able to advise the owner on what actions will be necessary to protect the property from excessive tax costs. The manager must be able to speak knowledgeably about taxes and assessments, ever keeping in mind the enormous impact that they have on a property investment. Ideally, the property manager will be skilled enough to administer a specific tax program for any type of shopping center.

Tax matters demand the property manager's administrative and analytical skills. For administrative purposes, the center manager must keep accurate records so that tax reports will be filed on time. The manager should also prepare tax calendars to ensure prompt payment. For analytical purposes, the manager who is entrusted with the finances of the investment must understand tax laws and know how they can harm or benefit the property owner's interests.

The main duty of the shopping center manager who has total responsibility for the administration of property taxes is to ensure that adequate funds are available to pay real estate taxes on or before the due dates. If possible, the manager should set up reserve funds for this purpose.

Next to assuring that taxes are paid on time, probably the most important tax-related duty for the manager is to analyze the tax bill. The first part of that job is to assess the value of the property. A local property assessor will put a value on the shopping center, and this value—the written assessment called the *tax bill*—is the basis for the real estate tax. An evaluation of the center's age, how much it has depreciated, the property's general classification, and the unit replacement costs will indicate specific characteristics of the property. But the property value also includes market value, which indicates how it compares to the competition. Therefore, the assessor will also study competing shopping centers, the economics of the area, population movements, neighborhood trends, and market conditions. Readers should recognize that these are all the same factors that the property manager analyzed during the market analysis to determine rental levels. This is as it should be since it is precisely the center's ability to attract tenants, its ability to command high rents, and finally, the owner's obligations to pay taxes—that, in essence, represents the shopping center's value.

A shopping center manager's general responsibilities in regard to the tax bill can be summed up by the following:

1. The manager determines, on a square foot basis, what the taxes will be at the shopping center.
2. The manager should be knowledgeable about factors at the property that are likely to affect the tax bill, such as the building's age, the success of the center relative to sales and tenant demand for space, the cash flow of the property before mortgage payment, the location value, and the replacement value of the building.

3. The manager should survey the competition and obtain information needed to convert each of these tax bills to a square foot basis.
4. Available information from other properties that are managed by the property manager, plus information from other properties under the administration of the manager's company, all relative to the square foot cost of real estate taxes, should be used.
5. With all of the above information, the manager can analyze the position of the shopping center, as it relates to taxes per square foot, and therein be able to recommend possible plans of action to the owner.

Readers may ask: Why should appraising and assessing the property be responsibilities of the property manager? Is valuation not the job of the appraiser, and is the tax bill not the job of the tax assessor? Both observations are true—but what is also true is that part of the property manager's job is to provide a check of both of these important statements. The local government will base the amount of the tax levied on the property on the appraisal; the tax rate is generally a percentage of the property's appraised value. The manager's evaluation is a monitor, which is intended partially to assure that the official statements are both fair and accurate. The property tax bill and the fair market value will be continual concerns for the local government, which wants a steady stream of revenue; and the property owner, who wants the property maintained at a high value but does not want to pay out large amounts in property taxes. As a result, the tax bill is often a cause for friction between the property owner and the local government.

The manager must also validate the total tax at which the assessor arrived. If the tax assessment of the property seems excessive, the manager should submit a statement of protest. If the assessment declares the protest invalid, an appeal to the next higher authority may be in order. The manager should follow similar steps for state property taxes.

To review, then, for tax purposes the property manager's two main responsibilities are to assure that there are always funds available to pay taxes when due, and second, to make sure that value appraisal and tax assessment of the property are accurate. Still, this excludes some of the property manager's other tax-related responsibilities. The property owner may be subject to other taxes, in part depending on the local laws. The following is a short discussion of some of the most common of these other taxes.

Personal Property Tax. Local ordinances may impose personal property taxes, in which case, the manager must file with the assessor, a schedule of all personal property that is subject to taxation. As such, the property manager should be familiar with local laws, in order to take advantage of accepted practices in the area. Here again, the manager is usually responsible for the prompt payment of any tax due.

Social Security Tax. Most property managers are responsible for collecting and paying social security taxes and for representing the property owner's interest and employee contributions. Therefore, the need for accurate and thorough records once again will emerge. The same applies to state unemployment compensation taxes. When federal excise taxes become payable, the manager must compile these records and then file them along with the tax payment.

Federal Income Tax. Most property owners include the income from their property with their personal federal income tax returns. Some property management firms, however, represent corporations, which must prepare and file federal income taxes as a separate entity.

In this capacity, the property manager functions as an accountant, able to advise the property owner on income tax regulations that will affect the return.

An understanding of federal income tax regulations, therefore, is another important part of the property manager's job. Some larger management firms have one full-time person on staff whose sole responsibility is to stay informed about federal income tax laws.

Excise Tax. In the operation of a shopping center, the property manager may be required to collect federal excise taxes. These are special taxes levied on certain "luxury" items, including possible dues and admissions, such as merchants' association dues, the sales from electrical lights, and charges for telephone use. When managing the shopping center also includes the operation of separate merchandise or service departments (restaurants, telephone switchboards, employee training seminars), the manager must investigate the laws that regulate the levying and collection of excise taxes. Many managers have been embarrassed to learn that they were unaware of certain excise taxes that were levied against their employers' properties.

Sales Tax. In states with a sales tax law, the manager must prepare a return and pay a tax for all taxable sales transacted under the manager's direct supervision. The property manager may have to collect sales tax on electricity resale, food and beverage operations, consumable goods—in sum, on any taxable goods sold in any operations that are under the management staff's direct supervision.

The Importance of the Lease Terms

As discussed in detail in chapter 8, "The Lease Document," the shopping center lease represents the only legal bond between the landlord and the tenant. The tax clause in the lease is a primary concern for the landlord because it gives the landlord the legal right to charge tenants for the increases in tax expenses. A lease without a clause that takes into account the landlord's need for an ever-rising income to pay for ever-rising taxes will serve to lower the earnings and overall value of the property. A landlord with several leases, none of which have increased-tax clauses, ultimately stands to lose thousands of dollars.

The landlord and tenant are not the only ones interested in the continued availability of funds to pay for taxes. The other interested party is the lender. The lender wants the assurance that the investor will continue to have an income, high enough above the costs of taxes, to meet principal and interest payments. For the benefit of all parties, then, in preparing a lease, the property manager must be certain that the lease includes a clause that will account for the recovery of taxes, as they increase.

Over the years, owners and managers have been quite ingenious in adding *tax escalation clauses (tax stops)* to leases. A tax escalation clause protects the property owner against the burden of future tax increases. Most such clauses are based on a specific cost of living index for reimbursing the owner. The most recent type of tax clause requires each tenant to pay all real estate taxes for its own space, from the start to the finish of the lease term.

An older method of recovery requests that tenants pay taxes above some specified level, for example, that they pay for taxes over $1.00 per square foot. Another method that is still common in older leases requires that the tenant pay a pro rata share of any increase in real estate taxes after an assessment in the full year, or some other agreed upon year.

Ideally, to limit administrative problems, the same method of recovery will be used for all leases at each center. Yet, much will depend on the negotiating power of both the tenant and the landlord at any particular time. These lease clauses, therefore, often vary among tenants within a center.

Some larger tenants may demand that tax escalation charges be taken directly from their percentage-rent overages. This works against the interests of the owner, however, since it reduces the amount of the owner's cash flow. During lease negotiations, the property manager should insist on clauses that require outright repayment of tax escalations.

A specifically worded lease will also allow the landlord to assess tenants for taxes on a pro rata portion of common area costs. At this point, the manager would probably do best to consult an attorney, who would know just how such a clause should be written and administered.

Conclusion

Shopping centers are susceptible to hundreds of risks everyday. Natural forces, hundreds of thousands of people walking in and out of its doors, an enclosed mall susceptible to any number of malfunctions, a structure filled with retailers and employees—all of these factors increase the number of risks on the property and the subsequent need for insurance. For many of these risks, insurance of the proper kind and amount will be the best method of protection.

Identifying the risks at the shopping center becomes the first step in establishing an insurance program. Static risks—those risks that occur on the property after the owner has taken the risk of investment real estate—permeate the shopping center. In accounting for risks, many managers use a decision-making model, such as the one that was presented in this chapter. In that model, risk management involves three steps: planning, action, and decision making. Each of these three steps is composed of several smaller steps.

After the manager has identified and analyzed the risks at the center, and both the manager and owner have agreed on how the risks should be handled, they next must agree on an adequate insurance plan to protect the property.

The scope of tax-related knowledge that property owners will expect from the property manager will depend on what role the owner wants the manager to assume. Taxes have a great impact on property investments, and a property manager with expert skills in tax analysis and administration will quickly be recognized as a highly valued professional. As the shopping center industry grows more complex, it has become more important than ever before that the manager possess a working knowledge of taxes and assessments and understand the impact that these factors have on property investments.

Taxes, insurance, and risk management are all basic to the continued profitability of the shopping center investment. The consumer who visits the center does not directly witness the property owner's tax or insurance program. Both programs are contained in the records of the property. Excellent programs of tax management, insurance, and risk management are essential to the continued availability of funds, which helps to maintain the shopping center as a profitable real estate investment.

Review Questions

1. What are some physical risks (loss exposures) that are present in a shopping center?
2. How can a risk management review serve the investment decision for a shopping center?
3. How can an insurance company aid the owner in reducing hazards?
4. What is the role of the insurance agent in preparing the center's insurance plan?
5. What are the three most important considerations in evaluating an insurance company? Discuss them.
6. Discuss the four factors that affect property insurance rates.
7. The property insurance contract with an extended coverage endorsement provides coverage for what additional perils?
8. What coverage is used to protect the owner from loss to heating or cooling systems?
9. Discuss the coverage that can protect an owner in cases of false arrest.
10. Why is it important that the property manager have a working knowledge of the appraisal and assessment of property?
11. What is a tax bill, and what are the property manager's general duties in regard to the tax bill?

12

Accounting and Reporting

The financial realities of a business are reflected in its budget. For a shopping center, it may seem odd that a few papers could be as important as the brick and glass that make up the structure. The records of a shopping center, however, represent much more than a "few papers." Some shopping center owners purchase insurance that will cover the loss of important records. To a shopping center owner, the budget and the accounting records of the property offer the clearest statement of the investment's financial condition. Excellent records of the investment's financial state are necessary to maintain a profitable shopping center.

The property manager who takes responsibility for an investment property, therefore, fills an essential fiduciary role. Efficient record-keeping procedures and reporting tools serve basic functions for the investment. They account for all of the property's cash expenses. As in most business decisions, the property manager must consider the tax consequences that relate to the operation of the investment.

Asset Management

At one time, property managers were primarily concerned with the smooth daily functioning of the property. The role of the property manager, however, has expanded greatly. Today's shopping center manager assumes much more than the day-to-day responsibilities of managing the property—and today many property managers could more accurately be called asset managers, as discussed in chapter 2. The asset manager prepares a management plan, which synthesizes all of the information obtained about the property, gathered from the analyses of the region and neighborhood, leases, financing alternatives, income tax consequences, and valuation. All of these factors affect how successfully a property will compete in the market—and how well the market will satisfy the needs of a profitable investment.

The word for shopping centers during the 1980s will be management. Shopping center investors face major concerns during the 1980s. In the early 1980s, the economy was plagued with numerous problems: Interest rates were high; energy costs for the common areas in malls continued to rise; high unemployment rates put great strains on a sluggish economy; and price increases in basic commodities reduced consumers' disposable incomes. Astute management may lead shopping center properties through these difficult economic times. The asset manager of the 1980s, therefore, must take an active role in the total operation of the shopping center. The asset manager is that rare person who can analyze all of the financial alternatives that affect a property's highest and best use, ever evaluating the best possible after-tax return for the investment.

Many property owners spend very little time on their own properties. Therefore, beyond asset management, the property manager still must oversee the daily functions of the center. Many investors own multiple properties, and time and logistics would make lengthy, regular visits impossible. Instead, they rely heavily on their managers' reports. A good relationship between owner and manager begins with clear communication. The manager's reports, therefore, must be accurate and complete.

Types of Accounting Systems

Several types of accounting systems are possible, but basically, they all can be classified as either manual or automated. A good accounting system stands as the foundation for accurate record keeping.

Most small firms that manage shopping centers establish manual systems. For such smaller operations, a manual system produces an adequate amount of information, within a reasonable amount of time.

Many larger firms, on the other hand, have ventured into automated or computerized accounting systems. These systems reduce bookkeeping costs and generate far more data than the manual method. Computers can handle a great deal of information quickly and efficiently. As more companies are turning to computerized systems, the cost is also declining somewhat, and today it is possible to purchase computerized equipment at moderate prices. Although computers are a significant investment, automated systems are quickly becoming realities for companies of all sizes.

If the management firm uses an automated system, the firm's decision makers can consider four alternatives: (1) a bookkeeping machine; (2) a service bureau; (3) time sharing; or (4) an in-house computer. The text will discuss each of these options briefly.

A bookkeeping machine can perform basic record keeping and limited calculations. It can administer tenant charges and receipts, and in turn, it can indicate each tenant's current balance. A bookkeeping machine can also maintain the necessary ledger accounts for the property. Although this type of system is relatively inexpensive, it has certain disadvantages. One drawback to the machine is that information is maintained on individual ledger cards, and it takes a significant amount of time for the manager to convert the information into reports. The system also creates difficulties in volume processing because the maximum efficiency of the machine corresponds directly to the individual speed and capabilities of the operator.

A second option of accounting makes use of a service bureau, which is a company that sells the use of its computer equipment. The management firm can contract with a service bureau and thereby, with a minimum investment, computerize its accounting system. The service bureau eliminates the high costs of purchasing and maintaining a computer.

Existing computer programs may be used, although many service bureaus help design custom software. Typically, the management firm batches its own information and sends the information to the bureau for processing. The results usually come back overnight. This system limits a firm's accessibility to accounting records, yet it does enable management firms to process large amounts of information quickly. Most service bureaus levy a charge for each transaction. The management firm must decide if this type of cost function serves its purposes most economically.

The third form of automation—time sharing—corresponds closely to the service bureau. With time sharing, however, the computer company sells the use of its computer by way of an in-house computer terminal. The initial costs for the property management company are low, since the only necessary equipment is a terminal, which connects to the central computer through telephone lines. This system has some advantages over a service bureau. One advantage is that the computer system provides instant access to information at all times. Also, the computer company bases costs on the amount of computer time used, the amount of time the terminal is connected to the main computer, and any information storage requirements. Therefore, firms that use the terminal less often will also be charged less. Still, the economic benefits that can be gained from this system will depend basically on the amount of volume that is handled by the management firm.

The final management alternative is for the firm to purchase its own computer system. In general, an in-house computer offers many advantages in terms of speed and flexibility. The in-house computer permits immediate access to all records and information. The price of computer equipment depends on the size of the system. A small business computer may cost only a few thousand dollars, but its capabilities may be severely limited. Other sophisticated systems can run into costs of hundreds of thousands of dollars. The practitioner who decides that the firm needs a custom software package also must realize that it will take several months before the computer company can design an appropriate program to meet the needs of the management firm. In any case, the property manager must work closely with the programmer to explain the firm's operations. The programmer should be able to design software that meets the specific needs of the management firm. Some advances have been made in "canned" software for property management. These are predesigned programs that the property management firm can purchase. These programs may require slight modification to fit a specific purpose. Proper software is one of the most important factors for a successful computer system. For some stable, financially grounded property management firms, a computer will help the firm significantly in providing clients with the quickest, most accurate, and most thorough service available.

To summarize what has been discussed so far, every management firm needs an efficient accounting system. The management firm must decide whether the business should have a manual or an automated system, based on the volume of business that the firm handles and the economic alternatives.

Automated systems are more expensive, but they are quicker and more efficient than manual systems. Small business computers are enabling many small firms to automate their records. Nevertheless, for many firms, manual systems will do the job adequately. The volume of business and the size of the firm serve as key factors in determining whether the firm can justify the high costs of an automated system.

With either system, the objective is to produce accurate, timely, and comprehensive reports for clients. Even what appears to be a very sophisticated computer will be unacceptable if it fails to produce information as quickly and precisely as is needed.

Chart of Accounts

A standardized and comprehensive chart of accounts sets the foundation for maintaining property records for any type or size of shopping center. Such a chart of accounts enables the management firm to analyze its operations at the center categorically. Although the chart of accounts should be thorough and consistent, it still must be flexible enough to allow for unexpected events that frequently arise.

The Community Builders' Council of the Urban Land Institute has published a valuable resource for shopping center managers. The publication, entitled *Standard Manual of Accounting for Shopping Center Operations*, contains a standard chart of accounts for income and expenses, with descriptions and definitions for every category. Most shopping center managers could adapt this information quite easily to their own operations. The publication also offers useful comparisons with the operations in other centers.

Many management firms today must be able to service the accounting needs of sophisticated property owners. Some of the automated accounting systems that were just discussed allow the firm to produce all of the necessary reports without high costs in time or money.

Exhibits 12.1 and 12.2 are examples of financial reports. Notice that the statement of income and expenses in Exhibit 12.1 presents income by categories both for the current month and for the year to date. The same data appear for each expense category. A chart of accounts is composed of a series of categories called *line items*, which permit uniform analyses of all sources of income and expenses. Following are examples of line items:

Operating Income—

Space rental. This figure is the total amount of rent that would be collected if all available space were rented. This does not include percentage rent.

Escalation. Additional rent collected as reimbursement for increases in fixed operating costs is included here.

Retail percentage income. This category includes percentage rent obtained from percentage lease tenants.

Operating Expenses—

Electricity. This includes the cost of electricity for lighting of tenants' spaces.

Cleaning supplies. This category includes the costs for all cleaning supplies, including those for restrooms, purchased by the shopping center owner.

Maintenance payroll. This category includes wages paid to maintenance employees (carpenters, plumbers, electricians, painters, and other craftsmen).

Supplies. This category includes the costs for all supplies used for the general maintenance of the shopping center.

EXHIBIT 12.1. *Cash Flow Statement*

For the month ending _____ , 19____

	Current Month			Year to Date		
	Actual	Budget	Var.	Actual	Budget	Var.
Receipts						
(List each classification as shown on budget)						
Add: Sale of assets						
Owner's capital						
Other capital receipts						
Total Receipts						
Expenditures						
(List each classification as shown on budget)						
Delete: Depreciation						
Add: Debt service amortization						
Add: Any capital expenditures						
Total Expenditures						
CASH FLOW						

EXHIBIT 12.2. *Income Statement*

For the month ending ——————, 19——

	Current Month			Year to Date		
	Actual	Budget	Var.	Actual	Budget	Var.
Income						
Minimum rent						
Percentage rent						
Common area maintenance						
Tax contributions						
Insurance contributions						
Sale of utilities						
Miscellaneous						
Gross Income						
Expenses						
Building maintenance						
Parking lot, mall, other common areas						
Central utility system						
Financing expense						
Advertising and promotion						
Depreciation						
Real estate taxes						
Insurance						
General and administrative						
Total Expenses						
NET OPERATING INCOME						

Regardless of the particular chart of accounts that the property manager uses, that chart should have certain basic items. The most common sources of income in shopping centers are the following:

1. Minimum or base rent.
2. Percentage rent.
3. Common area maintenance income.
4. Tax contributions.
5. Insurance contributions.
6. Sales of utilities.
7. Miscellaneous.

The following broad classifications represent those expense items that are common to shopping centers:

1. Building maintenance.
2. Parking lot and mall.

3. Central utility systems.
4. Office area services.
5. Financing expense.
6. Advertising and promotion.
7. Depreciation and amortization of deferred costs.
8. Real estate taxes.
9. Insurance.
10. General and administrative.

The Urban Land Institute's *Standard Manual* also charts the functional categories listed above into a more detailed set called natural divisions. The chart in Exhibit 12.3 shows the correlation between the functional categories and the natural divisions of expenses.

Once the manager establishes a chart of accounts, that chart will serve as the basis for reports to the owner, as well as for the budget for the investment. The manager can base budget projections on statements from past years, or if the project is new, on the expense statements from comparable operations. The chart of accounts also must offer a classification for expenses that tenants will pay. For example, in most shopping centers, tenants pay for common area maintenance costs. With a well-organized accounting system, the manager can bill tenants for charges as they are incurred. In general, a thorough but flexible chart of accounts is necessary if the owner is to have consistent and accurate financial reports of the investment.

Operating and Capital Budgets

Budgets are practical, essential records. The property manager should set up a separate financial record for each shopping center property. The budget establishes a spending plan or a standard for monthly or annual comparisons.

There are different methods that a center manager can use to set up a budget for the property. Most managers develop two such financial statements, an *annual operating budget* and a *capital budget*. The operating budget lists the property's recurring expenses—those that cover the everyday costs of running the property. A format for a sample operating budget appears in Exhibit 12.4. The capital budget projects expenses that will occur for major improvements to the property.

Throughout the year, the operating budget can serve as a guide that measures how well the property's expenses meet the projections. The manager then can compare each monthly

EXHIBIT 12.3. *Relationship of Natural Divisions to Functional Categories*

NATURAL DIVISIONS OF EXPENSE	10 Bldg. Maint.	20 Parking Lot, Mall & Other Public Areas	25 Central Utility Systems	30 Office Area Servs.	40 Financing Costs	50 Advertising and Promotion	60 Depreciation and Amortization of Deferred Costs	70 Real Estate Taxes	80 Insurance	90 Gen. & Adm.
01 Payroll & Supplementary Benefits	X	X	X	X		X				X
02 Management Fees	X					X				X
03 Contracted Services	X	X	X	X		X				X
04 Professional Services	X	X				X				X
05 Leasing Fees and Commissions										X
06 Materials and Supplies	X	X	X	X		X				X
07 Utilities	X	X	X	X		X				
08 Equipment Expense	X	X	X	X		X				X
09 Travel and Entertainment						X				X
10 Communications						X				X
11 Taxes and Licenses								X		X
12 Contributions to Merchants' Association						X				
13 Insurance									X	
14 Losses from Bad Debts										
15 Interest					X					X
16 Depreciation							X			
17 Amortization of Deferred Costs							X			X
18 Ground Rent					X					
99 Unclassified	X	X		X		X				X

report of income and expenses with that of the same month in past years. The budget should show the precise months when expenses will occur, since the costs probably will vary during different months of the year. December, for example, will generally require more money budgeted for promotion; perhaps

February, more money budgeted to pay for an additional cleaning staff; July, for added landscaping costs.

Managers can choose among a variety of methods as they establish an operating budget. Most common is an annual budget, with the year divided into months. Yet, some managers create a separate budget for each operating month. An annual cash flow budget provides another common format. In a cash flow budget, the manager estimates actual cash receipts and disbursements to determine cash flow. For example, debt service payments are considered disbursements, but depreciation is not. Similar to this is a monthly cash flow budget, which allows the property manager to know just how much money will be available each month. The budget will indicate the property's debt service and, in turn, will reflect the investment's cash flow.

Projection of Expenses. The property manager must estimate the center's operating expenses. *Operating expenses* are those funds that will be expended for the center's ongoing maintenance and operation. To make this projection, it is necessary to evaluate each of the expense line items in the chart of accounts, which was discussed earlier in this chapter. The experienced manager can estimate quite accurately the cost of maintaining and operating the property, based on the operating histories of the subject center and comparable properties and on market trends.

When percentage leases are in effect, the manager must also estimate each tenant's gross sales. The manager can project each tenant's annual sales by studying past operating performance and trends and, in turn, by applying appropriate changes to the budget. The manager should also take into account any new competition in the market area and the general condition of both the local and the national economy. With these assumptions in mind, the manager can project a fair and accurate percentage rent for each tenant.

The manager will also have to account for all vacant space at the center. The manager must estimate the length of time it will take to lease the vacant property, and then apply the market rents that prospective tenants are likely to pay.

After the manager has thoroughly examined each tenant's lease and vacancy and reviewed the expense accounts for the property, the operating budget can be completed.

Projection of Income. In making an accurate financial forecast of a shopping center's income, the property manager must compute the following items:

EXHIBIT 12.4. *Fiscal Operating Budget Format*

Fiscal 19____ Operating Budget

Category	Previous Year Budget	Current Budget	Estimated Actual	Proposed Budget
Income				
Minimum rent				
Percentage rent				
Common area maintenance				
Tax contributions				
Insurance contributions				
Sale of utilities				
Miscellaneous				
Gross Income				
Expenses				
Building maintenance				
Parking lot, mall, other public areas				
Central utility systems				
Office area services				
Financing expense				
Advertising and promotion				
Depreciation				
Real estate taxes				
Insurance				
General and administrative				
Total Expenses				
NET OPERATING INCOME				

	Gross possible rental income
Minus	Vacancy and rent collection loss
Equals	Adjusted rental income
Plus	Other income
Equals	Effective gross income

The shopping center's *gross possible rental income* is the income the center would generate if it were 100 percent occupied at rents set forth in the rental schedule. By studying the rents being paid in the local area for competitive shopping center space and measuring the desirability of space at the subject center, a market rent is established on a square footage basis. In forecasting the rental income stream from an existing shopping center, many other factors must also be considered:

Rents payable under existing leases.

Rent raises on renewals scheduled for the budgeted year.

A calculation of rent overages of retail tenants on percentage rent leases.

Losses due to anticipated turnover.

Anticipated escalation, Consumer Price Index, or pass-through charges.

Rent concessions.

The second part of the budget, the capital budget, contains nonrecurring costs—those costs that exceed the property's normal operating expenses. The capital budget will include any income from sale of assets, debt service payments against principal, and any costly improvements added to the property. One property owner may find it necessary to have the parking repaved; another may have to replace an air conditioning unit in the center; another may proceed with plans to enclose the center with a mall. All of these are examples of improvement costs that would be included in a capital budget.

Through regular inspections of the property, the manager can stay informed of capital items that need to be replaced or repaired. Shopping center owners are generally willing to pay for costly projects from their operating budgets, since they receive better tax benefits from operating expenses than they do from capital expenses. Capital costs can be depreciated but not deducted against regular income. It should be expected, therefore, that taxpayers and the Internal Revenue Service often differ on the matter of what constitutes a "capital improvement."

The manager should urge the owner to set up a reserve fund that would cover the costs for replacing any major item that has a finite useful life. The capital budget should list each outlay item and describe the work required, the estimated cost, and the time that each will involve.

Together, an annual operating budget and a capital budget offer an annual forecast for the center. Not all events can be predicted—and not all expenses can be projected. Yet, careful financial planning will help both the manager and owner deal with problems that eventually do occur on the property. The same holds true for any additional, anticipated income. If the owner anticipates a rent increase, the budget should specify the month that the increase will take effect.

However thorough the manager is in evaluating the property's finances, budgets are still only projections of income and expenses. As with any type of projection, there will always be some uncertainties. The manager has no way of knowing in advance, for example, that the building's basement will flood, causing hundreds of dollars of uninsured damage, or that two tenants will abruptly abandon their leases. Every budget requires some amount of "guesswork." But it is "guesswork" based on solid financial reasoning and past experience.

Neither the tenants nor the property owner wants a property that operates by a plan of "management by crisis." Together, the capital and operating budgets provide a planning device and a basis for evaluating the property's overall performance.

Breakpoint Calculations

In some cases, particularly in older leases, a specific calculation will be used to divide the financial obligations between the landlord and the tenant for various operating expenses that the two parties share. The breakpoint formula determines the maximum number of dollars spent before the tenant must begin to reimburse the owner fully. Real estate practitioners call this point the *breakpoint*. The owner must pay—partially or completely—all expenses above the breakpoint. The calculation for common area maintenance, for example, would read as follows:

1. Assume X is the breakpoint.
2. Assume each tenant who has a maximum on common area maintenance contributions has reached the maximum.
3. Let $T_1, T_2 \ldots \ldots T_N$ represent each tenant.
4. Let $P_1, P_2 \ldots \ldots P_N$ represent each corresponding tenant's pro rata percentage.
5. Then $P_1 (X) + P_2 (X) \times \ldots \ldots + P_N (X) = X$.
6. Let T_i represent any tenant who does not pay a pro rata share or has a maximum payment; such a tenant may pay a set annual amount or nothing.
7. Then set the product $P_i (X)$ = Set amount or maximum (in actual dollars).
8. The result is a linear equation with one unknown (X), which can be solved. Solving the equation for X will determine the breakpoint.

An example should help to clarify the breakpoint calculation:

T_1 — Pays 50% of common area maintenance (CAM) with no maximum payment.
T_2 — Pays 25% of CAM with maximum of $500 per year.
T_3 — Pays 100% per month set amount.

Accounting and Reporting　　　　　　　　　　　　　　　357

T_4 — Pays no CAM.

Formula—$(P_1 \cdot X) + (P_2 \cdot X) + P_3 \cdot X) + (P_4 \cdot X) = X$

$(.50)(X) + \$500 + \$1200 + 0 = X$

$.5X + \$1700 = X$

$\$1700 = X - .5X$

$\$3400 = X$

Therefore, all common area maintenance expenses over X will require a payment by the owner. In this example, the owner will pay 50 percent of all costs in excess of $3,400 annually.

Another way of expressing the breakpoint is to call it the point at which the owner must incur expenses for common area maintenance. The tenants who pay full pro rata shares will continue paying a portion of every dollar of expenses over the breakpoint. The sum of those pro rata shares, subtracted from 100 percent, will equal the amount of every dollar over the breakpoint that the owner will be required to pay.

The manager can perform a similar calculation to determine tax contributions. Some tenants will pay a full pro rata share of the taxes while others will pay only pro rata amounts of any increases. The portion of the tax expense that the tenants would be required to cover would include the following:

1. Let Z = current year's taxes.
2. Let B_1, B_2, ... B_N represent, for corresponding tenants (T_i), the base taxes. If the tenant pays a full pro rata share of the taxes, then let $B_i = 0$.
3. Let P_1, P_2 . . . . . . P_N represent each tenant's pro rata percentage.
4. $P_1 (Z - B_i) + P_2 (Z - B_2) + ... P_N (Z - B_N) =$ breakpoint.
5. Note: If $(Z - B_i) = 0$, then assign a value of 0 to $(Z - B_i)$.

The calculation can also be used to indicate the amount of money that the owner should be reimbursed for tax payments. The difference between taxes and the breakpoint then would be the owner's contribution. The manager can perform a similar calculation to find the breakpoint for insurance expenses.

Therefore, the breakpoint is useful to the extent that it identifies the owner's portion of the major expenses on the property. With the exception of debt service, it is taxes, insurance, and common area maintenance that will constitute the largest expense items for most shopping centers.

The property manager is generally responsible for paying invoices on time and for collecting tenants' rent payments. Every real estate investment must be backed by a steady cash flow to cover operating costs on a timely basis. Standard policies should be established to ensure that collection of tenant rent occurs systematically. Likewise, the manager should set policies and procedures for dealing with tenants who do not pay their rent on time.

Many property managers send monthly bills to their tenants. The terms of the lease establish the items that will be charged to the tenant. Besides a rent payment, most leases also reflect the tenant's pro rata charge for common area upkeep, real estate taxes, and insurance.

In some leases, the parties agree that the tenant will pay, without demand, any base or percentage rents. It, therefore, would be the tenant's obligation to pay these charges within a specific time frame. Enforcement remains the responsibility of the manager, although most tenants will probably comply with the lease terms automatically. Nevertheless, whatever the specific terms of the lease, generally the best system is for tenants to receive a monthly bill that lists charges. This means that payment becomes due on receipt of the bill. Billings also function as useful reminders to tenants.

A billing system helps the manager maintain accurate accounts and receive rent payments on time. Most leases require that tenants have their rents paid by or on the first day of the month, but the language of the contract should be specific on this point. Many shopping center owners allow some flexibility in the grace period during which they will accept late payment. Some permit a leeway period of up to 10 days. This policy has become common in shopping center management, largely because of the relatively slow in-house operations of many anchor and national chains who have many stores in different shopping centers. These companies must process their checks, which often must be sent from their home offices. The procedure, which takes only a few minutes in a small store, in a large operation can take several days.

Once the manager has established a due date in view of the grace period, tenants delinquent by that standard should be sent a notice, preferably on the day after the due date. The notice should demand immediate payment. If the manager does not receive a satisfactory response from the tenant within a specified number of days, more drastic action will become necessary. A second notice should go out to all such tenants, informing them that an attorney is now handling the case and will persist on collection and, if necessary, on eviction. A word of caution to property managers is in order here. The laws in many states clearly favor the tenant in matters of rent collection and eviction. In these situations, the manager must be careful not to violate any of the terms of the lease. Any delay of action or breach of the tenant's rights is likely to hinder the manager's efforts to receive the full amount due.

Property managers must dictate strict rent collection policies. The tenant who believes that the manager will ignore the penalty fee for slow payment will probably delay the mailing of each month's rent as long as possible. The property manager is probably to blame for leading the tenant to think that the property owner and management take such a lax attitude toward rental payment. Efficient rent collection generally requires that a policy be established before the signing of leases. The manager should inform new tenants, when they sign their leases, that rental payment is expected on the first day of each month.

In a similar vein, managers must be discerning in locating and approving tenants for the center that they manage. They should run credit checks on most prospective tenants, particularly those that are not national or have not developed a sound financial reputation. The credit investigations will offer one of the most important measures of the strength and stability of the tenant. The manager may be able to obtain a published statement or a Dun and Bradstreet report regarding a chain tenant's financial condition. If a credit reference is not available, which may occur with a very small tenant, the manager should request a financial statement from the prospect. The manager, in sum, can probably avoid most problems that arise from rental collection by painstakingly evaluating each prospect.

Tenant Gross Sales Reporting

The item in most shopping center leases that distinguishes them from other property leases is the percentage rent clause. As part of their agreement, the tenant agrees to pay the landlord rent based on a percentage of gross sales. A sample percentage lease clause appears in Exhibit 12.5. Most percentage leases require

EXHIBIT 12.5. *Sample Percentage Lease Clause*

Percentage Rent. In addition to the Fixed Minimum Rent hereinbefore provided for, TENANT covenants and agrees to pay, in monthly installments, to LANDLORD each lease year as "Percentage Rent" for the PREMISES, during the term of this lease and any renewal or extension thereof, without any deductions or setoff whatsoever, a sum equal to _____ percent (_____%) of the total amount of gross sales during such lease year in, upon and from the PREMISES in excess of _____ Dollars ($_____), which Percentage Rent shall be deemed a part of the rent reserved under this lease. The foregoing dollar amount shall hereinafter be referred to as the "minimum basis of sales."

(i) Payment of Percentage Rent. TENANT shall furnish to LANDLORD on or before the 10th day of each calendar month of the term, beginning with the second month, statements of the gross sales in, upon and from the PREMISES for the preceding calendar month. In the event TENANT shall be delinquent in furnishing LANDLORD such monthly statements for two (2) consecutive months, LANDLORD shall have the right, so long as said reports have not been received, without notice, to conduct an audit of TENANT's books and records and the cost thereof together with any charges occasioned thereby shall be the sole obligation of TENANT, which obligation shall be deemed Additional Rent hereunder. Percentage Rent shall be determined and paid monthly within Fifteen (15) days after the last day of each month, each such monthly period being hereafter referred to as a "Percentage Rent Period" (or fractional period thereof) with respect to gross sales during the preceding Percentage Rent Period. The amount of the payment of Percentage Rent shall be equal to the amount, if any, by which percent of the gross sales for said Percentage Rent Period exceeds one-twelfth of the annual minimum rent. On or before the last day of the month following the close of each lease year, TENANT shall furnish to LANDLORD a statement certified by a Certified Public Accountant employed by TENANT or by an officer of TENANT of the gross sales made in, upon and from the PREMISES during the preceding lease year, and at the same time, TENANT shall pay to LANDLORD the balance of Percentage Rent due, if any, for such preceding lease year, provided, however, that LANDLORD may at any time request, but not more frequently than once during any lease year, and TENANT is thereby obligated to provide to the LANDLORD, a statement, certified by a Certified Public Accountant, as to such gross sales. If the total amount of Percentage Rent paid by TENANT during any lease year exceeds the total amount of Percentage Rent due for such lease year, TENANT shall receive a credit equivalent to such excess which may be deducted by TENANT from the next accruing payment of Percentage Rent.

(ii) Books of Account. TENANT agrees to prepare and maintain on the PREMISES, or at its principal offices accurate books and records of the gross sales made in, upon and from the PREMISES, which books and records shall be kept in accordance with accepted accounting practice, and shall be open at all reasonable time to LANDLORD or its representative for the purpose of examining the same to determine the accuracy of the statements of the gross sales submitted by TENANT as aforesaid. The books and records of account shall also include all federal, state and local tax returns of TENANT relating to TENANT's gross sales. All books and records, including tax returns, with respect to gross sales for any one lease year shall be kept by TENANT and be open to LANDLORD's examination for a period of four (4) years following the close of such lease year. In the event an examination of the records of TENANT shall disclose that gross sales as reported in the aforesaid statements were less, by one percent (1%) or more than the gross sales actually made in, upon and from the PREMISES during any lease year, TENANT agrees to pay to LANDLORD the reasonable

(continued)

EXHIBIT 12.5. *(Continued)*

cost of any such audit. Any additional Percentage Rent found due and owing as a result of such audit shall immediately become due and payable. In the event such audit discloses that gross sales reported by TENANT were less, by three percent (3%) or more than the gross sales actually made in, upon and from the PREMISES during any lease year, LANDLORD shall, in addition to the foregoing rights, have the right to terminate this lease. LANDLORD shall have the right to inspect the records of TENANT in connection with sales made by TENANT from other stores operated by it, but only in the event such examination becomes necessary to ascertain the gross sales made by TENANT from the PREMISES.

(iii) Gross Sales. The term "gross sales", as used in this lease, shall be deemed to mean the aggregate gross amount of all sales of merchandise made and all charges for services performed by TENANT or any persons, firms or corporations on its behalf, or any subtenants, licensees or concessionaires of TENANT, from, in or upon the PREMISES, including orders taken upon the PREMISES for delivery from sources other than the PREMISES, and whether wholesale or retail, and whether cash or credit, and including the value of all consideration other than money received for any of the foregoing, less refunds for merchandise returned for which cash has been refunded or credit given; provided the sales price was originally included in gross sales. The amount of any sales and excise taxes whatsoever, and however imposed, computed or paid for sales from, in or upon the PREMISES, shall, to the extent included in sales, be deducted when determining gross sales. Merchandise transferred from the PREMISES to another store or stores of TENANT, or merchandise returned for credit to factories or jobbers shall not be included in determining gross sales. No deduction shall be allowed for uncollected credit or charge accounts.

(iv) Adjustment in Fixed Minimum Rent. In the event the Fixed Minimum Rent for any lease year or partial lease year shall be reduced or abated for any reason whatsoever, the "minimum basis of sales" for determining the amount of Percentage Rent shall likely be reduced proportionately.

---

the tenant to report gross sales to the landlord on a monthly basis—and to pay at that time any subsequent amount due. Most managers apply any balance due to the tenant, as credit applied to the next rent payment. This was fully discussed in chapter 8, "The Lease Document." Exhibit 12.6 presents a sample gross sales report.

With the tenant's report of gross sales, the manager can also find out how well each tenant is doing financially at the center. The gross sales, as recorded in the periodic reports, therefore, function as the center's "heartbeat." Strong sales reports from most tenants will generally indicate that the center is a healthy one. Periodically, most centers have one or two tenants that report poor sales, which could indicate many different things. It could be a seasonal trend, or it could be that the tenants' locations at the center are weak, or perhaps some tenants are doing a poor job in maintaining their spaces. The gross sales reports, therefore, besides establishing the percentage rent, also help the manager identify problems at the center.

EXHIBIT 12.6. *Gross Sales Report*

Center: _____
Tenant: _____
Reporting Year Ends: _____

Month	Year____ Sales Volume	Percent Increase	Year____ Sales Volume	Percent Increase
January				
February				
March				
April				
May				
June				
July				
August				
September				
October				
November				
December				

TOTAL _____ Annual % increase _____

Annual volume per square foot   Annual volume per square foot

[   ]   [   ]

Ideally, all tenants will report their gross sales monthly, although each lease specifies the required frequency. As the tenants submit their gross sales reports, the manager should file them, making comparisons with past months and years. This way, the manager will also learn of any emerging trends and unusual circumstances.

Some management firms have incorporated tenants' gross sales reports into their computer systems. In this case, the manager can compare each tenant's past and present sales volume, rank the tenant's performance in the center, or contrast the tenant to comparable tenants in other centers. Some firms have even designed computer software systems that bill tenants for the percentage rents that are due.

An analysis of gross sales reports can also help the manager determine whether a prospect would be suitable for the shopping center. The number of merchants in the market that sells a specific type of merchandise will indicate to the manager the need for one tenant. Basically, then, gross sales reports allow the manager to keep one record about the prosperity of the shopping center. The manager may spot problems and opportunities, ways to save money, conflicts, and solutions. Managers who find that some merchants at the center are having problems should do everything they can to help these tenants. The manager may suggest improvements in the areas of merchandising, advertising, or hours of operations. Most merchants who are having difficulties will be receptive to suggestions that have actually worked successfully in other operations.

Tenant Data

In addition to all of the tenants' payments, the manager should keep records of other information about the shopping center tenants.

For one, the manager needs to prepare a lease abstract for each tenant. A sample lease abstract appears in Exhibit 12.7. A lease abstract condenses all the essential terms of the lease on one convenient reference sheet. The abstract should contain such information as the date of the lease; commencement date; termination date; any rental concessions; unit location; total square feet; and the tenant's mailing address, telephone number, and legal name. The abstract should also note where

EXHIBIT 12.7. *Lease Abstract*

Location and Description

Center: _____   Lessee: _____
Lessor: _____   Store name: _____
Store dimensions: Lessee address:
_____ × _____
_____ × _____   _____
_____ × _____   _____
Store area: _____ sq. ft.   _____
Space number: _____   Billing address:
Store phone: _____   _____
Lessee phone: _____   _____
Store manager: _____   _____
Assistant manager: _____   Notice address:
                                 _____
                                 _____
                                 _____

Lease Data

Lease date: _____   Lease term: ____years ____mos.
Beginning date: _____   Ending date: _____

(continued)

EXHIBIT 12.7. *(Continued)*

Acceptance date: _____   Opening date: _____
Rent: _____ /sq. ft.   _____/mo. _____ /year
Percentage rent:
  1st breakpoint: ____% over _____ /year
  2nd breakpoint: ____% over _____ /year
  3rd breakpoint: ____% over _____ /year
  Less deductions: _____
  Report frequency:_____   Payments due:_____
Common area maintenance: Pays _____ per _____ annual maximum _____
  Estimated charge: _____ per _____
Taxes: Pays _____ % of (increased) taxes over base of _____ with
  estimated charge of _____ per _____
Insurance: Pays _____ % of (increased) insurance over base of _____
  with estimated charge of _____ per _____
Option: _____ (no.) _____ year term(s) at _____ same/ _____ increased
  rent

Lease Clauses

	Yes	No	Lease Locations
Common area maintenance	____	____	_____
Percentage rent	____	____	_____
Taxes	____	____	_____
Insurance	____	____	_____
Lessor repairs	____	____	_____
Lessee repairs	____	____	_____
Options	____	____	_____
Exclusives	____	____	_____
Sublet/assignment	____	____	_____
Merchants' association	____	____	_____
Utilities by lessee	____	____	_____

Lease Modifications

Amendments: 1) Dated _____;   2) Dated _____; 3) Dated _____

Assignments: 1) Dated _____   Assignor _____
                                            Assignee _____

Subletting: 1) Dated _____   Sublessor _____
                                            Sublessee _____
                                            Sublessee _____

Special Notes

                     Lessee: _____

                     Assignee/Sublessee: _____

any clause that directly affects the daily operation of the center appears in the lease. The manager might also note on the abstract the specific paragraph numbers of all repair clauses that delineate between the landlord's and the tenant's responsibilities. For those leases with percentage rents, the abstract will indicate the percentage that the tenant will pay and the sales base.

The managers themselves should compile the data to be recorded on the lease abstract. This will allow the manager to verify the accuracy of the information. Accuracy on the lease abstracts is essential, since the manager will often refer to the information on this form during the term of the lease. The lease itself is a long and detailed legal document. The abstract serves as a clear and condensed version of much of the same information.

Most shopping center leases require tenants to maintain liability insurance for their own premises. Generally, each lease specifies the required amount of minimum coverage. The manager must obtain from each tenant a certificate of insurance, which serves as evidence that proper coverage is being carried.

The lease may require the owner to be named as an additional insured. The manager can prepare a chronological list of the expiration dates of all tenants' insurance policies, which are not likely to coincide with lease expiration dates. Such a list will enable the manager, without a great deal of effort, to check whether each tenant has fulfilled this requirement of the lease.

The property manager should also maintain a list of all tenants' options and lease expiration dates. As explained in chapter 9, if a tenant's lease contains an option to renew, generally the tenant must exercise the option within a certain number of days before the lease expires. The tenant's failure to exercise this option will give the manager the right to renegotiate the lease or place a new tenant in the space. The manager, therefore, would have the opportunity to take immediate action should the tenant forfeit the option.

The property manager may want to set up a "tickler" file. Many business offices—from insurance companies to universities and sales forces—use a tickler system. The system offers useful reminders of important dates through the placement of special notes or tabs on dates when a specific activity must be conducted. For a property manager, the files can serve as a notice of dates that will require an action.

Managers will probably also find it worthwhile to establish billing ledgers for those expense items that tenants must pay according to the terms of their leases. For example, a common area maintenance billing ledger will list each tenant and show when each will be billed and the percentage rent that each will be charged. The same type of billing ledger can cover taxes, insurance, and utility chargebacks. A ledger system such as this will also verify to the manager that every tenant has received the appropriate bill at the appropriate time. Finally, these ledgers will provide a quick determination of the annual receipts from each category.

Lease expiration dates are essential information to the property manager, since lease terminations will affect the income and expense reports of the center. Ideally, tenants will be required to notify the manager of lease expirations at least 120 days before the termination of their leases. Most practitioners consider 120 days the minimum length of time needed to renegotiate with the current tenant or to find a new tenant for the space. If the management firm uses an automated accounting system, the manager can easily program it to list all expiring leases within a certain period of time. Option dates also can be programmed into the computer system.

Financial Reports to the Owner

Previous sections of this chapter focused on the methods that a management firm should follow in setting up an accounting system for a shopping center. It is difficult, however, to establish guidelines that will apply in all cases, since great diversity exists among different types of shopping center owners. As explained in chapter 2, ownership forms vary greatly, from single investors to partnerships and syndications, to sophisticated corporate institutions. Each of these entities has different objectives for investing in real estate as well as different means for doing so. Yet, all of these types of owners at the very least want financial reports that are easy to read and that are delivered on time. The manager should be equipped to provide as much information as the client demands, whenever the client demands it. The manager should be able quite easily to produce information when a record-keeping system has been set up, especially if the records are computerized.

Included with the property manager's daily reporting functions of the accounting systems are the following:

1. Maintain tenant billing records and apply proper records of collections.
2. Pay bills.
3. Send out monthly tenant statements.
4. Prepare monthly and year-end cash flow summary statements.
5. Handle utility bill payments.
6. Handle payroll and payroll taxes.
7. Assume responsibility for banking functions.
8. Make mortgage payments, together with tax and insurance escrows.
9. Keep records of security deposits.
10. Prepare budget reports, including monthly variance reports.

Basically, a comprehensive report to the owner should include the following items:

1. A current balance sheet.
2. An income and expense statement.
3. A cash flow statement.
4. Supportive documents and schedules for financial statements.

Some owners may not require all of these reports. In earlier years, most owners were content with a simple report of income and expenses. But that has changed. Many of today's owners of real property are sophisticated, experienced investors who demand all of the items listed above.

Step-ups in federal government regulations have led to even more strict accounting and disclosure procedures. One obvious example of a tighter federal regulation is that imposed on syndications' reporting methods. Property investors must also adhere to strict accounting laws when they receive special tax treatment for rehabilitation projects. There are still many other statements that property investors must submit regularly to the federal government:

Current balance sheet. This is a statement that shows all assets and liabilities of the property, which includes the current depreciated value of the property and the current loan balance.

Income and expense statement. A current month and year-to-date accounting of all income items and expense items must adhere to Internal Revenue Service regulations.

Cash flow statement. This is a current and year-to-date accounting of all receipts and disbursements that includes debt service payment, but excludes noncash items, such as depreciation and bad debt write-offs.

Supportive documents and schedules for financial statement. This statement includes rent roll, a detailed list of disbursements, prepaid rent, bank reconciliations, and explanations for any unusual items.

Conclusion

Throughout this chapter, the emphasis has continually shifted back to the all-important task of maintaining thorough and accurate records for the shopping center. That the center needs a good accounting and record-keeping system is not arguable; how the system is organized, however, will vary significantly among properties. The management firm must decide whether the company needs an automated accounting system to service its clients, or whether a manual one would suffice.

If the firm's decision makers decide to purchase an automated record-keeping system, they have four options to consider. These options are a bookkeeping machine, a service bureau, time sharing, or an in-house computer. The decision to purchase an in-house computer is a major one, since the systems are very costly. Yet, advanced technology has now begun to produce computer systems that are an affordable possibility, even for small firms. Computers provide the fastest, most accurate, and most thorough information-processing available.

After an accounting system has been established, the manager must develop a chart of accounts, which sets down a line-by-line report on all income and expense categories. Tenants' gross sales, besides establishing the amounts due for percentage rents, monitor the shopping center's overall successes.

An efficient accounting system will serve the shopping center for many years. The manager who provides the property owner with comprehensive and prompt financial reports is offering information about the property and is also assuring the owner that a true professional is managing the property.

Review Questions

1. How can the accounting and reporting functions affect the relationship between the owner and the property manager?
2. Discuss the merits of a manual accounting system versus an automated accounting system.
3. Which automated accounting system gives the manager the greatest flexibility?

4. Will a chart of accounts differ from one shopping center to another?
5. Discuss the distinction between the income and expense statement and the cash flow statement.
6. What purposes are served by the preparation of an operating budget? a capital budget?
7. When should an operating budget be presented to ownership?
8. Discuss the significance of "breakpoint" calculations for common area maintenance, taxes, and insurance contributions by the tenants.
9. What are the possible results from either an inconsistent policy on collections or no policy at all?
10. What important lease term items should be included on a lease abstract for proper input into the accounting system?
11. What particular report for a shopping center could be considered the heartbeat?
12. How could gross sales reports be used comparatively within a center and to other centers?
13. Discuss the types of reports that should be provided to the owner on a monthly basis.

13

What the Property Manager Should Know about Retailing

Shopping centers are retail communities. Ideally, the center will contain a mix of tenants that will satisfy the economic needs of the immediate trade area and will match its socioeconomic level. More than any other kind of real estate investment, a shopping center is the sum of its parts. Only in a shopping center does the investor depend so heavily and so directly on each tenant's commitment to profits. Retailing, in essence, is the reason that the center exists. In spite of all this, many shopping center managers know very little about retailing.

Readers have seen the property manager's role in maintaining the center property, in analyzing the region, in developing a new center, in understanding the owner's objectives, in preparing a management plan, in promoting the property, and in selecting a strong tenant mix. All of these are related to the center as a property investment. Yet, underlying these topics is a fundamental quality, and the distinguishing feature of the shopping center: It is a property filled with retail stores.

The purpose of this chapter is to describe, first, the unique relationship that exists between the retailer at a shopping center and the property manager. The text will then discuss the general problems that retailers, specifically shopping center retailers, are facing today, and how the manager can help the retailer find solutions to these problems. Although retailing is basic to the investment, the concern of this book is with property management. This chapter will show the property manager's relationship to retailers at the shopping center. It will show how the manager can understand the general problems that most retailers face, and the specific problems that they confront today.

Retailing Defined

Historically, retailing meant trading—buying and selling—and nothing more. A buyer and a seller bargained for a fair price. People bought items to satisfy their primary needs (food and shelter), and sellers supplied those products. Today, manufacturers produce, and retailers sell, the same items. The difference comes with the "package," whether that means the carton, the store, or the location. Companies spend billions of dollars each year, to convince consumers that one product or one store is better than another. Likewise, the shopping center owner tries to convince prospective tenants and consumers that one shopping center is better, more convenient, more complete, or more attractive than the one down the road.

Retailing has grown much more sophisticated since its early days. It has evolved into a field of "merchandising" and "operations"—systematic approaches to the promotion of merchandise and the daily functions that keep the store and its records in good order. In large stores, these tasks are divided by department, and by department managers and buyers. Computers now control inventories; advanced security systems protect the stores; and most anchor stores today are managed by skilled professionals, who understand the most sophisticated ways to operate a large store.

Nevertheless, the essential purpose of retailing—to provide the right item at the right time—remains the same. The retailer is as concerned as ever about finding the right location that shoppers will be willing to travel to and to sell the kind of merchandise that they will demand. This basic retailing service is called *time and place utility.*

Interdependence of Retailers, the Property Owner, and the Property Manager

A theme that has run throughout this book is that, among property investments, the shopping center is unique, largely because of the relationship that exists among the tenant, the landlord, and the property manager. Each tenant pays rent to the landlord, and the landlord, therefore, depends on tenants to produce a steady flow of income. As the overseer, the property manager depends on both the retailer and the landlord: The "overseer" manages the investment profitably and helps keep a steady stream of customers coming back to the stores.

Each party, in sum, depends on the others for its own success. In a regional center, although tenants will compete with each other, ultimately they stand together to complement each other and to attract a larger buying public. Just as all parties share an interest in seeing the center investment succeed, they also share an interest in seeing each individual tenant succeed. Each part, again, represents an important part of the whole. The property manager serves as the mediator, and in that role, must understand the demands of all parties, including those of retailers. Open communications are the starting point.

In most centers, the merchants' association offers the most effective way to communicate with all tenants on a regular basis. The purpose, advantages, and disadvantages of a merchants' association have been discussed in other parts of this book, in particular in chapter 10, "Advertising, Promotion, and Publicity." Ideally, the association will be a forum where tenants can work together for the common good in promoting the center; where tenants can regularly voice their concerns and complaints; and where the manager, in turn, can listen, respond, and inform.

Problems that Confront Retailers

A major trend of the shopping center industry throughout the 1960s and 1970s was for developers to build sprawling regional and superregional shopping centers, mostly in suburban areas. These centers, containing two, three, or even four major tenants, were extremely profitable for developers and retailers alike. A "bigger is better" mentality prevailed. Shopping center developers and anchor retailing tenants continued to build and expand in that spirit, assuming that bigger would always be better. Some of the superregional centers that were built contained four, five, and even six anchor tenants.

Developers of course, did not know that the population growth would be curtailed, that the price of fuel would skyrocket, that interest rates would go to record highs, or that the nation's economy would experience a severe recession. They did not know that many women would enter the labor force, or that large new discount stores would present stiff competition. This latter trend, considered a major problem for many retailers, is discussed in more detail later in this section. All of these factors, however, did occur, and did affect the shopping center industry.

In many suburban areas, the regional shopping center continues to thrive. The large department stores and the smaller satellites continue to draw a large, consuming public. Many patrons continue to visit the center on weekends, turning the activity into a daylong event. They browse, meet friends, eat lunch, and shop at the many stores. The center owner and retailing tenants alike maintain a healthy profit. Yet, the disposable incomes of most consumers are lower than they were a few years ago because incomes have risen slower than inflation. Although more women have joined the labor force, which, theoretically, should have increased disposable income per household, it has been found that most families are using this "extra" income as a way of maintaining rather than of improving their lifestyle. Many families indeed have found that financially it has become essential that the woman work outside the home. In 1982, 52 percent of all women actively participated in the labor force. This marks a major shift from 1950, when only about 35 percent of all women, and 1960, when 38 percent of all women were part of the labor force (U.S. Bureau of the Census).

In an economy of high unemployment, such as that of the early 1980s, consumers become ever more price conscious. As the supply of money tightens, many consumers spend money only on basic necessities—and still have a difficult time staying afloat financially. During difficult economic times, merchants quickly find that shoppers cut out the frills.

Since many shopping center sales depend on impulse purchases, center retailers, in particular, are affected, when the economy experiences a downturn. As more women have entered the labor force, another problem for retailers has developed: Fewer women have long, leisurely days to spend shopping, and many women now limit their shopping trips to necessity buying.

Another significant trend during the 1970s has reaped troubles for retailers, notably for department store retailers. Retailers have confronted strong competition from large discount chains. These stores, many of which are anchor stores in shopping centers, sell everything from hardware and clothing to jewelry and food. Most discount stores are chains that have been developed throughout suburban areas and therefore stand in direct competition with shopping center retailers. At one time, many retailers considered the discount stores "minor aggravations" and little more than that. That has changed radically, however, as consumers have become increasingly more satisfied with the merchandise and the services of discount stores. Inflation, recession, and high unemployment, which characterized the early 1980s, left consumers searching eagerly for bargains, a condition satisfied by the discount store. Therefore, the market that department stores once considered "their own" is now being shared with discount stores. Department stores are responding to the competition: Some are lowering their prices; others are simply retrenching, conceding some lines and items to the discounters. Some department store retailers still do not worry about the discount stores, insisting that the two markets are different. Many department store managers and owners are realizing, however, that the department store can no longer be "all things to all people." Instead, it must change its image, specializing its market and catering to a specific type of consumer.

The outlet center is a related trend that is becoming increasingly more common in suburban areas. Many real estate practitioners classify the outlet center as a shopping center in its own right. Still, the outlet center, which was described in chapter 7, "Tenant Mix," serves a very different function than a typical shopping center. The outlet center is a specialized center that generally sells high-quality merchandise at lower prices. Although they lack the diversity and extra attractions of a typical shopping center, these popular outlet centers have created keen competition for many center retailers. It is actually the lack of some of the "extras" of a shopping center—the lack of an attractive design, of an indoor mall with restaurants, or of special events—that convinces shoppers that they are "cutting out the frills" and saving money. Therefore, the outlet center is a threat to many retailers, and it is likely to remain so.

Other problems have troubled the retailing industry for years. Retailers notoriously have had problems with high turnover rates in personnel. The problem has been particularly serious for shopping center merchants. Most center business comes in the late afternoon, on weekends, and during evening hours, which means that many of the tenants depend on part-time help, which often represents a transient population. Many stores hire high school or college students, who may perform well on the job, but few of these students want to stay with the business for several years. This means that the retailer has the continual job of hiring and training. Many young people may be attracted to the "glamorous" retail world, but they soon find out that beyond the "glamour," retailing is plain, hard work. The hours are long, and compared to other industries, the wages are low.

There is also a trend away from the small, independent entrepreneur, a trend bemoaned and considered a problem by many in the retailing industry. The "new manager," employed by the large national chains that are so common in shopping centers, is in retailing for a career, not as an entrepreneur. The new manager resists working 72 hours per week—hours that the old-time entrepreneur simply expected. The new manager's main stake in the enterprise is generally personal pride. As a result, the industry on the whole lacks much of the fervent, tireless dedication that once controlled it. On the other hand, most of the new managers are highly skilled professionals who know how to operate a retailing operation at optimal levels. Therefore, many retailers consider this trend a healthy one.

Not all of the recent trends spell problems for retailers. There is still room for retailers' expansion and shopping center development. Although growth rates have slowed considerably, the often-forgotten fact is that the population continues to expand. The Bureau of the Census predicts that by 1985, the population will be about 5 percent larger than it was in 1980. Although the population has stopped growing at the extreme rates of the 1950s—and at the levels that demographers once expected—it nevertheless continues to grow. So, still there must be shopping centers to meet the ever-increasing demands. The real issue, therefore, is not whether to develop but rather how to develop. Haste and abundance, which once ruled the industry, are being replaced with careful planning and moderation.

Many specialty centers are being developed in renovated urban buildings. Specialty centers may cost less to develop, and to some extent, they are the answer to a declining population. The population, in general, appears to be moving away from the northern, traditionally industrial cities and is moving to the South and the West, to the "Sunbelt" regions of the country.

Specialty centers have been discussed in various parts of this book. For here, suffice it to say that the specialty center represents another concept in retailing. They are generally structures filled with boutiques and exclusive shops. There have been many successful specialty developments, but there have also been many failures. Specialty centers must be located in high-traffic locations, such as in a tourist area. People generally do not visit specialty centers on a regular basis for necessity purchases, and therefore, these centers must have unique shops and restaurants that will attract a consistently sizeable market.

The specialty center is not the solution for the expansion plans of anchor tenants—because most such tenants do not suit the quaint settings of many of these centers. The specialty center is also not the solution for the expansion plans of large numbers of retailers, because there is a limit to the number of specialty centers that can be built and can succeed in a small area. A shopping center developed from an old warehouse is interesting the first time, but the idea—as with all good ideas—can quickly be overdone. Remember that overexpansion and overbuilding became problems for regional shopping centers; these are problems that developers must learn to avoid. Finally, the developer must obtain financing for the speculative project, in an economy of high interest rates.

How the Property Manager Can Help Retailers

The property manager can help the retailer survive financially during these difficult economic times. First, however, it is important that property managers recognize some basic items that they *cannot* change. Managers cannot turn an ailing economy into a prosperous one. They cannot turn reluctant consumers into active buyers. A manager cannot prevent a potentially "deadly" competitor from moving into an area. A manager cannot turn a decaying neighborhood into a healthy one. The manager's steps, in sum, have less profound and less immediate impact, but these small steps add up. Besides, there never will be a few easy answers that will cure all of the problems in the economy. All efforts, it seems, must be small ones, and there are many small steps that the manager can take.

A note of warning is in order: The manager also cannot *direct* the retailer on how to maintain a more profitable store. Many shopping center retailers represent national conglomerates. Most of these stores have modern, sophisticated systems of operations. They can afford to hire highly skilled managers, and they are willing to pay for extensive training for their staffs. These stores will probably not be eager to hear criticism from a property manager whose "expertise" in retailing would be highly questionable. Many smaller retailers, too, are sole entrepreneurs who take great pride in their stores, and they want to operate their businesses their own way.

This often puts the property manager in a difficult position. When one tenant at the center is floundering, it affects the other tenants as well. Throughout this book, and again in this chapter, the same theme emerges: Each party at the center affects the others. All have an interest in their own prosperity and, to this end, in the long-term prosperity of the center. Nevertheless, some retailers will resent the property manager's help, no matter how well-intentioned or helpful the advice.

In general, property managers must remember that their own specialty is property and not retailing. They have an important role to play in maintaining the property, in assuring the smooth operation of the center, in guiding and overseeing—but not in meddling in the business of individual retailers. As might be expected, the property manager is forced to walk a delicate line.

Property managers not only manage property—they also manage people. Their dealings with retailers are one of their most important business relationships. It is retailers whom the property manager will work with everyday, and it is retailers who ultimately produce an income for the investment. Part of managing people is learning how to give criticism tactfully. Managers must remember that what they want from each tenant is cooperation, and tenants are far more likely to cooperate if they think they are being treated fairly and believe that responsibilities at the center go two ways. Different retailers attract different types of customers, they sell different goods and services, and they have different needs. The manager, therefore, must consider each tenant on an individual basis. Just as a good physician must do, the successful shopping center manager must probe for information from each tenant before prescribing a cure. By servicing the needs of each tenant through all stages of the investment, the property manager can operate a more efficient shopping center.

Constructive advice is usually appropriate. There are many areas where the property manager can offer useful, constructive suggestions. The manager's role in promoting the interests of retailers at the center is an ongoing one. It begins at the development stage and continues throughout tenant prospecting, lease negotiations, and the day-to-day operations of the property. In selecting a tenant mix, in most cases, the manager should maintain the position that competition among tenants gives the entire investment a boost and actually helps the tenants more than it hurts them.

Again, all parties involved share a common interest in maintaining a continued flow of consumers, and the manager should continually remind tenants of this. Only during the 1950s did shopping center developers embark on the new concept of competition within the center, and it generally has been beneficial to the industry. In most cases, competition increases the volume at all stores.

Another part of the manager's responsibilities is to insist that tenants abide by the terms of their leases. Store hours of 9 a.m. to 9 p.m. do not mean opening at 9:30 and closing at 8:45. Likewise, a sign restriction clause is in the lease for a reason, and tenants cannot be permitted to violate the terms of the clause. That is true for all of the terms in the tenants' leases. Standards must be set and enforced, and almost always, the manager will assume the duty of enforcement. Again, the shopping center is a single unit, and if it is to succeed as a property investment, all its "parts"—the tenants—must abide by the regulations.

The manager should also stay current on retail trends. If asked if there is a single step that the property manager should take that would help tenants at the center, many tenants would probably respond: "Know more about what we do," Most tenants do not expect the manager to be an expert on retailing, but they want someone who understands the pressures under which they operate. There are many periodicals about all aspects of retailing that the manager should read, as regularly as possible: *Women's Wear Daily, Footwear News, Franchising,* and *Chain Store Age* are among these. The manager should be aware of items that sell best during different seasons. The manager should know how high overhead costs are for different retailers.

Property managers will also be doing a great deal for the benefit of tenants by planning periodic special events. Chapter 10, "Advertising, Promotion, and Publicity," discussed many ways that the manager, the merchants' association, or the association's board of directors can plan special events. Especially effective are those events that revolve around a holiday or seasonal theme. The basic purpose of any promotional event is to attract shoppers who will become regular customers of the center. Art fairs, bake sales, and ethnic celebrations are only some of the many possibilities.

The manager may want to remind retailers of immediate selling opportunities, whenever they arise. If it is raining outside, for example, the manager might remind all retailers who sell umbrellas to bring some to the front of the store and perhaps suggest that the umbrellas be marked down 20 percent. If a fad is receiving a good deal of media attention—as the "hoolahoop" and miniskirts once did—the property manager might suggest ways to display the item prominently. There are many small ways that the property manager can advise retailers on how to improve their sales. But again, the manager must remember that between the two of them, the retailer almost certainly knows more about retailing. A property manager who "knows it all" is likely to create friction with the tenants.

Shopping center managers must recognize their own limitations. When it comes to legal and financial matters, the manager should refer the retailer to an expert. When tenants ask for help in putting together their financial plans, the manager should advise them to consult an accountant or a banker. Ideally, help will come before major problems develop. Professional assistance, therefore, would provide a preventive medicine.

Property managers should know the better retailers, merchandisers, and sales producers who will help in developing and maintaining an effective tenant mix. However, shopping center managers can create major problems for themselves, the owner, and the investment if they delve too deeply into the area of retailing. Retailing is the retailer's job, and in this aspect of the shopping center, most property managers function in ancillary roles.

Retailing Terms

Part of the property manager's job in understanding tenants' problems is understanding the language that retailers use. As it has been stressed throughout this book, the manager and the retailer need to understand each other. They need to communicate. They need, at some time, to "talk the same language."

The following is a case study that will show the situation of one retailer, and at the same time, point out the numerous terms that this retailer—and any other retailer—would use. The store is a men's clothier in a neighborhood center, located in Mayville, a secluded, rural town with 10,000 people. The store is called the Hub, and the owner is Mr. Peterson. The shopping center has a grocery store as the anchor tenant. There are only eight tenants in the center and no other men's clothiers. There is also a women's apparel store, a dry cleaner, a gift and card shop, a beauty parlor, a restaurant, and a snack bar. (The snack bar also sells convenience goods, cigarettes, candy bars—in sum, those items that consumers will buy from the nearest store, with the least possible effort and with little heed as to where they are making the purchase.)

It should be mentioned at the start that Mayville is a very unusual little town. Its population is small, but it has a large farm population, and were it not for the surrounding farm area, the city would not be able to support two fairly prosperous retailing areas—the downtown district and the shopping center. A major concern of Peterson's is his *market penetration*, which is the percentage of the men's clothing market in the trade area that the Hub can win.

Peterson has developed excellent *institutional advertising* for the Hub. This is advertising that attempts to enhance the image of the business rather than promote a specific product or service. On some items, the Hub stands apart from the competition, almost as an institution. There is one major competitor in the trade area, another high-quality men's clothing store, but Peterson has successfully conveyed the message that the Hub carries the finest quality suits. (Retailers commonly refer to men's suits simply as *clothing*.) The Hub's competitor carries high-quality merchandise, but it nowhere near touches on the quantity and selection of clothing at the Hub. When a man in Mayville needs a suit, he usually goes to the Hub.

When Mr. Peterson wants to promote a specific kind of shirt, he resorts to *promotional advertising*, an ad that he generally runs in the local newspaper. Peterson very effectively uses *price impression advertising* in his newspaper ads. Through skillful rotation and pricing of only a few items, he conveys the message to the public that Hub prices are generally lower than the competition. Peterson also uses *cooperative advertising*, which is when the manufacturer agrees to pay for part of the cost of advertising the product. Because of the prohibitive cost of TV advertising and the fact that Mayville has no radio station, Peterson has little concern with *media mix*, which refers to a retailer's distribution of the advertising budget among the various media. Peterson, in sum, understands the *promotional cycle*, which represents the various steps taken to introduce, sell, and clean out inventory of an item, or a line of merchandise.

Peterson runs the Hub with a philosophy of *balanced assortment*: Balanced assortment is a "model stock" that makes available what customers want at several different price levels, in proportion to what they demand. He also uses a *balance mix*, which is the proper mix of lines, classifications, and merchandise items at a variety of prices, all which appeal to the greatest number of customers.

Besides an excellent suit selection, Peterson sells the *basics*, which are items that a store should always have in stock, because consumers have a right to expect that they be in stock; for example, white T-shirts. He also carries an excellent *basic stock*—those items often referred to as the bread and butter assortment, items that enjoy a day-by-day consumer demand; and *ticket items*, which are high-priced items that are frequently sold by commissioned salespeople. For Peterson, that item is men's suits. Peterson pays one of his employees, Mr. Rogers, a commission because Rogers sells most of the Hub's clothing. Rogers has developed excellent skills in *concept selling*, which means that he is good at putting together wardrobes for customers. That is why Rogers also carries on a good amount of *personal trade*—which retailers commonly refer to as P.T. P.T. refers to customers who come into the store with the request that a specific salesperson wait on them. Rogers is also very much aware of the *Rule of Three*, a basic principle of selling: In showing merchandise to a customer, the Rule of Three holds that a salesperson should not have more than three items in view at any one time. More than three items will confuse the shopper.

Peterson belongs to the *National Retail Merchants' Association*, which is one of the largest retail trade associations in the world. He also subscribes to the services of a jobbers' association. A *jobber is* a wholesaler who buys merchandise from manufacturers and then sells it to dealers, who are usually retailers.

Peterson owns a small operation. He has no buyers or managers. He is a small-town merchant, and the Hub is his only store. He is, in fact, the Hub's owner, manager, advertising director, and buyer. Although his business lacks many of the sophisticated systems of a larger operation, Peterson applies many of the same principles to his own store. He sets specific buying limits for himself and puts many of the same standards on himself that a larger retailer would put on any manager or buyer. One of these controls is an *open to buy*, which tells a buyer how much to spend on a certain classification of merchandise at a specific time. Peterson has set a *stock-sales ratio* for the Hub of three to one, which is a common ratio in a retail store. The stock-sales ratio is the amount of stock it takes in a merchandising classification to achieve sales at a projected figure.

Another ratio that Peterson considers is the *selling cost ratio*. This is a percentage figure that results from dividing the amount of the selling payroll by the amount of sales in dollars. Besides Rogers, Peterson has eight people who are on the payroll. He, therefore, divides his total sales by nine, to arrive at the store's selling cost ratio.

Peterson faces a number of concerns that relate specifically to the business of retailing. First, he has large spaces in front of the main traffic aisles. These are spaces that he wants to use to the fullest. Here, he often displays appealing fashions, or he puts there small, inexpensive items that customers might buy on impulse. An *impulse purchase* is an item that customers often do not intend to buy but do so without first thinking about the purchase rationally. Peterson is well aware that, in his store, the bulk of income comes from expensive, more rational purchases, but he nevertheless displays these smaller items in an attempt to bolster his sales. Peterson is also very knowledgeable about the *fashion cycle*, which is the entire cycle that a fashion item goes through, from the buying, advertising, and replacement stages to its eventual termination.

Peterson has his income and expenses to consider. Above all, Peterson knows all too well how difficult it is to earn a steady profit in the retail business. Peterson has certain *fixed expenses*, which occur regularly and do not vary with business volume. For the Hub, these include rent and merchants' association dues. Peterson also has certain *variable expenses*, which he can, to some extent, control, and, in turn, increase his net profits. A variable expense is an overhead cost, such as labor or advertising.

Peterson must add a *markup* to all his merchandise. A markup is the difference between Peterson's purchase price and his selling price. Peterson uses the standard retailing *keystone markup*, which is 100 percent of cost, or 50 percent of the retail selling price. His *margin* is the difference between what he pays for an item and what it is sold for. (*Markon* is the same as markup.) Peterson's maintained market is the sum total of all markups, less markdowns, during a period of time. It is the average of all final markups on merchandise. Peterson's *initial markup* is the first markup that he takes on new merchandise.

Peterson often must take *markdowns*, which are reductions in the original buying price of various items. The "ideal markdown" is considered the reduction that will move merchandise quickly but not *too* quickly.

When the center sponsors special promotions, Peterson

might promote his shirts, which have been marked down in price considerably. The shirts are thus *leaders*, which are any products that, when offered at a certain price, have the capacity to pull people into a store. A good leader has mass appeal, requires frequent replacement, and is inexpensive, at least compared to most items in the store. Often, Peterson will promote a *loss leader*, which is a product that he sells below his own cost, in order to attract customers.

Peterson uses *Kimball tickets* on all his merchandise. This is a tag that contains inventory information.

On the other end of Peterson's accounting records is income. Peterson is concerned about the *breakeven point*, the point at which sales will be sufficient to replace merchandise and will pay all overhead expenses—but the point at which there is yet no net profit and no income. He has *gross sales*, which is the sum total in dollars of every sale that the store makes during a specific financial period, usually a calendar year. In most leases, it is this gross sales figure on which the percentage rent is based. Peterson's *net sales* is the amount left from the total sales after exchanges, refunds, and allowances have been taken into account. After Peterson has paid operating expenses and taxes, he has a *net profit*, which is the money that is *free and clear*—money that is left as Peterson's profit at the end of the financial period.

Peterson's concern now turns to selling, to the consumer, and to meeting the needs of the consumer. Creating an excellent first impression for the shopper is called *visual merchandising*, which involves everything that customers see as they approach a store and immediately after they enter. This includes the lighting, the floor covering, the fixtures—and, on the negative side, a cluster of employees standing around talking.

Peterson offers three *price lines* at the Hub—the top, middle, and bottom prices, thus offering general classifications of merchandise to shoppers. The *price points* are the specific prices within a price line. This is an important concept for Peterson to remember because consumers will buy more of a certain item at one price point (for example, $3.99) than at another (for example, $4.00).

When the Hub receives goods (*R.O.G.: receipt of goods*), Peterson nearly always pay for them at least 10 days after receipt. This entitles him to an 8 percent discount. Peterson usually takes an average inventory, which means totaling the beginning inventories for a specific period of time and dividing by the number of months that are involved.

Peterson has also agreed to display and sell handmade ties, which were sewn by a local senior citizens group. This is called *consignment selling,* and here the vendor agrees to take back goods if they are not sold within a specific period of time. Often, the store, as in the case of Hub, acts simply as an agent for the vendor. Retailers, however, can and often do add a profit margin to consignment goods. The Hub earns no direct profit from the handmade ties, but the store does a good public service.

Peterson is also concerned about the appeal of the anchor. He realizes that if the grocery store fails to draw customers, the shoppers may simply go elsewhere, which in Mayville, is the downtown district, the only place in or near the city where Peterson faces direct competition. There is a large, clean, well-stocked grocery store in Mayville's downtown. It is important to Peterson—as it is to the other retailers at the center—that the tenant mix be a strong draw, strong enough such that shoppers will choose it over the downtown area.

Peterson is satisfied that the grocery store effectively offers shoppers *self-selection,* which is the presentation of merchandise in such a way that the customer can select merchandise, usually without the help of a salesperson; and *self-service,* which includes anything in a store that makes it easier for customers to serve themselves, such as shopping carts and aisle designations. Before the shopping center was even built, Peterson carefully reviewed the grocery store anchor's *schematic,* which is a store's blueprint showing exactly where each section, fixture, and aisle will be located.

The anchor at the shopping center differs from the Hub in that it concentrates on *mass merchandising,* which is a self-service operation that displays and sells a wide mix of merchandise. In a mass merchandising operation, the displays tend to be very large, and customers often push carts to the checkout counters.

Peterson is aware of one glaring mistake that his downtown competitor makes: The retailer has fallen into the trap of *scatteration buying,* which refers to buying a classification of merchandise from too many buyers and not paying enough attention to the best lines. Peterson can take advantage of his competitor's flaw by avoiding it in his own store, by promoting the well-known, high-quality lines that the Hub offers.

Many men, when they buy a suit, will shop around before they decide on which one to buy. An item that people will shop around for, such as a suit or a stereo set or an item of furniture, is called a *shopping good*. Peterson has a problem here because he realizes that if the customer goes to the competitor, very likely because of the inconvenience, the customer will not return to the center for the suit. That is why the Hub must continually stress its superior quality of merchandise, convincing shoppers that, indeed, there is something well worth coming back to. Peterson constantly stresses to all his employees the *Three F's of Fashion:* fad, fabrics, and fit—standards that he wants them, in turn, to convey to consumers.

In many ways, the men's clothing store in Mayville's downtown district does present the Hub with stiff competition. It sells high-quality merchandise, although, as mentioned, its stock of men's suits is low. Its prices, however, are competitive with the Hub. The competitor is located on what is called a *spring street*, which is where many retailers are located along a main business artery.

As his competitor does, Peterson offers Hub customers *revolving credit*, which the customer can use over and over as long as payments are made regularly. Peterson charges an interest fee on the balance that remains at billing time.

Generally, Peterson's two primary concerns in managing the Hub are *merchandising*, which refers to getting the right merchandise to the right place in the right quantity at the right price at the right time; and *marketing*, which refers to everything involved in the movement of a product or service from the factory to the customer. These steps include packaging, transportation, merchandising, retailing, and advertising.

So, equipped with a very basic understanding of retailing, which involves a comprehension of everyday terms that retailers use, the property manager becomes an ever greater asset to shopping center investors and shopping center tenants. A hospital administrator cannot relate to physicians without a basic knowledge of their common language. A newspaper publisher must be able to speak in the vernacular of newspaper reporters. Likewise, shopping center managers need to understand the common words that continually enter into conversations with their tenants.

The Effects of Shopping Centers on Retailers

This chapter has discussed the unique interdependence that exists between retailers and the owner and manager at a shopping center. Just noted were all the ways that the property manager can help the retailer, ultimately to improve the profits of the investment. But what about the other side—what about the retailer's dependence on the shopping center? The question emerges: What have shopping centers meant for retailing?

It is no exaggeration to say that shopping centers have turned around the nature of retailing. At one time, the retail market was concentrated in downtown districts or in neighborhood shopping areas. Today, shopping centers represent over 60 percent of all retail sales. The fact is even more amazing, considering that shopping centers have been around little more than 60 years, and on a large scale, little more than 30 years. In just a short period, then, the whole concept of retailing has changed radically.

To a large extent, retailing has moved to the suburbs. The mall has become a part of American culture, and today it is not unusual for families to spend entire afternoons at the mall. In many ways, the mall has become the new social gathering place. High school students used to meet at the Malt Shop; now they meet at the mall. Families once took long drives on Sunday; now they go to the mall. The regional mall—the one-stop center for shopping, with theatres, restaurants, special displays, and an amazing variety of stores—has largely become the new retail center. The mall, in sum, has become an American institution.

Therefore, for most retailers, the mall has meant opportunities. Unfortunately, the trend toward shopping centers has taken business away from some small retailers. The national chain is generally on stronger financial footing, and unlike many smaller tenants, does not have the financial means to expand. The trend toward shopping center development has devastated many smaller retailers who cannot afford to move from the downtown area to the center. Because so many shopping centers have been built in outlying areas, the once-prosperous downtowns of some small cities have become ghost towns.

Yet, as it has been noted several times throughout this book, generally new businesses bring new traffic to an area. In most cases, large stores and shopping centers have added more than they have taken away in these cities.

The Future of Shopping Center Retailing

The success of shopping centers of the future will probably depend heavily on the abilities of retailers to provide efficient, skilled leadership. Retailers in all areas of the country are experiencing difficult times. The high cost of borrowing has put great strains on the retailing sector, and consumers' buying power has dwindled. Retailers must motivate their employees. They need to know what their market wants. They need to stay in touch with fads and trends. They need to know how to display merchandise effectively. They must know how to promote their own stores. Retailers, in sum, must know how to attract and keep an active buying public.

The growth in the number of discount stores will probably continue. Even when people are hard hit financially, they still will demand basic, consumable items. Discount stores do much to satisfy this need. Large, one-stop discount centers—selling everything from hardware to clothing, food, and books—are likely to prosper. High-fashion stores that sell discount-priced clothes will probably also continue to do well. Computer games, health food, and athletic equipment are other items that will probably continue to be strong sellers.

Ultimately, however, no one has special vision into the future, and so no one really knows what will happen to the nation's economy, to shopping center developments, or to the retailing industry. Even economists, with their complex understanding of the problems, do not come close to agreeing on solutions. In many respects, retailers must continue to do what they have always done: Provide goods and services at the right place and time, and continue to serve the public in a helpful, courteous way.

Conclusion

Shopping centers exist because retailers are willing to commit to long-term leases and to their own future in a retailing community. As all businesses suffer in a recessionary economy, it becomes more important than ever that property managers understand concerns that confront their tenants. Some problems have been around for many years. To name but a few: Retailers generally have a high turnover in personnel; new competition moving into the trade area poses a constant threat; and the tradition of the proud, hard-working entrepreneur is fading. With recent economic trends, other problems have emerged: As do other sectors in the economy, retailers face high interest rates; discount chain stores pose serious competition to many retailers; during the early 1980s, consumers' buying power dwindled dramatically—and these are still only some of the problems.

Despite the problems, there are ways of dealing with them, altering plans in a new financial scene. The property manager can gain a basic knowledge of retailing and thereby be a great asset to the retailer. The manager can put extra efforts into maintaining a clean, desirable shopping center. The manager can plan more special events that will draw more consumers, who in turn, may become regular customers.

Review Questions

1. What is the term that describes the essential purpose of retailing—that is, that which provides the right item at the right time?
2. What factors occurred during the 1980s that curtailed developers' plans to build regional shopping centers?
3. Describe the relationship between department stores and discount stores in a shopping center. Is the relationship generally an adversary one?
4. Discuss some of the major problems that confront retailers today.
5. What possibilities and what limitations can developers expect from a specialty center development? What special requirements are posed by a specialty center?
6. Discuss some of the ways that the property manager can aid retailers at the shopping center.
7. Define these retailing terms:
     market penetration
     balanced assortment
     open to buy
     basic stock markup
     margin
     loss leader
     breakeven point
8. Discuss the most significant ways that the shopping center industry has affected the retail industry.
9. Think question: What does the future hold for the retailing field in shopping centers, and what can retailers and property managers at shopping centers do to hold their share of the market?

Glossary

Absorption rate   The rate at which space is absorbed in a given locality within a given time period (usually one year).

Accounts payable contract   An insurance coverage associated specifically with the possible destruction of payment records.

Accrued depreciation   In appraisal, the difference between an improvement's replacement (or reproduction) cost and the present value of those improvements; the loss in utility of a property.

Ad valorem tax   Real estate tax that is based on a fixed proportion of a property's value.

Advertising   The act of attracting public attention to a product for the purpose of leasing or selling it.

Agent   A person who is authorized by another to act for another party within specific limits of authority.

Alarm system   An integral part of a building's security system, including fire-, burglar-, and intrusion-warning devices.

All-risk insurance   A policy providing coverage for every risk, except those risks specifically excluded by name in the policy itself.

Alteration (also **change of use**)   The process of changing the function of a structure without changing its exterior dimensions.

Amenity   A natural or manmade feature that enhances a property's attractiveness and increases the satisfaction of the user.

Amortization   The gradual reduction of debt by periodic payments of interest and principal over the term of the loan.

Analysis of alternatives   A study of a property to determine its highest and best use, including tests of economic feasibility for rehabilitation, modernization, or conversion.

Anchor tenant   A key shopping center tenant that will attract other businesses as well as the majority of consumers to the center.

Annuity   An assured and fixed flow of income.

Apportionment In an insurance policy, a clause stipulating that all companies insuring a property will divide any loss in proportion to the amount of insurance they carry.

Appraisal An estimate of a property's value.

Appraiser One who performs a formal, detailed estimate of a property's value.

As-is value A value placed on real property as the basis for the levy of real estate taxes.

Balanced assortment A "model stock" that makes available what customers want at several different price levels.

Balance mix The proper mix of lines, classifications, and merchandise items at a variety of prices, all which appeal to the greatest number of consumers.

Balloon loan A partially amortized loan in which the final payment is much larger than any of the periodic payments.

Band-of-investment method An approach to establishing a capitalization rate by weighing the return on investment required to cover mortgage interest and the return on investment required to provide a competitive return on equity.

Base rent The minimum monthly rental payments, as set forth in a commercial lease.

Basic stock In retailing, those items often referred to as the "bread and butter" assortment, items that enjoy a daily consumer demand.

Basics Those consumable items that a retail store should always have in stock, because customers have a right to expect that they be in stock.

Beneficiary In financing, a lender holding a deed of trust or promissory note as security for a loan; in insurance, one to whom the proceeds of an insurance policy are payable.

Boiler and machinery insurance Liability insurance coverage that applies specifically to the heating and cooling system in a building.

Book value The cost of a property, plus capital additions, less accrued depreciation charged off for income tax purposes.

Bookkeeping Maintaining the records of the financial accounts and transactions of a business.

Breakeven point In shopping center leases, the point at which the tenant's fixed rent is equal to its percentage rent. In retailing, the point at which sales will be sufficient to replace merchandise and will pay for all overhead expenses—but the point at which there is yet no profit and no income.

Brokerage clause A clause in many leases that assures the landlord that the broker will be paid only if the tenant actually takes possession of the space and pays rent.

Budget A written prediction of a building's income and expenses over a specific time period.

Bureau of the Census   A governmental agency within the U.S. Department of Labor that reports population by statistical areas and provides economic and demographic profiles every 10 years.

Cancellation   The rendering void or inoperative of a contract.

Canvassing (also **cold calling**)   Contacting current or potential users of shopping center space, about whom little is known, in an effort to locate prospective tenants.

Capacity   In insurance, refers to the insurer's ability to offer insurance policies and limits that meet the needs of the buyer.

Capital   Accumulated wealth, usually employed to produce additional wealth.

Capital appreciation   An increase in value.

Capital value   The estimated market value of income property based on the income capitalization approach, under which value is estimated by dividing annual net operating income by an appropriate capitalization rate.

Capitalization rate   The percentage at which net operating income is converted into an estimate of value.

Cash flow   The amount of spendable income from a real estate investment; the cash available after all payments have been made for operating expenses and mortgage principal and interest.

Central business district (CBD)   The main shopping or business area of a town or city, usually the place where real estate values are highest.

CERTIFIED PROPERTY MANAGER® (CPM®)   The professional designation conferred by the Institute of Real Estate Management on individuals who distinguish themselves in the areas of education, experience, and ethics.

Chart of accounts   A systematic series of income and expense accounts.

Chartered Property Casualty Underwriter (CPCU)   A professional designation for insurance agents.

Claims   In insurance, an insured's demand for payment as rightfully due. Also refers to the insurer's ability to offer insurance policies and limits that meet the needs of the buyer.

Coinsurance   A clause in an insurance policy used to penalize the underinsured. If a certain percentage of a property's value is not insured against loss, the property owner shares the risk of loss with the insurance company.

Commingle   To combine or mix together, for example, the management agent's funds with the owner's funds.

Commission   As compensation, a fee or percentage allowed to a salesperson, for example, a leasing specialist.

Common area   Any area within the legal boundaries of the shopping center that two or more tenants will use in common.

Common area charges clause   Clause that stipulates the amount that tenants and landlord will pay for the maintenance of the common area.

Comparative statement   Statement prepared by most management firms that compares the numerator, denominator, percentage increase, and the dollar increase in a fixed minimum amount.

Comprehensive general liability insurance   An inclusive policy providing the broadest protection against liability claims.

Concept selling   Selling an entire "concept" to a retail customer; in a clothing store, for example, helping the customer put together a wardrobe.

Conceptual stage   The initial phase of a project during which objectives are set.

Concession   Granting a reduction or allowance on rent in order to lease new space or to retain an existing tenant.

Consequential loss insurance   Insurance that protects the insured against the consequences of a direct loss, such as indirect physical damage or loss of income.

Consignment selling   Transfer of retail goods to an agent for sale.

Construction   For insurance real estate purposes, serves as one of the four factors on which property insurance rates are based, evaluating the material, layout, and design of construction.

Construction drawings (also **working drawings**)   Architectural and mechanical specifications drawn to scale and in sufficient detail to guide workers in constructing tenant improvements.

Construction loan   Funds borrowed on a short-term basis to pay for construction of improvements on real property.

Construction management   The supervision of tenant improvements by a firm or space-planning department specializing in this activity.

Construction stage   The developmental stage in which a project is actually built.

Consumer Price Index (CPI)   A figure constructed by the U.S. Bureau of Labor Statistics that measures consumer purchasing power by comparing current costs of goods and services to those of a selected base year.

Contingent business interruption   A form of consequential loss insurance coverage that provides the insured with payment for losses that indirectly affect the insured by interrupting business.

Continuous occupancy clause   A clause contained in many shopping center leases that requires the tenant to occupy the premises continuously throughout the term of the lease. The clause is intended to maximize the level of percentage rents.

Continuous operation clause   Clause that requires the tenant to keep the retail store fully stocked at inventory levels equal either to those when the tenant first opened for business, to the inventory level of stores that the tenant operates in other locations, or to similar stores in the area.

Contract of indemnity Insurance coverage designed to compensate the insured for a loss in such a way that there is neither financial gain nor loss.

Contract rent The rent stipulated in an existing lease, which may differ from the economic or market rent.

Contractor's liability insurance Coverage that insures a contractor's employees against injuries occurring on the job.

Convenience goods Goods such as cigarettes and candy bars, those items that consumers will buy from the nearest store with the least possible effort and with little heed as to where they are making the purchase.

Cooperative advertising When a manufacturer agrees to pay for all or part of the cost of advertising a specific product.

Corporation A form of business ownership by shareholders; used primarily to protect individuals from assuming full risks.

Cost approach (also **summation approach**) A method of appraising real property in which the value of the improvements is estimated on the basis of the cost of reproducing them, minus accrued depreciation.

Coverage For insurance real estate purposes, refers to the insurer's ability to provide the appropriate contract for risk exposures on a real estate property.

Crime insurance A type of casualty insurance that includes coverage for the perils of burglary, robbery, and theft.

Curable obsolescence The reversible deterioration of a building caused by deferred maintenance.

Curative maintenance (also corrective maintenance) Immediate repairs that must be performed in response to emergencies or service requests.

Damages The monetary compensation paid legally to a person who has suffered an injury or loss.

Debt service Periodic payments made on a loan, with each payment representing an amount for principal plus interest.

Debt-coverage ratio The ratio of a property's annual net operating income to the annual debt service on a loan.

Deductible The amount of loss sustained by the insured before the insurer assumes coverage.

Deed of trust An instrument used as security for a debt in mortgaging real estate by introducing a third party, or trustee, into the contract.

Default The failure to meet an obligation, either of a mortgage or a lease.

Deferred maintenance Inadequacies in maintaining and repairing property.

Delinquency Past-due rental collection.

Demand The desire in a given market to possess a commodity, combined with the ability to purchase it at the specified price. (See **Supply**.)

Demographic profile The characteristics of a human population including such factors as size, growth, density, distribution, and vital statistics.

Depreciation A property's gradual decline in use and value due to wear and tear and the actions of the elements; in accounting, the process of converting a fixed asset into an expense.

Design review The analysis of a proposed building's structure, to ensure its efficiency and profitability.

Development loan An interim loan, characterized by a short term and high interest rate, for the purpose of constructing improvements on vacant land; it usually provides for continuous funding throughout the construction period.

Direct mail A form of advertising through letters, cards, or brochures, sent by mail to prospective customers and which relies heavily on specialized mailing lists.

Discount point An amount equal to one percent of a loan charged by a lender for the use of capital in order to balance a submarket interest rate; also, the discount on a loan that is bought or sold.

Economic life The period of time a property can be used to produce assets or services.

Economic obsolescence A loss in value due to factors external to the property.

Effective gross income The anticipated income from real estate after an allowance for vacancy and collection loss.

Efficiency ratio The ratio of a building's net rentable area, which is the space used and occupied exclusively by tenants, to its gross area, which includes the building's core.

Ellwood Tables Computations of capitalization rates that take into account equity buildup resulting from regular amortization payments as well as loan terms.

Endorsement An amendment to an insurance policy affecting a change in its original terms.

Energy demand A building's total requirement for power during a given period.

Energy management The programs designed to reduce energy consumption and cut utility bills without jeopardizing tenant comfort or shortening the maximum engineered lives of a property's systems.

Energy performance standards The ranges of acceptable energy consumption, measured in Btus and based on geographic regions throughout the United States, as established by the American Institute of Architects Research Corporation.

Equal Opportunity in Employment Act A section of the Civil Rights Act of 1964 which prohibits all employers with 15 or more employees from discrimination in hiring, firing, or terms of employment on the basis of an individual's race, color, religion, sex, or national origin.

Equity participation loan Mortgage financing that, in addition to a fixed interest return, gives the lender the right to share in whatever benefits the equity investor/borrower receives.

Escalation clause A provision in a lease that guarantees automatic rent adjustments, usually based on increased operating expenses or a change in some index.

Estoppel clause A lease clause that sets forth the amount of rent that a tenant will pay and states that this amount constitutes the full and entire rent that the tenant will be required to pay for the premises.

Excise tax Special tax levied on certain "luxury" terms, including possible dues and admissions, such as merchants' association dues, the sales from electrical lights, and charges for telephone service.

Exclusive clause Clause in a lease that prohibits the landlord from leasing space in the shopping center to any tenant whose primary business is the sale of a specific merchandise or service.

Exposure A factor on which insurance rates are based, refers to the dangers that confront a shopping center.

Fashion cycle The entire cycle through which a fashion retailing item passes, from the buying, advertising, and replacement stages to its eventual termination.

Favored nation clause Lease clauses that offer a large concession to one tenant but not to any other tenant.

Feasibility study The analysis of a specific, proposed real estate project or program to determine if it can be carried out successfully.

Federal income tax A graduated tax levied by the federal government on annual income.

Fiduciary One who has a legal duty toward another because of an established relationship of trust and confidence.

Finish allowance A landlord's allowance for constructing tenant improvements; that is, what the owner allows to "finish off" a tenant space.

Fire insurance The most basic and essential type of property insurance.

Fixed expense An expense that occurs regularly and does not vary with business volume.

Flood An overflow of water that comes from a lake, river, or ocean.

Flood insurance Insurance purchased specifically to cover damage caused by floods.

Floor area   In a shopping center, defined as the total square feet of floor space in all store areas.

Foot-candle   The amount of illumination, measured by light meters at desk level, that comes from a lighting fixture.

Foreclosure   The legal process by which a lender can enforce payment of a debt by selling whatever right, title, or interest in a property the borrower had when the mortgage was executed.

Form   An extension to a standard fire insurance policy that provides coverage for additional risks.

Free and clear   Money that can be considered the owner's or a retailer's profit after all operating expenses and salaries have been paid.

Gap loan   A short-term, second loan that is used by a developer to make up the difference between a minimum loan amount and the maximum amount committed under permanent financing.

General liability insurance   Provides coverage for liability loss exposures faced by individuals and businesses. Common forms are general liability (personal, business, and professional); automobile liability; and employers' liability.

Goal   In a management by objectives program, a statement in broad and nonspecific terms of management's aims.

Gross possible rental income (also **gross scheduled rental income**) Income that a shopping center would generate if it were 100 percent occupied at rents set forth in the rental schedule.

Gross sales   The sum total in dollars of every sale that the retailer makes during a specific financial period, usually a calendar year.

Gross square foot (GSF)   A unit of measuring space, particularly useful in measuring and studying a shopping center's energy consumption.

Ground rent   Rent that is paid for the right to use and occupy the land under a property.

Heating, ventilation, and air conditioning (HVAC) system   The unit regulating the even distribution of heat and fresh air throughout a building.

Highest and best use   The most productive use to which real property may be put for the most desirable period of time, considering all economic factors.

Hold harmless clause   In a lease agreement, an indemnification provision holding the property manager harmless for liability arising from the property's operation.

Holdover clause   Clause that defines the appropriate action to take when a tenant fails to vacate the premises by the last day of the leased term when a lease renewal has not occurred.

Housekeeping   All the operations involved with keeping the entire property clean.

Improvement (also **capital improvement**)   A major replacement that becomes part of a property, halts deterioration of property and/or prolongs its life appreciably, and increases its value; must be capitalized rather than expensed.

Impulse purchase   A consumer purchase based on a momentary decision, rather than on a rational, carefully planned process. Many shopping center tenants depend heavily on consumers' impulse purchases.

Income capitalization approach   A method of appraising real property in which value is estimated by dividing the property's annual net operating income by an appropriate capitalization rate.

Incurable obsolescence   Irreversible loss in a building's value because of changing style or function.

Index escalation clause   A lease provision under which the rent rate is adjusted to reflect changes in a specified cost-of-living index.

Indirect damages   The loss of profits that result from direct damages.

Inflation   An economic condition occurring when the money supply increases in relation to goods; it is associated with rising wages and costs and decreasing purchasing power.

Initial markup   The first markup taken on a new item of merchandise.

Insurable value   The estimate of a property's value needed for purchasing fire insurance and related coverages.

Insurance   A contract binding a company to indemnify an insured party against a specified loss in return for premiums paid.

Insurance agent   A person who negotiates insurance.

Interest rate   The rate of return on (or cost of) borrowed capital, usually in direct proportion to the length of the loan term and the degree of risk assumed by the lender.

Interest-only loan   A loan on which only the interest is paid throughout its term; the principal is paid in full at the due date of the note.

Interim close   In lease negotiations, a temporary close.

Interim loan   Short-term, high-interest financing that can be used for new and existing projects.

Investment   The purchase of some form of property that will be held for a relatively long period of time, during which it is expected to increase in value.

Investment value   The worth of a property to a particular investor, based on predetermined criteria.

Janitorial maintenance   The services involved in the general upkeep and cleanliness of a shopping center's common areas.

Job specification   A list of the skills, experience, educational background, and working knowledge needed to fill a particular job within an organization.

Jobber A wholesaler who buys merchandise from manufacturers and then sells it to dealers, most of whom are retailers.

Joint venture A partnership established for a single business venture.

Junior loan Financing that is subordinate to a mortgage lien that precedes it, in the event of default.

Kilowatt-hour (kwh) A unit of electrical power consumption measuring the total energy developed by a power of one kilowatt acting for one hour.

Kimball ticket A retail tag that contains inventory information.

Leader A retail product that, when offered at a certain price, has the capacity to attract people into a store.

Lease A written document in which the owner of a property transfers the right to use and occupy the property to another for a specified period of time and in exchange for a specified rental rate.

Lease abstract A summary of the pertinent facts agreed to in the lease document.

Lease-up costs Expenses involved in obtaining tenants for a new building, including lease commissions, space studies, advertising, and promotional programs.

Leasing agent The individual in a management firm who is directly responsible for renting space in assigned properties.

Leasing plan The formal statement of the shopping center's rental rates and the types of tenants that would be suitable for specific spaces at the center.

Lessee The tenant in a lease.

Lessor The landlord in a lease.

Leverage The use of borrowed funds to acquire an income-producing asset in order to achieve a higher return on the equity invested.

Liability In insurance, a legal responsibility for injury or damage.

Liability insurance (also **third-party insurance**) A form of coverage in which the owner is the first party; the insurance company, the second party; and the person making the claim, the third party.

Lien The charge against a property, making the property security for the payment of a debt.

Life safety Refers to the physical safety both of the people on the property and of the building itself.

Limited liability An attribute of the corporation form of ownership; the individual shareholder is not liable for financial debts resulting from damage claims.

Loan constant The percentage of the principal amount of a loan required to pay off both the loan at its maturity and the amount of interest due at each installment.

Loan-to-value ratio The amount of a loan compared to the value of the real estate securing it.

Location   The comparative advantages of one site in consideration of such factors as transportation, convenience, social benefits, specific use, and anticipated patterns of change.

Loss   The amount of an insured's claim on an insurer.

Loss adjustment   The settlement of an insurance claim.

Loss exposure   A term that can be used for financial risks on a property.

Loss leader   A retail product that sells below the retailer's cost, in order to attract customers to the store.

Loss-of-income insurance   A policy that provides against loss of earnings as a result of an insured peril.

Maintenance   The process of preserving the shopping center property in a suitable condition to fulfill its intended purpose.

Management   The planned process of organizing, controlling, and administering a business enterprise; the persons in the organization who are engaged in management.

Management agreement   A document in which a property owner contracts the management of a property to an individual manager or firm and which details all rights and obligations of both parties.

Management plan   A strategy for a property's physical, fiscal, and operational management that is directed toward achieving the owner's goals.

Managing agent   One who supervises the operation of a property on behalf of the owner and in consideration of a management fee.

Manual bookkeeping   A system of record keeping involving the hand-posting of all financial transactions.

Margin (also **markon**)   The difference between what a retailer pays for an item and what it is sold for.

Markdown   Reductions in the original buying price of various retail items.

Market   The interactions between buyers and sellers.

Market analysis   A general study of market conditions that bear upon supply and demand and affect prices for a particular type of property.

Market area   A geographical region within which similar properties are effectively competitive.

Market data (also **comparable sales**) **approach**   A method of estimating value by comparing the property being appraised with comparable properties that have been sold recently enough to be used as guides for determining market behavior.

Market penetration   Percentage of a specific type of retail market—such as men's clothing—that a retailer can attract.

Marketing   All business activity involved in moving goods and services from producers to consumers.

Marketing plan   A short-term business tool, relying on scientific data, generated at increasing profits.

Marketing strategy Advertising and other techniques used to promote and lease a building's space.

Market price The amount actually paid in a real estate transaction.

Market rent (also **economic rent**) Rent that a property is capable of yielding if leased under prevailing market conditions.

Market survey The process of gathering information about specific, comparable properties and comparing it to data concerning the subject property in order to weigh its advantages and disadvantages and to establish market rent.

Market value A property's most probable selling price.

Markup In retailing, the difference between the retailer's purchase price and selling price.

Media mix An advertiser's distribution of the advertising budget among the various media.

Medical payments insurance Insurance coverage that reimburses members of the public who are injured on the premises, regardless of actual liability, for medical, hospital, and funeral expenses that result from their injuries.

Merchandising The process in retailing that involves getting the right merchandise to the right place in the right quantity at the right price at the right time.

Merchants' association An organization that advances the common interests of shopping center tenants in planning advertisements, promotions, decorations, etc.

Merchants' association clause A clause in many shopping center leases that establishes the dues and obligations of each tenant in regard to the merchants' association.

Mode of rent payment clause Clause in a lease that states that the landlord can refuse any rent payment that does not come directly from the tenant, and that the landlord can return the check from a third party, demanding payment from the proper account.

Modernization The process of upgrading a building's original or existing features to reflect technological improvements.

Mortgage A written instrument by which property is given as security for the payment of a debt or performance of an obligation.

Mortgagee The holder of a mortgage; one who loans money or advances credit on security for a loan or for the advance of credit.

Mortgagor One who owns an interest in real estate and who executes a mortgage on that interest as security for a loan or for the advance of credit.

National Retail Merchants Association One of the largest retail trade associations in the world.

Negotiation Dealings between two parties, particularly tenant and owner, in order to reach an agreement on price, quantity, quality, or other terms.

Neighborhood A grouping of similar or complementary land uses; commercially, an area in which land use is devoted principally to office buildings and retail establishments.

Neighborhood analysis The study of a neighborhood and comparison of it with the broader economic and geographic area of which it is a part, to determine why individuals and businesses are attracted to it.

Net operating income (NOI) The balance remaining after deducting a property's operating expenses from its effective gross income.

Net profit Money that is left as profit, after all expenses have been paid.

Net sales In retailing, the amount that is left from the total sales after exchanges, refunds, and allowances have been taken into account.

Notice clause A clause in a lease that establishes the proper method and time frame that the tenant must use for giving notice of leaving.

Objective In a management by objectives program, a quantitative statement concerning an achievement in a specific area of operation.

Occupancy One of four factors on which insurance rates are based; specifically, on the types of tenants at the center.

Occupancy level The percentage of rented space to the total amount of rentable space.

On-site manager The direct representative of management and ownership on the property site.

Open to buy A retailing control that tells a buyer how much to spend on a certain classification of merchandise at a specific time.

Operating expense escalation clause A lease provision under which increases in operating expenses are passed on to tenants on a pro rata basis.

Operating expenses The expenditures for salaries, taxes, insurance, utilities, maintenance, and similar items paid in connection with operating a building and which are properly charged against income.

Operating statement The primary record, which is produced by the management firm's accounting department, recording money received and money paid out relative to a property.

Option In a lease, the right to obtain a specific condition within a specified time.

Option to cancel Option granted to tenants that allows them to cancel their leases, given certain time limitations and conditions.

Option to expand Clause in a lease that gives a tenant the right to expand into adjacent space, thus allowing the tenant to accommodate a growth in business.

Option to extend An option that implies an extension of the lease term, without renegotiation or execution of a new lease.

Option to purchase A clause in a lease that grants a tenant the option to purchase the building it occupies at a specified period during the term of the lease.

Option to renew Option granted to tenants, giving them a renewal of their leases on the same terms and conditions. The option often implies, however, a renegotiation of rent or the execution of a new lease.

Option to sublease and assign Option that represents either the transfer of all of one tenant's rights, title, and interest in the property to a new tenant, with the latter assuming all of the obligations of the lease; or to a sublease, which is the transfer by the prime tenant of only a portion of its rights, title, interest in the leased estate, limited by the amount of leasehold area transferred or the length of the sublease term, or both.

Organizational chart A chart depicting the relationships, by job function or titles, among various members of a building's management team.

Over-building standards Improvements to a leased area that are installed at the tenant's expense.

Owner, landlords, and tenants (OLT) liability insurance Insurance covering liability arising from the ownership, maintenance, or use of the insured premises and operations necessary and incidental to it.

Package policy An insurance plan that combines many forms of coverage.

Partnership A form of business ownership, in which two or more partners pool finances and administrative skills.

Pass-through escalation clause Clause in a lease that passes on increases in operating expenses through a fraction that expresses the percentage increase. The numerator is the total square feet in the tenant's premises, and the denominator is the total square feet in the shopping center. The tenant's pro rata share equals the amount of the increase times the fraction.

Percentage increase Generally a fraction, with a numerator that indicates the index figure in December of each calendar year, and a denominator that indicates the figure in the month in which the tenant will begin to pay rent. The percentage increase in the CPI multiplied by the tenant's fixed minimum rent will reflect the increase in dollars, less any prior cost-of-living increases.

Percentage-of-loss deductible An insurance plan under which the deductible increases as the size of the loss increases, usually up to a specified maximum.

Percentage rent   Rent that is based on a percentage of the gross sales or net income of the tenant, often against a guaranteed minimum.

Performance evaluation   The periodic and realistic assessment of an employee's progress on the job.

Perimeter security   Security measures that protect the exterior of a shopping center.

Permanent loan   A long-term loan that either finances the purchases of an existing office building or replaces a construction loan.

Personal injury liability insurance   A policy that covers items such as libel, slander, discrimination, or wrongful eviction.

Personal property tax   Tax levied by local governments against personal property.

Personal trade (P.T.)   In retailing, refers to consumers who will request that a particular salesperson assist them.

Physical life   The length of time during which a building is a sound structure, depending greatly on the quality of maintenance.

Planning stage   A phase in the development of a building during which a design review is performed to ensure the property's efficiency and marketability. A feasibility study is conducted; financing is obtained; and leasing plans are made.

Point   A charge equal to one percent of a loan charged by the lender as a service fee or as additional interest.

Preleasing   The leasing of space in a project under construction in order to ensure a high occupancy level upon completion.

Premium   The periodic sum of money paid by an insured party on an insurance policy.

Price impression advertising   Conveyance of a general impression of a business or product through skillful rotation and pricing of items.

Price line   General classifications of price levels of retail merchandising.

Price points   Specific prices within a price line.

Primary financing   The first loan that is recorded on a property, which has a lien priority ahead of any other loan filed or recorded after it.

Prime rate   The interest rate, fluctuating with the availability of funds, at which commercial banks will lend money to their most creditworthy borrowers.

Prime tenant   A tenant who has signed directly with the landlord, as opposed to a tenant who has assigned or subleased.

Principal   The total amount of a debt outstanding, exclusive of accrued interest.

Print media   All media used for advertising prepared by printing; for example, periodicals, posters, and newspapers.

Pro forma   A financial projection for a proposed project based on certain specified assumptions and reflecting construction costs, financing, leasing rates, and operating costs.

Project critique An objective evaluation performed after a building's completion of its design, construction, and operational efficiency.

Promissory note A written promise to pay a sum of money that contains the amount of debt, rate of interest, schedule of payments, and the due date.

Promotional advertising Promotion of a specific product or brand.

Promotional cycle The various steps taken to introduce, sell, and clean out inventory of an item or a line of merchandise.

Property analysis A complete study of a real estate property, including its architectural design and improvements, physical condition, location, services, and tenant profile.

Property inspection A systematic process of examining a property in order to determine which items require physical maintenance.

Property insurance A policy protecting the insured against loss to property, income, or personal injury.

Property management A service profession in which someone other than the owner supervises a property's operation according to the owner's objectives.

Protection In insurance, a factor in rating policies that involves the property's loss prevention facilities or features of a structure. These could include sprinkler systems, fire walls, fire doors, parapets, heat vents, fire brigades, water towers, fire pumps, and secondary power sources.

Prospect A potential customer, or for leasing purposes, a potential tenant.

Prospecting The systematic search for potential tenants based on personal interactions, including referrals, canvassing, and cooperation with other colleagues in the business.

Public relations The activities, other than advertising, employed by a firm to promote a favorable relationship with the public in order to increase business.

Radius clause Clause in a lease that prohibits a tenant from opening and operating another business, whether competitive or not, within a certain radius of the shopping center.

Real estate The land and any improvements found on it; the term is often applied to nonagricultural property which accommodates individuals, business, and industry.

Real estate portfolio All real estate investments owned by an entity: a bank, investment organization, or other investor.

Receipt of goods (R.O.G.) Term used in the retailing trade to designate the receipt of goods.

Record keeping The overall process of accurately accounting for income and expenses in order to facilitate budgeting for future operations and preparing regular financial statements for the owner.

Regional analysis Identification of the general economic and demographic conditions and physical aspects of an area surrounding a shopping center and the trends that affect it.

Rehabilitation The restoration of improvements to a satisfactory condition without changing their plan or style.

Renewal clause An option giving a tenant the right to renew a lease for an additional period upon the expiration of the original term.

Renovation A general term covering the modernization, rehabilitation, or remodeling of existing real estate.

Rent A fixed, periodic payment made by a tenant to an owner for the exclusive possession and use of leased property.

Rent collection policy The set of procedures needed to ensure that tenants make rental payments on the day established in the lease document.

Rent escalation clause A provision in a lease that guarantees automatic rent adjustments for increased operating expenses.

Rent overage In retail leases, rent payments, usually a percentage of tenant sales, in excess of a guaranteed minimum.

Rent roll A report prepared regularly, usually monthly, that indicates the rent-paying status of each tenant.

Rent schedule The listing of each tenant area and its scheduled income.

Rental property operations insurance Insurance policies for income-producing properties that provide for specific kinds of coverage, such as valuable papers or rental value coverage.

Rent-up period The time following construction, renovation, or conversion that is required for a rental property to achieve specified occupancy rates and projected income levels.

Repair The general upkeep needed to maintain a property in its original condition and function.

Replacement cost In appraisal, the cost at current prices of constructing an existing building with one of equal utility; in insurance, a provision that insures a property at its replacement cost rather than its actual cash value, thus eliminating any deduction for depreciation.

Replacement index An alternative index for an escalation clause that is used, should the specified index be altered, or the Department of Labor change the statistical base of the index.

Reproduction cost The cost at current prices of constructing an exact duplicate of a building.

Restrictive covenant A clause in a lease that restricts the tenant's use of the property or restricts the landlord's leasing of space on the property.

Revolving credit A type of credit plan that consumers can use on a continual basis as long as regular payments of some minimum amount are made.

Risk management In insurance, the process of controlling risks and managing losses.

Roll-over loan A mortgage loan with a fixed rate for a set period of time, after which the interest is adjusted.

Rule of Three A basic principle of selling that says that a salesperson should not have more than three items in view of the consumer at any one time.

Rules and regulations Guidelines for the operation of a shopping center; for example, security requirements or after-hours entry.

Sales tax Tax levied on various goods and services that merchants are responsible to pay to the state.

Satellite tenant A shopping center tenant that stands in a secondary, ancillary position—both in size and location—to the anchor tenant.

Scatteration buying In retailing, refers to buying a classification of merchandise from several buyers and not paying sufficient attention to the best lines.

Schematic A store's blueprint which shows exactly where each section, fixture, and aisle will be located.

Secondary financing A mortgage that does not have first claim on the property securing it in the event of a default but is subordinate to any mortgage lien that precedes it.

Security deposit clause Clause in a lease that states both the tenant's and landlord's rights in regard to the amount of the deposit.

Self-selection The presentation of merchandise in such a way that the customer can pick out purchases, usually without the help of a salesperson.

Self-service Anything in a store that makes it easier for customers to serve themselves.

Selling cost ratio A percentage figure that results from dividing the amount of the selling payroll by the amount of the sales in dollars.

Service bureau A company that sells the use of its computer equipment.

Shopping center A group of commercial establishments planned, developed, owned, and managed as a unit related in location, size and type of shops to the trade area that the unit serves; it provides on-site parking in definite relationship to the types and sizes of stores.

Shopping good An item that consumers will shop around for, such as a suit, stereo set, or an item of furniture.

Social security tax Tax levied against employers for their employees' social security purposes.

Sole proprietorship Most basic form of financial ownership; one entity maintains complete ownership and control.

Special hazards insurance Property coverages that provide protection, in addition to the standard fire insurance policy and extended coverage endorsement, for specifically named risks such as floods, earthquakes, and water damage.

Special multiperil policy (SMP) An insurance policy combining both property and liability protection in one package.

Specific policy An insurance policy form written to cover a single item or type of property in one location.

Specific rate A scheduled insurance rate applied to special-use buildings, reflecting the condition and occupancy of the building at the time of inspection.

Spring street A street on which many retailers are located in a major business artery.

Stabilized income Income after adjustments are made for anticipated losses from vacancy and collection delinquencies.

Standard lease A lease form into which specific clauses or provisions may be written.

Standard Metropolitan Area (SMSA) A designation by the Federal Office of Management and Budget that applies to countries with at least one central city of 50,000 or more residents and any contiguous jurisdictions that are socially or economically within the central city.

Standard operating procedures (SOP) manual A handbook detailing all the policies, procedures, systems, and job functions that concern a property's operation.

Straight deductible An insurance plan under which the insurer pays nothing for losses that are less than a specified amount.

Subchapter S corporation An offshoot of the corporate form of ownership, in which members can choose partnership-type taxation.

Subordinate loan Secondary financing; in the event of default, the loan is junior to any mortgage lien that precedes it.

Subrogation clause In an insurance policy, a provision stating that if the insurance company pays a loss, the insured relinquishes to the company any rights to recover damages from the person who causes the loss, not exceeding the amount that the company pays to the insured.

Supply The quantity or amount of a specific commodity at a given price available to meet a demand. (See **Demand**.)

Syndication An association of individuals bound together by a business interest in which the members have a mutual interest.

Takeout loan A permanent mortgage loan that is funded at the completion of construction with the funds being used to pay off (take out) the construction lender.

Target marketing A sales program designed to attract specific tenant prospects.

Tenant One who pays rent to occupy or gain possession of real estate.

Tenant contract In a tenant relations program, an individual named by the tenant who is management's liaison with the tenant.

Tenant improvements Fixed improvements made to tenants' office space.

Tenant ledger A written record of tenant rental payments and additional damage charges.

Tenant mix The broad representation of retailers and various service units that occupy a shopping center.

Tenant relations A program, in large part dependent on sound maintenance procedures, that attempts to maintain harmony between tenants and management.

Term Duration of a tenant's lease; in some cases, a negotiating point between tenant and landlord.

Theft insurance A policy covering the repayment to individuals and businesses, victimized by burglars, robbers, embezzlers, and thieves.

Ticket items High-priced items that are frequently sold by commissioned salespeople.

Tickler file A record-keeping system that reminds the property manager of important dates.

Time and place utility A basic retailing service, to provide the right item at the right time.

Traffic control The orderly and safe regulation of people and materials entering and leaving a building.

Twilight zone In the shopping center industry, refers to the peripheral zone that lay between the city and suburbs.

Use clause Provision in a lease that restricts a tenant's use of the rental space.

Use factor The number of hours that a building is in operation in relation to the total number of hours in a given time period.

Use value A building's special value for a certain owner, based on that person's use of the building.

Utility A public service, such as gas, water, or electricity.

Vacancy rate The ratio of vacant space to total rentable area.

Valuable papers insurance Generally an all-risk policy that provides coverage for loss to specific valuable papers and records.

Vandalism and malicious mischief insurance An insurance policy covering losses caused intentionally by vandals.

Variable expense An overhead cost, such as labor or advertising.

Visual merchandising Involves all visual stimuli in a retail store that customers see as they approach a store and immediately after they enter.

Work order A record of maintenance work, usually stating what was performed to a building, by whom, where, the amount of time required, and materials used.

Workers' compensation insurance An insurance policy that covers payments that may be required by law to be made to an employee who is injured at work, regardless of who is at fault.

Wraparound loan An all-inclusive, secondary loan permitting the borrower to incorporate any existing debt with new financing under a single debt service payment made to the wraparound lender.

Yield Money earned as return on capital.

Zoning A public regulation determining the character and intensity of land use.

Select Bibliography

Creedy, Judith, and Wall, Norbert F. *Real Estate Investment by Objective.* New York: McGraw-Hill, 1979.

Cutler, Eliot R., and Reilly, John R. *The Antitrust Aspects of Restrictive Covenants in Shopping Center Leases.* New York: International Council of Shopping Centers, 1976.

Cutlip, Scott M., and Center, Allan H. *Effective Public Relations.* 5th ed. Englewood Cliffs, N.J.: Prentice-Hall, 1982.

Downs, James C. Jr. *Principles of Real Estate Management.* 12th ed. Chicago: Institute of Real Estate Management, 1980.

Halper, Emanuel B. *Shopping Center Leases and Store Leases.* New York: Law Journal Seminars Press, 1980.

Jaffe, Austin J. *Property Management in Real Estate Investment Decision Making.* Lexington, Mass.: D.C. Heath, 1979.

McKeever, J. Ross, Griffin, Nathaniel M., and Spink, Frank H. Jr. *Shopping Center Development Handbook.* Washington, D.C.: Urban Land Institute, 1977.

McMullen, Charles W. *Real Estate Investments: A Step by Step Guide.* New York: John Wiley & Sons, 1981.

Practicing Law Institute. *Shopping Centers Revisited.* New York, 1979.

Seldin, Maury, and Swesnik, Richard H. *Real Estate Investment Strategy.* 2nd ed. New York: Wiley-Interscience, 1979.

Sirota, David. *Essentials of Real Estate Investment.* Chicago: Real Estate Education Co., 1978.

Sternlieb, George, and Hughes, James W., eds. *Shopping Centers: USA.* Piscataway, N.J.: Center for Urban Policy Research, 1981.

Urban Land Institute. *Dollars and Cents of Shopping Centers.* Washington, D.C., published every three years.

Urban Land Institute. *Standard Manual of Accounting for Shopping Center Operations.* Washington, D.C., 1971.

For timely information about the shopping center industry and about real estate management in general, the following periodicals are recommended for regular reading: *Journal of Property*

Management, published every two months by the Institute of Real Estate Management; *National Mall Monitor*, published every two months by National Mall Monitor, Clearwater, Fla.; *Shopping Centers Today*, published monthly by the International Council of Shopping Centers, New York; and *Shopping Center World*, published monthly by Communication Channels, Atlanta, Ga.

Index

Essential Property Management Titles from IREM

The Condominium Community:
A Guide for Owners, Boards, and Managers

Managing the Office Building

Managing the Shopping Center

Marketing and Leasing of Office Space

Practical Apartment Management

The Practice of Real Estate Management
for the Experienced Property Manager

Principles of Real Estate Management

Expense Analysis:
Condominiums, Cooperatives & P.U.D.'s (annual)

Income/Expense Analysis:
Apartments (annual)

Income/Expense Analysis:
Office Buildings (annual)